Contemporary Philosop

B

Contemporary Philosophy

Each volume in this series provides a clear, comprehensive and up-to-date introduction to the main philosophical topics of contemporary debate. Written by
leading philosophers, the volumes provide an ideal basis for university students
and others who want an engaging and accessible account of the subject. While
acting as an introduction, each volume offers and defends a distinct position in its
own right.

Published Works
Contemporary Philosophy of Social Science
Brian Fay

Contemporary Philosophy of Mind
Georges Rey

Forthcoming
Contemporary Philosophy of Thought
Michael Luntley

Contemporary Philosophy of Religion
Charles Taliaferro

Contemporary Metaphysics
Michael Jubien

Contemporary Philosophy of Law
Dennis Patterson

Contemporary Philosophy of Physics
Simon Saunders

Contemporary Philosophy of Language
Kent Bach

Pluralism and Contemporary Political Philosophy
Daniel Weinstock

Contemporary Philosophy of Mind

A Contentiously Classical Approach

Georges Rey

Department of Philosophy
University of Maryland

BLACKWELL
Publishers

First published 1997

2 4 6 8 10 9 7 5 3 1

Blackwell Publishers Inc.
238 Main Street
Cambridge, Massachusetts 02142
USA

Blackwell Publishers Ltd
108 Cowley Road
Oxford OX4 1JF
UK

Library of Congress Cataloging-in-Publication Data

Rey, Georges.
Contemporary philosophy of mind / Georges Rey.
p.   cm. — (Contemporary philosophy ;)
Includes bibliographical references and index.
ISBN 0-631-19069-4 (hardcover : alk. paper). — ISBN 0-631-19071-6
(pbk. : alk. paper)
1. Philosophy of mind.   I. Title.   II. Series: Contemporary
philosophy (Cambridge, Mass.).
BD418.3.R69   1997
128′.2—dc20
96-21571
CIP

British Library Cataloguing in Publication Data

A CIP catalogue record for this book is available from the British Library.

Commissioning Editor: Nathalie Manners
Desk Editor: Deborah Seymour
Production Controller: Lisa Eaton
Text Designer: Lisa Eaton

Typeset in 10 on 12 pt Garamond 3
by Best-set Typesetter Ltd., Hong Kong
Printed in Great Britain by T.J. Press Ltd, Padstow, Cornwall

This book is printed on acid-free paper

For Karen

Contents

Asterisks mark difficult or tangential material that can be skipped without loss of continuity

Contents

List of Figures

Preface

This book is intended as an introduction both to recent work in the philosophy of mind, and to the foundations of the newly evolving field of cognitive science, which is – appropriately, I believe – replacing parts of the older topic. I am piously hoping that it will be accessible to anyone with an interest in the issues, but I suspect that its likely audience will be people with some background in basic "analytic" philosophy, for example, upper-level undergraduates and graduate students in most Anglophone universities. The treatment aspires to be continuous with science, not literature, and so would probably prove frustrating for those who prefer philosophy in more the latter form.

Although the focus is contemporary, the approach is classical in a number of senses. First, I take seriously what many philosophers have lately thought to be the misconceived classical problems of the philosophy of mind since at least Descartes: e.g. What is the nature of a mental state? How could matter have mental properties? How could those properties be causal? Secondly, I attempt to show how a certain, also much maligned traditional conception of the mind, can straightforwardly address those problems. That conception takes mental states to be real, highly structured, causally efficacious internal states of a system. I'm inclined to think that this conception is implicit in much ordinary talk, and certainly in the philosophical tradition going back even to the Greeks. It has been resisted in this century only out of desperation with what I think are quite inessential features associated with it, for example, empiricism, and an excessive fascination with the deliverances of introspection.

Lastly, the approach is "classical" in that it pursues a view about the nature of mental processes that, after forty years, is now (already!) being called "classical," the "computational/representational theory of thought" ("CRTT"), the view according to which thought involves computations over logically-structured representations encoded in the brain, sentences in a "language of thought."[1] Because of the failure of some premature assumptions that were initially made about the specific character of those computations, this approach is out of fashion in some quarters. I hope to show, however, that it has resources that no alternative seems to possess, resources that, not surprisingly, have yet to be fully mined in those brief forty years. Indeed, the main argument of this book is that a certain natural extension of CRTT, "CRTQ" (or a computational/representational theory of thought and qualitative states) makes possible an unusually unified, materialist theory of the mind.

Some might complain that there has not been enough space devoted to alternatives to my classical conceptions, e.g. to Wittgensteinian and Davidsonian approaches in philosophy; to connectionist and "dynamical" models in Artificial Intelligence; to neurophysiological approaches in psychology. Although I will discuss in passing some aspects of these alternatives (as will be evident, I'm actually fairly sympathetic to some of Wittgenstein's specific insights), there was simply not space for everything. Moreover, as I will indicate in those passing discussions, it has yet to be shown that these alternatives as wholes offer anything like the explanatory promise of the classical views I favor. In any case, there are now numerous volumes on these other approaches. There are surprisingly few these days defending the classical views.

Thus, I make no pretense to providing an entirely neutral discussion of the topics. Whether or not such a discussion is genuinely possible, I must confess that I would also find it boring. Both a writer and a reader are more engaged when there's a view at stake than when they try to hold themselves too far above the fray. But I hope I haven't been unfair to the alternatives, which I am at pains to discuss sometimes in detail, if only to set out my own views more sharply.

Some of the material in this book was originally supposed to appear as a book on consciousness that, however, *was* far too contentious to be usable as an introductory text, and far too expository to serve as a fully contentious one.[2] The unmarriageable material became happily separated when Jean-Michel Roy invited me to give six seminars at l'Ecole Normale Supérieure in Paris in 1993, as a way of introducing French students to the philosophy of cognitive science. Blackwell's Steve Smith thought the material presented there would serve well in their series on contemporary philosophy, something of an expansion of the introduction Barry Loewer and I wrote for our *Meaning in Mind: Fodor and His Critics* (revised portions of which made their way into the present work). I am grateful to Roy and Smith for these invitations and their encouragement – and particularly to Smith for his saintly patience awaiting the final version. The much more contentious material, mostly on consciousness, has made its way into a number of independent articles that I hope to fashion into a sequel to the present work.

Many of the views I express here have emerged from discussions with a good number of philosophers over many years. I think it was Steve Reich and then Bert Dreyfus who first got me interested in whether computers could have minds, and in Wittgensteinian reasons for thinking they couldn't. Rogers Albritton convinced me of the plausibility of much (if not, to his despair, quite all) of Wittgenstein's attack on the conception of the "internal world" that is too closely modeled on the familiar external one. But then Hilary Putnam (in his more realistic days), Michael Devitt and especially Jerry Fodor showed me ways nevertheless to sustain a realism about those portions of our mental talk whose explanatory role does seem to require it, a realism that, *pace* Dreyfus, did seem to involve thinking of mental states as computational. Most recently, Ned Block, Jerry Fodor, Joe Levine, and Brian Loar have offered often insightful resistance to the eliminativist view of phenomenal objects and properties that I nevertheless continue to advocate in the last chapter. Here, despite our many divergencies elsewhere, I have also benefitted from conversations with Dan Dennett, as well as from his early writings.

With regard to the manuscript of the present work, I want to thank my colleagues Michael Devitt, Michael Slote, and Michael Morreau, who read portions of drafts and made very useful suggestions, as did Jonathan Adler, Ned Block, Ramon Das, Charles Gallistel, Pierre Jacob, Joëlle Proust, and Juan Uriagereka. John O'Leary-Hawthorne and Ken Taylor read a complete early draft and provided much sound advice, some of which I hope I have heeded. Sally Bogacz was extremely helpful in discussing much of the empirical psychology, and she, Clare Sager, and Deborah Seymour, of Blackwell Publishers, carefully read the last draft and made numerous, sharp suggestions that greatly improved the final version. But my greatest debt is to Karen Neander for extremely sensitive and detailed comments drafts early and late: her ear for style and eye for argumentative lacunae caused me about six month's more labor than I had planned, but, all things considered, I'm immensely glad of it (and, in any case, the reader ought to be). I dedicate the book to her in warm appreciation.

Lastly, I want to thank the Graduate Research Board and the Department of Philosophy at the University of Maryland for financial support, and the Australian National University in Canberra, and the Centre de Recherche en Epistémologie Appliquée (CREA) of the Ecole Polytechnique in Paris, for their very generous hospitality during much of the writing.

Notes

1 A glossary containing many of the somewhat specialized terms and abbreviations used in this text is provided after chapter 11.
2 It was to be titled *Mind Without Consciousness: a Discrepancy Between Explanatory and Moral Psychology*, and was unfortunately cited in a number of places in print before I withdrew it from publication.

Introduction

1 A Renaissance of the Explanatory

The philosophy of mind is concerned with quite general questions about the nature of mental phenomena and their place in a systematic account of the world: what sort of thing is a pain, a thought, a mental image, a desire, an emotion? What is it for someone (or some*thing*?) to think, feel, deliberate, imagine, to be angry, in love, happy, or to be conscious? What essentially distinguishes a thinking being from something like a stone that presumably has no mental life at all? Could a computer made of plastics, silicon, and wires really suffer, or be afraid, or wish for its surfaces to be scratched? If so, would this be true no matter what the computer was made of? If not, what is so special about the stuff of the human brain? One reason these questions are regarded as "philosophical," as opposed to merely "scientific" is that there persists serious disagreement as to how we should even begin to answer them. Are we merely to introspect? Or reflect on our concepts and the meanings of our words? Are we (always? ever?) infallible judges of our own mental lives or the concepts we deploy in thinking about them? Or should we rely entirely on what scientists tell us: e.g. what psychotherapists tell us about our "unconscious" motives, what Skinnerians tell us about our behavior, or what neurophysiologists tell us about our brains? If someone can think up some experiments that would settle these puzzling questions that would be splendid. The trouble is that no one can – or, anyway, no one yet has – to enough people's satisfaction. There seem to be difficulties in how even to begin to think about the issues, and so they remain problems for the philosophy of mind (of course, I hope some of the suggestions I'll discuss in this book may help improve this situation).

The philosophy of mind is currently undergoing something of a renaissance, in that there is a re-awakened enthusiasm for many of the *explanatory* issues about the mind that the above questions would seem naturally to invite. These questions

1

were once quite prominent: Plato, Aristotle, Descartes, Locke, Hume, and Kant, were greatly interested in explaining, for example, what the mind must be like in order for it to have certain kinds of knowledge. But such questions became eclipsed during much of the present century. Only recently have they become the concern of a large number of researchers both in and outside of philosophy, particularly those working in the so-called "cognitive sciences" – linguistics, computer science, psychobiology, and experimental cognitive and developmental psychology – disciplines with which the philosophy of mind is now increasingly entangled, and with some of which this book will be concerned.

2* Explanation vs. Ontology and Ordinary Talk[1]

This interest in explanation is to be contrasted with two rather more specific concerns that dominated the field for much of this century, one, an *ontological* concern with what *stuff* the mind must be *made of*, the other, a *meta-linguistic* concern with the so-called "logic" of ordinary mental talk. Preoccupation with the latter arose in reaction to earlier preoccupation with the former, and both left the explanatory issues for a long time untouched. Thus, for many decades, the great debate in the philosophy of mind was the ontological debate between "material-ism"[2] (for example, "all that exists is matter, e.g. atoms, quarks, curved space-time") and one or another form of "dualism" (for example, "mental things, e.g. souls, pains, thoughts, exist over and above material things"). For instance, the early modern philosophers, Thomas Hobbes and René Descartes have often been taken to have been arguing about whether thought could consist of some mere material process. And early on in our century, there was extended debate about whether allowing thoughts as further entities in the world was compatible with the conservation of mass/energy.

Although much can be learnt from an examination of ontology, this preoccu-pation with it was unfortunate in a number of ways. In the first place, these positions have often been defined only *negatively*, each consisting largely in *denials* of the opposing view: materialists have wanted to avoid what they regard as the utterly unscientific mysticism they associate with dualism, and dualists to avoid what they regard as the philistine scientism they associate with materialism. Thus, materialism often comes to the view that there are no ghosts or other "spooky" entities; and dualism merely to the view that all is not matter. Rarely is a positive proposal made, and, when it is, it can be usually seen to be peculiarly unconvinc-ing: do materialists really want to insist on the truth of *present* physics? Do dualists really want to advance hypotheses about some mysterious non-spatial *substance*? Moreover, I shall argue, even when plausible, positive proposals are made, they can be shown to depend upon difficult explanatory issues that are not resolved by reflection on ontology alone.

Secondly, even if either dualism or materialism is sufficiently specified as serious, positive doctrines, they would appear to run the risk of what might be called the "What Chutzpah!" objection: what does anyone yet know about the mind, or about matter, that could justify a belief about the identification (or "reducibility"), or lack thereof, of one to the other? What entitles the dualist to claim that physics will *never* be able to explain the mental, or the physicalist that it *always* will? Suppose, by way of comparison, that someone proposed that some stars couldn't possibly be composed of selenium. Who are we (most of us, non-astronomers, non-chemists) to assert or deny it? What do we know about either the stars or the possible manifestations of selenium to make any reasonable conjectures? Now *perhaps* we do know something about mind and matter that we don't know about selenium and the stars. We shall consider such claims in due course. But the breathtaking generality of the claims, and the consequent difficulty in acquiring adequate knowledge of the issues, ought at least to give us pause.[3]

Thirdly, as we shall discuss in chapter 2, the issue of the relation of mental to physical phenomena has come to turn on what have turned out to be extremely delicate questions surrounding the logic of *identity*: of when it is, and when it isn't, appropriate to say that something (e.g. heat) which we may have conceived in one way is identical to something (e.g. mean molecular kinetic energy) that we may have conceived in another. There are complicated questions concerning identities not only between things that are very differently conceived (such as heat and mean kinetic energy), but even between things quite ordinarily conceived (statues and lumps of clay), as well as between their various properties, all of which must be clarified before we can begin to assess one of the main questions that has come to be associated with materialism: are all mental phenomena identical to some or other material phenomena?[4]

These are all good questions. But they are questions that, precisely because of their great generality, have little to do *specifically* with issues about the *mind*. No matter how these issues are settled, rather little will have been gained in any understanding of the mind. For if either materialism or dualism is true, we still might wonder *how* something – whether material or otherwise – might come to exhibit mentality: does a rock, a cockroach, a rat, or an orangutan have a mind? And, if it does, why? If not, why not? Neither materialism nor any of the various forms of dualism by themselves begin to answer these questions, and so they don't really constitute any serious *theory* about the mind: neither of them *per se* actually provides much in the way of *serious explanation* of any mental phenomena, or even much in the way of a program of research.

It might be thought that great strides are daily being made in explaining how the mind really is just a manifestation of the brain. And it's certainly true that the last decades have seen an explosion of knowledge about correlations between physical and mental phenomena. The popular scientific press regularly discuss experimental results relating, for example, decreased serotonin levels with depression, increased norepinepherine levels with more intense emotional experiences, and the activity in specific brain areas with specific mental states, e.g. vision and language processing. However, for all the impressive correlations that may be obtained in these ways – and, in some cases, all the relief from misery that exploiting them may bring – it has to be recognized that the cited physical correlates provide virtually *no serious explanation* whatsoever of the psychological phenomena. Aside from the nice correlation, how in the world are physical properties of the brain supposed to *explain* the specific thought *contents* ("Life is meaningless, not worth living") involved in depression? Would these same effects be had if the area were detached from the rest of the brain? Or from the rest of the body? Which parts? Why? What is it about the brain that explains a person's states having any *content* whatsoever? No doubt, if these correlations hold up, there is *some* explanation lurking here, and these correlations may well figure somewhere in part of it. But, as things stand, the correlations present mostly more data *to be explained*, not any genuine insight into the nature of the respective mental traits.

Impatience with the emptiness of this traditional ontological debate led a generation of philosophers, particularly under the influence of Wittgenstein (1953) and Ryle (1949), to deride even the possibility of a psychology couched in terms of an agent's internal mental states. In particular, they argued that the interest in it arose from a mistaken understanding of the "logic" or "grammar" of ordinary mental talk. As a result, from about 1950 to 1970, the "ontological" issues tended to be replaced by "meta-linguistic" ones: examination of mental phenomena *in the world*, such as *belief, desire, consciousness*, was replaced by detailed examination of the "language games" in which mental *words* – "belief," "desire," "consciousness" – were used.

Much was (and still can be) learned from the resulting heightened sensitivity to complexities and nuances of our ordinary mental talk. Unfortunately, however, it tended to occur at the expense of any further theorizing about the mental phenomena themselves. This was of a piece with a general embarrassment in philosophy about its pretensions to make *any* substantive claims about the world at all. The most that philosophy could be expected to do would be to clear up the confusions that by and large it itself engendered: as Wittgenstein put it somewhere: "philosophy is the disease to which it itself is the cure." Once we become clear about the logic of mental talk we will be cured of temptations to assert either materialism or dualism, or really to make any substantive conjectures about the nature of the mind at all. One of Wittgenstein's most famous phrases – "explanations to come to an end somewhere" appears at the very beginning of his later work, where he invokes it at the point of raising a question about how someone processes meaningful language:

4

"But how does [a shopkeeper] know where and how he is look up the word 'red' and what he is to do with the word 'five'?" – Well, I assume that he acts as I have described. Explanations come to an end somewhere. (1953:§1)

Gilbert Ryle went so far as to claim that:

[W]hen we are in a less impressionable frame of mind, we find something implausible in the promise of hidden discoveries yet to be made of the hidden causes of our own actions and reactions. (1949:325)

The view reached its perhaps most extreme form in the work of Wittgenstein's disciple, Norman Malcolm (1977), who emphatically rejected "the myth of cognitive processes and structures." For example, with regard to a cognitive explanation of such a phenomenon as a man or a child recognizing a dog, Malcolm claimed:

we could, just as rationally, have said that the man or child *just knows* (without using any model, pattern, or idea at all) that the thing he sees is a dog. We could have said that it is just a normal human capacity. (1977:168)

Perhaps one could "just as rationally" never ask for any explanations of anything at all: we *could* just say that it is a natural capacity of lightning to burn what it strikes. The question is whether we *can also* rationally ask for slightly deeper explanations, and, if we can, what those explanations might be. *Pace* Wittgenstein's dictum, it's not at all clear that explanation *needs* to *stop anywhere*: most scientific research no sooner provides an account of one phenomena (lightning) in terms of another (electrical discharge), then it begins to ask why *that* phenomenon occurs. Whether or not this might go on forever, explanations certainly don't appear to come to an end nearly as soon as these philosophers suggest. If anything characterizes recent cognitive science and a good deal of recent philosophy of mind as a whole, it's an explicit rejection of such claims as these of Malcolm, Wittgenstein, and Ryle. Serious explanation in these areas *begins* in trying to account for "normal human capacities," such as, for instance, vision, audition, reasoning, language acquisition, decision making, and motor control.

It is worth noting that, ontological caprices to one side, this steadfast avoidance of explanation is plausibly the essence of "dualism." For, if pressed, dualism is seldom defended as a thesis about a special "stuff" peculiar to mental beings: it most surely isn't the claim that there happen to be some sort of special particles – say, "mentons," in addition to protons – responsible for mental activity. The dualist's claim of an "irreducible" element to the mind is more radical than that; in the end it may amount to no more than the claim that the mind is somehow exempt from explanation as we encounter it in the natural sciences. This exemption is perhaps most evident in the case of very simple dualism, especially of the sort that Ryle (1949) characterized as committed to "the ghost in the machine." For, quite apart from whether there are any ghosts in or out of machines, one might still wonder how *possibly* any such ghost could manage to do the things it does: how does it manage to *see*, to *think*, to *conjure up images*, or (fail to) *overcome desires* for the sake of some recognized good. Believing in ghosts or immaterial souls is as may be, but it shouldn't be an excuse, which it too often is, to stop asking questions and demanding explanations.[5]

These explanatory lacks are, however, by no means limited to dualism. Too many materialists, intent merely on denying what they regard as dualism's superstitious belief in ghosts, also often fail to explain how it is that brains can do any better. After all, not just *any* brain is conscious – dead ones, or heavily anaesthetized ones aren't – and so we need an account of the further conditions that are necessary. But what further conditions could possibly make the difference between an unconscious and a conscious brain? Too often we are merely assured that consciousness is a property of a very "complexly organized" brain. We are seldom, if ever, told precisely wherein this complexity consists, much less how it could *possibly* account for consciousness (ocean waves are, after all, immensely complex physical processes, but presumably not a whit conscious). One finds people adverting to some unimaginably complicated organization in some as yet only dimly understood machines in order to avoid the worries that bother the dualist.[6] The ghost in the machine is merely replaced by "the complexity" in it.

3   Plan and Argument of this Book

One of the aims of the present book is to try to begin to exorcise this "complexity in the machine," along with the ghost. What I want to do is to try to be as specific as present theory permits about how *possibly* something, whether it be a ghost or brain, might have a conscious mind. This is a particularly vexing question, since, as a number of philosophers, beginning with Descartes, have noticed, there appear to be (in the nice phrase of Levine 1983) "explanatory gaps" between various physical and mental phenomena: it has seemed deeply mysterious how any arrangement of matter could possibly explain various features of conscious minds, specifically: rationality, intentionality, consciousness, and qualitative experience.

Chapter 1 will consist mostly in stage setting: we will consider some basic distinctions among mental phenomena (§1.1) and the three main strategies – reductionist, dualist, and eliminativist – for dealing with them (§1.2). We will also consider some general ground rules for choosing between these strategies: the need for non-tendentious (or non-question-begging) data (§1.3); the importance of fairness in not burdening the discussion with problems not peculiar to it (§1.4);

and some clarity about the nature of philosophical work of this sort in general, and its relation to empirical inquiry (§1.5).

In chapter 2 we will focus primarily on the lures of the dualistic strategies, considering first the nature of the explanatory gaps between physical and mental phenomena (§2.1–2.2), and then various arguments dualists have raised against traditional reductionist proposals. These include a variety of "Leibniz Law" objections to reductionist "identity theories" (§2.3–2.5), as well as the notorious problems of capturing "what it's like" to have various conscious, qualitative experiences (§2.6).

As compelling as many of the lures to dualism may be, however, there would seem to be an insuperable problem that confronts any straightforward dualist proposal: given the lack of any break in the physical, causal aetiology of an organism's bodily behavior, what reason is there to postulate non-physical mental causes as further causes of that behavior? They seem as superfluous to the motion of organisms as angels seem to the motion of the planets. This is the problem of the "lack of a causal break," which we will discuss in detail in §3.1.1. It has led some philosophers to embrace the startling proposal of (total) *eliminativism*, or the view that *there do not literally exist mental phenomena at all*. Although there are some quite strong statements of this view associated with the work of Paul Churchland (1981) for example, it can also be expressed in a more *instrumentalist* fashion, whereby mental descriptions are simply a useful tool for getting on with people, but should not be thought to apply literally and determinately to them (as in Quine (1960), Dennett (1978, 1987, 1991) and Kripke's (1982) interpretation of Wittgenstein (1953)).

For many, any such eliminativism may seem self-evidently absurd, even self-refuting: we will discuss so-called "transcendental" and "introspective" arguments to this effect in §3.2, and their tendency to beg the question against the eliminativist by appealing to tendentiously described data. We will linger especially on some surprising data showing introspection to be a lot less reliable in this respect than is ordinarily supposed (§3.2.2).

There is, however, one clear source of non-tendentious, at least *prima facie* evidence against eliminativism, what I call the "Standardized Regularities" exhibited by the results of common standardized tests of mental abilities (e.g. the SAT and GRE). While it's true that an eliminativist could count on non-mental sciences to explain, one by one, each individual mark on each individual test, it doesn't follow from this fact alone (and, indeed, it's by no means obvious) that she could hope to explain the impressive, law-like *correlations* among those marks across the millions of recorded tests by staying within eliminativist constraints.

But it's not for eliminativists' lack of trying. A good deal of twentieth-century psychology has consisted of a concerted effort to explain all human and animal intelligence without the aid of mentality: this was the aim of *Radical Behaviorism* ("RBism"), whose successes and failures we will discuss at length in chapter 4.

Now, it might be thought that RBism is old hat, of only historical interest. This would be a mistake. Because it was one of the most serious and concerted efforts to provide a non-mentalistic psychology, it exhibited quite vividly both the resources and limitations of such an approach, resources that more recent eliminativist efforts (e.g. Gibsonianism, Radical Connectionism) often lack, and limitations that they often fail to appreciate.[7] Even if it was (as we shall see) an ultimately inadequate account of intelligent behavior, it did force mentalists to be much more careful about the kinds of evidence and argument needed to establish specific mentalistic claims. We'll see, however, that RBism was nevertheless pretty much hoisted on its own petards: the RBists very own experiments on animal learning show that even rats are capable of intelligent behavior that RBism is unable adequately to explain.

But the data are not limited to rats. A particularly striking source of counter-evidence to RBism arises in the revolutionary work of the linguist Noam Chomsky (§4.2.1), who made vivid how the human case in particular stands in need of internal mental states for the representation and processing of natural language. In particular, Chomsky argued that what is needed is an account of rich, largely hidden internal structures of the mind, structures that have been systematically avoided by the philosophical movement that has most influenced Anglo-American philosophy, viz. empiricism (§4.2.2). Problems with empiricism seem to be what plague not only RBist, but any proposals that don't recognize a substantial innate mental endowment (§4.3).

Having specified in chapters 3 and 4 some of the crucial explanatory work mental states are needed to perform, we will begin in chapter 5 to consider different approaches to the analysis of mental phenomena. This will take us into the major discussions of twentieth-century philosophy about the "logic" of mental terms: how they are less grounded in introspection than people have supposed (§5.1); how their referential properties have been exaggerated, and can be accom-modated to "irreferentialist" proposals, treating, for example, phenomenal objects and properties not as real, but as merely "intentional-objects" (§5.2); and how their relation to behavior, a relation that *Analytical Behaviorism* ("ABism") took to be constitutive of their meaning, is mostly accidental (§5.3). This last view arose primarily out of a commitment to a verificationist theory of meaning generally, that, because it continues to influence even quite recent views, will receive separate discussion (§5.4).

ABism is widely thought to have been a failure. But out of its ruins there arose "functionalism," or a strategy for defining mental phenomena in terms of their *role* in a complete mental story that may be tied to the non-mental world in a variety of ways. However, it is an extremely abstract strategy that has been filled out in a surprising number of different ways. In chapter 6 I will set out some important features common to all functionalist approaches, turning in chapter 7 to distin-guish some of the major varieties. In keeping with the general methodology of

§1.5.2, I will endorse a "psycho-functionalist" approach (§7.1.3) that looks to empirically motivated explanation as the ultimate source of the appropriate functional analyses. I will argue that this leads us in turn to an externally anchored (§7.1.2), molecularist (§7.2.2) functionalism, that is to be contrasted with a "superficialist" (§7.2.4) functionalism that is arguably only a technical variant of ABism. By way of spelling out this view, I will then sketch a working proposal about the structure of a typical mind, what I call "Modest Mentalism." I claim that this kind of structure is what is needed to perform the explanatory work that mental phenomena are standardly invoked to perform and so provides a framework in which adequate psycho-functionalist analyses of these phenomena can ultimately be provided.

A valuable specificity is provided for Modest Mentalism by the computational/representational theory of thought ("CRTT") that has been proposed by a number of theorists, most notably Jerry Fodor (1975). Very roughly, this is the theory that having a mind consists in being *structured* or *organized* rather like a modern computer. The theory consists of two main ideas: that mental processes are *computational* processes defined over syntactically specified entities, and that these entities are *representations of the world* (i.e. possess semantic content). Both of these ideas have stimulated vast research programs over the last twenty years, which I will present only in their most general outline. In chapter 8 I will discuss the computational component; in chapter 9, the representational one; and in chapter 10 I will defend those programs against a number of objections that have been raised against them: "red herrings" that are based upon misunderstandings of the nature and scope of the view (§10.1); Searle's worries about his "Chinese Room" and "intrinsic intentionality" (§10.2); and the worries about idealization and "normativity" that have been raised by Saul Kripke and Daniel Dennett (§10.3). In passing, I will include in §8.8 a brief discussion of CRTT's most significant rival, radical connectionism ("RCON"). Its success would not affect any of the claims of the present book, which is concerned only with providing *one* plausible way to meet the challenges of dualism. However, indicating some of the difficulties faced by RCON provides an opportunity for noting seven crucial mental phenomena that CRTT, unlike RCON, easily begins to explain. Indeed, the capacity of CRTT to explain these phenomena helps meet the "explanatory gaps" regarding intentionality and rationality that we noted in chapter 1.

There remains the gap with the qualitative. In chapter 11 we will consider an extension of CRTT, CRTQ, that promises to account for such phenomena. We will start with a consideration of nested intentionality (§11.1), first person indexical subjectivity (§11.2), and an important distinction between central and avowed attitudes (§11.3), proceeding then to CRTQ's account of qualitative states as computational relations to representations that obey certain restrictions analogous to those on first-person indexicality. We will then consider how this account offers a clear, materialist explanation of many of the problems we discussed in chapter 2, e.g. privacy and privileged access (§11.4.1–.4.2), as well as the phenomena of "what it's like" (§11.4.3). Indeed, once we become clear about just which "phenomenal properties" are represented in sensation (§11.5), we will see that they are best regarded not as *real* properties at all, but as simply the "intentional-properties" championed by the irreferentialist (§11.6). There are a surprising number of good reasons for adopting such an unintuitive view (§11.6.1). Moreover, if phenomenal objects and properties are not real, then Kripke's Cartesian argument, although rightly capturing some of the modal properties of such phenomena, are ultimately ineffective against materialism (§11.6.2).

Although there is good reason to think that CRTQ may well be an ultimately correct account of qualitative experience, some peculiar problems remain. It seems difficult to rule out at least the metaphysical possibility of qualitative and intentional differences between functional isomorphs (§11.7.1), and, worse, there is the much more real possibility of "absent qualia," given arbitrary realizations of CRTQ or most any functionalist proposal (§11.7.2). I will conclude (§11.7.3) with some speculations about a kind of "behavioral" chauvinism in this regard that simply may be an unprincipled, but ineluctable, feature of our application of mental concepts, particularly as they play a role in our moral lives.

4 Why It Matters

A brief word about why philosophy of mind is important. Perhaps more so than any other area of philosophy, philosophy of mind impinges on a wide variety of issues outside of the subject. In the first place, philosophical views about the nature of the mind are inextricably bound up with our ordinary conceptions of ourselves. It's not like the case of, say, philosophy of mathematics, where ordinary arithmetic – and even most of mathematics – can be quite productively pursued and understood without deciding the philosophical question of just what a number *is*. Most popular conceptions of human beings involve substantial and controversial philosophical assumptions about the nature of, for example, the soul, the will, belief, faith, desire, emotions, subjectivity, consciousness, their relation to physical phenomena and their accessibility to scientific inquiry. Some of these can have fairly important consequences for our moral and political lives: philosophical views about the mental lives of fetuses, infants, and animals affect many people's ethical views about important issues such as abortion, infanticide, and the treatment of animals as sources of food and as subjects for medical (and cosmetic) experimentation (see, for example, Singer 1979 and Tooley 1983). At least one philosopher of considerable influence outside of philosophy, Richard Rorty (1979), has drawn from his philosophical views about the mental the conclusion that it is not "irrational to . . . deny civil rights to the moronic (or fetuses, or Martians, or *aboriginal tribes*)" (p. 190, emphasis mine).[8]

10

Quite apart from popular conceptions, philosophy also influences the kind of psychological research that is actually funded and undertaken. The hegemony of Radical Behaviorism for so many decades, for example, was due as much (if not more) to philosophical views about scientific explanation and the commitments of mentalism as to actual empirical successes of the theory of conditioned responses. Much current research in neurophysiology is undertaken out of a philosophical conviction that, since, for lack of ghosts, the mind must somehow just *be* the brain, the real science of it must be neuroscience. And throughout psychological research, one still encounters "operationalist" and "verificationist" assumptions that were the legacy of the Logical Positivism that flourished in philosophy half a century ago, but which has long been repudiated there and elsewhere (see §5.4). This is not to say that psychologists or funding agencies are particularly self-conscious about these influences; to the contrary, the influences can be all the more pronounced where they are unacknowledged and merely taken for granted as obvious truths. If these philosophical views turn out to be confused, psychologists might have reason to undertake very different kinds of research.

The connections between philosophy and psychotherapy are often quite explicit: Freud's continuity with the work of German romantic philosophers like Hegel, Schopenhauer and Nietzsche is legend, and many therapies today explicitly endorse various forms of mysticism. But even when the issues are more mundane, highly controversial philosophical views about the nature of mind can play a surprisingly important role. Consider the recent controversy surrounding Freud's work, and the related, more specific issue of "repressed" and therapeutically "recovered" memory (usually of sexual abuse in early childhood). *The New York Review of Books* ran some widely read exchanges on these topics in 1993 and 1994, that brought together a number of prominent intellectuals, ranging from philosophers to literary critics to psychoanalysts and developmental psychologists. The exchanges are well worth detailed study, if only for the light they throw on the considerable significance – not to mention the enormous difficulty – of issues in the philosophy of mind. To cite one such exchange, the philosopher Thomas Nagel wrote:[9]

> Much of human mental life consists of complex events with multiple causes and background conditions that will never precisely recur. . . . That doesn't mean that explanation is impossible, only that it cannot be sought by the methods appropriate in particle physics, cancer research, or the study of reflexes. We may not be able to run controlled experiments, but we can still try to make internal sense of what people do, in light of their circumstances, relying on a general form of understanding that is supported by its usefulness in countless other cases. . . . For most of us who believe in the reality of repression and the unconscious . . . the belief is based not on blind trust in the authority of analysts and their clinical observations but on the evident usefulness of a rudimentary Freudian outlook in understanding ourselves and other people. (1994a:35)

A leading developmental psychologist, Alison Gopnik, wrote a reply to Nagel, taking up a claim Nagel had cited, that "we conceive when we are very young of mental states on the model of corporeal entities . . . of a thought as a piece of food in the mouth or as faeces":

> Obviously, this claim would seem outlandish and absurd to common-sense psychology. More important, however, the nature of young children's thoughts about thought, their understanding and knowledge of the mind has lately been subject to a great deal of systematic experimental . . . investigation . . . that does follow precisely the canons that Professor Nagel protests should not apply to psychoanalysis. The research is replicable, public, generalizable and leads to specific testable predictions. . . . There is not even the faintest shred of evidence in any of this work that children ever think of thoughts as physical objects, let alone as faeces or food. In much the same way, of course, scientific psychology has found almost no evidence for the analytic accounts of memory that are currently causing so much real human misery. (1994:55)

The question is whether we should treat Freudian claims, and the issue of whether there is "repressed memory," as an issue to be treated like any other issue, say, in medicine, by the methods of objective science. As we shall see, this is an issue squarely in the philosophy of mind. And, as Gopnik rightly emphasizes, its resolution may make a serious difference to real human misery: either to possible victims of actual repressed abuse or to the individuals who might be wrongly accused of it.[10] (We will return to this issue in §10.3.4.) Sometimes philosophy matters.

Notes

1 The purpose of the rest of this section is to locate the approach of the present book in relation to previous approaches that may be weighing heavily on some reader's minds. The beginning reader might well read most of this section lightly, picking the discussion up seriously again at two paragraphs before §3, and returning to this section after reading the discussion of "irreferentialism" in §5.2.

2 Note that (*pace* Chomsky 1995), the word "materialism" in its present usage has long lost its association with "matter" specifically – thus, a materialist can often believe that everything is mass-energy. The view is often also called "physicalism": the words tend to be used interchangeably. Later (§6.4), I will use the terms to mark a distinction between two different ideas in this area.

3 Further chutzpah about the mental is often exhibited in many people's surprisingly strong (often divergent) opinions about whether ants, cockroaches, rats, porpoises, chimpanzees have minds, are conscious, can feel pains – without the slightest sense that the questions might be ones of fairly subtle scientific investigation.

4 In order to avoid prolixity and to remain as neutral as possible about issues when a stand may not be required, I will use "mental phenomena" to cover the broadest ontological range: mental objects, states, processes, properties (see §1.1.1) – even mental concepts and mental terms (§1.5.1).

5 In a similar vein, many people think that a central question that ought to be addressed in the philosophy of mind – it was early on addressed by Descartes – is the immortality of the soul: but whatever one's view of that issue, there still are the multitudinous questions about how souls, whether immortal, or mortal and material, manage to do *whatever* they do.

6 Or, as in Searle (1980a, 1984), they advert to entirely unspecified "biological properties." Whatever the ultimate merits of Wittgenstein's views of the mental, I think he does characterize well the traditional mind/body debate when he complains of "yet uncomprehended processes in yet unexplored mediums" (1953:§308), a remark that, as Wittgensteinians often correctly insist, applies as much to materialist as to traditional dualistic views.

7 As Ned Block put it to me, concurring about the moral to be learned from RBism, "Never again!"

8 Specifically, he argues that, since (according to him) modern science has shown that there are no real mental phenomena, no one could be making a factual error in supposing that aboriginals did or didn't satisfy some mental condition for the possession of rights – or, for that matter, whether trees or stones did. We'll discuss such "eliminativist" views in chapter 3.

9 As he acknowledges in a later letter expanding on his views, he is echoing views of other philosophers, specifically Wollheim, Hopkins, and Davidson. We'll discuss such interpretativist and instrumental views of mind in §3.1, returning to this quotation from Nagel in §10.3.4.

10 See Loftus et al. (1994) and Brown (1995) for evidence that indicates that scientific psychology is a bit more equivocal on this issue than Gopnik claims.

1
Preliminaries

1.1 Some Distinctions Among Purported Mental Phenomena

What are mental phenomena that are of such concern? I will argue shortly (§1.5) that it would be unwise to venture any sort of definition before having some theories in hand. Better simply to start with many of the things that are ordinarily regarded as mental, and see what order we can find in them. In §1.1.1 we'll set out some basic metaphysical and logical distinctions within which mental phenomena can be located,[1] turning in §1.1.2 to discuss two major kinds of mental phenomena, conscious states and propositional attitudes, that have proved philosophically troublesome. As we shall see in detail in chapter 2, they have each, in different ways, resisted incorporation into a physical account of the world, and this has given rise to three major views regarding their ontology: reductionism, dualism, and eliminativism (§1.2). Much of the philosophy of mind (and this book) is an attempt to adjudicate between these views. In the rest of the chapter, we'll set out some ground rules for the debate (§1.3–1.5).

1.1.1 *Language and metaphysics*

As I shall use the term "phenomena," it is the broadest ontological category, including concrete and abstract particulars, properties, types, tokens, states, events – and even all the linguistic ways we have of referring to these very different things (cf. §1.5.1). Such a broad category could invite confusion. However, where the occasion demands it, we can retreat to the different sub-categories it covers, as discussed below.

The world is commonly assumed to be filled with *individual things* (or "particulars"), such as atoms, molecules, mountains, molehills, people, cities. Most examples of particulars that come to mind, like those I've just mentioned, are of *"concrete"* ones that are located in space and time: within certain limits (involving vagueness and physical limitations), we can ask *when* and *where* an atom decays, a molecule is formed, a city exists, or a person lives. But there also seem to be clear examples of *"abstract"* particulars as well, for example, *numbers* and *sets*, that do *not* have spatio-temporal locations: it doesn't seem to make sense to ask *where* or *when* the number 7, or the set of odd numbers exists (7 couldn't have been hidden in the closet last March!). "Platonists" believe such entities exist; "nominalists" don't, although they have had a notoriously difficult time sustaining their case. Since this dispute is largely independent of issues in the philosophy of mind, I will assume what most philosophers who have thought about this issue presently assume, that such abstracta as sets and numbers do exist in the world independently of us.[2]

Whether concrete or abstract, we *designate* token particulars with *singular terms*, either *proper names* ("Sam," "London"), *numerals* ("101," "IV"), or *definite descriptions*, roughly speaking, noun phrases that begin with the definite article "the:" e.g. "the capital of England," "the largest star," "the square of 25." Other examples of singular terms are *demonstratives* ("this," "that"), *pronouns* ("he," "it") and, especially in logic, *variables*, arbitrary letters of the alphabet (usually, the letters "u" through "z") that function *inter alia* as genderless pronouns.[3]

Whether there really are *mental* particulars or not is a difficult question which we shouldn't try to answer just now. But there certainly *seem* to be: for example, there is *the pain* I had in my back a few minutes ago, or that bitter taste of tea last night. (Sensations regarded as objects in this way are frequently called "phenomenal objects.") And then there is *the particular thought* Galileo had one day, that the earth moves, a thought that probably caused some cardinal to fall into *a particular depression* that lasted two weeks. One reason for thinking of these "things" as particulars is that, as I indicated, they certainly seem to have *temporal* location. However, it's not clear that they really are in *space*: was the pain "in" my back in the same way that my spine is? Exactly where was Galileo's thought, or the cardinal's depression? "In their head," we may say, vaguely pointing to a general region, but with no clue how to specify its location any more precisely. We'll later consider ways of avoiding reference to many such peculiar mental particulars (§5.2.1).

One vexing problem in talk about "mental particulars" (if such there be) is that it is often ambiguous between "types" and "tokens." This is a distinction that has its home in thinking about language: for example, consider how many words there are on the next line:

Paris   Paris   Paris

It all depends upon what you're counting: there is one *type* word, but three *tokens* of it. Just so: "the taste of tea," or "the thought that the earth moves" could refer to a *type* mental particular, of which many *tokens* might exist in the same person at different times, and in different people at the same time. At least provisionally, tokens are the specific concrete particulars that have at least a temporal location; types are *sets* (or classes) of them.

A category of language and logic that plays a useful role in philosophy is that of a *predicate*, defined a little more generally than in high school grammar. After Quine (1972:145), we will take a predicate to be *the result of substituting variables for other singular terms in any indicative sentence.* Thus, by substituting "x" for "Socrates" in the sentence "Socrates is wise," one could construct the (1-place) predicate "x is wise;" substituting "x" for "Romeo" and "y" for "Juliet" in "Romeo loves Juliet", the (2-place) predicate "x loves y"; and, substituting "x" for "Romeo," "y" for "Juliet," and "z" for "the violin" in "Romeo gave Juliet the bow to the violin that belonged to his father," a (3-place) predicate "x gave y the bow to z that belonged to x's father."[4] Note that we needn't substitute variables for *all* singular terms in a sentence: in the last example, we didn't, although we could have, substituted for "the bow."

Why substitute variables for some singular terms and not others? It all depends upon what part of a sentence one needs to regard as seriously *referential*, as licensing *existential* claims. Presumably from "Romeo loves Juliet" we should be able to infer "Something (or someone) loves Juliet" and "Romeo loves something" (in logic: we can infer "$(\exists x)Lxj$" and "$(\exists x)Lrx$" from "Lrj"). Indeed, philosophers like to talk of the *values of a variable*: these are the things a predicate is *"true of,"* the *things* that *"satisfy"* the predicate; they comprise the predicate's *"extension."* In the case of 1-place predicates, the predicate is satisfied simply by the objects it is true of: thus, insofar as Socrates is indeed wise, the predicate "x is wise" is true of him; he satisfies the predicate; he is thereby a value of that variable, "x." In the case of 2- or more-place ("n-place") predicates, we say that *an ordered n-tuple* satisfies them: e.g. the ordered pair, ⟨Romeo, Juliet⟩, satisfies the 2-place predicate "x loves y"; the ordered triple, ⟨Romeo, Juliet, the violin that belonged to Romeo's father⟩, the 3-place predicate "x gave y the bow to z that belonged to x's father." Thinking of sentences composed of predicates in this way forces us to become self-conscious about precisely what things we are committed to talking about, the things to which, in Quine's (1953d) phrase, we are "ontologically committed."

Sometimes we don't want to become ontologically committed merely by virtue of using a grammatically singular term. There is no need to construct from "John lied for the sake of Mary," a 3-place predicate "x lied for y of z" since a 2-place one, "x lied for the sake of y" would surely do as well: there is no need to think of "sakes" as genuine *particular things*, as values of variables, in addition to the *people* who do things (as we say, as a *façon de parler*) for "each other's sake." Many cases however aren't so obvious and trivial. We'll see that we'll want to think carefully about which parts of our ordinary mental terms we should regard as genuinely referential: from "Ann complained of the pain in her back" should we construct "x complained of y in z," thus committing ourselves to *pains* as well as to Ann and her back? From a sentence like "John thinks that grass is green" should we construct a 1-place predicate "x thinks that grass is green," treating "that grass is green" as simply a non-referential part of a long predicate true of John, or a 2-place predicate "x believes y," true of John and a proposition (and what are *these*?)? "Irreferentalism" is the view that certain apparently referential mental terms shouldn't really be so regarded. We'll discuss this topic in detail in §5.2.

Thinking about predicates and their relation to the world has also seemed to many philosophers[5] to invite talk about "universals" like *properties* and *relations* in the world that correspond, respectively, to 1- and many-place predicates. For example, *wisdom* is sometimes thought to be the reference of "x is wise," *love* of "x loves y," and some harder to name, but just as real, relation ("*giving the bow of the violin of one's father*"?) of "x gave y the bow to z that belonged to x's father." Properties and relations are often distinguished from the *extension* of the predicate, which is the set of *actual* objects that satisfy it, or even the *comprehension*, which is the set of all actual and (if such there be) *possible* objects that *might* satisfy it. Thus, talk of properties and relations is often thought to be "*intensional*" ("with an s"), as opposed to extensional. *Wisdom*, for example, is to be distinguished both from the set of actual wise people (Socrates, Aristotle, . . .) and the set of *possible* but maybe *not actual* ones (Socrates, Aristotle, Zeus, Superman, . . .). One reason for distinguishing them is that it seems that two different properties could have the same comprehension: for example, *being an equilateral triangle* and *being an equiangular triangle* (which in geometry one proves are "equivalent"); or *being a round square* and *being even and odd*, the extensions of these latter two being empty in all possible worlds (the reader should keep such examples in mind; they will prove important at a number of places in our discussion, e.g. §9.4). Because they will aid in the exposition of a variety of material here, I shall allow that there exist *some* properties corresponding to *some* predicates, for example, properties that causally explain why things happen (e.g. a property of *having mass* that explains why bodies attract each other).[6]

A metaphysical category that *is* caught up in some of the most difficult issues in the philosophy of mind is that of "mental universals": *concepts, ideas, thoughts, propositions.* These, too, seem to figure in our accounts of the world: as Frege (1892/1952) pointed out, it seems natural to say that "the same thoughts are passed on from one generation to another." "Propositions," for example, seem to be what is "expressed" by different sentences in different languages ("Schnee ist weiss," and "La niege est blanche" express the same thought or proposition as "Snow is white"). They seem to be "composed" of concepts (e.g. the concepts [snow] and [white][7]). Yet they are not easily localizable: where is the concept of white? Where is the proposition that is expressed by two synonymous sentences? They can't be in only one of our heads, since we seem to be able to share them: you and I can both think "Triangles are also trilaterals," and, if we can, then the concept [triangle] is thought by us both. Moreover, whether concepts and propositions exist only with respect to mental phenomena is controversial. Many (e.g. Bealer 1982) claim that they are needed as the relata of logical relations: one proposition, e.g. [Socrates is wise] entails another, e.g. [Someone is wise]. We shall consider in due course whether propositions are needed for explanation in psychology (§5.2.4).

Still other metaphysical categories that are relevant to the mind are those of *states* and *events*. *Events* can be understood in a number of different ways, between which we needn't choose here. They could be regarded as just regions (or chunks) of space-time: the event of Brutus killing Caesar could be regarded as the portion of space-time consisting of, say, Brutus, his knife, and Caesar, beginning, say, at the moment that Brutus decided to plunge the knife and ending with Caesar's brain death.[8] Or it could be regarded as an ordered quadruple, or other composite, consisting of Brutus, Caesar, the relation of *killing*, and the Ides of March 44BC. *States* can be regarded as "boring events," events in which "nothing happens": so a particular state of being in pain for an hour is the same as the event of being in pain for that hour. Some philosophers think that much of our apparent talk about phenomenal objects could be better construed as talk about the events of having a pain or a thought during a certain period of time (cf. §5.2.1). Both states and events can be regarded as further particulars. Accordingly, *token* mental states and events (e.g. my having of a headache all day yesterday) have at least temporal location. *Types* of such states and events (that kind of headache; the longing for death) can be regarded, again, as sets of such tokens.

There are plenty of other metaphysical distinctions that are relevant to the mind, but they can be introduced as we go along. With the ones we have so far, we are in a position to consider one major distinction among mental phenomena, that between qualitative states and propositional attitudes.

1.1.2   Qualitative states and propositional attitudes

Conscious qualitative states are probably what first leap to mind when we think of mental phenomena. These are the states of mind of which we seem to be immediately aware and that are frequently associated with a particular "feel": sights, sounds, tastes, tickles, itches, pains, and a steady flow of thoughts, desires, memories, and imaginings. The "stream of consciousness" of these states seems filled with at least two kinds of phenomena that have seemed problematic, what I will call *phenomenal objects*, or the apparent objects of conscious experiences, e.g. *pains*, *tickles*, and *images*; and *phenomenal properties* or "*qualia*": [looking red], [feeling painful], [tasting like pineapple] (to be distinguished from the properties *in the objects* that may be the typical external *causes* of these qualia).

Some of the objects of conscious qualitative states are such things as thoughts, beliefs, and desires. These things, or states, are called the *propositional attitudes*; to

18

a first approximation, they can be defined as states represented by mental verbs that take *sentence complements* (a "that . . ." or "to . . ." clause) as their direct object, as in the case of "believe," "expect," "hope."[9] For example, a person can be in a state of thinking, believing, hoping, or expecting *that a friend will visit*. These sentence complements could be taken to be non-referential parts of what we might obstinately treat as 1-place predicates (e.g. "x hopes that a friend will visit"), or, alternatively, they could be taken to be substituents in 2-place predicates ("x hopes (that) y"), where the second-place invites reference to special objects called (propositional) *"contents"* (or *"propositions"*), to which the agent of the attitude is related. I postpone a principled stand on this issue until §5.2.4. Until then, it is worth noting that we do *seem* all the time to refer to the *contents* of people's thought, beliefs, desires, and these seem quite distinct from phenomenal objects and qualia: the thought that $73 + 29 = 102$ doesn't seem to feel different from the thought that $27 + 43 = 70$, and, even if it did, that would seem irrelevant: two people could have different thoughts that might feel the same to them, and the same thought might feel differently to them (some mathematicians think "in images," others "in words"). But, in any case, at least since Freud, it seems to be a serious possibility that many propositional attitudes may have no feelings attached to them at all, since they may be *unconscious*, at least in the sense that the person having the attitude may be entirely unable to report upon it (we will discuss some of the reasons for taking unconscious attitudes seriously in §3.2.1 and 9.6).

Much talk of propositional attitudes is actually ambiguous between the *state* of e.g. thinking, believing, hoping; the corresponding *relations* (thinking, believing, hoping); and the *content* to which the agent is thereby related. For example, a person's *belief* that *reindeer can fly* could be the *content*, [Reindeer can fly]; or it could be the state or the relation of *believing*, as opposed to *disbelieving* or merely *entertaining* that content. In order to disambiguate, I will follow the widespread convention of referring to the *relation* as the (propositional) *attitude*, and the claim that the agent is related to by virtue of being in that state as the *content* (sometimes "the object") of that attitude. The *state* will be separately indicated as such, i.e. the state of an agent bearing a certain attitude relation to a certain content.

Propositional attitudes can be divided into two broad types, *informational* ones that merely represent the world "neutrally" as *being* one way rather than another, e.g. belief, suspicion, imagining; and *directional* ones which motivate an agent to act in one way or another with regard to a particular way the world might be, e.g. preference, desire, hate.[10] In most discussions, philosophers use "belief" and "desire" as representative examples of each of these categories, but it shouldn't be supposed that anyone thinks that these are the basic or ultimate attitudes that figure in ordinary mental talk, much less in psychological theory. They are simply representative of those categories.

19

1.1.3 Rationality and intentionality

There are two important features of propositional attitudes that have been of concern to philosophers: their (potential) *rationality* and what has come to be called their *intentionality*. Rationality is the property an attitude has by virtue of bearing certain kinds of relations to evidence, other attitudes, and action: for example, a belief is rational insofar as it is supported by evidence (a belief that roses are red might be supported by a representative sample of red roses); an argument is rational insofar as it is supported by premises ("Socrates is wise" is supported by "All Greeks are wise" and "Socrates is a Greek"); and a decision might be rational insofar as it leads to the fulfillment of a person's plans or other desires (it's rational for someone to intend to learn French if she wants to get on with people in France).

Intentionality[11] is the property of propositional attitudes (and many things produced as a result of attitudes, like words and sentences) whereby they are *about things*, i.e. whereby they are *meaningful* or have a (semantic) *content*. The thought that tomatoes are red is *about* tomatoes (and maybe about *being red* as well), and it is thereby different from the thought that snow is white, which is about snow (and *being white*). We seem to be able to have thoughts that are about, well, just *anything* – or, anyway, anything we can think of!

Intentionality has been of special concern to philosophers because it exhibits a number of puzzling properties. One problem is specifying precisely the relation it is: what real relation (if any) *connects*, e.g. "cat" with cats, "dog" with dogs, "12" with twelve, and (perhaps) "is white" with whiteness? But another problem is specifying plausibly what sort of thing it is that an attitude could be a relation *to*. One might think that thoughts about Mark Twain are a relation between thoughts and the man Mark Twain. However, the man *Mark Twain* is identical to the very man, *Sam Clemens*. But, at least in one natural way of speaking, thoughts about Mark Twain aren't always thoughts about Sam Clemens: someone ignorant of the identity could have a thought that was about the one but not about the other (she might think that Twain was a great writer and sincerely profess to know nothing about Clemens).

Worse, some thoughts seem to be, well, "about *things*" that don't exist at all! Children regularly have thoughts that are *about* Santa Claus, the tooth fairy, and unspeakable creatures lurking underneath their beds; Ponce de Leon tramped through Florida swamps obsessed with thoughts "about" a wholly mythical "fountain of youth." Even we more savvy adults have thoughts about such things when we so much as *deny* that these things exist: after all, you can't very well deny that Santa Claus exists unless your denial is actually *about* Santa Claus! The things that thoughts are *about* are a curious lot, as is, therefore, this property of intentionality that seems to give rise to them. We'll return to this topic many times (see §2.5.6 for a fuller discussion, and chapter 9 for some theories of it).

1.2   The Metaphysics of Mind: the Three Main Approaches

Any ultimate explanation of mental phenomena will have to be in *non*-mental terms, else it won't be an *explanation* of it. There might be explanations of *some* mental phenomena in terms of others – perhaps *hope* in terms of *belief* and *desire* – but if we are to provide an explanation of *all* mental phenomena, we would in turn have to explain such mentalistic explainers until finally we reached entirely non-mental terms. Of course, there might be no such explanation of the mental: we might simply have to take certain mental phenomena as ultimate and unexplainable, but at least at the outset this would seem to be tantamount to an admission of defeat for the project of understanding the mind.

To what non-mental phenomena might we turn? On the face of it, theological, sociological, or economic phenomena presuppose mentality and so cannot explain it. The only plausible non-mental phenomena we know of are the biological, and, given what seems to be the explanation of the biological, the physical. Thus, in trying to provide an account of the nature of mental phenomena, a good deal of the philosophy of mind has come to be dominated by a specific metaphysical concern: to relate mental phenomena to physical phenomena. This has turned out to be tremendously difficult. As we shall discuss in detail in the next chapter, mental phenomena seem to exhibit a number of properties – like the qualitative feels, rationality and intentionality that we've just discussed – that no physical phenomena seem to exhibit. This has given rise to the fundamental problem in the philosophy of mind, the "mind/body problem" (or problem*s*, since, as we shall see, there are quite a number of different ones), and three metaphysical positions in regard to it: *reductionism*, *dualism*, and *eliminativism*.

1.2.1   Reductionism

One of the most important events in intellectual history was the development in seventeeth-century Europe of Newtonian mechanics. It seemed to offer a wonderfully elegant theory, not only of the motion of celestial bodies and the trajectories of missiles, but of *any* dynamical process in nature. The entire universe seemed to be describable in terms of the forces exerted by particles interacting in space and time, and, indeed, it seemed plausible to suppose that familiar macro-descriptions of the world, insofar as they were true at all, were necessitated by the truth of the underlying physical descriptions of those particles and forces. Details needed to be – and were – worked out as to the precise character of the particles and the forces between them. But, to many people, it seemed as if there were no limit to the power of this theory to explain any phenomena one observed.

Of course, there appeared to be two serious counterexamples to this claim: life and mind. "Vitalists" claimed that the phenomena of living things – metabolism, self-animation, reproduction – could not be accounted for by physical principles. These days at least, few people remain persuaded of this: the spectacular successes of molecular biology make it virtually certain that biological phenomena are just very special cases of physical phenomena.

The reductionist strategy envisions similar successes for psychological phenomena. According to the general reductionist strategy, mental phenomena are ultimately to be explained in various ways as physical phenomena. It's just a matter of empirical scientific advance, supplemented perhaps by a little philosophical therapy, to discover what those ways are. This is largely the strategy of this book, in which I will be exploring what I take to be the substantial insights that can be gained from thinking of the brain as a computer (although I shall also be at pains to indicate some of the serious problems that still remain).

A crucial terminological point that can be the source of much needless confusion: *reduction* is not the same as *elimination*! If a chemist succeeds in "reducing" claims about water to claims about H_2O, or a biologist "reduces" life to a certain complex chemical process, they have not for a moment shown that *water* or *life* don't exist: to the contrary, insofar as molecules of H_2O or those specific chemical processes genuinely exist, so do the water and life with which they have been identified! Similarly, if a philosopher or psychologist succeeds in "reducing" some mental phenomenon to a physical one, that doesn't for a moment entail that the mental phenomenon isn't perfectly *real*. It, too, is every bit as real as the physical phenomenon with which it is has been identified.

Confusion on this point is sometimes aggravated by a too solemn misreading of Bishop Butler's famous platitude, "Everything is what it is and not another thing." Searle (1992), for example, cites this platitude on behalf of what he regards as "the commonsense objection to any identity theory [of the mental with the physical] . . . that you can't identify anything mental with anything non-mental, without leaving out the mental" (p. 39). But, of course, someone who is identifying some mental with some physical phenomenon is patently *not* identifying the mental *phenomenon itself* with some genuinely *non-mental phenomenon*, since that would be obviously self-contradictory and would, indeed, violate Butler's maxim. What such an identity theorist is doing is linking mental with non-mental *terms*, in effect claiming that they refer to one and same thing, just as the chemist who identifies water with H_2O molecules is linking ordinary and chemical terms. Such identifications are arguably the very stuff of scientific advance: if they fall afoul of Butler's maxim, so much the worse for the maxim. But surely Butler didn't intend the maxim in this way. If the identity theorist's identification is in fact correct, then the mental phenomenon in question could not possibly have been "left out."[12]

Unfortunately, however, these very identifications do invite a different usage of the words "reduction" and "elimination" that seems to have exactly the opposite effect: after all, someone might argue, a successful reductionist program would succeed in "eliminating" mental *terms*, showing them to be *superfluous*, replaceable entirely by physical ones.[13] Scientific *reduction of the things referred to by ordinary terms* seems to invite an *elimination of the ordinary terms* themselves, at least in the sense that it makes them seem redundant and superfluous: who needs to talk about "water" any more if we can talk about "H_2O" instead? This latter view does *not* count as "eliminativist" as I (and most of the philosophers in the debate) will use the term: it's one thing to eliminate certain *terms* by replacing them with theoretically richer co-referential terms, quite another to eliminate the *very things* themselves that the old and (if the reduction is successful) the new terms still refer to. In any case, in using the terms "eliminativist" and "reductionist" the reader needs to attend carefully to whether the issue is about words or the things the words refer to.

We will discuss the genuinely *eliminativist* strategy in a moment. First, some mention of the standard *non*-reductive, *non*-eliminativist strategy, dualism.

1.2.2 Dualism

The general dualistic strategy despairs of there being any adequate reduction of mental to physical phenomena, and supposes there is an unbridgeable gulf between the two. Dualism has a number of historical sources: there are superstitious beliefs in ghosts, "auras" and/or immaterial "spirits;" and there are religious beliefs in angels and immortal souls. But it would be a mistake to suppose that all dualists are committed to any of these sorts of things. Many (perhaps even most) modern dualists are for the most part not concerned with either ghosts or immortality, but with fundamentally different aspects of reality exhibited by the mind that seem not to be capturable by the physical sciences. The project of explaining the mental in physical terms – indeed, presumably in any non-mental terms – is hopeless. Mental phenomena constitute a brute, basic feature of the world.

Most famously, the seventeenth-century French philosopher, René Descartes (1596–1650), claimed that human rationality couldn't be a physical process:

> [T]he rational soul . . . could not be in any way extracted from the power of matter . . . but must . . . be expressly created. (1637/1970:117–18)

And the nineteenth-century Austrian philosopher, Franz Brentano (1838–1917), claimed the same about intentionality:

> the reference to something as an object is a distinguishing characteristic of all mental phenomena. No physical phenomenon exhibits anything similar. (1874/1973:97)

The property we noted in the previous section of something's being "about" Mark Twain (as opposed to "about" Sam Clemens), or "about" Santa Claus or Zeus, is not a property any physical object can display. Many have found particularly Brentano's claim so compelling that they regard this (what is now called "Brentano's Thesis") as one of the cornerstones of their philosophy (e.g. Chisholm 1957).

More recently, Thomas Nagel (1986) has urged a dualism of properties (what he and others call a "dual aspect theory") that stresses the importance of the "subjective" as opposed to "objective" view of the world. He quite explicitly opposes the reductionist strategy that we shall largely be pursuing:

> The reductionist program that dominates current work in the philosophy of mind is completely misguided, because it is based on the groundless assumption that a particular conception of objective reality is exhaustive of what there is. Eventually, I believe, current attempts to understand the mind by analogy with man-made computers . . . will be recognized as a gigantic waste of time. . . . [T]here is no reason to assume that the world as it is in itself must be objectively comprehensible. . . . Some things can only be understood from the inside. (1986:16–18)

It is important to note that the issue here is not merely ontological, but essentially involves *explanation*. As Nagel wrote in the quote that we discussed in the introduction (§4), mental explanation "cannot be sought by the methods appropriate in particle physics, cancer research, or the study of reflexes" (Nagel 1994a:35). "Making internal sense of what people do" is to be a project involving not only a different ontology, but consequently a very different methodology than that employed in the physical sciences.[14] In a curious phrase that surfaces from time to time, psychology would be an "autonomous science."

There is something of a puzzle about knowing exactly what to make of such claims. We don't really seem to have precedents of any other "autonomous science" in at least the concrete realm. Arguably the "sciences of the abstract" – in particular, mathematics – are autonomous of any physical science, but claims about any one phenomenon in space and time do seem in one way or another connected to other claims about other phenomena. Moreover, it is not clear what it really means to say of any concrete phenomenon that it is, in and of itself, unexplainable in principle in further terms. As the example of, say, biology shows, phenomena thought to be inexplicable at one time turn out to be explicable at another; and it certainly would have been amazing had the phenomena of life really turned out to have not been explainable in physical terms. Of course, someone might argue that at least *physical* phenomena can't ultimately be explained – but even this isn't wholly clear: many physicists are eager to explain what have been taken so far to be the fundamental forces of nature (gravitation, electromagnetism, the strong and weak nuclear forces) in still more fundamental terms; and it's unclear just where the search for further explanation must really

24

stop. What would it be for a phenomenon to be, in and of itself, apart from our understanding, a metaphysically "brute fact"? Whatever it means, this seems to be the surprising claim that the dualist is making about the mind.

1.2.3 Eliminativism

It is precisely this kind of ontological and methodological irreducibility and autonomy of the mental that worries many philosophers who strive for some kind of unification in our emerging theory of the world. Thus, Quine contrasts his own attitude to Brentano's:

> One may take the Brentano thesis either as showing the indispensability of intentional idioms and the importance of an autonomous science of intention, or as showing the baselessness of intentional idioms and the emptiness of a science of intention. My attitude unlike Brentano's is the second. (1960:221)

At any rate, exasperation with both the difficulties of the reductionist strategy, and with what is often regarded as the extravagances of the dualistic one, has led many philosophers to question the reality of the problematic mental phenomena entirely. Just as the rise of evolutionary biology seemed to leave no place for God, so, for many eliminativists, does the success of physical theory leave no place for the mind (indeed, the debate today about the existence of the mind plays something of the role the debate about the existence of God played a century ago). If something can't be reduced to the physical, it has no place in a serious theory of the world.

The eliminativist strategy can seem to many people so preposterous as to not be worth entertaining seriously. As Kent Bach once put it, the eliminativist is actually denying the usual explanation of why the chicken crossed the road and why firemen wear red suspenders! Searle goes so far as to say that eliminativism is just "crazy . . . too insane to merit serious consideration" (1992:48). However, it should be borne in mind that eliminativism need not be regarded as a proposal about how people should ordinarily live and talk. It is an issue about what is to be taken seriously as *science*. Quine and other eliminativists are quite happy to speak a mentalistic *vernacular* in getting on in the world, just as they are happy to engage in pre-Copernican talk of "sunrises" and even assume a geocentric theory when navigating at sea, or lapse into sloppy Newtonian descriptions of a world they know to be strictly non-Newtonian. They regard mental talk, that is, as at best merely an *instrument*, allowing for useful prediction and manipulation of the behavior of certain objects we encounter, but not as strictly true or literally descriptive of those objects. We shall consider eliminativist proposals in greater detail in chapters 3 and 4, and I, myself, shall endorse some quite specific, limited eliminativist proposals both there and in chapter 11.

1.3 The Need for Non-tendentious Evidence

A crucial notion for adjudicating any debate, and certainly the one among reductionists, dualists, and eliminativists, is that of *non-tendentious evidence*. Suppose, by
way of analogy, that we were debating whether we needed to posit angels in order
to explain the motion of the planets (we suppose there is no plausible *reduction* of
angels to certain physical phenomena). The Newtonian denies it, claiming that all
the data regarding, for example, the position of the planets can be explained
merely on the more modest hypothesis of universal gravitation, an hypothesis for
which, moreover, there is abundant independent evidence. Imagine now that the
angelologist replies that the Newtonian can't explain *the angelic motion of the planets*
– the fact that it is being produced by angels – much less the fluttering of their
wings, or the love with which they do their pushing. The Newtonian can simply
reply that he sees no reason to think that there are such phenomena to explain: the
supposition that there are is of a piece with the very hypothesis under dispute, viz.
that there are angels pushing around the planets. The angelologist is begging the
question by appealing to tendentious data.

We'll see that opponents of eliminativism have to be careful to avoid just this
position of the angelologist, presupposing the very forms of mentality that the
eliminativist disputes. One reason for this is that if we were ordinarily asked to say
why we think anyone has mental states, we would point either to ourselves,
exclaiming that nothing could be more obvious than that, in one's own case, one has a
mind: that one is just immediately aware of having thoughts and feelings. However, if someone is seriously disputing whether something is the case, it is no help
simply to insist that it *obviously* is. At least if one is to meet the philosophical (and,
for many, the serious scientific) challenge, one needs to think of some sort of
reasons that could *justify* what one may, for all that, find obvious. After all,
consider how "obvious" religious fanatics often find *their* claims. Merely beating
one's breast and insisting one has mental states is no more effective than beating
one's bible and saying God exists because that book – the word of God, after all
– says He does. Of course, it might be thought that introspection about mental
phenomena enjoys here some special status. However, the eliminativist can provide good reasons for doubting that introspection is quite as reliable as people
suppose (§3.2.2).

Putting aside introspection, and turning to the case of establishing that other
people have minds, we would probably cite their *actions*: the fact that they
regularly engage in all manner of intelligent, deliberate activity. But such descriptions also beg the question: saying someone has performed the *action* of "raising her
arm" presupposes some kind of mental activity as its cause, in a way that describing it merely as "her arm rose" does not. Again, it appears that in our description

of the ordinary data we would cite, we are inclined to presuppose precisely what the eliminativist is disputing.

We will see that this demand for non-tendentious data will cut both ways: while much of our folk psychology is, I will argue, supportable by non-tendentious evidence, some crucial bits seem not to be. Some of our most cherished beliefs about the mind seem to far outrun the non-tendentious evidence that can be adduced for them. Specifically, most people are inclined to apply concepts of qualia, consciousness, free will and personal identity, for which, I submit that there is no non-tendentious evidence can be found. These concepts involve the "stronger mentalisms" that I address at the end of chapter 11.

1.4 The Need for Fairness

Many people come to the mind/body problems fresh – it may well be the problem that first grabs them in philosophy – without having thought much about other areas of philosophy. The mind/body problems are so numerous, complex, and difficult that they have a way of bringing out almost every other philosophical problem that can be raised anywhere. This is perhaps all to the good in the long run, since the mind/body problems can often give an urgency to problems that otherwise can seem academic and remote. But in the short run there is the danger of losing sight of problems that are *peculiar* to the mental. We shall see a surprising number of such instances as we proceed. In the light of this phenomenon, I want to try to abide in the present discussion by the following maxim:

Fairness Maxim for Philosophy of Mind:
   DON'T BURDEN THE MIND WITH EVERYONE ELSE'S PROBLEMS.
   Always ask whether a problem is *peculiar* to the mind, or whether the issue could equally well be raised in other less problematic areas. If it can be, settle it for those areas *first*, and *then* assess the philosophy of mind.

For example, if it turns out (as it will, see §2.5.7), that certain arguments against the identity of a mental with a physical state are equally arguments against the identity of salt with sodium chloride, or a statue with the lump of clay of which it is composed, this would not seem to be a fair argument to raise with special regard to the mind. It's not an interesting argument for any particular "dualism" about the mind that the same argument might make us dualists about salt or statues. Similarly, arguments about the causal efficacy of the mind ought first to be run by examples of causal efficacy in *other* macro-domains – e.g. geology, economics, biology – before special conclusions are pressed about the mind.[15]

27

1.5   Philosophical and Empirical Research

A worry that many readers might have at the outset is whether it is appropriate to orient the philosophy of mind to explanatory issues in the way that I propose. What is philosophy doing intruding on what is surely an empirical scientific task?

First of all, note that, as I've already suggested, *historically* philosophers did try to answer explanatory questions, or, anyway, took much of what they had to say to be part of some explanation. It is only in the twentieth century[16] that a sharp line has been drawn between "philosophical analysis" and "empirical inquiry," a line that many have protested is not principled, and may be of only bureaucratic interest (cf. Quine 1956b/1976).

Secondly, an adequate distinction between philosophy and science would require a much better theory of the nature of *both* those domains than anyone presently has available for *either* of them. The issues here turn out to be just as hard as any other questions historically called "philosophical."[17] Just to get some feel for the difficulty, ask yourself if anyone really has a satisfactory answer about how theories are confirmed in the empirical sciences; what the metaphysical presumptions are of the individual empirical sciences (try our best physics, quantum mechanics!); whether what mathematicians do is something fundamentally different from what physicists, or economists, or linguists do (whether what Einstein, or Kenneth Arrow, or Noam Chomsky do is empirical or conceptual). The fact is, we're all *very confused* about these questions: determining what *kind* of inquiry is appropriate to them seems to be every bit as hard as answering the problems themselves. And all of this is particularly true in the philosophy of mind, where issues about the nature of meaning and reason are themselves some of the very issues being examined.

Thirdly, there are specific problems with insisting from the outset on a sharp distinction between philosophy and science. One of the most troublesome problems in this regard involves an issue that is so near the heart of many of the mind/body problems that it really requires a separate discussion. This is the issue of the status of "philosophical analyses" and "scientific definitions."

1.5.1   *Constitutive analyses*

I have suggested that we'd like some kind of "analysis" of mental phenomena that would enable us to understand their place in nature. But what *is* an "analysis"? It would take us far too far afield to consider this question in any depth. But we do need to have an idea of what I shall be up to in much of the discussion of this book. I hope the following intuitive suggestions will be neutral to the disputes they are intended to help resolve.

What I think has been the underlying concern of philosophers from very early on, and in any case will be the concern of this book, are questions about the *constitutive nature* of various problematic phenomena. In his *Euthyphro*, Plato, for example, famously asked "Is what is holy holy because the gods approve it, or do they approve it because it is holy?," and proceeded to provide some reasons for preferring the latter alternative. Similar questions can and have been asked about other notions – virtue, justice, freedom, coercion, knowledge – and could in principle be asked about most anything: what makes a chair a chair, a duck a duck, or, as we will ask, a mind a mind? I submit that what we are interested in when we ask such questions are conditions that are *explanatorily constitutive* of the phenomenon being analyzed: we want to know what *makes* something an F; *by virtue of what* is it F? That is, I shall suppose that such constitutive "analyses" take the general form:[18]

x is F essentially by virtue of being G

where "G" is replaced by some explanatorily interesting constitutive claim. Some such questions receive fairly obvious answers:

x is a bachelor by virtue of being an unmarried adult male.
x is a US citizen by virtue of being either born in the US, being naturalized, or being the child of a citizen.
x is a chair by virtue of being a portable seat for one.
x is a renate by virtue of being a creature with kidneys.

Others are less obvious (if even correct):

x is knowledge by virtue of being a true belief produced by a reliable means (cf. Goldman 1986)
x is a just social rule by virtue of being rationally acceptable to the members of a society reasoning in ignorance of their specific positions in it (cf. Rawls 1971)
x is mean kinetic energy by virtue of being $mv^2/2$

Many philosophers have thought that these cases are simply ones involving legal or linguistic convention. And perhaps some of especially the first group are of this sort. But it would require a better semantic theory than anyone has yet proposed to show that all of them are. In at least some of these cases, the acceptability of the proposed analysis seems answerable to concerns other than merely recording people's actual usage of a term. There is some sort of normative appeal as well, to the effect that the analysis captures a way we "ought" to define the phenomenon, in some cases because so defining it somehow captures its "real nature" (a point to which we'll return shortly). If this is true, then it isn't clear whether the proper objects of analyses are our concepts or the phenomena in the world they sometimes pick out. However, I don't want to decide this difficult issue here. The exact nature of definition and "analysis" seems to me to await clarification of some of the very issues about meaning with which this book is concerned.

Neutrality on this issue is one of the reasons for my otherwise deplorably free use of the term "phenomena." As I've indicated, I use it as the broadest possible term for not only objects, properties, events, etc., but also for our means of referring to those things, viz. terms and concepts. Consequently, when I speak now of a "constitutive analysis of a phenomenon," this leaves open the question whether it's an analysis of a *concept*, the *meaning of a term*, or *a property*, or other metaphysical entity in the world. For much of our discussion, I submit, it will not be important which it is. If in some cases it turns out to be important, we can always retreat to the more specific category, distinguishing, if we like, for example, an analysis of a concept we deploy from an analysis of the corresponding property in the world.

Whatever one's candidate for analysis, it is crucial for the purposes of this book to distinguish an interest in analysis from other enterprises with which it can easily be conflated. A common confusion is between such analyses and mere *causal* theories of a phenomenon, between what *makes* something the sort of the thing it is, and what *made* it that sort of thing.[19] What *makes* someone a bachelor is being an unmarried adult male; what *made* someone a bachelor was, for example, his chronic indecision. For all its obviousness, this confusion is constantly a temptation with regard to the mental: as we shall see, when neuroscientists announce the discovery of some new neural correlate of a mental phenomenon (e.g. a 40 Hz oscillation in the visual cortex as a correlate of visual consciousness), it is often taken to be an answer to the question about the nature of the phenomenon. But, of course, a mere neural correlate may be as independent of the nature of a mental phenomenon as smoking is of cancer.

Sometimes the constitutive and the causal stories overlap: it's presumably constitutive of being a footprint that the print has been caused (in a specific way) by a foot (this case illustrates the constitutive question nicely, contrasting sharply with the case of smoking and cancer). We'll see that some important mental phenomena may be "aetiological" in just this way: e.g. intentional *action* may be physical motion caused (in a specific way) by certain psychological states. But this coincidence has to be established by some philosophical analysis, not merely by causal discoveries alone.

Another activity often conflated with constitutive analysis is the finding of "extensional equivalents." In a well-known passage, for example, Nelson Goodman (1951) wrote of the kinds of "constructional" definitions he was interested in pursuing in his work:

A constructional definition is correct . . . if the range of application of its definiens is the same as that of its definiendum. Nothing more is required than that the two expressions have identical extensions.   (p. 4)

On such a view, "creature with a heart" would suffice as a definition of "renate," since (let us suppose) there's nothing that's the one that's not the other: all and only actual creatures with kidneys are creatures with hearts; "renate" and "creature with a heart" are co-extensive (i.e. apply to precisely the same things in the world). One reason for being dissatisfied with such definitions is that they don't cover possible cases: it would seem to be perfectly *possible*, or at any rate *intelligible*, that there are renates that don't have hearts. Goodman is undaunted:

We do not require that the definiendum and the definiens agree with respect to all cases that "might have been" as well as to all cases that actually *are*.   (p. 4)

since, as he famously argues, "the notion of 'possible' cases, of cases that do not exist but might have existed, is far from clear" (p. 5).

Although one might agree that modal notions like possibility and necessity aren't as clear as one would like, it is by no means clear that science or human knowledge in general can dispense with them. As perhaps my first invocation of my Fairness Maxim, I want to proceed in the philosophy of mind with some presumption that some kind of sense can be made of modal notions and that their deployment is innocent enough until proven otherwise.

Moreover, finding even an expression that is *necessarily* co-extensive (one that applies to all and only the same *possible* objects) won't suffice for the purposes of analysis: as we noted earlier, "even and odd numbered" is necessarily co-extensive with "round and square" – they both refer to *nothing* in all possible worlds – but neither is remotely a satisfactory analysis of the other. Indeed, this would seem to be the reason that analysis, unlike necessary equivalence, is *asymmetric*: "unmarried eligible male" may define "bachelor" but not *vice versa*: "bachelor" is no sort of analysis of "unmarried adult male."

One advantage of pursuing constitutive analyses is that they permit *partial* suggestions to be illuminating even in the absence of fully adequate ones. For example, it might be very difficult to find analytically necessary and sufficient conditions for something's being a chair. As Fodor once mocked the definition "portable seat for one": what are we to say about a chair with a tack? Clearly, despite this example, "portable seat for one" is a perfectly good contribution to an analysis, even if it isn't quite a sufficient condition. Or some conditions might contribute a sufficient condition for an analysis without being necessary: being a conscious, reasoning, self-reflective agent may be sufficient for being a person in the moral sense, but it is not at all clear whether it's necessary. By contrast, mere extensional equivalences, whether about actual or possible objects, are more all or

31

nothing affairs: being told a merely extensional necessary condition on being a person – e.g. not being the number 17 – or merely an extensionally sufficient one – being Julius Caesar – might be entirely uninteresting. Constitutive analyses are supposed to indicate conditions that, *inter alia*, are theoretically illuminating: they contribute to an understanding of what a phenomenon *is* in a way that mere extensional equivalence need not do.

One last, cautionary point: the belief in constitutive analyses, real essences, or in necessary and sufficient conditions for the application of a concept is often thought to be undermined by the existence of difficult, borderline cases for its application. Now, it certainly cannot be denied that the world is full of genuine borderline cases: is drizzle rain? Are middle class people rich or poor? How many hairs must someone lose to count as bald? Arguably, the world doesn't supply determinate answers: all *kinds* in the world, whether natural or unnatural may have indeterminate boundaries, and it may be up to human decision to draw boundaries as needed on any particular occasion. *This doesn't for a moment imply that all applications of concepts are up to human decision or that there are no defining essences of the phenomena they pick out!*[20] "Unmarried adult male" may be a perfectly excellent analysis of "bachelor" despite the fact that there are plenty of cases in which it's indeterminate whether someone fits that description or not. All that's reasonably required of an analysis is that the extension of the analysis coincide with that of the analysandum "umbra for umbra, penumbra for penumbra" (Quine 1960:41).

1.5.2 Analyses of explanatory concepts

However, if philosophical analyses are constitutive, "by virtue of" analyses, fully adequate ones are pretty hard to come by. Note, first, that most people can't define the vast majority of the terms that they use perfectly well in reasoning and communication: try defining not only "chair," but "table," "pencil," "sparrow," "tuberculosis" – not to mention the standard philosophical examples of, e.g. "freedom," "justice," "piety," "knowledge" – and see if what you spontaneously come up with really matches all and only the cases you would want on careful reflection to include. Research in this area suggests that what's readily available to people are mere "reference fixers" (Kripke 1972): descriptions, stereotypes, memories of exemplars that appear adequate in context to "fix the reference" of a term, e.g. to distinguish what one is thinking about from rivals in that context, but aren't remotely adequate as analyses of the term (or phenomenon to which the term refers). Thus, to take a standard example, the reference of "water" is fixed by common beliefs about the potable liquid that fills rivers and seas, though no one would take these features to be remotely defining of it.[21]

More importantly, as Putnam (1962b/1975a, 1975b) suggested (resuscitating an idea of Locke 1690/1977), many good analyses actually await empirical investigation. Our use especially of terms that refer to phenomena appropriate to scientific investigation – such as the terms for natural kinds (water, salt, stars), natural processes (combustion, digestion, metabolism), diseases (tuberculosis, cancer) – are often used by scientists expressly *ignorant* of their proper analysis: it's often one of the goals of scientific research to *provide* them.[22] Thus, it is empirical scientists who have *discovered* that e.g. "water" is best defined as H_2O, "salt" as NaCl, and "polio" as the active presence of a particular sort of virus. At any rate, it is their investigations that have provided the best answers to the questions about the *nature* of water: what it is *by virtue of which* something would count as water, and *why*, under all possible circumstances.[23]

Someone might protest that looking to empirical theories for the definition or analysis of a term flies in the face of the traditional assumption that analyses should be *a priori*, establishable by philosophers independently of empirical research. After all, it might be argued, isn't analysis of what one means by a term something that must be available to a scientist *prior* to empirical investigation in order to determine just what the investigation is about? To be sure, *something* must determine what it is that a term or concept refers to; but it appears that it needn't be a full analysis known to its user. Indeed, Putnam (1975b) makes an extremely important suggestion to which we will specifically want to return in considering analyses of mental terms and concepts: competent users of natural kind terms like the above *know that they may well not know* how properly to define a term, and rely on experts to do so.[24] As Grice (1965) independently suggested, one's grasp of such a term "leaves a blank space to be filled in by the specialist." Perhaps there's an *a priori* component to any such analysis (cf. Bealer 1987); but it may amount to little more than a recognition, *a priori*, that an adequate analysis will be empirical.

Turning to the mental, it appears that many of our concepts are constrained by the *explanatory* work we expect them to play, and we get by day to day by accidental features that serve merely as reference fixers for the discussion. Notions like [belief], [desire], [perception], [reasoning] are presumed by many to play some important role in the explanation of human and animal behavior, but most people – including philosophers and psychologists – would be loathe at this stage to offer any adequate definition of them (but see §7.1). So it is not unreasonable to suppose that, just as in the case of the concepts of chemical elements, adequate analyses of them will depend to some extent upon the structure of an actual empirical psychology. It is for this reason that I postpone considering analyses of mental terms to chapter 5, until *after* we've begun considering the explanatory role they are supposed to play.

However, clearly not anything is permitted from the outset. Scientists in their initial investigations must be constrained *somehow*: they couldn't find out that water or god or a mental state was just *anything*; scientists presumably couldn't discover that water was the cube root of two, or that pains were park benches. What constraints are there? Mustn't there be *some* rules prior to the investigation to guide it, that determine that it is the "same phenomenon" in the end that one was wondering about at the beginning?

Settling these questions unfortunately requires getting clearer than anyone is about some of the very topics that are at issue in this book, in particular, about the issue of "aboutness" or intentionality. The question is of a piece with the difficult question of whether there is a separable "meaning" component of our thoughts and assertions, and a corresponding distinction between "analytic" claims (or claims that are true or knowable by virtue of meaning alone), and "synthetic" ones (claims true or knowable by virtue in part of the way the world happens to be). We will touch on some aspects of these issues in §9.1.2. For the nonce, and because so many of the people we will discuss have assumed there is such a distinction, I will assume there is one as well. But I will not assume that how we *access* it is unproblematic. In particular, I will not assume that "philosophical intuitions" about what is and is not possible are anything like an infallible guide. Intuitions can be defective in many ways. They can have a number of sources – prejudice, theoretical commitments, lack of imagination – other than the rule that actually governs the use of a concept. What we need to do is to try to ferret out the conditions that define a term at least in part by considering the best explanation of those intuitions, proceeding with them until we are presented with an argument that undermines them.[25] Intuitions are probably not the last word in an account of our conceptual competence, but they are a good first word, and will have to do until we can think of better access to what may well be quite subtle facts about the organization of our minds.

In any event, the project of providing constitutive analyses has been especially difficult in the case of mental phenomena, in part because of the yet unclear explanatory role they are being asked to serve, and in part because they exhibit a number of striking peculiarities that have thwarted easy analysis. After considering some of the explanatory work mental phenomena are needed to perform (chapters 3 and 4), we will consider a number of approaches to such analyses (chapters 5–7). But first we turn to consider some of the striking peculiarities mental phenomena exhibit, and the controversies that have informed all efforts at analysis of them.

Notes

1 Some terminology: "Metaphysics," as I (and most philosophers nowadays) use the word, refers simply to very general issues about the nature of the world (e.g. what it is to be real, to be an object or a property), and, in this sense, could be regarded as continuous with physics and other sciences – it's just more general. A related word, "ontology," refers to the specific area of metaphysics concerned with what things *exist* (e.g. objects, properties, facts, events).

2   See Quine (1953a: essay 1). People interested in seeing how to avoid apparent reference to numbers might consult Hartry Field (1978).

3   This is all quite rough. There are other ways of forming definite descriptions, e.g. by use of the genetive (e.g. "Charlie's aunt"), and sometimes *indefinite descriptions* can serve as singular terms ("I saw a man come into the room"). A controversial case is that of *sentence complements*, e.g. "that . . ." clauses, as in "John thinks that elephants snore": does "that elephants snore" designate a particular thing, say, a "thought" ? More below.

4   As this last example shows, where there is intended co-reference (as between "Romeo" and "his"), we can substitute a variable of the same letter type.

5   Not Quine (1953a: essay 1), who would insist on restricting reference to values of variables, and in any case sees no need of properties or relations. Keeping within his restriction, believers in properties would need to say that every predication, "Fa," really should be read as "a has the property F" (cf. Bealer 1982).

6   Committed nominalists, however, could replace all such talk of properties by talk of predicates being satisfied by particulars.

7   I shall use expressions enclosed by square brackets to designate the mental universal expressed by the expression: thus "[snow]" designates the concept expressed by the word "snow." Whole sentences express propositions: thus, "[Snow is white]" designates the proposition expressed by the sentence "Snow is white."

8   I don't mean to take sides on the thorny issues surrounding the identification of events and actions. See Davidson (1980), Goldman (1970), Thomson (1977) and Kim (1976) for sophisticated discussions.

9   This is only a first approximation: some attitudes (e.g. *attending to, noticing, loving, hating*) may also take as a direct object something in the world outside of the mind, e.g. one notices *a person*, or *his tie*. Note that the issue about sentence complements here could be cast in terms of whether we should treat them as singular terms.

10 Descartes (1649/1911:340) draws a related distinction between "passions" (informational) and "actions" (directional). Note that some attitudes, e.g. *hate the fact that . . .* , may be both.

11 Two exasperating, terminological cautions: (1) this use of "intentional" is to be distinguished from its use to characterize action, as a near synonym of *"deliberate"* (as in, e.g. "She intentionally raised her arm"); an *intentional act* in this latter sense might well be caused by an *intentional* state in the sense discussed in the text; and (2) "inten*t*ional" (with a "t") is to be distinguished from "inten*s*ional" (with an "s"), the latter referring to a certain *approach* (and the kind of entity it posits) in semantics that is contrasted with "exten*s*ional" approaches (and entities). We've already touched on the motivation for inten*s*ions in noting in §1.1.1 that two predicates (e.g. "x is round and square" and "x is even and odd") could have the same extension in all possible worlds. An inten*s*ional semantics is for this and other reasons sometimes recommended for understanding talk of inten*t*ional states, but this is controversial, as we shall see in §9.2.4.

12 Searle may have been misled on this point by a (characteristically) facetious remark of Fodor's (1987:97) – "If aboutness is real, it must really be something else" – that he quotes disapprovingly (1992:51). Clearly all Fodor is interested in here is doing for

intentionality what, for example, the chemists did for water, or the molecular biologists are doing for life.

13 Shoemaker (1975:306–7) and Block (1978/1990:445) sometimes write this way.

14 Some of what Nagel says here echoes claims that may be familiar to many people from the social sciences. Max Weber (1922/1978), for example, famously wrote of "Verstehen" (or "empathic," "interpetative") explanation, which he claimed was fundamentally different from a "causal" explanation. It would take us too far afield to consider whether Weber and other "Verstehen" sociologists are committed in this way to dualism, but the interested reader should bear this possibility in mind.

15 For example, it is because this requirement seems to me not yet to have been adequately met in the discussions of Kim (1993) and Davidson (1970/1980) that I shan't be devoting much space to their arguments in this book.

16 This oversimplifies: philosophy has often been distinguished from empirical science throughout its history, but the distinctron is rarely clear with regard to the structure of the mind – were, for example, Plato, Hume, and Kant *really* not making empirically testable speculations about the structure of the mind? It's certainly not hard to envision empirical consequences of them: see, for example, the discussion of the connection between behaviorism and empiricism in §4.3 below. In any case, the view that they weren't is as controversial as most any other question in what generally gets called "philosophy."

17 Elsewhere (Rey 1993d), I try to begin to address them, but only to show just how much more in the dark we are than people have supposed.

18 Note that the general form of analysis does not commit us to definitions being only a property of terms, although it will sometimes be convenient to talk about terms. Definitions and analyses seem to me often better thought of as properties of concepts. But, the latter being very controversial, there's no need to labor the point here.

19 I owe this latter wording to Jerry Fodor. In his (1975:6–7) he distinguishes the *conceptual* from the *causal* story of "what makes Wheaties the breakfast of champions": the former is given by "the fact that it is eaten (for breakfast) by non-negligible numbers of champions" ; the latter by, for example, "the health-giving vitamins and minerals that it contains." Perhaps the confusion between the causal and the constitutive is encouraged by the temptation to use "by virtue of" in either case: "Wheaties is the breakfast of champions by virtue of (being eaten by champions)/(containing vitamins)." This is why one has to focus on *constitutive* "by virtue of" claims.

20 I beat the drum about this issue since it is so persistently ignored. Dennett, for example, repeatedly uses examples of borderline cases to argue against the existence of biological essences – see Dennett (1995a:37–9, 95, 201–2) – as well as against realism about mental states (see §10.4 n. 30 below). See also Smith and Medin (1981:31) and Wittgenstein (1953:§66–7) for other instances of this error.

21 The research here is both "philosophical" – e.g. Wittgenstein (1953), Kripke (1972), Putnam (1975b) – and "empirical" – e.g. Rosch (1973), Smith and Medin (1981) – some of the latter being directed towards confirming Wittgenstein's (1953:§66ff) speculation about "family resemblances." The term "reference fixer" is due to Kripke (1972). Whether a reference fixer could ultimately function to actually fix reference in the absence of some background analytic rule somehow governing a person's judgments is an issue that remains open (see Bealer 1987 and Rey 1993d for discussion).

22 "Natural kind" terms that figure in scientific theories provide the clearest examples of our analytic ignorance. But it's important to note that it can arise even with non-scientific terms, e.g. terms for unusual artifacts, like "cyclotron" and "viola da gamba," which many people use knowing full well that they don't know how to define them.

23 In Locke's (1690/1977:III–vi–6) terms, what scientists seem to discover in such cases are the "real essences" of things, as opposed to the mere "nominal" essence with which we are ordinarily acquainted. He provides as an example of the latter, the nominal essence of gold as "a yellow malleable metal." But from at least that example, it's unclear why nominal essences count as any essences at all. It is for this reason that I regard analysis as a search for "real" essences.

24 Putnam (1975b) proposes a "Principle of the Division of Linguistic Labor," according to which we defer to experts for adequate definitions. Since in many cases it may not be clear just who the experts are, or even whether there are any, I prefer what I call the "Principle of Acknowledged Ignorance" that I present here (and discuss further in Rey 1983).

25 As Bealer (1987) rightly pointed out, it was just linguistic intuitions that drove Putnam and Kripke in the first place to think that the definitions of natural kind terms often awaited empirical research. Schiffer (1987:40) also rightly emphasizes the fact that scientists alone don't settle the nature of natural kinds: one needs a *"philosophical theory"* that identifies a kind with properties found to be shared by members of the kind.

2

The Temptations to Dualism

Why think there are mind/body problems? Why think there is any more difficulty integrating mental phenomena into a physical account of the world than there is integrating, say, geology or biology? In this chapter, I want to answer this question by discussing various considerations that have led people to be tempted by dualism. Many of these have to do with there being some salient properties of the mental that are not obviously possessed by anything physical. However, I think that the underlying problem is that there seem to be what Levine (1983) calls "explanatory gaps" between many mental and any physical phenomena. In §2.1, I will set out these gaps, turning, after some slightly technical stage setting (§2.2–2.4), to discuss in detail specific features of the mental that make these gaps seem unbridgeable (§2.5–2.6).

2.1 Explanatory Gaps[1]

Philosophically troublesome explanatory gaps arise in any domain in which it seems impossible to imagine how phenomena in one domain could be explained by phenomena in another. At one point, it seemed that there was such a gap between the living and the non-living: prior to Darwin and biochemistry, it seemed impossible to imagine how the intricate organization and adaptability of organisms could arise in a purely physical world. We are still in such a position with respect to the phenomena of mind. It seems impossible to imagine how purely physical processes could give rise to the rationality and intentionality of propositional attitudes, and to conscious, qualitative states.[2] Wittgenstein (1953) vividly captures some of this perplexity in a famous passage:

> The feeling of an unbridgeable gulf between consciousness and brain process:
> . . . When does this feeling occur . . . ? It is when I, for example, turn my attention

in a particular way on to my own consciousness, and, astonished, say to myself: THIS is supposed to be produced by process in the brain! – as it were clutching my forehead.   (1953:§412)

It is important to see that the problem is not an ordinary scientific one, e.g. of merely thinking up a theory that accounts for all the data; of thinking up experiments to distinguish rival hypotheses; of finding the practical means (e.g. finding subjects) to run experiments one has thought up. Psychology has those problems too – indeed, when thinking about the status of psychology as a science, it is important to bear in mind how it suffers a lot more than other sciences from quite boring practical problems. For one thing, there are obvious *moral* constraints on experimenting on the primary source of data, human beings and (many have urged) even most higher animals. We can't just systematically produce and raise people in carefully controlled conditions the way we can raise fruit flies and see what differences in behavior differences in conditions would elicit (think of how easily certain Freudian theories could begin to be tested were this not so!). For another, the physical system that seems in one way or another crucially responsible for mental phenomena, the brain, is an incredibly compact, staggeringly complicated network of some 100 billion neurons connected by some 100 trillion fibers, that is both morally and practically inaccessible to unconstrained experimentation. Theorizing has therefore to be extremely ingenious, based upon a data pool far more restricted than in most sciences. But, while these are all real problems that do make psychology particularly difficult, none of them are particularly *philosophical*. The philosophical problem arises, here as in many other places, when we imagine that all these problems were solved, and we consider what we would think had we world enough, loose morals, and time, and could avail ourselves of all imaginable data. For what we would make of it? What possible hypotheses might such data confirm or disconfirm that would really begin to explain the mental?

By way of contrast, note that most other familiar phenomena do not pose such a problem. Consider, for example the following standard explanation of the expansion of ice when it freezes:

Water is one of the few substances that is less dense as a solid than as a liquid. While other materials contract when they solidify, water expands. The cause of this exotic behavior is, once again, hydrogen bonding. At temperatures above 4°C, water behaves like other liquids, expanding as it warms and contracting as it cools. Water begins to freeze when its molecules are no longer moving vigorously enough to break hydrogen bonds to neighboring molecules. As the temperature reaches 0°C, the water becomes locked into a crystalline lattice, each water molecule bonded to the maximum of four partners. The hydrogen bonds keep the molecules far enough apart from each other to make ice about 10% less dense (have 10% fewer molecules for the same volume) than liquid water at 4°C. When ice absorbs enough heat for its temperature to increase to above 0°C, hydrogen bonds between molecules are disrupted. As the crystal collapses, the ice melts, and molecules are free to slip closer together.   (Campbell 1987:41–2)

The text goes on to provide similar explanations of the cohesion and surface tension of water, its specific heat and its heat of vaporization. For our purposes, it doesn't really matter whether these explanations are *true*: it's enough that they are plausible, and, most importantly, that they are the very models of an illuminating explanation. If they are true, then we do in fact have a substantial understanding of the target properties of water.

As the same text goes on to show, this sort of explanation seems to be increasingly available for a wider and wider range of phenomena, both on the large ("macro") scale – as in the emergence of life, processes of respiration, digestion, reproduction – and the very small ("micro") scale – as in the chemical bondings themselves, the structure of atoms, the interactions among sub-atomic particles. The explanations do not always proceed *directly* from, say, quantum physics to respiration. There are explanatory "levels": micro-physics, macro-physics, chemistry, biology, anatomy and physiology. But the laws and features of each level seem in principle explainable by the laws and features of the lower levels. Indeed, it has become even plausible for physicists to speculate about a "TOE," or grand, unified "Theory of Everything" on which all other successful explanations ultimately rely (see Hawking 1980, Weinberg 1992). These are theories that would unify all the fundamental forces of nature – gravitation, electromagnetism, the strong and weak nuclear forces – into one force and explain how this one force diversified into the distribution of forces and mass-energy that we encounter.

Of course, we don't yet have a TOE. There are deep problems about how to understand some of our most fundamental theories, particularly, quantum mechanics, which a flourishing "philosophy of physics" addresses. But even within science, there are certainly myriad phenomena that we don't yet know precisely how to explain, much less control: how cancer cells proliferate, how bumble bees manage to consume enough food to fly, why people catch "the common cold." But it's significant that, with a little thought, we can easily *imagine possible accounts*. Even someone ignorant of the details of, say, digestion could make up at least a *possible* explanation of the way food is converted to nourishment: food makes its way through the esophagus, to the stomach and eventually to the intestines, along the way undergoes a variety of chemical changes that extract certain substances and pass them on via the circulatory system to various bodily cells. We know how in principle this explanation *could* be continued in virtually endless detail, until we would arrive at basic physiochemical – perhaps even quantum mechanical facts that seem to apply across nature. Of an afternoon, one could probably think up a dozen different conceivable accounts. And we look forward to empirical scientists telling us eventually which of these or other conceivable stories is actually *true*.

The impressive achievement of modern science is that it is increasingly able to do this for almost any phenomenon one can think of.

Except, apparently, for the phenomena associated with minds. Putting aside for a moment some recent advances that will be the subject of the present book, it seems extraordinarily difficult to imagine even *one* possible physiochemical explanation of even the most humdrum mental phenomena: e.g. the fact that you and I both understand (most of) the words on this page; that we have *experiences* – for example, of the surface of the page, the color of the paper, the temperature of the air around us; that we frequently have thoughts and wishes and hopes and expectations about a vast range of phenomena, past and future, near and far.[3]

Try constructing an explanation of any of these phenomena along the lines of the explanation of the expansion of ice, or digestion. How would it go? Consider ordinary perception, say of a very ripe tomato. A good deal is known about the behavior of light which, emanating from some source, is reflected from the tomato in predominantly long wave frequencies that enter the lenses of your eyes and are focused on your retinas. From there, certain impulses caused by those frequencies (as well as the previous state of your retina) are transmited along the optic nerve to the visual cortex and then to other regions of the brain. But, however detailed and illuminating the physical story of neuronal transmission may be in many ways, it seems either to leave out the mind, or leap to it without argument. The problem was put quite graphically some years ago by the physiologist, Charles Sherrington:

> The chain of events stretching from the sun's radiation entering the eye to, on the one hand, the contraction of the pupillary muscles, and, on the other, to the electrical disturbances in the brain cortex, are all straightforward steps in a sequence of physical "causation" such as, thanks to science, are intelligible. But in the second serial chain there follows on, or attends, the stage of brain-cortex reaction an event or set of events seemingly incommensurable with any of the events leading up to it. The self "sees" the sun; it senses a two-dimensional disc of brightness, located in the "sky," this last a field of lesser brightness, and overhead shaped as a rather flattened dome, coping the self and a hundred other visual things as well. Of hint that this is within the head there is none. . . . The supposition has to be, it would seem, two continuous series of events, one physio-chemical, the other psychical, and at times interaction between them. (Sherrington 1906/1947:xx–xxi, quoted in Place 1956/1991:34)

Neuroscientists are supplying us with an abundance of facts about neural pathways and neurotransmitters, and *psychologists*, as well as most everyone else in their daily life, are supplying us with an abundance of facts about our minds: what we tend to like and dislike, the kinds of perceptual and cognitive illusions to which we're prone. But what is the *connection* between the two? How does having a certain pattern of excitation in one's limbic system *explain* an experience of hunger? Or a pattern in one's visual cortex, an experience of red? Or a pattern in one's frontal lobe, a memory of one's childhood home? What *makes* that pattern hunger, or that stimulation a memory *of that very home one had as a child?*

Perhaps the two events are nicely correlated in a particular person, so that when and only when a particular area is stimulated she remembers her childhood home. But mere local *correlation* isn't explanation: the tides are correlated with the position of the moon, but until we had a theory of gravitation that fact was not an *explanation*, but a *datum*. A perennial complaint philosophers have raised against much neurophysiology is that the mere discovery of psycho-physical correlations offers us no understanding of *why* the correlations obtain, in particular of just how possibly specific brain processes could be responsible for the specific psychological processes with which they are correlated.[4]

This discrepancy between explanation and mere correlations is an indication of the explanatory gap that seems to exist between mental and physical phenomena. Consider again the account of the expansion of ice: once you understand the claims about the intensity of hydrogen bonds, their locations, and the greater space the colder molecules take up, the lesser density of ice is a *mathematical/geometrical consequence* of those claims. That is, given that a quantity of water is *comprised* of a multitude of H_2O molecules with determinate forces existing between them, then the mathematics of part/whole relations (merology) determines that, other things being equal, that multitude will take up greater space below $0°C$.[5] As Levine puts it, in a good explanation of this sort, the micro-facts *upwardly necessitate* the macro-scale facts about the properties that water displays: e.g. the facts about the micro-forces between the individual molecules imply that they should move over each other quite easily, giving rise to the familiar phenomena of fluidity and non-compressibility. Given enough of the laws and those microfacts, water would *have* to be fluid and non-compressible.

Levine argues that it is precisely this necessitation that is lacking, for example, in the case of sensations:

> No matter how rich the information processing or the neurophysiological story gets, it still seems quite coherent to imagine that all that should be going on without there being anything it's like to undergo the states in question. Yet, if the physical or [informational] story really explained the qualitative character, it would not be so clearly imaginable that the qualia should be missing. (1993:129)

Consider by way of recent example, the Crick and Koch (1990) claim that visual consciousness is correlated with a 40 Hz oscillation in layers five and six of the primary visual cortex. Paul Churchland (1995) goes so far as to claim that this is a plausible account of consciousness.[6] That it isn't, that something still is lacking, can be appreciated by simply thinking of such an oscillation *outside of a living animal*, say, in a radio or sine-wave generator. Should such a device oscillating at such a frequency really be counted as conscious? This seems preposterous. If it is, then the 40 Hz oscillation can't itself be the explanation of consciousness: as the examples show, it is at least possible that the oscillation should occur without consciousness: the oscillations don't *necessitate* consciousness, in the way that molecular bonding necessitates freezing.

Moreover, even if we allowed that certain states, as a matter of brute fact, just possessed conscious qualitative content, Levine (1983, 1991) claims there would still be a problem of explaining why they possessed one content rather than another: why should a certain state give rise to a sensation of *red* rather than one of *green*? To *middle C* rather than *middle G*? Why couldn't those sensations be switched in someone's mind even while the neurophysiology remains the same (why couldn't the "color wheel" be rotated 180°)? What *ties* a particular sensation to a particular neural state? Here, too, there seems to be an explanatory gap that no one seems to be able to think of any way of filling.

Similarly, Descartes' (1637/1970) claim, which we quoted in the previous chapter on behalf of the non-physical character of rationality – that it can't be extracted from matter – can be read as calling attention to a similar gap. Descartes was well aware that mechanical contraptions could be devised to emulate this or that specific intelligent behavior. What he thought was impossible was the creation of a mechanical device that was *universally rational* in the way that human beings seem to be.

> [A]lthough machines can perform certain things as well as or perhaps better than any of us can do, they would infallibly fall short in others, by which means we may discover that they did not act from knowledge, but only from the disposition of their organs. For while reason is a universal instrument which can serve for all contingencies, these organs need of some special adaptation for every particular action. (Descartes 1637/1970:116)

Even in this day of clever chess-playing computers and navigation systems, it is by no means clear that we have conclusively shown him to be wrong. No one has yet seen clearly how to program a machine as *generally* intelligent as we seem to be (but, as we'll discuss in chapters 8–11 below, we have perhaps somewhat better grounds for optimism here than were available to Descartes).

The "Brentano Thesis" that we also cited can be read as noticing a similar gap with regard to intentionality. To get a feel for why this has seemed plausible to so many philosophers, simply ask yourself: just what physical relation *would* explain how, for example, the word "snow" refers to snow, "cat" to cat, "Caesar" to Julius Caesar? Of course, there are *conventional* relations; but conventional relations are mediated by *minds*; and so the question becomes, what physical fact makes it true that some state of a person's mind is *about* snow, or cats, or Julius Caesar? It doesn't seem to be any sort of *local* physical relation, since we and words can refer to most anything anywhere in the world, and over eons – why, apparently faster than the speed of light! Worse, we can refer to abstract things like the number twelve that are not in space or time at all; and even to – things? – like Santa Claus, or round squares that don't exist at all, neither concretely nor abstractly.[7] Although there is perhaps ultimately a story to be told (we will examine some suggestions in chapter 9), few philosophers are under any illusion that anyone has yet told it.

Quine (1960:chapter 2) discovered a particularly difficult feature of this latter gap. Suppose you were to encounter highly intelligent creatures on Mars who used a word "gavagai" rather in the way we use the word "rabbit": for example, when a rabbit passes by they point and exclaim, "gavagai!" Quine ingeniously argues that all the evidence we could adduce for translating "gavagai" as "rabbit" could equally well count as evidence for translating it as meaning "undetached rabbit part"; or "temporal slice of a whole rabbit"; or "Rabbithood instantiated once more," translations that seem intuitively incompatible with one another (his argument trades on the fact that all these expressions are necessarily co-instantiated: wherever there's a rabbit there are undetached rabbit parts, time slices of whole rabbits, and rabbithood is instantiated). The case is very like the one we mentioned above when we wondered what physical facts could determine whether it's a red or a green sensation someone is experiencing at a particular time. Just as it's hard to see how any physical facts necessitate an experience of red rather than green, it's hard to see how they necessitate thinking of rabbits rather than of their undetached parts.[8]

It is important to see that the problems, particularly in these cases, of sensation and translation are not merely *epistemological* ones of trying to decide which story it is *reasonable* to believe. As Quine himself has emphasized, in any interesting theoretical enterprise we are always in the position of having to choose between rival theories on the basis of data compatible with each of them. The problem he and Levine are raising is a *metaphysical* one of seeing how the physical facts *necessitate* the mental ones, whichever of the alternative stories we might decide to believe.

But maybe the problem is not with the world but with *us*. It's important to notice that the existence of these explanatory gaps does not itself entail anything like dualism. The gaps, after all, could simply be gaps in our way of *conceiving* phenomena in the world, and not in the worldly phenomena themselves: they could all be a result of some limitations in the way we have of *thinking* about the world: the right way of thinking about the issues simply hasn't yet occurred to us.[9] But it is also possible that the gaps do reflect something about the phenomena themselves. In any case, philosophers have not been shy about specifying particular properties of the mental that they argue no physical phenomenon could possibly possess. These are best appreciated by seeing how they have been cited as objections to the most straightforward reductionist proposal, the so-called psycho-physical "identity theory." In §2.2 I will discuss some general features of such an ontological claim, spelling out the identity theory specifically in §2.3, as well as an important constraint on claims on identity, "Leibniz's Law" (§2.4). In §2.5, we will then consider the many "Leibniz Law objections" the dualist has reasonably raised against the identity theory, as well as a related objection regarding the status of qualitative states (§2.6).

2.2   Monism, Dualism, . . . , N-alism

Although, for reasons I've sketched in the introduction, the traditional ontological issues about the mind may well turn out to be less important than many have supposed, they bear examining if only fully to appreciate and then resist their lure. In particular, it is worth understanding what has led people to make what seem like quite extraordinary ontological claims about the world, of a sort that they would seldom make in any other domain of inquiry. The most famous such claim is that of traditional "dualism," or the view that there is something very special about mental phenomena that sets them apart from anything physical. Precisely what this claim even amounts to will be the subject of this chapter. As I mentioned in the introduction, it tends to be merely a *negative* thesis: a denial of "materialism" or "physicalism" (I will use the two terms interchangeably until §6.4), or the doctrine that all phenomena are physical phenomena. Consequently, we will get a better grip on dualism by trying first to understand what a physicalist initially wants to say, considering then the many reasons that a dualist would want to deny it.

Ontological questions are questions about what exists, and, to a first approximation, physicalism is a *monist* theory: it is the claim that there is *one* basic kind of substance out of which everything in the world is composed. There are other monist theories: *idealism* is the view that everything is not matter, but rather *ideas*, a suggestion historically associated with the work of Berkeley and Hegel. The considerations that lead people to such a view are, however, by and large quite distinct from those that arise in the mind/body problems.[10] Since this view concerns *any* empirical phenomena – rocks, stars, or people – it does not raise issues peculiar to the mind, and so, by our Fairness Maxim, is not a concern here. The only monist theory we shall consider is physicalism.

Physicalism could be contrasted not only with "dualism" but also with what might be called "tri-alism," which sometimes posits God as still a further substance different from both mind and body. And, of course, there could be 4-alism, 5-alism. . . . However, as the number increases, the interest of the view begins to diminish, particularly if it were to turn out, say, that arguments for mind being different from body were also arguments for dollar bills being different from bits of paper or mountains being different from collections of atoms. Indeed, we will see shortly (§2.5.7.1) that some of the arguments for dualism could be regarded as equally arguments for what I shall call "N-alism," or the view that there are n

45

number of different kinds of things in the world (dimes, dollar bills, mountains, molehills), for an arbitrarily large number n.

In order to begin to come to grips with any of these ontological claims, one needs to specify the *category* of phenomena about which one is making a monistic or dualistic or n-alistic claim (where the "categories" are the distinctions among e.g. "objects," "properties," "states," "events" that we discussed in §1.1.1). Many philosophers are eliminativists with respect to one category of thing, but reductionists with respect to another. Thus, Descartes spoke of a dualism of *substances*: there was a mental substance, "mind," in addition to physical substance. He and many others have also claimed that there were non-physical *objects*, like "immortal souls"; some people even believe in (presumably non-physical) "ghosts"; and it has certainly seemed vivid to many people that there are such things as *pains*, *itches*, *tickles*, *after-images*, *mental images*. But many recent opponents of materialism have balked at these claims, regarding them as extravagant. They might well be *eliminativists*, for example, about *ghosts*, and maybe even about any mental *substance*, and restrict their dualism merely to *properties* or *aspects* of ordinary physical objects (§2.6). And they might or might not then be dualists about the *events* composed of, say, physical objects with these aspects. And we'll see later that someone might be an eliminativist about *pains*, or *mental images*, but a reductionist about pain or imagistic *experiences*. So in considering various ontological views, whether monist, dualist, reductionist, or eliminativist, it is a good idea always to be prepared to specify what category of phenomena, among such alternatives, one has in mind.

2.3   Physicalist Reduction

The physicalist view that all is matter needs to be spelled out a little if we are to engage the issues that are specific to the mind/body problems. For our purposes, it might be more precisely defined as the view that the only things that exist are the things required for the truth of physical theory: any universe of things that satisfies the claims of physical theory satisfies the claims of *any* other true theory. Now if one looks only casually at what sorts of things are required for physical theory in general, it certainly appears that one needs a great deal more than mere "matter." Precisely what one needs is a matter of much controversy that is independent of issues about the mind and so needn't detain us here.[11] We shall simply assume that it includes what it appears to include: not only elementary particles, mass-energy, waves, atoms, molecules, forces, points in space/time, but also (perhaps surprisingly) various *abstract* objects, e.g. numbers, sets, and properties, since, so far as anyone has yet been able to show, physical theories are standardly expressed in a way that commits them to such things. For example, physics is committed to arithmetic, which seems committed to *abstracta* such as numbers when it says such things as "There is a positive square root to 16," "There are an infinite number of prime numbers"; and its causal explanations appear to appeal to such *properties* of objects as their *mass* and *charge* ("It is because of *the opposite charge* of the particles that they attract one another").[12] Just what numbers and properties are, and whether they themselves can be explained physically, is an issue we won't attempt to settle (except to note occasionally that, especially in the case of properties, the issue is conspicuously unsettled).

For simplicity, the physics I will have in mind is Newtonian. Of course, that theory has itself been refuted on entirely physical grounds. Not only Relativity Theory, but quantum mechanics has challenged some of its basic assumptions about causation, locality, and the determinacy of events. We could pause here and try to spell out these changes and provide a more up-to-date characterization of physicalism. However, there are at least two reasons for not doing so: (1) there remain fundamental problems in the interpretation of current physical theory. As one of the leading quantum physicists, Steven Weinberg, has recently put it:

> Everyone agrees on how to use quantum mechanics, but there is serious disagreement about how to think about what we are doing when we use it. . . . Most physicists use quantum mechanics every day in their working lives without needing to worry about the fundamental problem of its interpretation.   (1992:77, 84)

But even were the problems in the interpretation of quantum mechanics to be ironed out, it is by no means clear this would be any help to the philosophy of mind, since (2) the differences between Newtonian and quantum theory have yet to be shown to be at all relevant to the nature of the mind. As Weinberg adds:

> Quantum mechanics has been overwhelmingly important to physics, but I cannot find any messages for human life in quantum mechanics that are different in any important way from those of Newtonian physics.   (1992:78)

Nagel (1986), otherwise keen to make room for a special role for the mental in the world, also notes:

> Even if, as some physicists think, quantum theory cannot be interpreted in a way that permits the phenomena to be interpreted without reference to an observer, the ineliminable observer need not be a member of any particular species like the human, to whom things look and feel in highly characteristic ways.   (1986:16)

There are, to be sure, those who think otherwise, and argue that there are such messages to be had (e.g. Lockwood 1989, Penrose 1989). For reasons that will emerge from our discussion, I find such claims extremely doubtful. I suspect a dangerous tendency to suppose that all mysteries are the same, "Grand Mystery," and to engage in more than a little explanation *obscurium per obscurius* (explaining the obscure by the still more obscure).

Consequently, for the greater part of the present discussion, by "physics" I shall mean Newtonian mechanics and let the burden fall on those who would hope that Relativity Theory or the obscurities of quantum mechanics would illuminate what is more likely only a peculiarity of the mental.

2.4   Identity and Leibniz's Law

If we are to make sense of monism, dualism, and other n-alisms, we had better have some idea of how we're counting, and in particular of when we are willing to count "two things" as really "one." This last question is a question of *identity*, and we need to linger a moment over this seemingly innocuous, but notoriously troublesome notion. After all, as so many writers on the mind often remind us, there is Butler's maxim: "everything is what it is and not another thing." Do such trivial laws really have significant consequences for the mind?

An ambiguity that bedevils almost all discussions of identity is the ambiguity between *types* and *tokens* that we discussed in §1.1.1. *Tokens* of things, recall, are *individual* things, e.g. copies of books, that have a location in space and time: it makes sense to ask when and where they have occurred. *Types* are, for our purposes, *classes* of all tokens that are similar in some respect: thus all copies of *Moby Dick* consist presumably of the same words in the same order, despite their having many other physical differences. Similarly, we can talk about the same *type* mental state, in which case it seems pretty obvious that different people could share it: different people can both have experiences of the *type*, e.g. pain. But we could also talk about the same *token* mental state, and here it might be much less clear whether two people might share *it* (perhaps Siamese twins could do this; perhaps telepaths could). In considering the question "Are pains physical things?" we have to be clear whether we're asking whether the *type* of thing, pain, is identical to a physical *type* of thing, or whether merely every *token* pain is some (or other) physical *token*. For the time being, I shall presume we are talking about tokens; we shall turn to talk of types only later in chapter 5.

Token identity claims do commit us to more than we might initially notice. For example, it is an important logical truism, to which we shall have occasion to return a number of times, that if anything x is identical to something y, then whatever is true of x is also true of y. Shakespeare put it best: "A rose by any other name would smell as sweet." Logicians put it thus (where "F" is any predicate):[13]

If x = y then (Fx iff Fy)

Thus, if Juliet = my rose, then (my rose smells sweet iff Juliet smells sweet). This truism is known as "Leibniz's Law," or the "indiscernibility of identicals."[14] It can also be expressed more cumbrously at a meta-linguistic level as a claim about substitutions:

> *Leibniz's Law (meta-linguistic version):*
> if two expressions, "a" and "b" refer to the same thing, then they may be substituted for one another in any sentence, *salva veritate*.

where "salva veritate" means, not "saving truth," but "saving truth *value*": truths remain true, falsehoods false. Thus, if "Juliet" and "my rose" both refer to the same thing, then in any sentence containing "Juliet" (e.g. "Juliet is fickle") one could substitute "my rose" (yielding "My rose is fickle"), without changing the truth value of the original sentence (if "Juliet is fickle" were true/false, "My rose is fickle" would be correspondingly true/false as well).

Now, insofar as the materialist *identifies* mental phenomena with physical phenomena, she must come to grips with this law. It turns out not to be always easy to do so. The next long section, §2.5, will be devoted to considering a range of problems – spatiality, privacy, phenomenology, and intentionality – that seem to present Leibniz Law problems for such an identification.

2.5 The "Identity Theory" and Its Leibniz Law Difficulties

The simplest version of materialism is often expressed by what has been called the "Identity Theory," the view that any mental phenomenon is identical to some or other physical phenomenon. Perhaps the baldest recent statement of it occurs in the work of Searle (1992):

> The famous mind-body problem, the source of so much controversy over the past two millennia, has a simple solution. This solution has been available to any educated person since serious work began on the brain nearly a century ago, and, in a sense, we all know it to be true. Here it is: Mental phenomena are caused by neurophysiological processes in the brain and are themselves features of the brain. (1992:1)

Indeed:

> Some philosophers . . . fail to see that the mental state of consciousness is just an ordinary biological, that is, physical feature of the brain. (1992:13)

49

Searle is by no means the first to have propounded the thesis. It certainly begins to surface in Hobbes (1651/1961:chapters 1–3), and is championed by many eighteenth-century scientific writers, such as Priestley (see Passmore 1965). As Chomsky (1995) points out:

> The basic contention of Priestley and other 18th Century figures seems uncontroversial: thought and language are properties of organized matter – in this case, mostly the brain, not the kidney or the foot. It is unclear why this conclusion should be resurrected centuries later as an audacious and innovative proposal. . . . Every year or so a book appears by some distinguished scientist with the "startling conclusion" or "astonishing hypothesis" that thought in humans "is a property of the nervous system, or rather the brain," the "necessary result of a particular organization" of matter, as Priestley put the matter a long time ago. (1995:10)[15]

In any case, J.J.C. Smart (1962/1991) certainly introduced the thesis into the contemporary discussion when he advanced his "psycho-physical identity thesis" at least with regard to sensations: they are, he claims, "nothing over and above brain processes," just as "lightning is a certain kind of electrical discharge" (pp. 170–1). Thus, pains, beliefs, experiences of falling in love, and emotions are simply identical to some or other physical phenomenon.

If materialism is expressed in terms of an identity theory, however, it immediately risks falling afoul of a number of objections occasioned by application of the aforementioned Leibniz Law. For there seem to be properties of mental phenomena that physical phenomena lack, and in some cases properties of physical phenomena that mental phenomena lack.

2.5.1   Rationality and language

We've already mentioned rationality with regard to the explanatory gap, and observed how merely the existence of such a gap doesn't entail dualism. Descartes, however, doesn't think there's merely a gap in our understanding, but a fundamental gap in the world: it cannot "in any way be extracted from the power of matter" (1637/1970:118). It's difficult to find in his texts a compelling argument for this particularly strong conclusion, over and above merely the difficulty he observes for imagining a machine capable of reason. But he does call attention to what do seem striking facts about people, in contrast to the rest of nature, that do present a challenge to any identity theory.

Descartes' dualism about reason arose hand in hand with the emergence of the mechanical theory of nature that he himself did much to promote. Indeed, he was one of the first to pursue the suggestion that infra-human animals ("brutes") were "mere machines":

[I]f there were machines with the organs and appearances of a monkey, or some other irrational animal, we should have no means of telling that they were not altogether of the same nature as those animals.

Humans are, however, very different.

Whereas if there were machines resembling our bodies, and imitating our actions as far as is morally possible, we should still have two means of telling that, all the same, they were not real men. First, they could never use words or other constructed signs, as we do to declare our thoughts to others. . . . Secondly, while they might do many things as well as any of us or better, they would infallibly fail in others, revealing that they acted not from knowledge but only from the disposition of their organs. For while reason is a universal tool that may serve in all kinds of circumstances, these organs need a special arrangement for each special action. (Descartes 1637/ 1970:116)

Putting aside the better grounds we have today for being slightly more optimistic about the potentialities of machines, why should Descartes be impressed by these facts? The suggestion seems to be that reason is *unrestricted*: it seems to *transcend* at least any limitations the physical world might impose. Of course, one might wonder what the evidence might be for *that* (see §4.3). But there are the following interesting facts about us that, we shall see later, play an important role in contemporary theories of mind:

(i)   both reason and language are *productive*: a normal human being seems capable of understanding a potential *infinity* of different sentences and the thoughts that they express. Thus, if one merely had time and patience (and longevity) enough, one could understand indefinite continuations of the childhood sentence, "This is the gnat that lived in the sock that lay in the closet that was at the foot of the stairs of the house that Jack built": although at a certain point it might be difficult to keep the whole thing in your mind at once, there's an important sense in which almost anyone could understand precisely the thoughts that such sentences express;

(ii)   people's language use is (to use a phrase Chomsky deploys in this connection) "creative": people are able to produce and understand arbitrarily novel sentences of their own language. This, after all, is at least *one* reason we write and read. We are not always producing and encountering the same sentences over and over again, but ever new ones – and they're not random: despite their novelty they are usually intelligibly appropriate to the context in which they occur;

(iii)   people's concepts go far beyond their sensory experience. An example Descartes discussed in his Sixth Meditation, is our concept of a chiliagon, or thousand-sided figure: although someone might suppose the idea of a triangle is capturable by a visual image of a three-sided figure, few would claim that a visual image could distinguish the thousand sides. Our ideas are not tied so closely to our

51

sensory apparatus. Indeed (as we observed in remarking on intentionality), we can conceive all manner of non-physical things, and even things that don't exist in any way at all.

Now, Descartes' conceptions of the potentialities of physical devices seem to have been limited to simple reflexes and devices for reception, storage, and transmission of sensory signals,[16] a limitation that is shared even today when people speak of someone's mere "mechanical" responses. Armed with only such conceptions, certainly these three phenomena would be difficult to explain. Indeed, it required a conceptual revolution to imagine the power of modern computers, and even now it is by no means easy to account for these phenomena.

2.5.2 Free will

Related to reason's apparent freedom from physical limitations, there was also the apparent "freedom of the will," the peculiar kind of freedom associated with many human decisions. Consider a paradigm case of thoughtful human action, say, a choice to lie to the tax authorities about one's income; or, to take a famous example from Sartre (1973), a choice to join the French Resistance to the Nazi occupation or stay home and take care of one's ailing mother. What seems striking about such cases is that they don't seem to be cases in which one's decision is *caused* in any obvious way by antecedent conditions. It certainly doesn't *seem* in such cases as though the considerations that one marshals – "Lemme see: there's this much to be said for risking my life and joining the Resistance, this much for staying home with Mom" – *automatically* bring about the action. They are surely relevant; but the decision itself seems to be something additional. After all the pros and cons are in, one just "makes up one's mind." One may have a strong desire to stay home, and yet still choose to act contrary to it; one may even think a certain course of action best, and yet, notoriously, fail to act upon it.[17] People sometimes succumb, but at least sometimes they appear to resist acting on (what they take to be) their strongest desires, doing instead what they *choose*: sometimes they do so for moral reasons; sometimes for prudential ones; sometimes for mere reasons of etiquette; sometimes on no basis whatever – perhaps, as Slote (1989) has emphasized, they "have enough," and are "satisficers" not "maximizers" of their satisfactions (sure, I would enjoy another piece of cake; I even can detect in myself a strong desire for one. But I've decided not to take one all the same).[18]

Of course, someone might argue that this just shows that the desire to take the next piece of cake – or to cheat or stay at home – wasn't "strongest" after all. Perhaps: but if this claim is not to be vacuous,[19] we would need some independent evidence of the greater strength of the relevant desire, and, on the face of it, it doesn't really seem that the strongest desire does always win. What does win? Well: a "choice," what seems to be a "free choice."

Such "freedom" isn't confined to outward behavior. To a surprising extent people seem to be able to "decide" what to believe. This isn't true for all beliefs – I can't decide to believe that I'm presently on Mars, or that I'm a hippopotamus. But consider some ingenious argument a philosopher might provide for some claim that contradicts some long-standing piece of commonsense: say, that material objects don't really exist independently of us. The argument might be presented as an iron-clad deduction from principles that, when they are articulated to you, you feel you have every reason to accept; and the philosopher might try then to persuade you that you therefore *must* accept the conclusion: "logic will grab you by the throat."[20] But in fact logic does no such thing: you are free *not* to draw the conclusion; you are free simply "to think about it," and, later, to choose to reconsider any one of the premises you perhaps had too readily conceded.[21]

But what kind of material process could allow for this "freedom"? Any specific material process either is caused by an antecedent one or is probabilistic in a determinate way (as in the emission of an α particle): in neither case do we seem to obtain any kind of grip on any process of *decision* or *choice*. Needless to say, this has made many worried about the basis for moral responsibility. But quite apart from sorting out that issue, there is simply the psychological pattern of specifying precisely what sort of material process a decision or choice might be. The occurrence of such processes is then at least a *prima facie* example of a mental process that has a property not possessed by any physical one.

2.5.3   Spatiality and phenomenal objects

Perhaps a more obvious sort of counterexample to the identity thesis would seem to be provided by reflections on *spatial* properties. Descartes writes in his Sixth Meditation:

> [T]here is a great difference between mind and body, inasmuch as body is by nature always divisible, and the mind is entirely indivisible. For, as a matter of fact, when I consider the mind, that is to say, myself inasmuch as I am only a thinking thing, I cannot distinguish in myself any parts, but apprehend myself to be clearly one and entire; and although the whole mind seems to be united to the whole body, yet if a foot, or an arm, or some other part, is separated from my body, I am aware that nothing has been taken away from my mind. . . . But it is quite otherwise with corporeal or extended objects, for there is not one of these imaginable by me which my mind cannot easily divide into parts.   (1641a/1970:196)

Conceivably one might quarrel with Descartes' insistence on being something "quite single and complete:" don't we talk all the time about "split personalities" and "part saying yes, part saying no?" But this talk is pretty clearly metaphorical: we don't really think on the face of it that it's possible, literally, to cut up a mind just as we might a body, say into two parts, one "three times bigger than the other." Indeed, it seems pretty obscure how even to begin to talk of the "size" of the mind (say, in cubic inches), or what a cut into three parts, one twice as large as the other two, would come to. The mind certainly *seems* to have no genuine spatial properties at all.

Ironically enough, the very mental phenomena that *do* seem to admit of spatial properties present special difficulties in this respect. Mental images seem to have spatial properties that, for all that, seem not to be located in ordinary physical space! At any rate, they at least seem to have properties that no available physical object has. If I form a mental image of a tiger, then the image would seem in at least some ways to be like a painting: the tiger image would be, for example, longer than it is high, and it would have many orange and black stripes. But, now, just where in the relevant physical space is there anything with those properties? If I'm merely "forming an image in my mind," then it's surely not on the retina. The only plausible place to begin to look for it would be in my brain: but is there really any chance that a surgeon would find anything there that was appropriately tiger-shaped with *black and orange stripes*? No surgery on anyone's brain has ever turned up anything with remotely such properties – and even if they did, one might wonder how it managed to get incorporated into a person's mental life: there is no reason to think that an image seen by a neurosurgeon examining your brain is identical to the image *you* "see with your mind's eye."

These spatiality problems have taken on a special urgency recently in view of a variety of psychological experiments that strongly suggest that people have some kind of access to imagistic representations that they seem regularly to inspect and even "rotate" in the course of solving problems. Thus, in a pioneering experiment of Roger Shepard (1982), subjects were trained to discriminate whether two images presented in rapid succession were rotations of one another: it turned out that the time it took them to respond was proportional to the angular displacement of the image![22]

It is extremely difficult to resist the temptation to think that in such cases the subjects are actually rotating something "before their mind's eye." But what possibly could this thing be? It seems as improbable that there's actually something *rotating* in one's brain as that there's actually a black and orange striped image there when someone is imaging a tiger. Consequently, such experiments can seem to invite dualism with a vengeance. Confronted by these problems, many philosophers have claimed that, corresponding to many properties that are normally attributed to objects in space, there are "phenomenal" properties and "phenomenal" objects that we "directly" experience in our mind: thus, corresponding to the redness of tomatoes, there is the "phenomenal redness" of our recollected image of a tomato, and it's this phenomenal redness we also experience in "red" after-images, and dreams of red flowers, the dream and after-images themselves being examples of phenomenal objects (recently the word "qualia" has come to be used for phenomenal objects and qualities fairly indifferently). And the claim for many is that phenomenal properties exist in some "phenomenal," non-physical world. We'll return to this issue in §5.2.2 and §11.5, considering less extravagant interpretations of this data. For the nonce, it's important only to feel its pull, and the difficulties it presents to a facile materialist theory of at least mental images.

2.5.4 Privacy

Besides either lacking spatial properties, or having them in a peculiar "non-physical" fashion, mental images illustrate another feature that many people have thought distinguished many mental states from any physical ones. It's not merely that mental images are in a special non-physical space, but that this space seems also to be *essentially private*: I can't hope to experience your mental images or anyone else's, and no one else can hope to experience mine. Your images exist in "your space," mine in mine, and we can learn of each other's only "indirectly," by inference, e.g. from such experiments as Shepard's.

"Privacy" is not peculiar to mental images. It also seems true for pains, sensations, qualia, as well as for most any conscious thought or feeling. Indeed, it is hard to resist the suggestion that what we are each doing when we introspect our conscious lives is surveying an essentially private world of such phenomenal objects, states, and properties to which we have a specially privileged access. If this is true, then it would seem to present a serious obstacle to any materialist theory: for any material process is presumably objective and publicly accessible.[23]

One simple way to appreciate the problem is to compare a hole in a tooth with a pain in a tooth. Someone could wonder whether the hole in hers was larger or smaller than the one in her brother's. If she really cared enough to find out, it's perfectly clear what she might do. For example, she might have a dentist measure how much of some common substance could be inserted into each cavity. Or both teeth might be extracted and measured in a good light. But what is she to do if she wonders whether *the intensity of the pain in her tooth* is more or less than that of her brother's? How are the pains to be "extracted" and compared? Holes in teeth are objective and public in a way that pains in them seem not to be.

The epistemological point is crucial. The problem here is *not* the simple verbal problem that neither the woman nor her brother can have the same pain, since one person's pains are "by definition" not another's: of course there's a sense in which I can't have *your* pains, because if they did they would be *mine*; but that seems no more an argument for privacy than the fact that (as Nagel (1965/1971:100) put it) I can't have *your* haircut. The privacy that is a serious issue for the dualist is a peculiarly epistemic privacy that not even telepathy or brain fusions would seem to overcome. For even in such outré cases, there would still seem to be an epistemic gap. The woman wondering about whether her toothache was as bad as her brother's is not likely to be satisfied by being assured that she was "telepathizing" her brother. She could still wonder whether it *appeared* to her as it *appeared* to him. But how could she or her brother ever really definitively compare the intensities, since they could never put themselves in the same epistemic position to each of them? Insofar as the inner objects of conscious experience are exhausted by a person's conscious introspection, they would seem to be entirely available to her in a way that no one else's experiences could ever possibly.

At least since Descartes, many philosophers have sought to specify the "internal," sensory things of whose existence they were "absolutely certain," on which they could carefully try to base their (for some, less certain) knowledge of the external world. Leave aside the feasibility of the project. The distinction between the sensory experiences that we somehow know "directly" and other things that we seem to know only inferentially seems striking and important, and one which any adequate theory of mind should explain. It should specify what the "objects" of our immediate thought and knowledge are, the items with which we are, in Russell's (1912a) phrase, "directly acquainted." But questions about "the objects of thought" begin to bring us to some of the deeper properties of the mind, which are exhibited by another Leibniz Law argument that is associated with Descartes.

2.5.5 Descartes' argument: the fallacious version

Descartes makes in his Sixth Meditation another argument that has long fascinated philosophers, particularly since it seems to many people to put its finger on several very tenacious intuitions about the mind. It runs as follows:

> I know that everything which I clearly and distinctly understand is capable of being created by God so as to correspond exactly with my understanding of it. Hence the fact that I can clearly and distinctly understand one thing apart from another is enough to make me certain that the two things are distinct, since they are capable of being separated, at least by God. . . . Thus, simply by knowing that I exist and seeing at the same time that absolutely nothing else belongs to my nature or essence except that I am a thinking thing, I can infer correctly that my essence consists solely in the fact that I am a thinking thing. . . . [O]n the one hand I have a clear and distinct idea of myself, in so far as I am simply a thinking, non-extended thing; and on the other hand I have a distinct idea of body, in so far as this is simply an extended, non-thinking thing. And accordingly, it is certain that I am really distinct from my body, and can exist without it.   (1641a/1970:26)

This argument is open to a number of interpretations, a standard one that convicts it of a simple fallacy, and a more sophisticated one that seems interestingly valid, although many have questioned the truth of its premises. The simple fallacy, however, turns on a further, extremely important feature of mental phenomena that we've already mentioned in the introduction, their *intentionality*, whose logical intricacies we will begin to explore in the next sub-section. Only after that exploration will we return to the sophisticated version of Descartes' argument (§2.5.7).

The fallacious version of the argument could be expressed as follows:

(1) My mind has the property of being conceivably unextended

(2) My body does not have the property of being conceivably unextended;

therefore   (3) my body ≠ my mind.

Now this argument is patently invalid. The same form of argument could defeat almost any identity claim. Consider, for example, the identity of Mt. Everest with the highest mountain on earth. By parallel reasoning, we could argue:

(1′) The tallest mountain has property of being conceivably different from Mt. Everest.

(2′) Mt. Everest does not have the property of being conceivably different from Mt. Everest.

therefore: (3′) The tallest mountain ≠ Mt. Everest.

Indeed, in general, for any x and y for which (1G) and (2G) are true, (3G) would be true:

(1G) x has the property of being conceivably different from y.

(2G) y does not have the property of being conceivably different from y.

therefore   (3G) x ≠ y.

By the same reasoning, the morning star couldn't be identical with the evening star, Mark Twain couldn't be identical with Sam Clemens, and the square of 14 might not be 196! Clearly something has gone wrong.

2.5.6 Intentionality and referential opacity

What has gone wrong has to do with some of the specific problems associated with the general phenomena of intentionality that we noted earlier when we cited Brentano's famous dictum to the effect that no physical phenomenon exhibits "reference to an object." Whatever one thinks of his bold metaphysical thesis, he was certainly right to call attention to some striking peculiarities about "reference" that have troubled philosophers and logicians for some time, and which, as we shall see, have the deepest significance for an understanding of the mind.

In the first place, notice that, although "x refers to y" would initially appear to be a two-place relation, like "x kicks y" or "x kisses y," it is by no means obvious precisely how this can be so. If a relation actually obtains between two things, the things had better actually exist: you can't kick things that don't exist – you can't kick Pegasus or Santa Claus! But it would appear that you can nonetheless *refer* to Pegasus or Santa Claus: indeed, one might think you'd better be able to do that if you're even so much as going to *deny* that they exist! So reference would seem to be a very peculiar relation, and intentionality – the property of our mental states whereby they refer or are "about" things – would seem to be a peculiar property of mental things that would certainly not appear to be a property any mere physical thing could possess.

Not only do intentional mental states seem to allow reference to the non-existent, they also appear to violate the very Leibniz Law that we have been trying in this chapter to respect. At least on one natural reading of them, ordinary ascriptions of propositional attitudes to people exhibit what has come to be called *"referential opacity"*: you cannot substitute in their complementation clauses (e.g. the "that . . ."clause that follows the verb) co-referential singular terms *salva veritate*.[24] Recall the meta-linguistic version of Leibniz's Law:

> if two expressions, "a" and "b"refer to the same thing, then they may be substituted for one another in any context *salva veritate*.

thus:

and

(4) John thinks (Paris = Paris)
(5) Paris = the Capital of France

do not entail:

(6) John thinks (Paris = the Capital of France)

For John could know the former as a trivial truth, but know nothing about France. You can't substitute the co-referential terms, "Paris"and "the Capital of France" in the complement clauses of a mental verb like "thinks" *salva veritate*. And so, propositional attitude ascriptions seem on their face to present violations of Leibniz's Law.

Related to violations of Leibniz's Law, is an apparent violation of another logical truism, existential generalization: if some individual, Sam, is bald, then surely *something* is bald (in logic: Fa $\Rightarrow$ ($\exists$x)Fx). But now consider:

(7) John thinks Zeus will punish Hitler

This certainly doesn't entail

(8) ($\exists$x)(John thinks x will punish Hitler),

58

since, for lack of Zeus, there would in fact be *nothing* of which John's thought is true; i.e. (8) would be false.[25]

Both the failure of substitution and the failure of existential generalization suggest that terms inside the complement of an attitude do not actually *refer* to things in the world in the way that they ordinarily do outside such complements. Somehow, they play some other role. Philosophers have many suggestions: Frege claimed that in such case they referred to their "sense" (*Sinn*); Quine, that they referred to *themselves* (i.e. the words are being *mentioned* not *used*). Since it's the *words* themselves (or their senses) and not their *ordinary* referents that are being referred to in the complements of attitude terms, the occurrences of "Paris"and "the Capital of France" in those complements need no longer be taken to be co-referential (after all, the *quoted* expressions)

"Paris"   "the Capital of France"

are *not* co-referential: *they* refer not to the same city, but *to different spelled expressions*). Thus, when we say that John thinks Zeus will punish Hitler, what we are really saying is that John in some way thinks the *sentence* "God will punish Hitler" is true. We need not decide between these and many other theories of attitude ascriptions here. It suffices for our purposes only to notice the availability of such theories to explain opacity and so preserve Leibniz's Law.

Referential opacity is an absolutely crucial property of the attitudes and/or their typical ascriptions, to which we shall return again and again, not only in understanding arguments like Descartes', but also in coming to understand crucial features of mentality itself. We shall see later on that it plays an important role in motivating the computational theory of thought.

At some point, the reader is likely to wonder why, in view of all these apparent exceptions, one should hold on to Leibniz's Law at all. One reason is that, when one thinks about it, it seems so obvious that one begins to suspect that these exceptions are systematic. And we will see that there do seem to be interesting explanations of them that permit the original law to be preserved. But readers can judge for themselves whether in the end they are convinced by the received wisdom about how to deal with these problems: many of the questions surrounding them are still very much open and subject to lively debate.

2.5.7* *Kripke's version of Descartes' argument*[26]

Many people think that Descartes was too clever a philosopher to have really been guilty of missing the issue of referential opacity (even if he wouldn't have noticed it in anything like our terms). As a number of writers (e.g. Wilson 1968) have noted, there is a much more interesting interpretation of his argument that turns on the notion of "essence" or properties that are *necessary* to something's being the very *particular* or *kind* of thing it is. For example, it is no accident that you can't find the number 5 underneath the tablecloth: the number 5 is not possibly a concrete object located in space and time, just as a stone is not possibly an abstract object *outside* of space and time. 5 is *essentially* abstract; a stone is *essentially* concrete. Suppose now that we make Descartes' not implausible assumption that, at least in the case of "clear and distinct ideas," essential properties were revealed by exercises in conceivability; that is, F is an essential property of x iff one can't clearly and distinctly conceive of x without conceiving of it being F. If we accept this assumption, then an interesting argument emerges that has been advanced in modern dress by Saul Kripke (1972).

Along the lines of the view of Putnam's that we discussed in §1.5.2, Kripke suggests a semantic view that enlarges the role of the scientist in determining the referential and modal properties of ordinary words. For example, when children learn the word "water" they usually don't learn its chemical composition, H_2O. What they may learn instead are "reference fixers" e.g. descriptions of water that are sufficient to pick water out in the limited contexts in which they find themselves. Thus, they may learn that "water" is the transparent liquid that fills the seas and comes out of kitchen faucets. But these features are often *entirely accidental* features of water: it's perfectly possible for water not to have filled the seas or issued from faucets.

But, asks Kripke, are children in the same situation in the case of pain? In the case of *that* term, he claims, reference is typically fixed by reference to an *essential* property of pain: the phenomena of *feeling painful*. Unlike the case of "water," where we feel free to refer to the phenomenon that happens in this, but maybe not in all possible worlds, to fill the seas, in the case of "pain" Kripke claims we do not enjoy a similar freedom. We ordinarily cannot say, "And by 'pain' I mean the phenomenon that in this, but perhaps not in all, possible worlds feels to me painful." The painful feeling whereby we fix the reference of "pain" is, claims Kripke, *essential* to something's being a pain in the way that, say, the appearances of water, whereby (in a context) we might fix the reference of "water," are not. A pain necessarily feels painful; water doesn't *necessarily* fill the seas or quench our thirst (cf. Descartes' claim that he is immediately aware of his essence as a thinking thing, but not as essentially extended).

Kripke's version of Descartes' argument can now be put thus (I simplify for brevity). Consider *a particular pain*, P, that a physicalist proposes to identify with some particular physical brain state B (I use "the very thing" to emphasize the fact that the claims are about the *very objects themselves*, and not *relative to how we describe them*[27]):

> (K1) The very thing that is pain P is necessarily painful, just as the very thing that is a stone is necessarily matter;

(K2)   The very thing that is brain state B is not necessarily pain-ful, just as the very thing that is a stone is not necessarily a doorstop.

therefore   (K3)   The very thing that is pain P ≠ the very thing that is brain state B.

This argument is not fallacious or straightforwardly refutable by common sense. Note that, unlike the earlier fallacious version, it is not deployable against ordinary identity claims. Consider, for example:

(K1')   The very thing that is Bill Clinton is necessarily Bill Clinton;

(K2')   The very thing that is the US president is not necessarily Bill Clinton;

therefore   (K3')   The very thing that is Bill Clinton ≠ the very thing that is the US president.

Here, the argument doesn't go through, since the second premise, (K2'), is false: after all, *the very thing that is the US president*, i.e. Bill Clinton, *is* necessarily Bill Clinton! (Remember: Kripke's premises depend upon focusing on the very objects themselves, not on how we happen to be describing them.)

Consequently, criticism of this argument will involve questioning the plausibility of the premises. Is it really true that a pain – or the state of being in pain – is in fact necessarily painful? Do pains, so understood, really exist? We will return to this question in §11.4.

2.5.7.1* *Constitution or identity?*   The above argument, however, may prove a little too much. In a footnote at the end of his discussion, Kripke observes, "Similarly, it can be argued that a statue is not the hunk of matter out of which it is composed" (1972:354 n73), since after all, it is possible for the hunk of matter to exist without being a statue (indeed, arguably, the statue is necessarily a statue, but the hunk of matter isn't). That is, what Kripke's argument calls attention to is the need for care in applying the actually slightly technical notion of *identity*. It is by no means clear in what way ordinary objects are identical with the "sum of their physical parts." To take a famous argument from Plato, suppose we identified a vase with its molecules. But then also suppose someone breaks the vase and makes a statue of the pieces. If the vase = the molecules, and the statue = the very same molecules, then, by the transitivity of identity, the vase = the statue, and this is patently false.

There are a number of solutions to this puzzle – one might identify the vase with the molecules at a time, or with a certain space/time region – or, alternatively, one might say *not* that the vase is identical to the molecules, but rather that it is *composed* of them: the "is" in "the vase is just a lot of molecules" might be taken to be an "is" not of identity, but of "composition." Much progress could probably be made on the mind/body problem without taking a stand on this delicate issue.[28] I raise it only to caution the reader against too readily supposing that Leibniz Law arguments can be so easily deployed against the Reductionist proposals.

Kripke does suggest that the relation of mind to body can't be handled on the analogy of a statue to a hunk of matter:

> A theory that a person is nothing over and above his body in the way that a statue is nothing over and above the matter of which it is composed, would have to hold that (necessarily) a person exists if and only if his body exists and has a certain additional physical organization. Such a thesis would be subject to modal difficulties similar to those besetting the ordinary identity thesis. . . . A further discussion of this matter must be left to another place.   (1972:354 n73)

But (to my knowledge) he nowhere returns to this discussion. He ends the footnote with an acknowledgement of the relevance of functionalism to the issue, but aside from claiming that it's a view that he has "little tendency to accept," he presents no argument against it. We'll see more precisely the bearing of that view on his discussion in §11.6.2.

I hasten to use this occasion also to invoke my Fairness Maxim, not to burden philosophy of mind with everyone else's problems. If it turns out that a Leibniz Law argument against the identity of a mental with a physical phenomenon would tell equally against the identity of a vase and its molecules, one can be fairly confident the argument is more about the logic of identity than about the nature of the mind.

2.6   Qualia and "What It's Like"

Other objections have been raised to the identity theory, but less with respect to the category of mental *objects* (like pains), than to the category of *properties*. Although Leibniz Law objections could be raised here as well, the requisite thinking about *properties of properties* is awkward. Moreover, it's not really property *identity* that's at issue, since, as we'll see, the problems could arise no matter how properties are identified.

Jerome Shaffer (1963/1991) noted that, even if the identity of, say, a certain experience and a brain state were to obtain, there would still be an issue about the different *aspects* of the one state, the mental aspect and the physical aspect. It is, after all, only because the noticed aspects are *different* that the identity could count as the empirical discovery that proponents of the identity theory standardly take it to be. After all, if the mental aspect, M, of having a pain were identical to a physical aspect, P, then how would the thought that M = P be different from the thought that P = P (or, for that matter, M = M)? But if M and P are different, then it would seem we now have a dualism of aspects, if not of the states themselves. Shaffer writes:

[T]ake the case where a person reports . . . the having of an after-image. . . . Now it seems to me obvious that, in many cases at least, the person does not notice any *physical* features – he does not notice that his brain is in some particular state. . . . Yet he does notice *some* feature. Hence he must notice something other than a physical feature. (1963/1991:178)

So put, however, Shaffer could be thought to be begging the question against the physicalist: for isn't a physicalist someone who would want to insist that *all* features of anything are indeed physical features? Just because those features aren't ordinarily specified in terms of the brain doesn't make them the less physical, any more than the fact that the word "metabolism" doesn't occur in the description, "the first feature mentioned in the biology book" entails that the first feature mentioned in the biology book isn't in fact a metabolic one.

Why are many people nevertheless tempted to think that mental features couldn't be identical to physical features? Again, an epistemic issue seems crucial. In a number of famous articles, Thomas Nagel (1974/1991) and Frank Jackson (1982, 1986/1992) point out that knowing all the "objective, scientific facts" about some mental being would still leave out an important kind of knowledge of that being that arises only with respect to mental beings: and this is knowledge of phenomenological properties, or, in Nagel's famous phrase, "knowledge of what it's like" to be a being of that sort.

Jackson's "knowledge argument" involves a woman (who has become famous in the literature as "Mary") who understands all there is to understand *scientifically* about the causation of color perception in human beings, but who, having been color-blind since birth, doesn't know "what it's like to see red." Let us suppose that in later life medical technology discovers a way to endow her with color vision. Jackson argues:

Physicalism is . . . the thesis that [the actual world] is entirely physical. This is why physicalists must hold that complete physical knowledge is complete knowledge simpliciter. . . . It seems, however, that Mary does not know all there is to know. For when [she acquires color vision and sees] a color television, she will learn what it is like to see something red, say. (1986/1990:392)

Nagel illustrates a related point by considering the problem of "knowing what it's like to be a bat." On the assumption that bats have experiences, but noting that they engage in a kind of perceptual process – "echolocation," or essentially a sonar system of detecting reflections of their own shrieks – that seems fundamentally different from any process in which we humans engage, Nagel writes:

> It will not help to try to imagine that one has webbing on one's arms . . . that one has poor vision, and perceives the surrounding world by a system of reflected high-frequency sound signals. . . . Insofar as I can imagine this (which is not very far), it tells me only what it would be like for me to behave as a bat behaves. But that is not the question. I want to know what it is like for a bat to be a bat. Yet if I try to imagine this, I am restricted to the resources of my own mind, and those resources are inadequate to the task. (1974/1991:423)

He generalizes from cases like this to the conclusion:

> If physicalism is to be defended, the phenomenological features must themselves be given a physical account. But when we examine their subjective character it seems that such a result is impossible. The reason is that every subjective phenomenon is essentially connected with a single point of view, and it seems inevitable that an objective, physical theory will abandon that point of view. (1974/1991:423)

Like the Shaffer argument, Nagel's and Jackson's arguments draw attention to an important *epistemological* fact from which they draw *metaphysical* conclusions: someone could know all about the physical world, including her own brain, and still be missing what would seem undeniably to be certain further facts: for example, how red looks, and what it's like to be a bat.

2.7 Summary of Problems So Far

Summarizing our discussion so far, then, we have raised six *prima facie* Leibniz Law objections to the identity theory, six properties of mental phenomena that appear not to be properties of any physical phenomena:

1. Rationality
   Universal reason transcends any properties of mere matter.

2. Free will
   Human decisions seem not to be caused in the way that physical events are.

3. Spatiality
   Thoughts don't seem to be located in physical space; mental images seem to be located in a space of their own.

4. Privacy
   Some mental phenomena (e.g. the pain in one's tooth) don't seem to be publicly observable in the way that any physical phenomena (e.g. the hole in one's tooth) are.

5. Intentionality

Thoughts seem to be *about* things in a way that no physical thing seems to be. Indeed, thoughts can be about *non-existent* things, and exhibit a referential opacity that no physical thing seems to exhibit.

6. Being essentially mental

Mental things seem essentially mental in a way that no physical thing seems to be.

In addition, we have seen that there are reasons to think that the physical facts don't exhaust the facts of the world, since there seem to be the phenomena of:

7. Subjectivity and qualitative content

It's possible to know all the physical facts of the world and still not know "from the inside" what it's like to see red or be a bat.

And over all these there hover:

8. The explanatory gaps

Physical facts don't seem to upwardly necessitate facts about qualitative experience, rationality, or intentionality.

The task of a physicalistic reduction is to show how, despite appearances, these eight phenomena *could* be explained on a physicalistic hypothesis, or, alternatively, how they aren't really genuine phenomena. We shall be undertaking this task in the chapters that follow (I shall return to this list to judge how well we have fared at the end of chapter 11). We turn first to a simple, radical proposal, that there don't exist any mental phenomena to worry about in these ways at all!

Notes

1 For both the term, and several of the ideas suggested by it, I am greatly indebted to discussion with Joseph Levine (see his 1983, 1991, 1993). Chalmers (1996:chapter 2) takes up Levine's point and elaborates it in interesting ways, providing the basis of his dualism (which neither I nor Levine endorse). An unfortunate terminological point for our discussion: "explanatory gaps" of the sort to be discussed here are to be distinguished from "causal breaks" of the sort to be discussed in §3.1.1. The latter involve breaks in the *physical mechanism* for bringing about certain changes, as seem to occur in magician's acts. As will become clear, an *explanatory* gap may, but need not, involve a causal break of this sort.

2 Or explained at all: in the kinds of cases we shall be considering, it is hard to see what alternative to material explanation there might be; cf. §1.2 and Teller (1984).

3   Derivatively, insofar as phenomena involve the interactions of many minds – as in sociology, economics, history – our explanations are similarly truncated. But there could be ways, of course, that a macro-science such as economics could by-pass psychology and the mind-body problems by sufficient idealization away from facts about the minds of any particular individuals.

4   Neurophysiologists themselves can be sensitive to this issue, distinguishing the anatomical classifications of the brain from functional ones (as in DeGroot and Chusid 1991:1).

5   Searle (1992) misses this point, arguing that "the apparent 'necessity' of any scientific explanation may just be a function of the fact that we find the explanation so convincing" (p. 101). He also wrongly supposes that the necessitation doesn't occur in the case of the inverse square law of gravitation. But it clearly does: *given* the inverse square law, then *as a matter of mathematical mereological necessity*, apples near the earth will fall to it, and objects with a certain momentum at a certain distance will orbit it (*ceteris paribus*). Of course, the inverse square law "does not show why bodies *have to have* gravitational attraction" (p. 101): that would be the task of, for example, a TOE, which showed how the inverse square law of gravity was (conceptually) necessitated by some deeper laws.

6   Note that Crick (1994:245) makes no such claim, but seems content to describe the finding as a "neural correlate."

7   Note that Santa Claus is not an abstract object nor an idea – neither abstract objects nor ideas can tumble down chimneys! Besides: *they* exist – but he presumably doesn't! See Quine (1953a:essay 1) for a superb discussion of this ancient problem.

8   As we noted already in §1.2.3, Quine's reaction to this problem is quite the opposite from Brentano's: where Brentano sees such problems as inviting a form of dualism, Quine sees them as a reason for eliminativism.

9   See McGinn (1991) for interesting suggestions in this regard. McGinn speculates that human beings may simply not be endowed with the right concepts for understanding the relation of the mental to the physical. Loar (1996) suggests that the difficulty may be due to the peculiar "demonstrative concepts" that are involved in introspection.

10 They are largely motivated by concerns about the knowability of the world, and whether there could be facts so independent of us that we could in principle never know them: for example, whether everything we take to be our waking lives could actually be a dream. We will consider this concern as it arises with regard to the mental in discussing verificationism in §5.4.

11 Thus, we needn't tarry over the many foundational problems about the nature of matter and causal interaction that have plagued modern physics from its beginnings in the work of Descartes and Newton. Chomsky (1995:4–5) suggests that these foundational problems vitiate any discussion of a supposed "mind/body problem." However, as I hope my characterization of physicalism allows, one may raise this problem no matter how the *general* problems of physics are to be resolved: for the question will still arise whether there is anything *special* about the mental.

12 See Field (1978) for proposals for avoiding numbers, and Quine (1953a:essay 1) for avoiding properties.

13 And "iff" abbreviates "if and only if," as in "Someone is in Washington D.C. if and only if she is in the capital of the United States."

14 After Gottfried Leibniz (1646–1716). This truistic law should not be confused with its more controversial *converse*, "identity of indiscernables": if (Fx iff Fy) then x = y. That is, if everything that is true of x is true also of y, then x = y. This claim turns on what one would say about the possibility of perfectly replicated universes, an issue that has no bearing on the present discussion.

15 Note that Chomsky (1995) goes on to acknowledge nevertheless the explanatory gaps that still exist, adding that these reiterations of Priestley's claims

> seem close to truistic – and as uninformative as truisms tend to be, since the brain sciences, despite important progress, are far from closing the gap to the problems posed by thought and language.   (1995:10)

16 It is a fascinating irony that Descartes seems to confine his dualism to the powers of reason and language: *sensation* and even imagination seem to him physically unproblematic (see, for example,1641b/1970:212 and Wilson 1978 for discussion). As we'll see, the problem nowadays is almost entirely the reverse: many people are prepared to suppose that computers could *think*; but *feel*?

17 Dennett (1978a:essay 16) provides a subtle and excellent discussion of the issue of "making up one's mind."

18 And sometimes we act on no reason whatsoever, as when we dance with joy, scream in rage, or just twiddle our thumbs. See Hursthouse (1991) for a splendid discussion of this interesting category of "arational action."

19 It would be circular to insist that a person always acts on her strongest desire if the only possible evidence of that being the strongest desire is that she indeed so acts.

20 – to cite the line Lewis Carroll (1895/1995) has Achilles scream to the obdurate Tortoise who refuses to draw a deductive consequence from an argument. This brief and charming article is well worth reading in connection with the present issue.

21 I am indebted to Jim Woodward for making this point vivid to me.

22 See Kosslyn (1980) for a rich discussion of these and many other similar results.

23 In a surprisingly verbal maneuver, Searle (1992:97ff) simply avoids this problem by claiming that *all* physical phenomena possess a "subjective" aspect. The problem remains: what reason is there to think so, apart from the existence of conscious mental beings like ourselves?

24 The metaphor of "transparency" and "opacity" originates with Russell and Whitehead (1912/1960:§I-appendix C) and is much discussed by Quine (1956a/1976), and then by a veritable industry of others. Think of the "light of reference" in a normal, "transparent" context shining through to the *object* being referred to, but the light being stopped somehow by the referring expression itself in an "opaque" one.

25 A footnote for the really dedicated: what has just been said is in fact not *always* true. There is another way of reading propositional attitude ascriptions whereby they are *not* referentially opaque. Consider:

> (9-1) Whoever the mob wants to get, it will get.
> (9-2) The mob wants to get Leftie
> (9-3) Leftie = Sam Spade

therefore	(9-4)	The mob will get Sam Spade
indeed	(9-5)	There is someone the Mob wants to get.

The inference from (9-1, 2, 3) to (9-4 and 5) seems valid. In order to keep the issue straight here, philosophers have distinguished "transparent" from "opaque" readings of these expressions. In a "transparent" reading, the applicability of an attitude ascription doesn't depend upon *how the things mentioned inside the object of the attitude are described*; in an opaque one it does (see, for example, Quine (1956a/1976), Kaplan (1969) and Richard (1990) for a taste of the full complexity of the issues here).

26 I should caution scholars that I am simplifying the actual argument Kripke provides for ease of exposition. Even so, the section is slightly more difficult than others, involving some relatively subtle philosophical intuitions. It could be omitted without interrupting the rest of the discussion (I return to the topic only briefly in §11.6.2, also an optional section).

27 In philosophical jargon, they are "*de re*" modal claims – claims about *the objects themselves* – not "*de dicto*" ones – claims that depend upon how we *describe* the objects.

28 See, for example, Wiggins (1971) and Yablo (1987).

3
Eliminativism: Philosophical Issues

3.1 From Dualism to Eliminativism

The arguments of the preceding chapter all raise problems for a simple reduction of mental to physical phenomena. If they are correct, then it would appear that the emerging physical theory of the universe is false and that there really are special, non-physical phenomena of mind that take place outside physical space. Understandably, many philosophers and scientists have found this an unacceptable conclusion: it has seemed to them to be virtually an argument for a belief in ghosts. But what are they to do? How are they to answer the dualist's often quite serious objections?

Apparently, it wasn't until the twentieth century that anyone actually considered the interesting, if desperate solution of *denying the existence of mental phenomena entirely*. Total *eliminativism* about the mind is the view that there simply are no mental phenomena whatsoever: no beliefs, desires, hopes, feelings, pains, tickles, pangs of love, displays of courage, or even (what the reader at this point may think she is beginning to experience) feelings of depression or despair. Although one finds anticipations of the view in the work of Watson and Skinner, it has probably never been stated so plainly as by Paul Churchland (1981/1990) when he proposed taking seriously

> the thesis that our common-sense conception of psychological phenomenon constitutes a radically false theory, a theory so fundamentally defective that both the principles and the ontology of that theory will eventually be displaced, rather than smoothly reduced, by completed neuroscience. . . . [It] is a stagnant or degenerating research program, and has been for millennia.   (1981/1990:206–11)

Believing in mental states, he likes to suggest, ought to go the way of belief in the Greek Gods, or phlogiston, or a luminiferous ether. Similar views have been expressed by Quine (1960), Feyerabend (1963/1971) and Rorty (1965).

There are some who would object to thinking of our ordinary beliefs in mental phenomena as any sort of *theory* at all.[1] It certainly doesn't ordinarily *seem* to be a theory. Wittgenstein captures at least the phenomenology of understanding other people when he claims:

> We do not see facial contortions and make inferences from them (like a doctor framing a diagnosis) to joy, grief, boredom. We describe a face immediately as sad, radiant, bored, even when we are unable to give any other description of the features. – Grief, one would like to say, is personified in the face.   (1967:§225)

And, in a often cited passage, he writes, "I am not of the *opinion* that someone has a soul; my attitude towards him is as towards a soul" (1953:178).

Of course, someone might argue that, despite this phenomenology, people are engaged *unconsciously* in inference (a suggestion to which we will return in chapter 8). However, whether or not this is true, it still might be philosophically interesting to regard mental beliefs as comprising a theory, and ask whether, if it were one, what reasons could be adduced for thinking it is true. Certainly there are times and places in the world where there have been no mental states; perhaps here and now is one of them. Moreover, even if we ultimately reject eliminativism about *all* mental phenomena, answering the eliminativist challenge may help keep us honest about the phenomena we do accept: we may become clearer about reasons for believing in some of them, and see reasons to reject others, much as a more traditional scepticism about, say, the existence of the external world has often led to insights and cautions about reasoning in that domain.

3.1.1   The lack of a causal break

The most serious argument for eliminativism proceeds from exasperation with the many problems we've noted facing reductionism. But why should that lead to eliminativism? If those problems are so insoluble, why not opt for dualism?

Historically, discussions of dualism often were excessively caught up with worries about ghosts, parapsychology, and the problems such phenomena might or might not pose for such principles as the conservation of mass/energy. And there are genuine problems here in trying to make sense of how dualistic mental phenomena could causally interact with physical phenomena. But there is no need to tarry on these sometimes excessively arcane arguments here. For there is an argument that cuts through such speculations and presents a problem for most any form of dualism and a serious argument for eliminativism. If correct, it shows that if physicalistic reduction really does fail, and dualism is the only option for believing in the mind, then we *would* have abundant reason to give up on mental talk. It might be called the "no causal break argument" (not to be confused with the arguments about the existence of "explanatory gaps" discussed earlier in §2.1).

70

Recall the example discussed in §1.3 of the debate between a Newtonian and an angelologist regarding the motion of the planets. In that case, it appears that the angelologist is at a distinct disadvantage, since he can provide no non-tendentious evidence for his positing of angels. At least as regards the motion of the planets, there is nothing describable independently of the theories under dispute that can't be explained a lot better by Newton's theory of gravitation. By way of contrast, consider a particularly narrow-minded Newtonian – call her NN – who believes gravitation is all you need to explain anything, and is arguing with a standard physicist who believes in electromagnetism. How might NN be refuted? Again, by appeal to non-tendentious evidence. Simply hold a paper clip to a lodestone (a natural magnet) and ask NN to explain why it doesn't fall to the earth as her theory would predict. Note that the existence of this datum – the clinging of the paper clip to the lodestone – does not presuppose the truth or falsity of either theory under discussion: it can be observed and described without presupposing any of the terms or concepts of either NN's theory or an electromagnetic theory, which might, though, be the best theory that explains it. Given this (and, of course, a mass of other) data, gravitational theory alone can be shown to be explanatorily inadequate. We need to posit electromagnetism.

Now the dualist is engaged in a similar kind of debate with the eliminativist: the dualist – like both the angelologist and (as we will call him) the electricist – is positing further phenomena that he claims are required in a complete account of the world. But in which position is he? Is he in the position of the angelologist, positing entities that serve no explanatory need, or in the position of the electricist, supplementing an inadequate materialist theory?

If *this* is the debate between the dualist and the eliminativist, however, the dualist is in an extremely vulnerable position. For it seems to be a striking fact about people and animals that *all of their non-tendentiously described behavior could be explained in principle by reference to physical properties alone.* All the motions of their bodies, from the bat of an eyelash to the thrashing of a limb to the complex contractions of the human larynx, the scribblings of pens and the tappings of computer keyboards, could be perfectly well explained by reference to the electrical impulses along nerve fibers that preceded them. These firings in turn could be explained by earlier neurological events, which in turn could be explained by earlier events extending back into the past in the same way that any other physical event can be. We have absolutely no reason to believe that there is any break in the physical explanation of their motion. As Quine (1960) put it in a famous passage:

> If there is a case for mental events and mental states, it must be just that the positing of them, like the positing of molecules, has some indirect systematic efficacy in the development of theory. But if a certain organization of theory could be achieved by thus positing distinctive mental states and events behind physical behavior, surely

71

as much organization could be achieved by positing merely certain correlative physiological states and events instead. . . . The bodily states exist anyway; why add the others? (1960:264)

Of course, it *could* turn out otherwise, if, say, there were any satisfactory evidence of so-called "parapsychological" phenomena, e.g. telepathy, telekinesis, clairvoyance. If there were such phenomena, then existing physical theory would certainly appear to be inadequate: we would indeed be in the position of our gravitationalist confronted with the non-tendentiously describable causal breaks explainable only by electromagnetism. But there is no evidence of such phenomena (or so most current philosophers of mind assume). Moreover, even if there were, it is unclear how it would bear upon the explanation of vast amounts of perfectly normal human and animal behavior where such evidence seems even less likely to arise.

But it might be thought that there is plenty of normal human and animal behavior that *does* require mentalistic explanation. Someone might insist, "There are all the things that people *say*, the content of their *thoughts*, their *loves* and *quarrels*, or just the *intelligence* with which humans and many animals *act*. While physics can explain motion – why my arm rises – surely only a dualistic mentalism can explain action – why I *raised* my arm." The eliminativist can simply reply: all the italicized expressions are *tendentious*, begging the very question of the applicability of mentalistic talk that he is disputing. "But didn't you yourself begin this book with an observation of an explanatory gap between the physical and the mental? What about all the objections to a physicalistic reduction that we considered in chapter 2: don't they appeal to phenomena that can't be explained by physics?" All those discussions operated on the assumption that there *were* minds – that there were phenomena of rationality, intentionality, privacy, thoughts, and images outside a physical space, and these are now the very phenomena the eliminativist is calling into question. In a way the modern puzzle about the mind could be put this way: *how can there be an explanatory gap between the mental and the physical given that there is no causal break in a physical account of the world?*

Of course, perhaps causal breaks will turn up: maybe they already have, and I'm just exhibiting my ignorance. But the philosophically interesting point would remain: what if there weren't? Does anything we say ordinarily, or even theoretically, about the mind – short, of course, of dualism – really turn on whether there are such breaks, so that, if there are none, then belief in mental states would be as idle as belief in angels? I think few parties to the debate actually think so, but it's a question worth asking whenever the debate is raised.[2]

One recourse that many dualists have tried at this point is to claim that mental phenomena are not really causally efficacious. There are historically two forms this claim has taken: Leibniz proposed the doctrine of psycho-physical "parallelism," whereby mental phenomena are neither caused by nor the cause of any physical phenomenon. And Thomas Huxley (1893) proposed merely "epiphenomenalism": mental phenomena are indeed caused by, but still don't cause any physical phenomena:

> All states of consciousness in us . . . are immediately caused by molecular changes of the brain-substance. It seems to me that . . . there is no proof that any state of consciousness is the cause of change in the motion of the matter of the organism.   (1893:244)

The view persists in recent discussions. On behalf of the worries about facts about qualitative experience that are left out of any physical account of the world (§2.6 above), Jackson (1982) defends the view that "qualia cause nothing physical but are caused by something physical" (p. 134), and one finds the view in different forms commonly among non-philosophers such as Jackendoff (1987:25) and Velmans (1991).

Recalling our Fairness Maxim, it is important to understand these doctrines as somehow peculiar to the mental. Parallelism and epiphenomenalism are not particularly interesting doctrines about the mind if they apply, as some might well be tempted to apply them, to *any* macro-theory, such as economics or astronomy ("After all," they might argue, "the only causation is physical causation at the micro-level; any apparent macro-causation is an illusion" and/or, "Well, there is upward causation from micro- to macro-phenomena, but not *vice versa*.") Unfortunately, few of the discussants of these doctrines ever make their policy about non-mental phenomena very clear in this regard.[3]

Supposing, however, that these doctrines *are* being advanced as peculiar to the mind, an immediate difficulty of both parallelism and epiphenomenalism is why anyone should believe either of them: if a mental phenomenon has *no* physical effect, then it would certainly appear that nothing physical should be able to provide any evidence whatsoever of anything mental. The mind would seem to be as badly off as "parallel" or "epiphenomenal angels" that are posited – now not to explain anything at all! Why on earth believe in any such things?

The dualist might reply that, unlike angels, at least in one's own case one is *directly aware* of mental phenomena, e.g. of one's own present thoughts and sensations. We will consider such epistemic claims shortly (see §3.2.2 below). Whatever the merits of such appeals in *one's own case*, it should be clear that they would seem to be of no utility at all in justifying anything like the rich mental claims we ordinarily make about anyone else. That is, this suggestion invites with a vengeance the traditional "problem of other minds": why should anyone think that *anyone else* has a mind? Insofar as mental phenomena can really have no physical effects, they clearly can't be responsible for any of the physical behavior that I observe about anyone else; and since observation of others' physical behavior is all I have to go on in presuming them to have mental states, I again have no reason to think *anyone else* has mental states.[4]

Thus, if dualism is taken literally as the positing of non-physical mental phenomena in addition to the phenomena of physics, it risks very nearly the fate of an angelic theory of planetary motion: if mental words refer to non-physical phenomena, we have no more reason to believe at least in other minds than we do in angels. Dualism invites eliminativism, at least about others.

But doubts about the mind can be raised in one's own case as well. One source is reflection on the apparently "normative" nature of much mental ascription.

3.1.2   *Normativity and interpretavism*

The most basic feature of mental talk that seems to many people to be ineliminably normative is the fact that beliefs can be *true* or *false*: they are susceptible to a notion of "mistake" that, many argue, cannot be captured by a mere scientific description of a person's brain states or behavior. I do not want to assess this argument at this point – different aspects will be discussed in §9.2 and §10.3, after some larger theoretical apparatus is in place – but only indicate the eliminativist conclusions to which its proponents are led.

Kripke (1982) has perhaps made the case for this point most simply. Since it was inspired by his reading of Wittgenstein (1953), from whom he takes some pains to distance himself, it has come to be called the "Kripkenstein" argument (all references to this composite figure are to Kripke 1982). Consider what makes it true that someone who claims to be "adding" is following the usual rule (R1):

(R1)   For every pair of numbers you're presented, provide the *sum* of those numbers.

Kripkenstein wonders what distinguishes this person from someone who, also claiming to be (as he puts it) "adding" is actually following a different rule:

(R2)   For every pair of numbers you're presented, provide the *sum* of these numbers, unless you're presented 68 and 57, in which case provide 5,

a rule he calls "quadding".

One sort of answer is a simple *behavioral* one: a person is obeying (R1) rather than (R2) if, were she to be presented with 68 and 57, she'd say "125" and not "5." However, as it stands, this answer won't suffice: for her saying "125" instead of "5" is perfectly compatible with her actually trying to obey rule (R2) and *making an error* (due perhaps to her having misheard, or having made a slip of the tongue, or a confusion about how to follow (R2)). As Kripkenstein notes:

> Suppose I do mean addition by "+". What is the relation of the supposition to the question how I will respond to the problem "68+57"? The dispositionalist gives

a descriptive account of this relation: if "+" meant addition, then I will answer "125". But this is not the proper account of the relation, which is normative, not descriptive. The point is not that, if I meant addition by "+", I will answer "125", but that, if I intend to accord with my past meaning of "+", I *should* answer "125". (1982:37)

Everything depends upon what determines what rule she *intended* to follow. But what determines that?

A tempting answer is an introspective one: a person just knows, immediately by introspection, which rule she intends to be following. But how does she know this? When presented with a rule does she imagine every possible case of its application and imagine how it is to be applied in that case? But rules, especially arithmetic rules like (R1), apply to *a potential infinity of different cases*: all possible pairs of numbers! And these obviously can't be surveyed by finite beings like ourselves (we'll consider this introspective answer further in §5.1.1).

Kripkenstein argues that no purely *descriptive* account of what the person does, has done, or even would do under specific circumstances will decide the issue, and appeals, instead, to the *normative standards* of the person's community:

> Wittgenstein proposes a picture of language based, not on *truth conditions*, but on *assertability conditions* or *justification conditions*: under what circumstances are we allowed to make a given assertion? . . . [I]f one person is considered in isolation, the notion of a rule as guiding the person who adopts it can have *no* substantive content. . . . The situation is very different if we widen our gaze . . . and allow ourselves to consider him as interacting with a wider community. Others then will have justification conditions for attributing correct or incorrect rule following to the subject. (1982:74, 89)

Thus, whether someone is following a particular rule or not depends upon the normative conditions of the community in the context of which the individual's behavior is understood. There is no fact about the individual's mental life in this respect beyond such community relative evaluations.

Quite apart from Kripkenstein's worry about rule following, the idea that our understanding of people is in some way *normative*, or evaluative, pervades a great deal of contemporary discussion. Donald Davidson, for example, defending what might be called an "interpretavist" conception of psychology, stresses the sense we need to make of the *whole* of the set of attitudes we ascribe to a person, whereby we try to make them "make sense." In a well-known passage, he writes that, in general, in ascribing attitudes to people (or "interpreting") them:[5]

> we must work out a theory of what he means, thus simultaneously giving content to his attitudes and to his words. In our need to make him make sense, we will try for a theory that finds him consistent, a believer of truths, and a lover of the good. (Davidson 1970/1980:253)

However, in doing this, we are committing ourselves to norms that are not dictated by the physical description of the world:

> It is a feature of physical reality that physical change can be explained by laws that connect it with other changes and conditions physically described. It is a feature of the mental that the attribution of mental phenomena must be responsible to the back-ground of reasons, beliefs, and intentions of the individual. There cannot be tight connections between the two realms if each is to retain allegiance to its proper source of evidence . . . (Davidson 1970/1980:253–4)

One can no more determine the right mental descriptions from the physical descriptions of the world than one can in general derive claims about how things *ought* to be from a description of how they *are*.

In a number of influential discussions, Dennett (1978a, 1987) seconds these normative conclusions:

> As many philosophers have observed . . . a system's beliefs are those it ought to have, given its perceptual capacities, its epistemic needs, and its biography . . . , [its] desires are those it ought to have, given its biological needs and the most practicable means of satisfying them . . . [where] "ought to have" means "would have if it were ideally ensconced in its environmental niche." (Dennett 1987:48–9)

This normativity renders the mental (or being what he calls an "intentional system") as something less than objective:

> deciding on the basis of available evidence that something is (or may be treated as) an intentional system permits predictions having a normative or logical basis rather than an empirical one. (Dennett 1978:13)

From which fact he draws the startling conclusion:

> Intentional theory is vacuous as psychology because it presupposes and does not explain rationality or intelligence. (Dennett 1978:15)

So much, it would appear, for the pretensions of a mentalistic psychology.

3.1.3 Instrumentalism

Do eliminativists really want to suggest that *we stop using mental words entirely?*! Of course, if we took seriously Churchland's comparison of mental talk to talk of phlogiston and the ether seriously, it might seem pretty wrong-headed to persist in it. But there is a more generous interpretation: the eliminativist can think of mental talk *instrumentally*, as a convenient way of thinking about the behavior of certain things, just as mariners can often navigate geocentrically, or biologists can think of an animal as designed, without committing themselves to the *truth* of the claims (e.g. that the earth is fixed and motionless; that animals didn't merely evolve) that such talk might appear to involve.

Daniel Dennett has been the most prominent proponent of an instrumentalist approach. He advocates treating mentality not as a theory about any *actual* states of a system, be it person or machine, but rather a "stance" – he (1971/1978, 1987) calls it the "intentional stance" – that one takes towards certain things for the purpose of prediction and control. For example, when we are playing with a chess playing computer, it is often useful to take such a stance, thinking of the machine as wanting to win, planning strategies, favoring sacrifices, etc. But:

> [T]he definition of intentional systems I have given does not say that intentional systems really have beliefs and desires, but that one can explain and predict their behavior by ascribing beliefs and desires to them. . . . The decision to adopt the [intentional] strategy is pragmatic and not intrinsically right or wrong. (1971/ 1978:7)

Indeed, "there is no objectively satisfiable sufficient condition for an entity's really having beliefs" (1978:285). To use a phrase that has come to have increasing currency in the discussion, there is "no fact of the matter" about whether a system really does or doesn't have mental states, any more than there are natural facts of the matter about the constellations in the sky: they are mere patterns that can be discerned from a certain specific angle by creatures like us, and may be useful for navigation, but they have no role to play in the causation and explanation of any actual phenomena in the world.[6]

Presumably, this position about the mental is not to be regarded as simply a consequence of a *general* instrumentalism about all (or most) scientific postulations. The examples of geocentricism and a biological design are examples of strict fictions against a backdrop of general scientific realism, in particular, realism about those phenomena that are required for any (non-question-begging) causal explanatory purposes. So the question for the mental realist at this point is whether there are serious causal explanatory purposes served by the postulation of mental states. Beginning in §4.4, I shall argue that there are.

3.2 Philosophical Objections to Eliminativism

Philosophers and psychologists have employed a number of strategies to meet the challenges posed by eliminativism. They range from purely philosophical arguments based upon what it could possibly be rational ever to believe, to arguments based upon introspection, to arguments based upon empirical evidence of the sort gathered by natural science. This distinction between these strategies is not one it would be easy to spell out in general: the distinction between philosophy and science is one of the more controversial issues that have plagued philosophy from the outset, and has recently proven especially difficult to draw (§1.5). I invoke it only as a pragmatic distinction between two styles of argument that are connected in different ways with actual empirically testable results. We will examine the more philosophical arguments in this chapter, considering first the so-called "transcendental arguments" (§3.2.1), and then arguments from introspection (§3.2.2). I will argue that no version of either of these strategies has yet been sustained, and that its proponents invariably either neglect the resources available to the eliminativist, or beg the question against it. However in §3.3, I will turn finally to a source of genuinely non-tendentious data that has not been sufficiently appreciated in traditional discussions, which, although it may not succeed in establishing dualism, may well present the eliminativist with a serious challenge that is not easily met. I will then turn in chapter 4 to the more purely empirical arguments about whether mentalism is or is not required to account for this particular kind of data.

3.2.1* Transcendental arguments

Generally speaking, transcendental arguments attempt to show that eliminativism is incoherent because the theory itself presupposes the existence of minds. The argument is "transcendental" insofar as it transcends any particular empirical evidence; but it is not quite *a priori*, since it requires the existence of the theory, argument, or theorizer as a premise. In a useful discussion of eliminativism, Barbara Hannan puts the idea driving the transcendentalist thus:

> It is at least arguable that certain concepts (such as matter, space, cause, effect, before, after) could not possibly prove to have no application to reality, since they are necessary in order to experience anything at all. Concepts referred to as part of "folk" semantic and psychological theories, such as *meaning* and *belief*, are arguably necessary in an analogous way – necessary not for the experience of empirical reality, but necessary for the experience of the person or self as rational agent. (1993:171)

Descartes' *cogito* was in this sense a transcendental argument: he claimed not that it was *a priori* that he existed, but that any doubt or denial that he existed would presuppose his existence, i.e. the truth of the very thing he was doubting or denying. The present case is not far from Descartes': denying there are minds would seem to be something only a mind could do; and so the denial is "self-stultifying." Proponents of such arguments have included Malcolm (1968), Baker (1987), and Boghossian (1990a,b). (The conundra here aren't always strictly *logical* ones. Baker calls the contradictions *pragmatic*: contradictions of someone *asserting* that, for example, no one *asserts* anything.)

It is not hard to feel the pull of such arguments. On the face of it, it would be logically contradictory to say things like the following:

(E1)   People falsely believe that people believe things;

since this entails:

(E2)   People believe that people believe things, but it's false that people believe things;

which entails:

(E3)   There's something people believe, but it's not the case that there's something people believe;

which is clearly contradictory.

Now there may well be some eliminativists who've expressed themselves in this way. In the passage we quoted above, Churchland (1981/1990:206–11), for example, writes happily of "our commonsense *conception* of psychological phenomena," and how it constitutes a *"false theory,"* comparing it to other *mistaken theories*, like the phlogiston theory of combustion. All these italicized words seem to involve the very mentalisms he is proposing to reject: they seem on their face to involve people *believing* things! He does suggest replacing our ordinary talk by "übersätze" (p. 220), but their specification is left sufficiently vague that it is impossible to tell whether they involve mentality and intentionality or not (we'll consider related suggestions of his in §4.3 and §8.8).

A related incoherence threatens Dennett's appeal to the intentional stance, and Kripkenstein's appeal to social norms. For example, Dennett (1991a) proposes that intentionality be treated as a dispositional (what he calls a "lovely") property on the model of a dispositional analysis of color (where something is red iff it is disposed to affect standard observers in a certain way). However, any such analysis risks appealing to the very intentional notions being analyzed: if something has beliefs only if *something else is disposed to "treat it" (i.e. think of it) as though it does*, then we seem at least to have an infinite regress of appeals to *believers*. For the analysis,

x believes p iff
   (someone (else?) would believe that x believes p)

would at least require expansion as:

x believes that p iff
(someone (else?), y_1, would believe that
(someone (further?), y_2, would believe that
(someone (still further?), y_3, would believe that . . .
. . . and so on))) . . .)

Similarly, when Kripkenstein (1982) looks to "social agreement" to establish what rule a person is intending to follow it would seem he would be confronted with the very problem is he trying to solve. "Social agreement," after all, is ordinarily agreement in intentionally characterized states: people are *believing* the same thing, and *think* they are. If we are unable to establish that any one person is following a specific rule, how is an appeal to the rule *many* people take themselves to be following going to be any help?

Can eliminativists avoid such difficulties? Appreciating the resources that eliminativists have at their disposal will throw into sharper relief the empirical explanatory issue that seems to me to be the really serious issue on which the question of eliminativism ought to turn.

First of all, note that merely *pragmatic* contradictions will be of no interest in the present discussion. A pragmatic contradiction is one concerned not with the *truth* of a claim (a *semantic* contradiction), but with its *assertability*: thus it is pragmatically, but not semantically contradictory for someone to utter the words "I am not uttering words right now." Similarly, there is a difficulty of someone *claiming* that no one claims anything only if she also wants to claim that she is claiming *that*. But she needn't do that. She may have an alternative account of what is going on when she is doing what people *ordinarily describe* as "making claims." Of course, *we*, who don't share her views and may not even understand them, may not be in a position to say what she *is* doing according to *her* account. But that may very well be *our* problem, not hers. (On the other hand, she presumably does *owe* us that account.)

Paul and Patricia Churchland have compared the situation to the apparent difficulty one might have in explaining non-vitalist biology to a convinced, seventeenth-century vitalist, who believes a special vital spirit was a necessary condition for life. One can imagine such a person arguing:

> The anti-vitalist says there is no such thing as vital spirit. But this claim is self-refuting . . . for if the claim is true, then the speaker does not have vital spirit and must be *dead*. But if he is dead, then his statement is a meaningless string of noises, devoid of reason and truth.   Churchland (1981/1990:222)

But, as the Churchlands observe, obviously this latter argument begs the question against the anti-vitalist. Although I am not in the end convinced that it is quite as easy as the Churchlands suppose to account for human functioning in non-mental terms as it is in non-vitalistic ones, the analogy is well taken. The eliminativist must not, without substantial argument, be burdened in her characterization of herself with the very idiom she aims to reject.

But the eliminativist is, of course, under an obligation to say *something* about the activities normally described in mentalistic ways, even if those ways are to be described ultimately in non-mentalistic terms. Peoples' arms *do* to rise when they "raise" them, and they do make specific noises when they "talk." What specifically is to be the account of these motions and noise?

Although neither Dennett nor Kripkenstein present much indication,[7] some eliminativists have been quite energetic in this regard. The most famous effort to provide an account of our motions and noise was provided by Radical Behaviorism ("RBism"), whereby talk of mental states is replaced by talk of the dispositions of an organism to produce physically described behaviors in response to physical stimuli. We will examine this theory in detail in the next chapter (§4.1). What the transcendentalist is claiming is that any such effort is doomed *a priori*. But can RBism really be refuted so easily? What could the RBist say about what people are doing when they are "believing theories" that are "true" or "false"?

A well-known RBist effort in this regard is Quine's (1960:chapter 2) replacement of talk of "beliefs" by *dispositions to assent*, or to *utter* certain sentences in certain circumstances. Dispositions can be regarded as physical properties of a thing that make certain hypothetical claims true: solubility is a disposition of salt to dissolve in water if certain normal conditions obtain. *Sentences* are just sequences of certain sounds and marks, and theories are just sets of sentences. Someone can have a disposition to utter tokens, and assent or dissent (say "yes" or "no") to them, in response to various sorts of stimuli: "stimulation from an inferometer once prompted Michelson and Morley to dissent from the . . . sentence 'There is ether drift'" (Quine 1960:36). That, at any rate, is all that the RBist needs to say. Indeed:

> If we are limning the true and ultimate structure of reality, the canonical scheme for us is the austere scheme that knows no quotation but direct quotation and no propositional attitudes but only the physical constitution and behavior of organisms. (1960:221)

So instead of talking about people *believing* in mentalism, the eliminativist can talk instead of people being disposed to utter (or assent to) the sentences of folk psychology. Such dispositions may seem a pretty poor substitute for belief as it is ordinarily understood; after all, Germans ignorant of English can believe the same things as Englishmen ignorant of German. But, Quine notoriously replies, so much the worse for determinate relations of translation! This is indeed why the RBist is best construed here as an *eliminativist* about belief, not a reductionist. The burden is now on the transcendentalist to show that such an eliminativist recourse is *incoherent*. But it's hard to see how the postulation of dispositions to make certain noises under certain circumstances could be charged with *that*.

The eliminativist, however, owes us a replacement not only of talk of *belief*, but also talk of *being mistaken*, of mentalism being *false* and of his own non-mentalistic theory being *true*. These would seem to be notions that are paradigmatically *semantic*, and so entangled in the very properties of *intentionality* that many have thought posed problems for a physical account. Merely explicating "believe" by "disposition to utter" won't free us of what's problematic about the mind, if the sentences uttered are themselves irreducibly semantic. The eliminativist needs to eliminate not only belief *states*, but also their *complements*, insofar as they involve semantically valuable *contents*. And it is not immediately obvious how it is possible to do this while persisting in talking of truth, falsity, and mistakes.

At this point, however, the eliminativist can avail herself of what have been variously called "redundancy," "disquotational," or, more generally, "deflationary" semantic theories.[8] These are theories that pointedly avoid analyzing the predicates "x is true" and "x is true of y" and "x refers to y" in any fashion that takes them express a "robust," "real," causally efficacious property in the world. Rather, they are construed as mere logical devices, permitting us to replace an utterance of one sentence (appropriately "believed" in Quine's sense) by an utterance of another sentence that quotes the first: " 'Snow is white' is true," after all, seems simply another way of saying "Snow is white." This suggestion has been worked out in impressive detail in the work of the logician, Alfred Tarski (1902–1985), who defines for a formally specified language what it is for a sentence to be true in it. Specifically he defines a language, L, and a predicate "x is true-in-L under interpretation y" in such a fashion that we can specify for every sentence of L its truth condition, where an "interpretation," is simply a pairing of names with objects, and predicates with sets. For example, if an interpretation, i_{25} paired "s" with Socrates and "Wx" with the set of wise things, then it would follow that:

(S) "Ws" is true-in-L under i_{25} iff Socrates is wise.

The interesting, and by no means implausible claim of the disquotational theory, is that *this sort of definition of "truth" is ultimately all that's needed for an account of the meaning of "true" in English.* In particular, it doesn't require any of the traditional intentional talk of "correspondence with facts," "coherence at the end of science," or "causal/referential connections between words and the world" that the eliminativist may be anxious to avoid. This further talk may well define *another*, "*robust*" notion associated with the word "true," but there's no need of any such notion in any explanatory theory of the world.

I don't mean particularly to defend this deflationary theory here. It is enough that it is not incoherent, and is applicable to the kinds of claims the eliminativist wants to make, in particular, the claim that there are no contentful states. The eliminativist may say, for example, that nothing satisfies the predicates "is true" or "refers"; or she may say that those predicates don't refer to any real properties, and/ or that sentences containing them are not even truth-conditional. These latter claims can have the superficial appearance of self-contradiction: the eliminativist appears to be using the very truth-conditional talk she rejects. But that appearance can be dispelled by carefully distinguishing robust from deflationary ways of understanding that talk: for example, the eliminativist is not saying that it's *robustly false* that any sentence has robust truth-conditions (which would be paradoxical); rather, she is merely saying that it's *deflationarily* false.[9]

Of course, the above reliance by the eliminativist upon a disquotational theory of truth does have its peculiarities. Suppose the sea were to shape sand into a token of the sentence "Snow is white." The eliminativist would seem to be committed to claiming that that token, too, would be true-in-English iff snow is white. This seems a little wild, attributing semantic properties to objects that, pre-theoretically at least, would seem clearly to lack them. But perhaps there's no harm in it. Why, after all, should the eliminativist care?

Well, she might not have to care for *transcendental* reasons; but she might have to for *empirical* ones. For it would appear that, unlike the productions of the sea, ordinary English speaker's productions of "Snow is white" are not entirely *accidentally* related to snow's being white. For the most part, it's no mere *coincidence* that English speakers tend to utter it when asked such questions as "What's the color of snow?," whereas it would be clearly a coincidence were the sea merely to so shape the sand. Robust semantic and intentional properties may not be needed in order for the eliminativist to be *coherent*, but they may be needed in any adequate *explanation* of non-accidental facts about the noises that she and other human beings produce. But, to establish this, we need to look beyond *transcendental* arguments to serious, *empirically grounded* theories of those beings and those noises.

3.2.2 *Introspective arguments*

By this time, the reader is likely to have grown fairly exasperated with the discussion; for isn't the empirical evidence for mentalism really about as obvious as any evidence could possibly be? Indeed, the incoherence of eliminativism would seem to follow from what seems virtually a first principle of anyone's philosophy: that we each know in our own cases that we are thinking things. Descartes (1641a/ 1970) famously proclaimed "I see clearly that there is nothing which is easier for me to know than my mind" (p. 157). Thought being "whatever is in us in such a way that we are immediately conscious of it" (1641b/1970:52), he took as one of his certainties, his "clear and distinct idea" of himself as a "thinking thing" (1641a/1970:190). It can seem as though whatever knowledge we do have would be undermined if we didn't know this. As the neurophysiologist John Eccles (1966) put it:

> Conscious experience is the immediate and absolute reality. . . . My conscious expe-
> rience is all that is given to me in my task of trying to understand myself; and it is
> only because of and through my experience that I come to know of a world of things
> and events.   (1966:315)

And Chalmers (1996) rejects eliminativism "as being in conflict with the manifest
facts" (p. 164), since:

> [W]e are surer of the existence of conscious experience than we are of anything else
> in the world. . . . We know about consciousness more directly than we know about
> anything else, so "proof" is inappropriate.   (1996:xi–xiii)

Indeed:

> Consciousness is not an explanatory construct, postulated to help explain behavior or
> events in the world. Rather it is a brute explanandum, a phenomenon in its own
> right that is in need of explanation.   (1996:188; see also p. 196)

But what are we to make of such claims? Can a view like eliminativism be
refuted quite so easily, by merely digging in one's heels? Is there really no room
whatever for discussion? One is reminded of those theists who declare God not
an explanatory construct but similarly a "directly experienced" explanandum
("through revelation," after all) and likewise claim that "proof is inappropriate."

With regard to such appeals, either to God or to the mind, it is important to
distinguish the *metaphysical* claims being made about *the existence* of God or
consciousness, themselves, from the *epistemological* claims about how we *know* about
them. These latter are often slipped in as if they were of a piece with the
metaphysical ones – and perhaps they are, in the sense that *if* the metaphysical
claims *were* true, then the epistemic ones *might* be as well. But the atheist and
eliminativist, demanding non-tendentious evidence for the metaphysical claims,
are surely entitled to equally non-tendentious evidence for these further epistemic
claims as well: one doesn't escape begging a metaphysical question merely by
begging an implied epistemic one instead. So the question is whether we have any
such evidence for Descartes', Eccles', or Chalmers' (not to mention the theist's)
epistemic claims.

Well, we might ask generally what kind of knowledge we obtain from introspection? Of course, this question is of a piece with many of the questions being
raised in this book, and so any full answer would probably beg some of our
questions one way or another. However, there happens to be evidence about the
reliability of introspection that is neutral to many of our disputes. In a well-known
article, Richard Nisbett and Timothy Wilson (1977) reviewed a wide range of
experiments that show that what people at least take as direct, introspective
knowledge is a lot less reliable than they ordinarily suppose.

Subjects have been shown to be sensitive to, but entirely unaware of, such factors as cognitive dissonance,[10] expectation,[11] numbers of bystanders in a public crisis,[12] pupilliary dilation,[13] positional and "halo" effects[14] and subliminal cues in problem solving and semantic disambiguation[15] (Maier 1931; Zajonc 1968; Lackner and Garrett 1972). Instead of noticing these factors, the subjects frequently "introspect" material that can be independently shown to be irrelevant to the causation of their behavior. Indeed, even when explicitly asked about the relevant material, they will deny that it played any role.

The positional effect, for example, consists in people being sensitive to the position of articles in an array from which they are asked to choose: 52 subjects asked to choose between what were (unbeknownst to them) four *identical* pairs of nylon stockings presented in a left-right array. They tended overwhelmingly (four to one) to choose the right-most pair, without one of them mentioning position as affecting them. Indeed:

> When asked directly about a possible effect of the position of the article, virtually all subjects denied it, usually with a worried glance at the interviewer suggesting that they felt either that they had misunderstood the question or were dealing with a madman.   (Nisbett and Wilson 1977:244)

Other experiments deal with systematic errors in reasoning and the demonstrably mistaken accounts subjects provide of them (Wason and Johnson-Laird 1972); and cases of hypnotic suggestion in which subjects respond to whispered commands and even to "painful sensations," of all of which they claim to be unaware (Hilgard 1977).

Perhaps some of the most dramatic, and philosophically interesting phenomena undermining the absolute reliability of introspection are those of "blindsight" and "anosognosia." Blindsight occurs in patients who have suffered damage to their visual cortex and who claim not to be able to see various stimulus materials that have been presented to them; nevertheless, they can be shown to score well above chance when they are forced to "guess" at what they may be seeing (Weiskrantz 1986). Anosognosia occurs in patients suffering from various sorts of brain damage that demonstrably undermine their normal psychological functioning, who will sometimes report no awareness whatsoever of their deficiencies (they are "agnosiac" about the "diagnosis" of their states). Young (1994), for example, reports the case of a woman painter who was prosopognosiac (unable to recognize faces), and had to laboriously reason from the apparent age, sex, and other cues in her (earlier) paintings, who they were paintings of, but who denied she suffered from any recognitional deficit![16] And people with, for example, stroke damage to one hemisphere, will ignore one half of their body (e.g. shaving only one side of their face), but without any awareness of doing so (see Bisiach and Luzzatti 1978).

Of course, one philosophically important implication of this research is that it provides substantial evidence for the existence of unconscious mental states, an issue that we will discuss in §9.6. But another even more intriguing implication, is the hypothesis Nisbett and Wilson consider by way of explanation of many of these phenomena:[17]

> We propose that when people are asked to report how a particular stimulus influenced a particular response, they do not do so by consulting a memory of the mediating process, but by applying or generating causal theories about the effects of that type of stimulus on that type of response. They simply make judgments . . . about how plausible it is that the stimulus would have influenced the response. (1977:248)

They speculate that such causal theories may originate not in any special inner knowledge, but in popular theories about people that they acquire growing up in a particular culture.

Such a hypothesis has received further support in the developmental literature. In a recent article, Gopnik (1994) reports experiments with three-year-olds that suggest that

> children make errors about their own immediately past [belief] states that are similar to the errors they make about the states of others . . . even though [they] ought to have direct first-person knowledge of these past states. (1994:7)[18]

She concludes:

> The important point is that the theoretical constructs [about the mind] themselves, and particularly the idea of intentionality, are not the result of some first-person apprehension that is then applied to others. Rather, they are the result of cognitive construction. (1994:10)

She goes on to suggest that, as we mature, we may become so knowledgeable and reliable about people and ourselves generally, that we become totally unable to notice anything but the grossest inferential steps on which that knowledge nevertheless relies. With respect to many of our own mental states, we seem often to be in the position of "expert" chess-players, medical diagnosticians, or water dousers who often take themselves to be sensing very sophisticated information in their domains "directly" (p. 11).

For present purposes, there is no need to endorse either Gopnik's or Nisbett and Wilson's speculations unequivocally. Clearly there are *some* first-person states – for example, sensory ones, like pain – about which people do seem to have some special first-person apprehension. What we obviously need in order to sort out these from the unreliable cases are much more fine-grained theories about the actual information processing details underlying introspection: just what are the processes that intervene between, say, stimulation of one's nerve ends, report on the character of that stimulation, and memory of that stimulation even just a few seconds later? What is the relation of introspection to attention, short-term and long-term memory, and to the deployment of either innate or learned concepts and theories of mental processing?[19]

This speculation need not be limited to cases in which one is merely introspecting one's mental *processes*;[20] they could involve various general theories about the nature of perception, sensory experience, even dualism itself, which many people are uncritically inclined to believe. Indeed, a question that has concerned many philosophers, and to which we will critically return in §5.2 and §11.6, is whether people are right to think that, when they introspect, they are aware of internal *objects* (pains, tickles) or *properties* (being painful, looking red) at all. Perhaps, as Wittgenstein (1953) plausibly suggested, we are merely in the "grip of a picture" of an internal world uncritically modeled on the usual external one (we'll return to this suggestion in both §5.2 and §11.6 below). In any case, it is certainly a serious possibility that we are in the grip of such pictures and, like Young's painter, simply anosognosiac about it. Insofar as this is a serious possibility, the strong epistemic claims of writers like Descartes, Eccles, and Chalmers about our "direct knowledge" of certain mental phenomena cannot be taken at face value. Their "introspections" may well be commiting them to metaphysical claims that introspection alone could never be in a position to establish.

Actually, these experimental results on introspection can be taken merely to dramatize what on reflection ought to be an unsurprising logical point: that sentential operators like "it is directly/introspectively/infallibly knowable that p" do not necessarily iterate. I might *directly/introspectively/infallibly know that p* without *directly/introspectively/infallibly knowing that I directly/introspectively/infallibly know that p*. Claims to know something directly, introspectively, or infallibly may require empirical support beyond any such claims themselves.

In a related vein, there is not equal reason to believe in the actual applicability of *all* ordinary folk mentalistic terms. Many philosophers bandy about such terms as "belief," "desire," "thought," as though it were perfectly obvious what they referred to. But some reflection on actually constructing a psychological theory of our states and behavior might well invite caution about whether these are really the right terms, that there really are states answering to them. Is people's behavior really caused by *beliefs* and *desires*? People can *believe* things, but "forget" them at any given moment; *desire* can include passing *preferences, wishes, thoughts about what one ought to do* that can be entirely ineffective in producing behavior. Steve Stich (1983) takes many of the above mentioned experiments showing people's unreliability about their own mental states to undermine the folk notion of belief, claiming that they show there are no such things as beliefs. Whether he is right or wrong about this, such arguments should at least give one pause: precisely *which* mental phenomena entitle us to a philosophical confidence about their existence that could outweigh any possible empirical arguments the eliminativist might advance?[21]

One might put the point this way: in view of the at least serious *possibility* raised by these experiments that people's introspections are far more fallible than we ordinarily think, a burden is placed on a defender of any contested introspective report to show that it is reliable, that it did in fact issue from a reliable process, and that it wasn't merely the imposition of a popular mentalistic theory. Now, in many ordinary contexts in which eliminativist challenges are not being raised, this burden may be easily discharged: we don't have reason to think people are unreliable about ordinary sensory reports. But when the eliminativist raises the sorts of *motivated* doubts that we have considered, the burden is increased. In discharging this burden the introspector will have to assume the falsity of the very eliminativism that he hopes his introspections will refute! That is, he will have to show that the process of coming to think he is a thinking thing is in fact a reliable process; but that will presuppose the truth of the very theory that the eliminativist is challenging. So in relying on introspections to refute the eliminativist, the introspector is simply begging the question against her.

3.3   Standardized Regularities

In allowing the eliminativist, in the section before last, to resort to a disquotational theory of truth, we observed that he would be unable to distinguish between *accidental* and *non-accidental* entokenings of a sentence. This observation suggests another approach to answering the eliminativist challenge to produce non-tendentious evidence for mental states. While it does seem that there is no denying that every *motion* of every animal could be explained in physical terms, it is by no means obvious that every *non-accidental pattern* in the behavior of animals could be so explained. It is worth noting this distinction as it seems to arise in many sciences.

Consider some non-accidental patterns that can be observed in biology. Although the presence of, say, fur in every *individual* mammal could be explained merely in terms of physics, it is by no means obvious that we can similarly explain the *pattern* of fur in some but not other animals. It would seem that we can acquire insight into *that* pattern only by supplementing physics with evolutionary biology: the reason that all and only mammals have fur is that some common ancestors of all present mammals all had fur and their having fur significantly increased the probability of their having descendents, as opposed to their ecological competitors. There is no question that, were such an explanation correct, we would acquire an insight into the non-accidental pattern of furry creatures by citing this pattern of biological evolution. But it is by no means obvious that this pattern is one that could be derived from a quantum mechanical account of the world alone: we need to see that some, but not other molecular structures count as specific genotypes, and that having fur increased the probability of that genotype being reproduced over its relevant competitors. Perhaps there is *some* way that this latter explanation could ultimately be obtained from physics: but it certainly appears that in order to understand this *level of organization of the world* we need to advert to such phenomena as "having fur," "genotype," "competitions in an ecological niche," and so on.

Are there such patterns in the case of psychology? One might think so, but the trouble with the ones that will immediately come to mind is that they will probably involve the very vocabulary of the mind that the eliminativist will reasonably find tendentious. For example, a great deal of the evidence we might ordinarily adduce for human capacities does depend upon intentional characterization: *actions*, not mere movements. When at the end of the previous section I mentioned the non-accidental features of normal utterances of "Snow is white," I used locutions like "utter," "in response," and "query," all of which need to be intentionally understood if the claim is to be correct, all of which seems to violate the requirement for non-tendentiousness. In terms of a figure that recurs in many discussions of the mental, there can seem to be no escape from the "intentional circle": the use of one intentional idiom presupposes the use of another, and there is no way to secure any independent, non-intentional purchase on any one of them.[22]

Such claims may make for grand philosophy; but a little reflection on the complexities of ordinary mental phenomena suggests that things aren't quite so neat. There are numerous intrusions into the intentional circle, numerous places where a purely physical phenomenon seems to require a mentalistic explanation. For example, people characteristically *blush, giggle, laugh, cry, tremble, become sexually aroused* often in reaction to certain sorts of phenomena that would be hard to explain in any other way than intentionally. Laughter, after all, isn't always due to mere physical tickles: usually you've got to "get the joke." Tears aren't always merely the effects of the likes of onions: usually they have to do with the *meaning of the news*. Such connections between the mental and the physical can be quite specific: belief in immediate danger can induce a rush of adrenalin; belief that one is receiving "tender, loving care" can induce the secretion of specific endorphins. How can we hope to explain such obvious connections than by appealing to mental states with their intentional properties? Is it really a serious possibility that a joke has its effect quite independently of how the punch line is understood? Such phenomena, then, as laughter and tears begin in this way to serve as non-tendentious evidence of the mental states that are plausibly their best explanation.

Such evidence can be systematic. There now exists a small industry of deliberately constructed "standardized" tests of mental capacities, e.g. (in the United States) the notorious Scholastic Aptitude Tests (SAT) and Graduate Record Exams

(GRE) administered to millions of high-school and college graduates each year. The standardization consists in the fact that the data say, questions and answers – are characterized *independently of interpretation*: the "questions" and "answers" are *physically specifiable* as strings of identically printed shapes on the "question" page, and patterns of graphite rectangles on the "answer" sheet of a sort that can be "read" by a simple machine. That is, although they are the very paradigms of intentionally produced objects, the regularities involved happen also to be characterizable *in entirely non-mentalistic*, indeed purely physical terms.

What is particularly interesting about such data is that, despite the decline of scores over the years, the relations among these data are statistically spectacular: the graphite patterns across subjects tend to be the same, and there seem to be law-like relations between the "question" and "answer" sheets. Suppose, for example, the "question" sheet contained the following:

#24: Suppose there are 120 pigs in pen A, 19 pigs in pen B, and no pigs in C; and suppose Jones took 10 pigs from A and 9 pigs from B and put them all into pen C: how many pigs would now be in pen C?
  (a) 120
  (b) 19
  (c) 10
  (d) 9

Not only would a statistically significant number of subjects fill in the rectangle on the "answer sheet" next to "(b)" just under "#24," but were (b) changed to read "9" and (d) to read "19," then we can predict that the same subjects would fill in the rectangle next to "(d)" instead. And there are innumerable similar law-like relations for each of the items, as well as between them (switching "#24" with "#62" would occasion a similar switch of the corresponding "answers").

There are other striking features. In general, the output – or the phrases correlated with the graphite boxes – stands in a variety of *relevancy* relations to the input – the interrogative sentences or paragraphs that preceded the array of output alternatives. The best example of a relevancy relation is *correctness*: the output is the correct answer to the question posed in the input. For example, if the stated problem asks how many apples result from combining 203 apples in one box with 17 apples in another, the answer very likely to be produced happens to be the correct answer.[23]

But there are other relevancy relations that are brought out by beginning to employ some modest mentalistic vocabulary: the output could be the answer that is merely commonly believed to be the right answer ("What's the largest city in the world?" "New York"), or an answer that many people will mistakenly think to be the right answer because of a certain common error in reasoning. Designers of these tests often deliberately include "bait" answers that poorer thinkers will select. For example, they might include an instance of the gambler's fallacy ("Suppose a coin has come up heads fifty times in a row. Is the probability increased, decreased, or unchanged that it will come up heads on the next throw?") Indeed, there is now a substantial body of experimental literature confirming what logic teachers have long known: that people are often irrational. Even after explicit tutelage to the contrary, they're liable to the gambler's fallacy, disregard of background frequencies, bias towards recent examples, inconsistent reactions to different descriptions of the same situation, and favoring of positive instances in confirming a generalization.[24] But the important point here, as logic teachers also know, is that the errors aren't *random*: there are patterns, some of them captured in the standard "fallacies" chapters in elementary logic texts. And the fallacious answers of this sort usually display as much "relevance" as correct answers do.

It is important in this connection to distinguish "irrational" from "non-rational" responses. It is likely that some of the above deviations from perfect rationality are due simply to simple physical limitations or breakdowns: thus, the "recency effect," and other failures in memory, explicit computation, and imagi-nation may be due simply to limitations of the brain. Let us confine the word "non-rational" to such cases. What is interesting about the familiar fallacies exhibited by bait questions, however, is that, again, although they can be *described* non-mentalistically, it is not at all clear that they can be *explained* non-mentalistically. They are "irrational": i.e. non-rational in a way that is to be explained by reference to content-bearing states. Fallacious gamblers and people who confuse necessary with sufficient conditions are making errors that seem to be capturable only conceptually. It is because they have a complex set of (some false) beliefs about the "tendency" of random events to "even out" in the not so long run that they bet as they do; it is because they often misunderstand conditionals as biconditionals, or deductive for inductive reasoning, that they reverse necessary and sufficient conditions.[25] At any rate, the fallacious answers to the puzzle questions are also non-randomly related to those questions.

Now, of course, none of these predictions can be made with utmost certainty: subjects can be perverse, they tire, and, in the case of most of these actual tests, there are deliberately some questions that are too hard for most subjects to answer. But if we were interested not in *distinguishing* subjects' abilities, but discovering their commonalities, we could make the tests easier, allow the subjects more time, more coffee, and greater incentives ("$100 for every correct answer!"). And we could increase the range of abilities tested in this way by including non-verbal stimuli, and arranging for non-verbal responses. (Note that mentalists can de-scribe what they are doing using our ordinary vocabulary, so long as the data that we ultimately produce in this way are not tainted by our mentalistic interpreta-tions.) It should be clear that with enough controls of this sort the above statistics would asymptote: the answer sheets would converge to type identity, actually and (under switching of "questions") counterfactually. In short: the statistical results are already spectacular, and could be made more so by relatively trivial adjustments. I shall refer to such statistical results as *"standardized regularities."*

Now, one of the primary tasks of science is to explain *significant statistical regularities*: it is rare that science is concerned to explain merely *particular* cases – e.g. a particular person's going to a store – that are so often the diet of philosophy. While *every particular instance of the above regularities may indeed have a physical explanation, it is by no means clear that these regularities do*. For how would that explanation go? Is there any reason to believe that *all* of the people who satisfy these regularities share some distinct physical property that those who wouldn't do so lack? Do all and only these subjects have a certain serotonin levels in their brains? Or perhaps neurons arranged in certain geometric patterns? Perhaps, but it is extremely hard to think of a genuinely plausible candidate.

The most concerted effort to explain intelligent regularities in human and animal behavior was Radical Behaviorism. Unlike the arguments of this chapter, this is a largely empirical theory, a scientifically serious attempt to account for empirical data like the standardized regularities without invoking mental states. We turn now to consider its empirical promises, and ultimate failure.

Notes

1 Recently, there has been much discussion about whether in our day to day understanding of other people we rely on some theoretical inferences, or rather on "simulations" of how others feel by putting ourselves in their shoes (see Gordon 1986, and Davies 1994). The present discussion is neutral on this issue, making no claim about day to day thought processes.
2 We will see, however, that the lack of a causal break can be an argument for *some* restricted eliminativist claims to be discussed in §11.6 below.
3 See Kim (1993), and Block (forthcoming) for discussion of just this point.
4 Jackson (1982) replies to this objection by comparing the situation to other situations in which one argues "from one effect back to its cause and out again to another effect":

> Consider my reading in *The Times* that the Spurs had won. This provides excellent evidence that *The Telegraph* has also reported that the *Spurs* won, despite the fact that (I trust) *The Telegraph* does not get the results from *The Times*. (1982:132)

But the trouble with the analogy is that, unlike the inference about *The Telegraph*, in the case of other people *we have no reason to believe the cause goes out again to a similar effect* – unless, that is, we're simply prepared to generalize irresponsibly (and how far? to chimps? to rats? to spiders?) from our own case.
5 It is unclear whether Davidson would draw eliminativist conclusions from these claims. On the one hand he seems to endorse Quine's "indeterminacy of translation,"

which is standardly understood eliminativistically; on the other hand, he claims to be a token materialist, which would appear to be a species of reductionism. Sorting out the different strands in Davidson's discussion – indeed, really any serious Davidson exegesis – is far beyond the space of this book. The interested reader should consult, for example, Antony (1989).

6   Of course, there are "conventional" facts about the constellations (Scorpio is just that apparent region of the sky people call "Scorpio"), and so presumably, for Dennett, about the mind. It's notoriously difficult to pin Dennett down about the status he accords the mental. In his (1987:72) he tries to distinguish his view from instrumentalism and fictionalism about the mind, but doesn't reconcile what he says there with all the things he says elsewhere (e.g. in the above quotes, and at 1987:39). I think the comparison with constellations comes closest to the view that all the quotes suggest (see also his 1978a:18–19, 21–2, 106, 281–2), a view that I call "Patternalism," and whose relation to the rest of Dennett's work I discuss at length in Rey (1995b).

7   Indeed, it would be distinctly out of character with their interest in *Wittgenstein* to do so, since *this* project, of replacing mentalistic with non-mentalistic explanations, would certainly be anathema to him.

8   See Tarski (1956), Quine (1970), and Horwich (1990) for useful discussions and defenses of this approach.

9   Devitt (1990) and Devitt and Rey (1991) argue that Boghossian's (1990a,b) transcendental argument turns on not recognizing this option. Boghossian (1990b:277, 278n14) appears to concur.

10   In cognitive dissonance experiments, subjects can be induced to revise even low-level perceptual beliefs (e.g. about whether two obviously unequal lines appear so) when they conflict with (as it turns out, the insincere) testimony of peers (Festinger 1957).

11   Expectation of meeting someone can be shown to positively affect ratings of that person on a number of dimensions (Darley and Bershied 1967).

12   People's willingness to come to the aid of others in distress can be shown to be proportional to the numbers of bystanders but without the subjects being aware of that fact affecting them (Latané and Darley 1970).

13   Males' preference for female faces can be shown to be a function of the dilation of the faces' pupils, without the males being aware of it being a factor (Hess 1975).

14   These are effects where subjects can be shown to prefer stimuli to which they have been previously exposed (Nisbett and Wilson 1977).

15   In experiments in problem solving, subjects can be shown to be sensitive to cues presented in their peripheral visual field that are crucial to the solution, without any apparent awareness of the cues (Maier 1931, Zajonc 1968). In disambiguation experiments, ambiguous sentences are presented to one ear and disambiguating material is presented below conscious threshold to the other: subjects interpret the sentences in accordance with this latter material of which they nevertheless remain unaware (Lackner and Garrett 1972).

16   See Young (1994) and Block (1995) for further discussion.

17   A version of this important hypothesis was also suggested much earlier by Sellars (1956), but merely as a philosophical possibility, without the empirical support Nisbett and Wilson provide.

93

18 The experiments involve, for example, asking three-year-olds who have been recently fooled by some appearances, what others would think when presented with the same appearances, as well as what they themselves previously thought. Up until around four years, children claim that they *did*, and that the others *would*, believe the *truth*. Gopnik reports similar results and conclusions in Wimmer and Hartl (1991).

19 Ericsson and Simon (1984/1993) address some of these questions systematically in reply to Nisbett and Wilson's findings, emphasizing our greater reliability about states at the very time they are occurring, as opposed to even temporally close memories of them and speculations about their causal role. Ericsson (1993:42) raises similar issues with regard to Gopnik's discussion.

20 Ericsson and Simon (1984/1993) and others have reasonably argued that many of the above examples involve the agent's opinions about causal processes responsible for a mental state, and not the mental state itself. The point remains that it is not obvious, much less introspectively available, just which sorts of states and processes are reliably reported introspectively.

21 Chalmers (1996) does claim that:

> we have very good reason, quite independent of any considerations about [the] explanatory irrelevance [of consciousness] to believe that the epistemology of experience is special, and very different in kind from epistemology in other domains. Many have spoken of our "direct knowledge" of our "acquiantance" with experience.   (1996:197)

But, although he is right to suggest that there is non-tendentious evidence for the existence of *some* kind of special epistemology for (what ordinarily gets called) experience, he hasn't begun to show that that evidence requires anything like the traditional dualistic explanation that he endorses and which the eliminativist doubts. He needs to show that the *best explanation* of that evidence involves a direct acquaintance with *non-physical mental phenomena*. Given that he concedes the "no causal break" argument of this chapter and regards at least consciousness as indeed "causally irrelevant" (see 1996:179), it would seem very difficult for him to do so. For a non-dualist explanation of the evidence of *some* special epistemology of experience, see §11.4 below.

22 For many, this has been tantamount to "Brentano's thesis": cf. Chisholm (1957) and Quine (1960:221).

23 "Correct" here, by merely a disquotational theory of truth, per §3.1 above. That is, the correlation is between answers of the form "p" and (the fact that) p.

24 See Wason and Johnson-Laird (1972), and Kahneman et al. (1982).

25 Dreyfus and Dreyfus (1986) reasonably speculate that many of the errors subjects make in the above experiments may be due to the artificial conditions of the experimental setting, conditions that may not correspond to the often ill-defined conditions under which the human cognitive capacity has evolved. The errors are still errors on this account; but they would still be mentalistically understood, as involving, for example, "points of view" (p. 48).

4

Eliminativism: Empirical Issues

In the last chapter, we considered some relatively philosophical arguments for the existence of the mind and found them at best inconclusive, but, more usually, simply question-begging, persistently assuming the applicability of the very mentalistic vocabulary that the eliminativist doubts. We did finally uncover some interesting, non-tendentiously describable phenomena that certainly would *appear* to require the positing of minds. But this evidence is at least partly empirical: it depends upon the existence of physically describable regularities in human behavior – what I called the Standardized Regularities – that, at least so described, are not establishable by reason alone. Moreover, it is an empirical question whether these regularities could be explained with or without the positing of minds. In this chapter, I want to consider this empirical question in detail. Can eliminativists make good on their claim to explain these and all other regularities in human and animal behavior without appealing to mental states?

This question requires extended discussion, if only because *non*-mentalistic theories of human and animal functioning have been developed at such length in the twentieth century. By far, the most concerted such effort was that of so-called *"Radical Behaviorism"* ("RBism"). We will examine that theory in some detail, considering the immediate problems raised by the very experiments on animals that RBists themselves often performed (§4.1), turning then to the prospects of extending the account to human functioning. Here we will consider the impressive data and arguments that emerge from Noam Chomsky's revolutionary discussions of natural language (§4.2). We will then raise a *general* problem dramatized by that work that all eliminativist theories like RBism seem to face, viz., an excessive commitment to certain assumptions of traditional empiricism (§4.3). The failure of these assumptions affords at least one strong *prima facie* reason for the postulation of mental processes (§4.4).

Throughout most of the first half of the twentieth century, it did appear to many philosophers and psychologists in England and America that the best approach to explanation of the intelligent regularities exhibited by humans and animals was some or other form of "behaviorism." The view was that psychology should concern itself only with the overt *behavior* of an organism. After all, behavior constitutes all that we ordinarily *observe* of other people and animals; the mental vocabulary we use would seem to have been learnt largely in connection with that observed behavior; and at least some of our intuitions regarding the mental can be shown to correspond closely with behavioristic claims (we will examine these claims more closely in §5.3). In any case, it seemed to most scientifically minded psychologists that the only prospect for a *objectively testable* science of psychology was one that eschewed the relatively fruitless, subjectivist methods of introspection, and devoted itself only to explaining publicly observable behavior.

There are actually three very different views associated with the word "behaviorism": there is *radical, analytical,* and *methodological* behaviorism. *Radical Behaviorism* ("RBism") is the attempt to explain the rational regularities without any appeal at all to mental expressions, but, instead, in terms of stimuli, responses, and reinforcements. *Analytical Behaviorism* ("ABism," sometimes also called "Logical Behaviorism") is the attempt to analyze any mental expressions that do occur purely in terms of stimuli and (dispositions to) response. Note that these are entirely different, logically independent claims: RBism is an *explanatory* claim, proposing a *non*-mentalistic account of animal behavior; ABism is a *"semantic," "philosophical"* claim about the meaning, or *analysis* (§1.5) of mental terms and concepts. RBism is largely motivated by an *eliminativist* interest, in particular, an interest in explaining animal behavior *without* appealing to mental states. ABism is a *reductionist* enterprise: it welcomes mental states, claiming that they are nothing but (i.e. are identical to) behavioral dispositions.[1] As we shall see, however, the two views did become oddly intertwined, theorists often being led to the one to escape the deficiencies encountered in the other (§4.1.5). In order to keep things straight, I shall postpone discussing ABism until the next chapter (§5.3) in which we will discuss philosophical analyses of mental terms more generally.

"Methodological behaviorism" is a view somewhere between RBism and ABism. It is a methodological stricture to the effect that all objective scientific procedures in psychology should concern themselves only with the external behavior of organisms. This was a reaction specifically against nineteenth-century introspectionism, although it can also involve a stand more recently against the relevance of any neurophysiological data. It is certainly not committed to RBism (mental terms are allowed in explanations, so long as their application is grounded in *some or other* behavior); but nor is it committed to actually *defining* mental terms behaviorally (there need be no *single* type of behavior common to all cases of a particular type of mental state). It is closest to a view that I call "superficialism," which I will discuss in §7.2.4. In this chapter I will focus only on RBism.

The failures of RBism are so widely acknowledged these days that one might wonder what is served in rehearsing them. An appreciation of RBism is useful for two reasons. First of all, there can be little doubt that meeting the challenge posed by RBism raised mentalistic hypotheses to a much more careful and sophisticated level of articulation and defense than had previously been imagined. The experiments alone were often subtle and ingenious, and provided a model for later psychological experimentation that has proved indispensable for serious mentalistic theorizing. Secondly, there are a number of ideas underlying behaviorism that one can find persisting in many more recent theories that have ostensibly moved beyond it, for example, Gibsonianism and Radical Connectionism (§4.3). It will be useful in examining these later theories to be alert to their susceptibility to the same problems that doomed RBism.

4.1 Radical Behaviorism and Its Problems

Radical Behaviorism (RBism) emerged from the work of Edward Thorndike (1874–1949), John Watson (1878–1958), and Ivan Pavlov (1849–1936), receiving its most energetic development by B.F. Skinner (1904–90) and attaining considerable precision in the work of Clark Hull (1884–1952). It has its source in traditional empiricist theories of the mind, according to which the mind at birth is a *tabula rasa*, or blank tablet on which experience forms sensory "impressions." "Ideas" are derived from experience and are welded together to form complex ideas by a process of "association," which closely tracks the presentation of those experiences in reality. Thus, certain sights, sounds, and tactile sensations become associated in experience to form the idea of a material object; and certain associations of "contiguity, succession and constant conjunction" form the idea of causation (Hume 1734/1978).

This traditional suggestion, though right in spirit, suffered from a major defect, viz. a reliance upon peculiar "private" entities, ideas, and sensations which, for the kinds of reasons we've discussed, didn't seem to many to serve as proper objects of scientific inquiry. To remedy this situation, RBists proposed studying not associations among "ideas" but among physically characterizable *stimuli* to sense organs, and physically characterizable muscular *responses*.

It seemed improbable, moreover, that all intelligent behavior could simply be a reflection of mere frequency effects among stimuli in the environment. There needed to be some process by which ideas *became* associated, particularly with appropriate behavior, some kind of "glue" that held different stimuli and responses together. After all, not just any stray associations in experience are useful for an organism. RBism tried to provide this glue by offering a principle of selection among them, namely Thorndike's "Law of Effect." For our purposes, it can be stated thus:[2]

The Law of Effect: The probability of a response R following a stimulus S is increased/decreased if pairs ⟨R,S⟩ have been followed by positive/negative reinforcements, F, in certain patterns (e.g. intermittently) in the past.

For example, should a particular movement like pressing a paw on a lever (=R) when a light is on (=S) be followed intermittently by the presentation to a hungry animal of a food pellet (=F), then the probability of the animal pressing its paw on the lever when the light is on in the future will be increased. Such are *rewards*. Negative reinforcements are either the *absence* of positive reinforcements, or actual *punishments*, which also reinforce, but in the opposite direction: the probability of the R given S is *reduced* if pairs of S and R have been followed by punishment in the past (and they do so in somewhat different patterns. One or two trials with a severe punishment, e.g. an electric shock, are often enough to secure a pronounced decrease in the probability of R, given S).

As Skinner frequently stressed, the Law of Effect is very nearly the biological principle of Natural Selection, extended now beyond the persistence of traits that are genetically inherited to the persistence of acquired behaviors in individual animals. Just as from a random generation of genetic mutations certain ones are selected by virtue of meeting an environmental test of "survival of the fittest," so from an essentially random generation of responses in an animal certain ones are selected by virtue of being reinforced when they occur after certain stimuli.[3]

How could this simple law, however, stand a chance of explaining the full range of intelligent animal behavior? The central idea was an extension of the associationist strategy of building complex ideas from simpler ones, only now it was a matter of building not complex *ideas*, but complex *responses*. These could be built up out of simpler responses by "response chaining," whereby stimuli associated with a reward themselves become reinforcers, and so available for the conditioning of *further* responses (they become "conditioned reinforcers"). Thus, a rat conditioned to press a lever on hearing a bell, could now be conditioned by *the sound of the bell itself* to produce further responses given further stimuli, say, doing a little dance on seeing a red light, which is then followed by the bell, which is then followed by food if the rat presses the lever. Discrimination of complex stimuli would similarly be built from discrimination of simpler stimuli, through either a chain of discriminations of simpler stimuli, or by "stimulus generalization," whereby novel stimuli are treated as "of the same kind" as earlier ones (a notion to which we will return in §4.3).

Now, the Law of Effect is undoubtedly true of *some* animal behavior, and chaining responses in this way is no doubt sometimes effective. Skinner achieved remarkable successes using it to train animals to engage in all manner of curious behavior: for example, rats to run mazes, pigeons to play ping-pong, pigs to push shopping carts around supermarkets. And it seems to play an important role in explaining a variety of persistent behavioral patterns such as gambling and drug addiction, as well as in extinguishing them, as in "behavior modification therapy." For our purposes, the issue is not whether such applications occur or are a good idea, but whether they offer a theoretically adequate paradigm for understanding the full range of intelligent animal behavior. If RBism is to provide the basis for eliminativism, it must maintain that *all* intelligent behavior is produced in this way.

Problems with the Law of Effect emerge in the first instance from the RBist experiments themselves.[4] Contrary to popular belief, it's not only human behavior that resists RBistic explanation; the theory doesn't even really work for the rats. The main problem is that the probability of a response can be increased in ways other than by the Law of Effect. There are at least four classes of phenomena that present immediate difficulties for the law: *latent learning, passive learning, spontaneous alteration,* and *improvisation.*

4.1.1   Latent learning

Latent learning occurs when an animal learns *without reinforcement.* Rats that were well sated with, for example, food and water were allowed to run around in a maze for ten days *without* any reward, sometimes being placed in the maze at arbitrarily different points. Subsequently, when they were hungry again, they were introduced into the maze and were able to learn to find the food that was now placed in it much faster than rats not previous exposed (Tolman and Honzik 1930; Gl:127). The probability of their emitting the appropriate responses had evidently been increased without prior reinforcement. Similarly, monkeys presented with a complex hinge, requiring the undoing of several pins and bolts to free it, learned to do so with no special reward other than "the fun of it" (Harlow 1950; Gn:80). And indigo buntings learn something about the position of the stars while still in the nest, despite not using this information for navigation (and so, *a fortiori*, not for any reward) until they are much older (Emlen 1969). Again, in all these cases the probability of the animal producing the appropriate response was greater than that of animals that had not been previously exposed to such stimuli, but without any history of reinforcement.

Not only can learning occur without reinforcement, but, if the stimuli are not presented in the right *critical period*, it cannot occur even *with* it! When the buntings were raised without a view of the night sky during their fledgling period and then released into the world as adults, they:

> never oriented consistently with respect to the night sky, regardless of their migra-
> tory condition. By the time the knowledge of the stars was of use to them, they could

no longer master it. . . . The learning of the stellar configuration cannot be concep-
tualized as [Skinnerian] "selection by consequences." At the time of learning, there
are no consequences, and by the time the animal is equipped to benefit from what it
has learned, it is no longer capable of learning it.   (Gallistel 1990:85–6)

Similar results emerge from Thorpe's (1950) and Lorenz's (1981) famous studies
of *imprinting*, where birds produce specific reactions to stimuli, such as moving
animate objects, only if those stimuli are presented in early youth. Should the
stimuli not be presented *then*, presenting them in adulthood even with reinforcement will be of no avail: some adult song birds can't learn their species song if they
haven't heard it in their youth before they were capable of singing (Marler 1970)
(a feature of animal learning that seems also to be true of language learning in
humans; see below).

4.1.2   Passive learning

Passive learning occurs when an animal learns *without* antecedently producing the
requisite *response*. Thus, rats can learn a maze merely by being pulled through it in
a transparent trolley car (McNamara et al. 1956, T:181; Gleitman 1963): i.e. the
probability of their running the maze correctly at a later time is greater than that
of rats who were not previously exposed. But, of course, when they're in the basket
they do not execute anything like the responses that will take them through the
maze. Similarly, rats were trained to run a maze with two distinctive goal boxes;
subsequently the rats were *placed* directly in one of the goal boxes and shocked.
When they were set again at the beginning of the maze, they avoided the shock-
box, despite the fact that the *responses* leading to that box had themselves not been
extinguished – *those* responses had previously led to food; what had led to shock
was merely their *writhing in the hands of the experimenter* who had placed them there
(Tolman and Gleitman 1949, T:251).

4.1.3   Spontaneous alteration

Not only can rats learn without reinforcement or response, they can sometimes
respond in ways that *defy* their conditioning history. In "*spontaneous alteration*," an
animal actually *avoids* emitting the response that has recently been reinforced.
After having found food at a particular location, for example, hummingbirds
will go *somewhere else* to find more food (Kamil 1978, Gl:163). Rats presented
with a number of paths of equal length to a goal will vary their routes,
although invariably in ways that advance their approach to the goal (Dashiel 1930;
Gn:163). The phenomenon is most dramatically displayed by rats in a "radial
maze," consisting of eight pathways radiating out in all directions from a central
location:

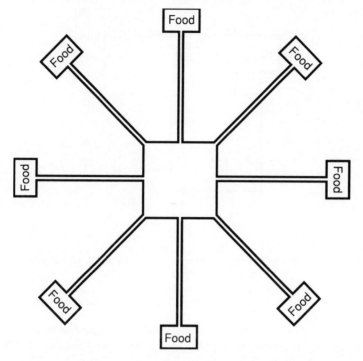

Figure 4.1 Radial Maze (after Dashiel 1930). Rats finding food in one arm tend not to revisit that arm until they've visited all the others.

Baits are placed at the end of each arm, and a record is kept of how many paths the rat takes before finding all of them. Olton and Samuelson (1976, Gl:160) found that they seldom revisited an arm until they had – at random – visited *all eight*. That is, they seem not to be matching responses to stimuli, but "keeping track" of "where the baits are." The Law of Effect seems not only inadequate to account for such cases; it actually seems to be disconfirmed by them!

4.1.4   *Improvisation*

The flexibility of animals responses beyond the Law of Effect is not limited merely to exploration. Animals engage in outright improvisation: appropriate behaviors are produced that have neither been produced nor reinforced before. Thus, rats will take *short-cuts* for which they have not been trained. For example, rats were trained to run the maze of figure 4.2a:

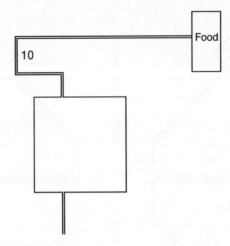

Figure 4.2a Long Route Maze (after Tolman et al. 1930:13; see M:409). Rats were trained to take the long route to the food box.

taking a round-about route to the goal box, which was illuminated by a light bulb. When the circular portion was replaced by the fan of paths as in figure 4.2b:

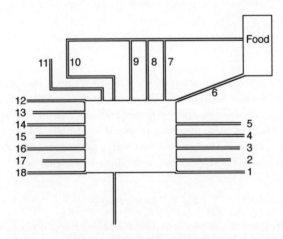

Figure 4.2b Short Cut Introduced in Long Route Maze (figure 4.2a). More than a third of the rats trained to the long route, took path 6 when path 10 was subsequently blocked and all the paths were offered to them.

102

36% of the rate took path 6, which led in a 45° bee-line to the goal (Tolman et al. 1930; T:162).

Indeed, animals apparently refuse to be tied to specific physical responses. Rats will *swim* a flooded maze after being taught to *run* it (McNamara *et al*. 1956, T:181): the body motions being quite different, RBists owe us an account of why the pairings of stimuli and responses in the running period should generalize to swimming. More remarkably, rats will transfer their learning to a maze's *mirror image*: in an experiment of Köhler's, rats trained to run a maze were better able than rats not so trained, to learn a maze laid out with pathways left/right reversed (T:179)!

Such results suggest that what the rats have learnt is not any mere sequence of responses to stimuli. Tolman (1948) argued they must have developed some sort of "internal map." More recently, Gallistel argues that they must be computing their location by a process of "dead reckoning," whereby they exploit a vector algebra for space: they keep track of how *long* they've moved in a specific *direction*. He points out that this seems strikingly true of animals in the wild: desert ants will forage in a winding path up to 100 meters from their nests, and then, once they find food, will take a bee-line home (Gl:59). Goslings, led or transported by roundabout routes in unfamiliar territory up to 1.5 kilometers from their homes, make their way back directly (von St. Paul 1982, Gl:65).

Passing beyond issues of navigation, we've already noted with regard to latent learning that monkeys presented with a novel, complex hinge, figure out how to undo several pins and bolts to free it (Harlow 1950, Gn:80). Köhler (1926, Gn:128) demonstrated even more remarkable improvisation in chimpanzees: they would use sticks as rakes to secure food that was outside a fence; and then as poles, which they would climb up in order to snatch food that was out of reach, grasping the food just as the stick toppled over! In all of these cases, the *responses* – i.e. the sequence of muscular motions required to execute the acts – are by no means physically type-identical between prior and test trials. So the animals must have learnt something other than merely to repeat certain physically typed responses.

4.1.5 *Responses of RBists: epicycles and mentalistic re-description*

RBists, of course, did not take these challenges lying down, and often made elaborate replies to them. By far, the most sophisticated efforts were those of Hull (1943). Space forbids considering both the full ingenuity of his proposals and the further experiments that in turn refuted them. A typical example was his proposal of a "divergent habit family hierarchy" to account for short-cut behavior observed in the maze of figure 4.1. Based on its exploration of space in general, an animal forms a hierarchy of sequences of responses of, say, increasing length; when a shorter sequence is blocked, the animal tries the next longer sequence unless presented with stimuli that once again prompt the shorter sequence (e.g. an opened gate). However, Tolman and Honzik (1930) and Caldwell and Jones (1954) (T:167, M:271) showed the inadequacy of such a proposal by constructing the three path maze of figure 4.3:

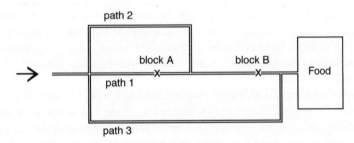

Figure 4.3 Nested Path Maze (after Tolman and Honzik 1950:223; see M:271). Rats trained to run path all three paths, pick path 2 when path 1 is blocked at A, but path 3 when it is blocked at B.

According to the Hullian proposal, there should be a corresponding hierarchy of responses whereby the rat should favor the responses that lead it down path 1 to those that lead it down 2 or 3. And when path 1 is blocked at A, it's true that the rats then tried path 2. But what happens when the path is blocked at B? The rats also encounter this in trying path 1, but then, instead of resorting to path 2, they try path 3 instead! Evidently they 'figured out" that the block at B was a block not only to path 1, but to path 2 as well: the response hierarchy was trumped by what Tolman called their "insight" into the structure of the maze. As Gallistel (1990) remarks, commenting on similar results regarding spatial location:[5]

> Results like these highlight the difficulties with theories that conceive of learning in terms of "selection by consequences" (Skinner 1981) – that is, theories in which the concept of reinforcement and the law of effect play a pivotal role. . . . When the more advanced mobile organisms – arthropods and vertebrates, at least – move, they generally do so by reference to a cognitive map of their environment. The map records the geometric relations among the points, lines, and surfaces that define the macroscopic shape of the animal's behavioral space. . . . The currently perceived sensory characteristics of the goal position become important only at the last moment, when the animal calculates that it is at the correct position and begins to look for the expected goal characteristics. (Gallistel 1990:162, 171–2)

Such talk of "insight" and "maps" of course, begins to imperil any eliminativist ambitions of RBism. Talk of "maps" is talk of inner *representations*; and that, on the face of it, is talk of *intentional* states, states that have *content*. However, the more we suppose that an animal is in some way exploiting some sort of internal representation, the less we need to adapt an eliminativist RBism to all these recalcitrant phenomena. Indeed, the efforts of RBists to explain the apparent exceptions to the Law of Effect came to many to seem no better than the efforts of Ptolemaics to account for the motion of heavenly bodies, an effort that became otiose as a more elegant, heliocentric theory – in the case of the mind, a representational theory – emerged.

This becomes particularly evident in the human case. Picking up on an example of Skinner's (1957:38), Dennett (1978a:66–70) provides an apt and amusing discussion of the difficulties besetting a RBist attempting to explain why someone mugged in New York hands over his wallet: instead, why doesn't he do any number of things that are more likely to have been previously reinforced with the stimulus "Your money or your life!," like giggling, or yawning?

> The Skinnerian must claim that this is not truly novel behavior at all, but an instance of a *general sort* of behavior which has been previously conditioned. But what sort is it? Not only have I not been trained to hand over my wallet to men with guns, I have not been trained to empty my pockets for women with bombs, nor to turn over my possessions to armed entities. None of these things have ever happened to me before. I may never have been threatened before at all. . . . [Skinner] must insist that the "threat stimuli" I now encounter . . . are similar in some crucial but undescribed respect to some stimuli encountered in the past which were followed by responses of some sort similar to the one I now make, where the past responses were reinforced somehow by their consequences. (Dennett 1978a:69)

Of course, it is not *impossible* that there is a story of prior threat stimuli and responses of the requisite sort. But the burden is squarely on the RBist to supply it. Indeed, RBism has always seemed most implausible in the human case – again, not because people are not conditionable (they surely are); but because there seems to be such an immense range of behavior that doesn't seem remotely susceptible to such an explanation: consider simply the immense range of questions one could ask on a standardized test, and the improbability of explaining the corresponding range of responses by conditioning.

Another strategy to which RBists increasingly resorted was to begin to allow mentalisms to creep into their explanations. An obvious example was the effort of many (e.g. Berlyne 1950, Glanzer 1958, T:249) to account for latent learning, by appeal to "exploratory" and "curiosity" drives: novel stimuli cause a drive for producing further stimuli, which will diminish as such further stimuli are received. Initially, such terms are introduced ostensibly in purely S-R terms. But, as Taylor rightly remarks:

> The suggestion that we can account for exploratory behavior as a set of stimulus-response habits is almost unintelligible. For the set of responses which an animal will use in exploration include a vast range . . . running, sniffing, walking around, jumping on top, pushing with his paw. We cannot account for the emission of all

these by saying they are conditioned to stimuli having the property "novelty", for the problem is of explaining *which one* will be emitted. . . . It is Nissen (1954) who has seized the nettle, and postulated that this behavior is "autonomously motivated", i.e. just occurs for its own sake, [speaking] of a "drive to perceive" and a "drive to know".   (T:249–50)

Despite his widely publicized rhetoric denouncing mentalism, Skinner was often the most flagrant abuser of thinly disguised mentalistic descriptions:

> The artist . . . is reinforced by the effects his works have upon . . . others . . . [his] verbal behavior . . . reach[ing] over centuries or to thousands of listeners or readers at the same time. The writer may not be reinforced often or immediately, but the reinforcement may be great.   (Skinner 1957:206, 224).

As Chomsky (to whose work we will shortly turn) remarked in reply to Skinner (1957):

> When we read that a person plays what music he likes (1957:165), says what he likes (1967:165), thinks what he likes (1957:438–9), reads what books he likes (1957:163), etc. *because* he finds it reinforcing to do so, or that we write books or inform others *because* we are reinforced by what we hope will be the ultimate behavior of a reader or listener, we can only conclude that the term "reinforcement" has only a ritual function. The phrase "x is reinforced by Y (stimulus, state of affairs, event, etc.)" is being used as a cover term for "X wants y," "X likes Y," "X wishes that Y were the case," etc.   (Chomsky 1959/1964:558)

Sometimes Skinner does try to cleanse our vocabulary of mentalisms; but he fails to notice that he is merely substituting one mentalism for another:

> The fact that operant conditioning seems to be "directed towards the future" is misleading. Consider, for example, the case of "looking for something." In what sense is the "something" which has not yet been found relevant to the behavior? . . . . In general, looking for something consists of emitting responses which in the past have produced "something" as a consequence. . . . [It] is not a further description of his behavior but of the variables of which his behavior is a function; it is equivalent to "I have lost my glasses," "I shall stop doing what I am doing when I find my glasses," or "When I have done this in the past, I have found my glasses."   (Skinner 1950:89–90)

But how is the equivalent an improvement? Quite aside from the problem of novel responses – doing something *other* than what has produced "something" as a consequence in the past – "losing" one's glasses is no more a physical relation than is "looking for": one loses one's glasses when one doesn't *know* where they are, and *finds* them when one does – even if they were all along *physically* right on one's nose!

106

The problem of mentalistic description has seemed to some to be so pervasive in our ordinary description of particularly human behavior as to be insurmountable. Hull, himself, didn't presume that he would cleanse behavioral theory of all mentalisms; but he did think that any that were used could be ultimately be "deduced" from purely physical descriptions of "colorless movement and mere receptor impulses":

> An ideally adequate theory even of so-called purposive behavior ought, therefore, to begin with colorless movement and mere receptor impulses as such, and from these build up step by step both adaptive and maladaptive behavior . . . [This] approach does not deny the . . . reality of purposive acts (as opposed to movements), of intelligence, of insight, of goals, of strivings, or of value; on the contrary, we insist upon the genuineness of these forms of behavior. We hope ultimately to show the logical right to the use of such concepts by deducing them as secondary principles from more elementary objective primary principles.   (Hull 1943:25–6; quoted in T:114)

Thus are RBists driven to *analytical behaviorism* (ABism) the view that all mental terms can be *analyzed* in terms of relations among physically described stimuli and responses. That is, although RBism is logically independent of ABism, defenders of RBism came to rely on ABism in view of the mentalisms that invariably emerged in their accounts. We'll consider ABism and its problems at some length in the next chapter (§5.3).

Whatever the prospects of RBism in dealing with the problems raised so far, they become decidedly dimmer when we look at a particularly interesting bit of behavior exhibited by human beings, the behavior surrounding the production of language and people's responses to it. This is a particularly crucial bit of behavior for purposes here, since any prospect of a non-mentalistic account of the Standardized Regularities – which involve processing of linguistic stimuli – will obviously have to include an account of it. In his book *Verbal Behavior*, Skinner (1957) sketched such an account, which was subjected to a famous review by the then young linguist, Noam Chomsky (1959/1964). Although the review was (to many minds) devastating by itself, what really led to the decline of RBism was the spectacular research program that Chomsky and his followers began to develop from the fifties down to the present. The evidence and theoretical arguments adduced by Chomsky are so important, both in their own right, and for seeing the problems for eliminativism, that they deserve special discussion.

4.2   Chomsky

Every now and then there occurs a figure in the history of thought that completely revolutionizes the way people have thought about a domain, often by making plausible certain possibilities that were not taken seriously prior to the time. Thus,

Galileo and Descartes proposed a mechanical theory of nature; Darwin an evolutionary theory of speciation; Marx an approach to human society in terms of class struggle; and Freud an approach to psychology in terms of unconscious, often surprising, sexual motivations. It's important to note that such figures are not significantly diminished by the failure of the *specific* proposals they have made. What is interesting about Galileo, Darwin, Marx, or Freud is not whether they have the last word about the truth in their particular domains, but that they have called attention to certain kinds of facts, distinctions, and possible hypotheses that, once noticed, cannot again be seriously ignored.[6]

Noam Chomsky is without a doubt such a figure. Although he is (as he acknowledges) resurrecting ideas that were suggested by Plato and championed by the eighteenth-century rationalists,[7] he found a way of advancing these ideas as serious scientific proposals about the structure of the mind. Whether or not his specific hypotheses about language are true, the *kinds* of facts about linguistic structures and innate capacities to which he has drawn our attention are now an essential ingredient of our psychological understanding. At the very least, they point to fundamental inadequacies of RBism and render the prospects of any other eliminativist program unlikely in the extreme. In §4.2.1 I shall consider a few representative samples of the exquisite evidence to which Chomksy and linguists since have called our attention; in §4.2.2.4 I will turn to some distinctions and hypotheses that he argues are needed to account for this evidence; and in §4.2.5 I will indicate some of the further research on non-linguistic capacities that his suggestions have inspired.[8] In §4.3 I will discuss how his arguments raise a general problem for classical empiricism and thereby undermine the prospects for any successful eliminativist program. Indeed, the failures of behaviorism and the insights of Chomsky all point to the need for mind (§4.4).

4.2.1   The evidence

The first, and in some ways the most striking of Chomsky's contributions in this area, was his bringing to our attention a wide range of perfectly ordinary facts about language that are, in a phrase he (1968:22) borrows from Wittgenstein (1953:§129) "hidden because of their simplicity and familiarity (one is unable to notice something – because it is always before one's eyes)." These facts reveal a sensitivity of language speakers to fairly elaborate grammatical structures that do not seem in any way to be a *physical* feature of normal linguistic stimuli, and which it seems absurd to suppose that people are in any way conditioned to discriminate.

Chomsky begins by citing what normal English speakers would or wouldn't find grammatically acceptable, their "linguistic intuitions" about grammatical phenomena. Now it might be thought that such a reliance on intuitions is a species of the very introspectionism that we argued in chapter 3 merely begged the eliminativist's question. However, given the method of standardized tests that we discussed in §3.3, it's easy to imagine eliciting these intuitions by multiple choice questions on such tests, and citing the patterns of responses to the paired questions as the relevant non-tendentious data.

The basic fact to notice about our linguistic intuitions is that we are all disposed to discriminate an indefinitely vast set of stimuli that count as the grammatical sentences of one's language. For starters, all English speakers would accept as grammatical:

(1a)   The dog bit the man.
(1b)   John hoped that Bill took a ferry.
(1c)   Millions of years ago, dinosaurs roamed the planet.

but not:

(2a)   *Dog the bit man the.
(2b)   *That Bill John ferry the hoped took.
(2c)   *Years millions dinosaurs, the ago roamed dinosaurs planet.

(the "*" is the linguist's way of indicating an ungrammatical sentence). But not all cases are so blatant. Grammatical sentences also include:

	3a)	I asked what time it is.
	3b)	I asked the time.
and	3c)	I wondered what time it is.
but not:	3d)	*I wondered the time.

We can say:

	(4a)	He gave his money to the library.
	(4b)	He gave the library his money.
	(4c)	He donated his money to the library.
but not:	(4c)	*He donated the library his money.

And we can ask:

	(5a)	Who do you think that Mary loves?
	(5b)	Who do you think Mary loves?
and	(5c)	Who do you think loves Mary?

but, mysteriously, not:

	(5d)	*Who do you think that loves Mary?

(Apparently the "that" in (6d) *must* be deleted, even though "think" ordinarily takes a "that.") As now several generations of linguists will attest, determining even roughly what the principles are that distinguish grammatical from ungrammatical English is no easy matter.

The RBist might, of course, claim that the grammatical sentences are discriminated by "chaining" responses to each of the basic elements of a sentence, words and/or morphemes ("-ible," "un-"). In the first place, however, such a proposal would not distinguish a sentence from a mere association of words, like "salt, pepper," "left, right, up, down," "north, south, east, west."[9] Secondly, Chomsky raised a serious difficulty for any such account: the structures of indefinitely many grammatical sentences of English are not constructible by *local links alone*, in the way that would be required if the structures were built up by response chains. An easy set of examples is presented by familiar sentences involving bifurcated logical particles, for example, sentences of the form "Either . . . or__" or "If . . . , then__". If the word "either" appears at some place in a sentence, then "or" must appear at certain (not just any) points later. One simply can't say:

(6)   *If, John, who hates tomatoes, but loves oranges, hopes to live well.

(7)   *Either John will go to the movies and Sally will stay home.

One needs an "or" to appear at certain places somewhere in (7): for example, before another *whole sentential clause* of the sort that also needs to follow (maybe with a "then") the last words in (6). But, this would seem to be in principle beyond the power of any local chaining device,[10] which can only build on *immediately contiguous* links (e.g. the next response in a chain). Pinker puts the point nicely, imagining such a device building up sentences from lists of words it has encountered in the past:

> To satisfy the desire of a word early in the sentence for some other word late in the sentence, the device has to remember the early word while it is churning out all the words in between. And that is the problem: a word-chain device is an amnesiac, remembering only which word list it has just chosen from, nothing earlier. By the time it reaches the *or/then* list, it has no means of remembering whether it said *if* or *either* way back at the beginning. From our vantage point, peering down at the entire road map, we can remember which choice the device made at the first fork in the road, but the device itself, creeping antlike from list to list, has no way of remembering.   Pinker (1994:94–5)

Worse, such bifurcated logical structures can be indefinitely *embedded* in themselves and each other. Consider the following horrible, but still perfectly grammatical sentence from a leading RBist, Quine (1936/1976:95) himself:

(8)   If if if time is not money then time is money
        then time is money then if time is money then time is money.[11]

Since this sort of embedding of conditionals within conditionals seems to have no upper bound, a chaining device would need to consult increasingly long lists in order to process such sentences. Of course, such lists of sentences, most of which have never been encountered, are not part of the learning history of any organism.

Indeed, it appears that, as Pinker points out, "a sentence is not a chain but a tree" (p. 97). That is, sentences seem to have a structure of dominance and subordination that is captured best by the "tree" structures familiar to many of us from "diagramming sentences" in "grammar" school. For example, (1-a) and (1-b) might be diagrammed as in figure 4.4:

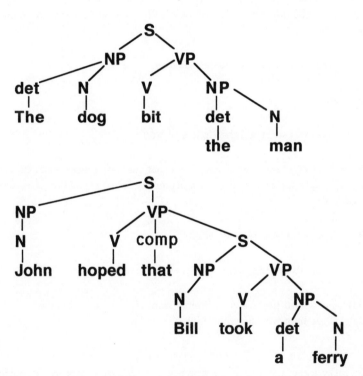

Figure 4.4 Typical "Tree" Diagram of a Sentence. A sentence ("S") divides into a noun phrase ("NP") and a verb phrase ("VP"). An NP further divides into a determiner ("det") and a noun ("N"); a VP further divides into a verb ("V") and another NP, or, in the case of attitude verbs, a complementizer ("comp") and another S, which further sub-divides along the same lines.

Such structures can also be represented by nested, labeled bracketings of ordered n-tuples, e.g.:

$$\langle\langle\langle \text{John}\rangle_n\rangle_{np} \langle\langle \text{hoped}\rangle_v \langle \text{that}\rangle_{comp} \langle\langle \text{Bill}\rangle_n \langle\langle \text{took}\rangle_v \langle\langle a\rangle_{det} \langle \text{ferry}\rangle_n\rangle_{np}\rangle_{vp}\rangle_s\rangle_{vp}\rangle_s$$

All that's important is that there is some representation of the *ordering* and consequent "dominance" relations between various labeled constituents.

These tree structures play a central role in a speaker's understanding not only of the ways in which more complex sentences are composed of simpler ones, but in understanding a variety of relations among the sentential constituents. Consider, for example, the phenomenon of *anaphora*, whereby pronouns can pick up the reference of other phrases, especially nouns. Permissible anaphoric relations turn out to be heavily constrained by sentential structure, not capturable by a mere *physical* relation among the constituents. Thus, one might suppose that a pronoun should refer merely to a physically prior "antecedent" in a sentence, so that

(9a)   John was surprised that he had won.

could mean

(9b)   John was surprised that John had won.

But consideration of other sentences shows that the "antecedent" can't be merely what has literally appeared earlier in the sentence, since (9a) and (9b) could also be expressed as:

(9c)   That he won surprised John.

where "he" can also refer to John. But they could *not* be expressed as:

(9d)   He was surprised that John had won.
(9e)   That John won surprised him.

since, here, neither "he" nor "him" can refer to "John."[12]

Chomsky argues that the only way to begin to adequately capture this phenomenon is to recognize that all the sentences of (9) have (at least) the underlying structure:

$$\langle \ldots x \ldots \langle \ldots y \ldots \rangle\rangle$$

for example,

$$\langle \ldots \text{John} \ldots \langle \ldots \text{he} \ldots \rangle \rangle$$
or
$$\langle \ldots \text{he} \ldots \langle \ldots \text{John} \ldots \rangle \rangle$$

and that there is a principle that permits replacement of noun by pronoun beginning in the innermost structure(s) – e.g. the *subordinate* phrases – *first* (1968:38–9).[13] That is, we must understand (9a–c) to be of the form:

$$\langle \text{John was surprised} \langle \text{that he had won} \rangle \rangle$$

which *permits he* to be the same person as John, and (9d) and (9e) to be of the form:

$$\langle \text{He was surprised that} \langle \text{John had won} \rangle \rangle$$

in which *he* cannot be the same as *John*.

Such examples might lead one to think that linguistic principles are just elaborations of conventions of the sort one learns in school, and might have been instilled therefore by some sort of training that might be ultimately characterized in RBist terms. However, the evidence of actual language learning flies in the face of any such conditioning story. In the first place, it seems that humans exhibit the same dependence on a "critical period" that we noted earlier to be true of Marler's (1970) song birds: "ferral" children deprived of exposure to language prior to puberty seem unable to be trained to grasp grammar thereafter. Moreover, anything like "reinforcement" for speaking grammatically even among normal children is either non-existent or ineffective. Brown and Halon (1970) showed that very young children tend to be "reinforced" not for their *grammar* but rather for the *informational content* of what they say. Thus, a typical exchange of a mother and a child, observing a cat on a chair, might proceed:

CHILD:	Momma isn't boy, he a girl.
MOTHER:	That's right.
CHILD:	And Walt Disney comes on Tuesday
MOTHER:	No, he does not. (Pinker 1994:280)

Moreover, even when grammaticality *is* attended to, the child often doesn't understand the issue. Pinker cites a typical experience of the psycholinguist Martin Braine, who:

tried for several weeks to stamp out one of his daughter's grammatical errors. Here is the result:

CHILD: Want other one spoon.
FATHER: You mean, you want *the other spoon.*
CHILD: Yes, I want other one spoon, please, Daddy.
FATHER: Can you say "the other spoon"?
CHILD: Other . . . one . . . spoon.
FATHER: Say "other."
CHILD: Other.
FATHER: "Spoon."
CHILD: Spoon.
FATHER: "Other . . . spoon."
CHILD: Other . . . spoon. Now give me other one spoon?

Braine wrote, "Further tuition is ruled out by her protest, vigorously supported by my wife." (Pinker 1995:281)[14]

It is difficult to imagine much more straightforward evidence against RBism. Perhaps Braine ought to have tried chocolates or electric shocks as reinforcements – but then one would be deprived of an account of how the typical child, lacking such obvious reinforcements, *does* eventually master grammar!

In fact, the vast majority of permissible or impermissible constructions that Chomsky considers are decidedly not explicitly taught or learnt. Although, as we just saw, children do make errors, these fall into fairly regular patterns that also betray their obedience to structure sensitive rules. For example, children over-generalize the regular rules for the past tense to even those irregular verbs whose past tense they have already learnt (well after learning that "went" is the past of "go," children nevertheless regularly begin using "goed", as in *"He goed to the store"; see Pinker and Prince 1988:136–7 and Pinker 1994:273–6). However, unless they are confused about who's who, neither children nor adults say "He was surprised that John had won" to mean "John was surprised that he had won," or happily begin a sentence with "Either" and not follow it at certain places with an "or".

Particularly vivid examples of untutored structural sensitivities are afforded by colloquial contractions, which are, of course, not only not explicitly *taught*, but are actually often *discouraged* in explicit instruction. Consider, for example, the odd restrictions on the contraction of "want to" in most English dialects:

(10a)   Who(m) do you want to see?
(10b)   Who(m) do you wanna see?
(10c)   Who(m) do you want to see John?
(10d)   *Who(m) do you wanna see John?

For some reason that has surely never been noted in anyone's "training," the "want to" in (10a) can be contracted to the "wanna" of (10b), but not in (10c) to yield (10d).[15]

114

Chomsky's (1955b:22) explanation of this particular phenomenon also illustrates another important fact about sentence structure that challenges RBism: there can be elements in a sentence, called "traces," that are *patently not part of the physical stimulus*. Chomsky argues that in questions like (10a) and (10c) there is a trace marker that indicates the place of the noun phrase marker (indicated by a "t") to which the interrogative "Where" or "Who" applies. The sentences are really understood (or internally represented) as:

(10e)   Who do you want to see t?
>   cf. You want to see *Shirley*.

(10f)   Who do you want t to see John?
>   cf. You want *Shirley* to see John.

Supposing contractions are prohibited across even unpronounced elements of a sentential representation, the contraction is blocked in (10f), while still permitted in (10e). Needless to say, the prospect of any RBist account of "response chains" linking such invisible and inaudible links is virtually nil.

Some have reasonably complained that peoples' "intuitive" judgments about grammaticality, on which so many of the arguments like the above are based, are notoriously unreliable, particularly as indications specifically of *grammar* – as opposed to *semantics*, *pragmatics*, or other features of language. Of course, some intuitions may be a lot more or less reliable than others. Sorting out which ones to trust plausibly goes hand in hand with providing any theory of the domain that explains the intuitions one way or another. But, fortunately, the data are by no means limited to intuition. A wide variety of other kinds of evidence have been adduced for the psychological reality of at least structural descriptions. In a classic experiment, Fodor and Bever (1965) presented subjects with normal grammatical sentences in one ear, accompanying them by short bursts of noise ("clicks") presented in the other, and asked them to indicate where in the sentences the clicks occurred. For example, clicks were presented at the locations indicated by the numbers in:

⟨⟨That ⟨he ⟨was happy⟩⟩⟩⟨was ⟨evident ⟨from ⟨⟨the way⟩⟨he smiled⟩⟩⟩⟩⟩⟩
>   1 2   3   4   5   6 7 8 9

(where brackets, as before, indicate grammatical constituents). Subjects were good at identifying the position of clicks when they occurred at location 5, the major phrase boundary (marking the complex subject of the sentence), but poorer at identifying their position elsewhere. Indeed, all the others tended to be *mis*heard as occurring closer to position 5 than they in fact occurred (see Clark and Clark

1977:54–5 for discussion). What is crucial for our discussion is that the "break" is in no way a *physical* break – there is absolutely no *physical* interruption of the speech stream at position 5: what "break" there is exists only "in the hearer's mind" (and only if they know English).

More recently, a number of EEG and PET scan studies[16] have revealed distinctive patterns of electrical activity at just those points in a subject's reading of a string of words at which it becomes ungrammatical (as distinct from merely semantically or pragmatically anomalous), as well as at points when a phrase (such as "Who" in "Who you do wanna see?") must be held in memory while the reader of it awaits the "trace" that it indexes (the "t" in "Who do you wanna see t?"). It seems that, contrary to the underlying intuition behind most forms of behaviorism, not only does the mind impose distinctions that are not part of the physical stimulus, but there are issues of mental representation that are demonstrably not issues merely of behavior (we will return to this point in §7.2.4).

If a revolution is to be successful, there must be more than grumbling about the problems with the *ancien régime*; some positive proposals need to be made in its place. Chomsky has not wanting in this regard. In addition to these straightforward evidential difficulties for RBism, he also proposed an alternative theory, indeed, an alternative conception of the appropriate subject matter of linguistics and psychology. I will touch only upon a few of the most important aspects of that conception here.

4.2.2   Competence vs. performance

For a variety of reasons having to do not only with the sorts of worries about the mind that we have discussed, but also with the then prevailing positivistic conceptions of science generally, RBists insisted that psychology should be a theory of *publicly observable behavior*. Roughly speaking, serious scientific theory was supposed in the business not so much of *explanation* by reference to hidden mechanisms, but rather of merely *predicting* publicly observable phenomena[17] generally. In the case of psychology, the only publicly observable phenomena that is ordinarily available is overt behavior. Chomsky challenges this conception, calling attention to an important feature of scientific practice that had been given short shrift by both postivists in general, and RBists especially.

An important question to ask in doing any science is what is a fit topic for research. Sometimes, of course, there are merely *practical* interests: it would be nice to know tomorrow's weather and which horse is going to win at the races. However, sometimes our interests are more *theoretic*: we'd like to know *the principles underlying* weather change or the speed of horses. For this purpose, predicting the *actual* weather, or winner of a race from day to day, may be the wrong place to look. One does better to step back from these particular phenomena and try to abstract and isolate the many different factors involved in their production: e.g. general principles of the musculature of animals, growth, aging, nutrition, as well as the physics of moving bodies quite generally. Most ordinary phenomena – weather and horse races are obvious examples – turn out to be the result of a *massive interaction* effect of a number of different principles operating at once. It's not that *some* predictions of actual phenomena aren't relevant: what one wants (and what scientists spend great quantities of time and money preparing) are experiments in which one tests the effects of one principle unconfounded by the effects of the others: e.g. the fall of a feather or a stone in a vacuum, the pressure of a gas in a sealed and uniformly heated container, or the scattering of particles in a Wilson cloud chamber.[18]

A moment's reflection strongly suggests that human behavior is obviously much more like the weather than like the free fall of a stone. At least on its mentalistic face, speech behavior in particular would seem to be the result of the interaction of an overwhelming diversity of factors: intention, motivation, habit, interpersonal sensitivity, intelligence, rhetorical ingenuity, wit, speed. A person's grasp of grammar is only one background condition among these many factors. If this is true, then the ordinary flow of speech, a person's "verbal behavior," would seem to be as unlikely a source of theoretic insight as would the fall of a leaf in a tropical storm. What we need to do is to study each of the factors in relative isolation, and only then consider how they might interact with one another in actual episodes of speech production and comprehension. Thus, we need to study, *inter alia*, speakers' grammatical *abilities*, or, in Chomsky's phrase, their *competence* (or competen*cies*, given there are doubtless many different ones), not their *performance*.

Of course, RBists *could* claim to be studying a kind of competence: they could claim that, really, the only systematic factor determining speech behavior is the past history of conditioning. The trouble is that this seems so wildly implausible; and can be shown to be so when one turns to what would appear to be the best, relatively *unconfounded* cases for such a theory, for example, the above effort of Martin Braine to correct his child, or all the attempts reviewed earlier to test RBism generally by highly controlled experiments on rats. The theory is in the position that Galileo's or Newton's would have been in, had feathers continued to fall more slowly than stones even in a perfect vacuum.

In the case of language, it is particularly obvious that people's linguistic performance does not match what (by their own lights) their competence with the language would prescribe. Listen to the actual flow of noise in a normal conversation, and note the number of extraneous noises (coughs, "um"s and "ah"s, sniffles, snorts, giggles), linguistic tics ("Like, I was, you know, like, going to the store, when, like, this man, you know, like, came up to me . . ."), as well as false starts, interruptions, mid-sentence changes of mind, and simply outright speech errors. The actual speech behavior of people in ordinary life only intermittently consists in the production of *perfectly grammatical sentences*. Moreover, in their lifetime, human beings will encounter and produce only a tiny fraction of all the sentences they can understand. It would seem as arbitrary to limit linguistics by these accidental facts about actual speech production as it would be to limit a person's grasp of arithmetic to the actual sums and absent-minded errors they produce in their daily calculations.

4.2.3   *Creativity and productivity*

As we already noted, competent speakers seem to be able to understand an enormous, indeed, indefinitely large number of sentences of their natural language. Well, one hypothesis is that they resort merely to a vast look-up table, like the entries in standard trigonometry tables. But this seems implausible in the extreme. For another striking fact about people is that, aside from special ritualistic speech (prayers, incantations), *people daily produce and understand masses of sentences they've never either produced or encountered before*, a fact that Chomsky calls the "creativity" of language use. This fact is, of course, the main reason people bother to talk, listen, and read at all, and how they manage to extend their learning beyond their own immediate experience.

Moreover, not only can people understand an indefinitely large number of sentences, it appears that they have at least the competence to understand a potential *infinity* of them. For example, children routinely understand how to continue such constructions as:

(11a)   This is the house that Jack built;
(11b)   This is the rat that lived in the house that Jack built.
(11c)   This is the cat that chased the rat that . . .
(11d)   This is the dog that chased the cat that chased the rat . . .

and so forth, in a sequence for which the child seems unable to conceive any upper bound. Even more transparently, anyone can *understand* at least the truth conditions of any in the following boring repetitions of ordinary sentences:

(12a)   Snow is white.
(12b)   Snow is white and snow is white.
(12c)   Snow is white, and snow is white, and snow is white, and snow is white and snow is white.

and so on (and similarly for the other logical connectives: "or," "only if," "if and only if").[19] So one question to raise is: what do all these potentially infinite numbers of grammatical sentences have in common that permits finite beings like ourselves to understand them?

The best – perhaps the only – explanation of this remarkable fact is that people is some way have recourse to *productive* or *generative* rules, a little like the "recursive" rules for generating all the well-formed formulae of logic, e.g.

(L) If σ is a formula, then so is "-σ"

   If σ and τ are formulae, so is "σ & τ"

The rules are "recursive," since they can be applied over and over again to produce more of the same kinds of things they specify: thus, iteration of the negation rule on its own products specifies a potential infinity of formulae, "-σ," "--σ," "---σ," . . . A language is "productive" insofar as it can be captured by such rules. Natural languages (and our competence with them) certainly appear to be productive in this sense. For Chomsky it is the task of linguistics to specify the recursive rules.

Of course, apart from the existence of the sentences as merely abstract objects produced by formal rules, the infinity here is only potential: no one will ever encounter an actual sentence a trillion words long, and, even if they did, they would probably die (of boredom alone) before actually processing it. And there are other limits on processing: most people "saturate" on repetitions of a single word, and so have trouble appreciating that

(13) Police police police police police police police

is a perfectly good sentence of English.[20] The point is that our *competence* is productive: they *could* understand such a sentence, or a sentence a trillion words long, but for the fact that they'd saturate or die first.[21] Of course, we could choose to limit our grammars accordingly, and rule out of the grammar trillion word sentences, and sentences like (13). But this would be bad science, failing to carve nature at its joints. Such things as the length of our lives, our susceptibility to boredom and saturation would seem to be factors as *independent* of grammar as they are of our ability to do arithmetic. Constraining a theory of our grammatical – or our arithmetic – competence to only the finite cases with which people will actually contend would miss the underlying patterns that generate them. It would be like abridging Kepler's laws about the elliptical orbits of planets to accommodate the perturbations caused by their mutual gravitational fields and passing comets (see §10.3 below).[22]

4.2.4 *The poverty and corruption of the stimulus*

With astounding rapidity, children come to have a command of a language that seems every bit as productive as that of the local adults. Even children's very first word combinations fall into standard syntactic categories. Studies show that 95% of the two-word combinations initially uttered by children are properly ordered:

they say "All dry," "No pee," not "Dry all," "Pee no" (Pinker 1994:268). This ear for the grammatical continues into longer strings: despite the saliency to adult ears of childhood errors (like "Can you broke those?" "What he can ride in?"), apparently errors occur in only up to 8% of the opportunities for making them; abstracting from non-linguistic noises, 90% of most children's utterances are grammatical (Pinker 1994:272). And, of course, by the ages of four or five, they have a practically endless appetite for such constructions as "This is the x that y'ed the z that . . . that lived in the house that Jack built." In any case, they are capable of understanding an indefinite number of constructions that they have never heard before on the basis of a very small subset of them.

Now, it is an elementary logical point that there are infinite number of languages that are compatible with that small subset (say, the subset the child has heard before her fourth birthday): for starters, there's the very simple language that consists *only of that subset and nothing more*! But no child so much as considers such a possibility. A finite child can only consider a finite number of possibilities, and so the question needs to be addressed as to why children settle so readily on the particular grammars that they do, why, indeed, all children converge on what seem to be the "natural human languages."[23]

Moreover, as we noted in distinguishing linguistic competence from performance, people misspeak, fail to complete sentences, change their utterance intentions in mid-sentence, and generally garnish their speech with all manner of extra-linguistic noise. Given this fact and given the sometimes distorted speech adults engage in when speaking "baby talk" to children, the actual stimuli children receive consist of often *bad* examples of grammaticality, a fact which makes it even harder to see how grammars could be mastered on the basis of experience or training.[24] Children would seem to be in the position of someone trying to learn the rules of some elaborate game, like Chess or Go, from a sample of games in which only a very few of the permissible moves are made, and in which one in every ten or so moves is illegal!

This argument from "the poverty and corruption of the stimulus" is one of the main arguments Chomsky adduces on behalf of his famous thesis that the basic principles of grammar (what he calls "universal grammar") are *innate*. Given how radically underdetermined our linguistic abilities are by the evidence provided in the short period in which we acquire them, human beings must be born heavily biased towards acquiring a very few of the infinitude of possible languages – much as Marler's (1970) song birds are disposed to acquire only the songs of their species. Indeed, increasingly the focus of concern for linguistic theory is simply to provide an account of the "language acquisition device" ("LAD"), or an account of how it is that children in so short a time can learn to recognize and produce the actual sentences they do.

It's worth noting that Chomsky's argument here is simply an application to the case of language of a famous insight of one of his philosophy teachers, Nelson

Goodman. Consider in addition to the usual predicate "x is green," the infinite series of predicates, defined as follows:

x is $grue_0$ IFF (x is green and observed before the year 3000AD or otherwise blue)

x is $grue_1$ IFF (x is green and observed before the year 3001AD or otherwise blue)

x is $grue_2$ IFF (x is green and observed before the year 3002AD or otherwise blue)

. . .

x is $grue_n$ IFF (x is green and observed before the year 3000AD $+$ n years, or otherwise blue)

As Goodman (1956) noted, any finite observation of emeralds ever made by the human race thus far (before the year 3000AD) is *logically compatible* with (indeed, could be taken to confirm) any of the infinite number of hypotheses: "All emeralds are $grue_0$," "All emeralds are $grue_1$," . . . , "All emeralds are $grue_n$," as well, of course, as "All emeralds are green." Why do we prefer this last to any of the infinite other hypotheses? It appears we are somehow innately endowed to prefer only a few out of the infinite totality of possible predicates compatible with our finite empirical observations.[25] What Chomsky did was to apply this insight of Goodman's to the far more complex case of natural language, where we seem also to be innately biased to prefer only a few out of the infinite totality of possible languages.

4.2.5 Extensions of Chomsky's program

Chomsky's own research has been confined largely to linguistics.[26] His ideas, however, have stimulated research across many cognitive domains in which overwhelming evidence has been adduced for the innateness of a variety of conceptual structures. Spelke (1991) let infants witness a ball falling behind a screen; when the screen was removed, they gazed longer when the ball was shown *beneath* a table than when it appeared *on top of it*, or when it appeared *unsupported in mid-air*: apparently they are innately disposed to think that objects can't pass through one another, although they are not particularly disposed to believe in gravity – despite the fact that non-penetration and gravity have been equally present in their limited experience. In a similar experiment, Wynn (1992a) had 5-month-old infants observe an object become occluded by a screen, behind which another object was shortly added. When the screen was removed, the infants gazed longer when only one object was visible rather than two; and, *mutatis mutandis*, when two objects appear after one has been removed from an original two. Infants seem to be capable of at least rudimentary addition and subtraction.[27]

Or, consider the philosophical chestnut, the "Molyneux problem": would people congenitally blind, but newly sighted, visually recognize the shapes they had only previously encountered by touch? Rationalists were disposed to think they could; empiricists that they couldn't. Meltzoff and Borton (1979) blindfolded 29-day-old infants, and allowed them to suck on either bumpy or smooth pacifiers; after the blindfold was removed, the infants gazed longer at the visual image of the pacifier they had sucked. Apparently, infants are born with the ability to identify shapes cross-modally.

Investigation of young children's developing cognitive capacities in general is presently one of the most fruitful avenues of research on the structure of the mind. In addition to the work of Spelke and Meltzoff on the infant's understanding of the physical world, Carey (1985) and Keil (1989) have investigated the child's developing conceptions of living things, artifacts, and – most interestingly for the philosophy of mind – psychological phenomena. Although the evidence is at this time still quite complex and inconclusive, it appears that children readily grasp distinctions – between reality and pretense, between objects and pictures of them – that arguably only an innate grasp of intentional distinctions would permit.[28]

4.3*   Eliminativism's Roots in Empiricism

The problems with RBism are not peculiar to it. As Chomsky has pointed out at length, the problems with RBism can be traced to classical empiricist assumptions that underlie both it and most other eliminativist proposals. It is worth pursuing this connection to appreciate the problems that any eliminativist proposal must ultimately face.

What Chomsky's arguments seemed to show is that human linguistic competence required some sort of substantial internal mental structure as part of the innate endowment of the child. Such a claim flew in the face of what had been for about two hundred years the prevailing orthodoxy in philosophy and psychology – and, many thought, any right-minded science: *empiricism*, or the view that all knowledge and concepts were based on experience. According to that view, the human mind was a "*tabula rasa*" on which experience etched impressions, from which were derived our ideas and knowledge of the world. So exiguous were the internal mechanisms of mind that were needed to bring about these results, it was not surprising that RBists thought they could be replaced entirely by the association mechanisms of a stimulus-response psychology. That that particular mechanism seems to have failed did not by itself discourage the empiricist idea, which, as we'll see, survives in other eliminativist proposals.

Empiricism is actually associated with a number of claims. Two of the most important ones are: (1) that all knowledge of the world must ultimately be *justified* on the basis of experience; (2) that all knowledge in fact *originates* in experience.

The first needn't concern us here.[29] The second concerns us only insofar as it involves a crucial corollary, that all *concepts* are derived from experience; or, as Hume (1734/1978) put it, "there is no idea without a corresponding impression." A descendant of this assumption plays a critical, if often only implicit role in RBism, and can be found underlying most other eliminativist successors to that view. But this will take a moment to show.

In §4.1.5, we noticed that RBists recognized early on that they couldn't confine themselves to simple physical descriptions of stimuli, responses, and reinforcements. Animals don't learn merely to repeat precisely *the same physical motions* for which they've been reinforced; nor are all the stimuli or reinforcers to which they develop a response *physically* identical: the different retinal patterns formed by even so simple an example as a cube, seen from now this, now that, perspective are by no means a physically delimitable lot. The question arises, however, as to what constraints there are on the descriptions of the stimuli, as well as of the responses and reinforcements. Can we describe these variables as we like? This can't be right if the RBist is to be an eliminativist: presumably *mentalistic* descriptions aren't allowed (even if, as we saw, the RBist is constantly tempted to re-introduce them).

But the problem goes far beyond merely mentalistic description. A crucial point to note is that *the further that the generalized descriptions diverge from physical descriptions, the less illuminating RBist explanation will be*. This point can be best made by considering, first, the notion of a *transducer*: this is any device that transforms a physical magnitude of one form systematically into a physical magnitude of another by virtue of physical laws. Microphones, for example, are transducers that transform sound waves into electromagnetic waves that other transducers, for example, radios, transform back into sound. Animal sense organs consist, at least in part, of just such transducers, transforming, for example, sound and light waves into electric impulses along visual and auditory nerves. Now, so long as RBists set out their case with examples of conditioning animals to approximately transducible properties, like *color* and *shape*, the Law of Effect promises to afford an illuminating explanation of the resulting conditioned behavior: after all, if color is understood as nothing more than reflection of particular wave-lengths, and shape as a specific spatio-temporal property, it isn't hard to imagine physically characterizable transducers that might be sensitive to them, and association networks that might link the output of such transducers to certain muscular contractions. Although such sensitivities could also be explained mentalistically, they do not *need* to be so explained.

However, suppose the descriptions of S are "glimpses of victims of the Holocaust," of R, "campaigning against Neo-Nazis," and F "moral satisfaction"; or just the Ss, Rs, and Fs needed to specify the Standardized Regularities, i.e. "glimpses of 'question #24'," "filling in the corresponding rectangle," "prospect of $100 given a correct answer"? Even if the Law of Effect did manage to link these phenomena so described, it would, by itself, explain rather little: we should reasonably want to know how an organism managed to become sensitive to what are from a physical point of view *extraordinarily heterogenous* Ss, Rs, and Fs.[30] Explanations in terms of such variables would be of little interest if it turned out that one couldn't imagine the mechanisms that could be responsible for them. As Chomsky notes, the issue that concerns him is not between those who think evidence is limited to behavior, and those who think there is some other source, but rather *the complexity of the input/output function* that the psychologist needs to postulate:

> The differences that arise between those who affirm and those who deny the importance of the specific "contribution of the organism" to learning and performance concern *the particular character and complexity of this function*, and the kinds of observations and research necessary for arriving at a specification of it. (Chomsky 1959/ 1964:549; italics mine)

A recurrent temptation in this regard is to attempt to paper over this problem of the detection of non-local properties by appealing to an undefined notion of "similarity." Thus, RBists tried to meet the difficulty with their notion of *stimulus and response generalization*: animals treat new stimuli as "the same" as old ones, and emit "similar" responses to "similar" reinforcements. It's important to see that such claims, as they stand, are *entirely empty*. Similarity comes only in *respects*. Any n things are similar in *some* respect, if only in the respect of *belonging to any set that has those n things as members* (thus, the number 3, tomato juice, and Caesar's right thumb have in common the fact that they all belong to the set {3, tomato juice, Caesar's right thumb}, cf. Goodman 1970). ("Similarity" is what might be called a "crutch" word – "novelty," "creativity" are others: they convey information only by allowing us to lean against some other, usually implicit, information.) If RBist appeals to "similarity" are to have serious explanatory content, the relevant respects, i.e. properties, must be specified; but this is simply to re-state the problem we were raising for the view: how can it account for the *properties* to which organisms are sensitive?

This problem is not limited to RBism. Another less famous but still influential eliminativist approach at least to perception was the "Ecological Realism" of the psychologist, J.J. Gibson (1904–79). In his last book, Gibson (1979) wrote:

> In this book the traditional theories of perception have been abandoned. . . . . Not even the current theory that the inputs of the sensory channels are subject to "cognitive processing" will do. The inputs are described in terms of information theory, but the processes are described in terms of old-fashioned mental acts: recognition, interpretation, concepts, ideas, and storage and retrieval of ideas. These are still the operations of the mind upon the deliverances of the senses, and there are too many perplexities entailed in this theory. It will not do, and the approach should be abandoned.

What sort of theory, then, will explain perception? Nothing less than one based on the pickup of information. . . . My description of the environment [in earlier chapters] and of the changes that can occur in it implies that places, attached objects, and substances are what are mainly perceived, together with events, which are changes of these things. To perceive these things is to perceive what they afford. (1979:238–40)

What is it to perceive what they afford, or, as he calls such properties, "affordances"?

The *affordances* of the environment are what it *offers* the animal, what it *provides* or *furnishes*, either for good or ill. . . . Note that [the properties of being] horizontal, flat, extended, and rigid would be *physical* properties of a surface. . . . Terrestrial surfaces, of course, are also climb-on-able or fall-off-able or get-under-neath-able or bump-into-able relative to an animal. . . . There could be other examples. The different substances of the environment have different affordances for nutrition and manufacture. . . . What other persons afford comprises the whole realm of social significance for human beings. (1979:127–8)

It would appear that *any* property that human beings can discriminate can be regarded as an affordance, and so "perceived" without "recognition, concepts, ideas." But, if we are to have no intermediary processes that explain how a physical system could discriminate all the arbitrarily complex properties humans routinely detect, then we have no explanation of those remarkable abilities. We have only a description of the problem and a rejection of mentalistic solutions (see Fodor and Pylyshyn 1981 for further discussion).

There is a systematic problem here. An organism's sensitivities begin to present difficulties for any purely physicalistic proposal once one considers the detection of *non-local, non-physical properties by local physical agents*. It appears to be a fundamental fact about the kinds of entities that include people and animals that their causal interaction with their environment is entirely *local* and *physical*.[31] For example, in the case of human beings, their ability to detect an indefinite variety of phenomena in their environments is confined to (depending on how you count) six or seven sense modalities, or transducer systems. Now, as animals become more "intelligent," the relation between the input and output becomes increasingly complex, and it becomes increasingly difficult to see how the animal must be constructed so as to to be able to produce that output, given the input. As Gallistel (1990) points out, RBist theories that don't take into account internal processing face difficulties in accounting for the path-alternation behavior we discussed earlier:

The information that one has found and eaten food at a given place may lead to the avoidance of that place in the short run (within a sequence of visits) but the return to that place in the long run (in a new sequence of visits). Models of learning that make intelligible this sort of use of the information provided by experience need to assume that the animal can represent more about the structure of its past experience than is readily represented within the confines of traditional associative theories . . . For example, successful models need to assume that the animal can represent the *temporal structure* of that experience – how long it has been since it last found food at a given place. (1990:164)

Indeed:

[T]he representation of temporal intervals in rats and pigeons appears to be a rich one, in the formal sense of rich. Successful computational models of timing behavior appear to require decision processes that employ operations isomorphic to the addition, subtraction, and division of represented intervals. (1990:586)

But how does an animal keep track of "temporal structure" in a way that enables it to perform these computations and so sensitively modify its behavior? What must its brain be like to do this? For starters, it had better somehow *represent* events as having specific temporal properties, and then somehow *store* those representations for further use in combination with other such representations in ways available for executing the vector algebra of dead reckoning. Understanding mechanisms that could be sensitive in these and other ways is one of the fundamental problems for any psychology, RBist or otherwise.

Moreover, human sensitivities to stimuli are not confined to non-local properties. What the evidence adduced by Chomsky and his followers show is that human beings are sensitive to such properties as [noun phrase], [verb phrase], [trace marker], [possible co-referential anaphor] that are in no plausible sense *physical properties* of the stimuli. The problem with them can be brought out by imagining trying to build a device to detect them. What kind of mechanism could possibly mediate physical stimuli and grammatical output? *Noun phrases patently do not share any transducible property: it would seem nomologically impossible to rig a device to be sensitive to all and only noun phrases in any way other than by "building into" the device the principles of grammar, and, with them, at least representations of the relevant grammatical categories (e.g. noun phrase, verb phrase, sentence complement) over which those principles are defined.* And no one knows yet what one specifically has to "build in" to a device to make it sensitive to any of the plethora of other non-physical properties to which people are obviously sensitive: e.g. timidity, audacity, pomposity; being a picture of a duck; being composed by Beethoven or painted by Braque; being a fall in corporate profits, a Swedish citizen, a proposal of marriage, a declaration of war.[32]

A venerable strategy for dealing with this problem is to show that *every complex property to which an animal is sensitive is a truth-function of locally transducible properties.* Thus, [duck] might be regarded as some truth-function of [fluffy], [feathered], [quacks], etc. Since truth-functions can easily be mirrored by physical devices, it would seem that we could then explain such sensitivities without positing a mind.[33] As a thesis about properties and concepts, this comes to the famous (conceptual) "reductionist" program of classical empiricism.[34] Traditional empiricism took the truth-function to be *conjunction*, what they called "association." "Logical" empiricism (positivism) attempted to deploy the others (disjunction, conditionals), proposing to analyze at least all cognitively meaningful concepts in terms of logically necessary and sufficient conditions for their verification, conditions that were ultimately to be spelled out in terms of (presumably transducible) sensory conditions. There are notorious problems with this strategy, some of which we touched on in §1.5, others of which we will discuss further in §5.4. One basic problem worth mentioning here is that many of the properties/concepts to which we are sensitive seem pretty clearly to *transcend* the sensory evidence we adduce for them: the ordinary concept [duck] is decidedly *not* the concept of anything fluffy, feathered, quacking etc. It's simply not true that "if it quacks like a duck, waddles like a duck, and swims like a duck, it's duck": makers of mechanical toys and decoy ducks aren't, after all, making serious contributions to *zoology*! Ducks, like many other natural kinds, need be *implanted in the world* in the right way: a duck is (to a first approximation) the progeny of ducks and anything that can mate with them, whether or not it has the characteristic look or quack.

It is sometimes thought that Wittgenstein (1953:§66) presented an alternative to empiricist reduction with his famous account of "family resemblance" concepts. We shouldn't, for example, ask for some feature or respect by virtue of which all games are similar to all other games; but rather we should appreciate how games "form a family" of cases with overlapping similarities, no single feature being shared by all. Inspired by Wittgenstein's work, Eleanor Rosch (1973) and her followers have proposed "prototype" theories, according to which membership in a category is determined by "distance from a prototype or exemplar," or share enough of some cluster of features. On this view, for example, robins are "better" birds than are penguins since robins (are believed to) share more prototypical properties of birds than do penguins. However, insofar as such proposals do (often unselfconsciously) restrict the permissible "resemblances" that a system considers, the only modification they make of the traditional empiricist program is that they allow for the truth functions to be numerically *weighted*: nearness of a prototype is still determined by satisfying one or another cluster of transducible properties, but simply to varying *degrees*. (We'll see in §8.8 how radical connectionists' proposals seem also to rely in this way on what might be called "stochastic" empiricist reductions.)

Whether or not concepts possess such prototype or family resemblance structure, it should be noticed that this is not a *solution* to the problem of property detection, but simply another aspect of it. Indeed, it's an aspect that makes the problem even harder to solve, since "family resemblances," like the RBists notions of "stimulus generalization" by "similarity," *can go off in any direction*: *anything* bears a "family resemblance" to a game; but obviously not anything actually counts as one. The question has to be faced: why do normal English speakers ordinarily proceed to include parchesi, solitaire, and psychological interactions, and not, e.g. ducks, photosynthesis, or sub-atomic reactions.

It's not impossible that some sort of empiricist reduction strategies might ultimately work for many properties. But the failures of the past ought to give us pause. Philosophers since Hobbes and Locke have pursued empiricist reduction programs for several hundred years without appreciable success. We'll see at the end of the next chapter (§5.4) that there seems to be good reason for their failure: their chief inspiration, a "verificationist" theory of meaning, is independently problematic. In any case, it is one thing to imagine that such reductions are somehow possible, quite another to provide ones, and to specify mechanical devices that could mirror them and that would actually work for the staggering set of properties to which humans are sensitive. This in a way is the problem Descartes was noticing when, in the quotation we cited early on (§1.1.1), he expressed scepticism that any machine could be made so versatile as to be able to respond to the wide variety of circumstances with which humans are typically presented. He was probably right about the need in this regard for *a mind* – what we hope to show, of course, is that it doesn't follow that we need a special non-physical *substance* to satisfy that need.

4.4 The Need for Mind

"But what good would a mind do?" it might well be asked. That's a terrifically good question, and one that an eliminativist might rightly charge traditional mentalists with not having sufficiently addressed. The traditional mentalist claims, roughly, that people have "ideas" or "representations" (the latter term has come to replace the former) and an "ability to reason" whereby, on the basis of perception, they confirm or disconfirm the application of those representations to reality and alter their behavior to satisfy their needs and desires. Thus, to take some of the examples of the previous sections, it is because we have fairly elaborate representations of grammatical structure that we can understand sentences with multiply embedded logical structures. It is because our minds in some way realize principles for combining those representations in systematic ways, increasingly complex representations being constructible from simpler ones, that we exhibit "productivity" and "creativity" in our thought. It is because we have ideas/representations about space, time, and causality, psychology, and social life that we can detect an indefinite range of non-local properties, e.g. regarding long-dead dinosaurs, distant stars, declines in profits, and declarations of war; and it is because of the ways in which we can rationally combine these representations of the world with representations of what we want that, reasoning practically, we can figure out ways to satisfy those wants. But what is an *idea* or *representation*, and what is *reason*, that they enable us to do such things? How on earth is this supposed to work? Appeals to ideas without mechanisms can seem too easy, nearly vacuous.

Some of the air of vacuity can begin to be dispelled by noticing the enormously complex explanatory network in which these appeals to ideas are made. Think of the intricate tangle of such claims that comprise the ordinary "folk psychology" that we deploy with sometimes considerable subtlety in explaining and predicting the behavior of friends, enemies, shopkeepers, politicians, historical figures, or just other drivers on the road.[35] Lest all this "behavior" be regarded as involving question-begging "action" descriptions ("saying things," "retaliating," "driving to one's destination"), note that such folk psychology is the only explanation we know of that stands the remotest chance of explaining and predicting the Standardized Regularities: why are there the commonalities in graphite patterns across the millions of the SAT answer sheets? Well, the subjects of the tests *saw* and *understood* the instructions on the question sheet, *representing* the sentences in certain ways and not others; *preferred* to get as much money as they could; *believed* that the more correct answers they provided the more money they'd get; *reasoned* logically, arithmetically, and even *fell for* common fallacies; and, as a result of all these processes, they *deliberately filled* in the same boxes on the answer sheet. This is a pretty rich explanation, one that, note, provides us with an enormous amount of predictive control over the results (e.g. suggesting myriad places to interfere in the process and obtain different results).

But, if we are to take this explanation seriously, we still need to ask (1) what *seeing, understanding, preferring, believing, representing* are that they could have this explanatory force, and (2) how could such phenomena result in physical events such as the moving of a hand and the filling in of a graphite square? Particularly given the lack of a causal break in the usual physical explanation that we discussed in §3.1.1, what's the relation between these and the usual physical phenomena? That is, we need to answer the questions that are the subject matter of this book. We will now look at some traditional answers to these questions. In the next chapter we will consider various proposals that have been made about how to address the first question. Settling on one, we will then turn to a recent answer to the second (chapters 6 and 7).

I should emphasize from the start, however, that it is by no means clear precisely what final shape the correct mentalistic explanation of the phenomena we have considered might take, or that there is *one* form that would have to be deployed in all the cases that we have considered. I think it would be absolutely amazing – really, *almost* inconceivable – if something very like the above folk psychological explanation of the Standardized Regularities wasn't largely correct (What are we being asked to believe? That the subjects didn't *read* the questions? That they didn't *want* to make any money? That they didn't *know* how to add 2 and 2? That none of these things had anything to do with the ways they moved their hands?). But nothing that's been said so far establishes that a similar sort of explanation is *equally* plausible about the various behaviors of rats running a maze, desert ants navigating by dead reckoning, buntings learning the layout of the night sky, chimpanzees attaching poles to obtain food, or even children acquiring their native language.[36] A persistent controversy that is by no means yet settled concerns precisely what representations are necessary for understanding language. It seems fairly clear from the evidence we've considered that some sort of representation of *the grammatical structure* of a sentence is needed in order to account for people's sensitivity to it. But need people actually represent the *rules* of grammar themselves? It may be enough merely that they process internal representations *in accordance with the rules*, without representing them?[37] If so, perhaps their knowledge of grammar is more a matter of "knowing how" to do something, than "knowing that" such and such is the case (cf. Devitt and Sterelny 1987).

In any case, pending a clearer understanding of mental states, there is no particular reason to leap to the postulation of *beliefs*, or *reason*, or *understanding*, per se, in all these cases. The most that *these* phenomena suggest is that RBism is inadequate and that *some* sort of postulation of internal computations on representations is required. Whether all such postulations amount to postulations of full blown mental states awaits a clearer understanding of the nature of mental states, which is the subject of the next three chapters.

Notes

1 There is ample room for confusion on this point however, since often ABists represent themselves as denying the existence of mental things – "the ghost in the machine" – that they take dualists to be positing. Briefly, the situation is a little like that of an "atheist" who might either "eliminate" God by simply saying, "He doesn't exist," or, alternatively, might "reduce" Him by identifying "Him" with, say, certain feelings religious people have. Disputes between eliminativists and reductionists often can have this somewhat equivocal quality (see Quine (1960:265–6) and Rorty (1965) for discussion).

2 The original statement of the law occurs in Thorndike (1911). Skinner (1938:21–32) revised and refined it in many ways irrelevant to purposes here. An excellent recent discussion can be found in Gleitman (1986:102–33).

3 Some terminology: the responses that are selected in this way Skinner (1938) called "operants," since they involved ways that an animal "operated" on an environment that secured reinforcement. This process of "operant conditioning" was Skinner's distinctive contribution over "classical conditioning," where the response was *elicited* (e.g. salivation by hunger in Pavlov's dogs), rather than being spontaneously *emitted*. This is crucial here for the RBist account of the range of intelligent responses, just as it is in evolutionary theory to account for the range of adaptive traits, without relying

on the presence of an already existing intelligence (or designer). Skinner also sometimes calls his approach "functional analysis": this should not be confused with the altogether different "functionalist" approach to the mind to be discussed below.

4 Much of the content of my discussion is gleaned from rich discussions of the vast experimental literature in Munn (1950), Taylor (1964), Gleitman (1986), and, especially, Gallistel (1990). Where possible, I cite the original experiment, indicating the text source as "M:," "T:," "Gn:," or "Gl:" respectively. I make no pretence of beginning to do justice in this short space to the complex discussions of such experiments that took place over some sixty years. I only want to indicate some of the main problems, especially as they bear on eliminativism (which was by no means always – indeed, over time ceased to be – a leading concern of all the experimenters).

5 He is echoing here earlier proposals of Tolman (1948).

6 Which is not to say that many of the particular claims of these figures have not held up: many of Galileo's observations, and an impressive number of Darwin's, still stand.

7 As well as suggestions of earlier linguists such as Jesperson (1924) and Harris (1951), and formal techniques derived from modern symbolic logic.

8 It is impossible to provide the reader with anything but a taste of the philosophically relevant points here. To begin to do justice to the Chomsky revolution generally, the reader should consult Steven Pinker's (1994) superb introduction to it (one of the very few popular books on a technical topic that doesn't seriously compromise its material). Chomsky, himself, has made some non-technical presentations of his main conclusions (see especially 1968, 1980, 1988), but they are often highly polemical, requiring some familiarity with his opponent's views. Lightfoot (1982), Radford (1988), and Haegeman (1994) offer useful introductions to the technical work.

9 This is no trifling problem: see Kant's (1781/1968:B142) attempt to distinguish "judgments" from associations, as well as Russell's (1904/1938:§54) struggle to distinguish a sentence from a list. We'll return to this issue in §8.8 below.

10 Or "Markov machine," as such devices are generally called. The general argument here is set forth in Chomsky (1957).

11 Of course, to make this (logical truth!) intelligible, it helps to indicate the grouping not indicated in ordinary speech or writing: If (if (if (time is not money) then (time is money)) then (time is money), then (if (time is money) then time is money)). A less philosophical example of multiple embeddings (in this case of bifurcated verbs with prepositions) is provided by Pinker (1994:97): "Daddy trudges upstairs to Junior's bedroom to read him a bedtime story. Junior spots the book, scowls, and asks, Daddy, what did you bring that book that I don't want to be read to out of up for?

12 Which is how linguists are prone to put it (see e.g. Lasnik 1989). Of course, any philosopher might be quick to object, "but suppose the speaker didn't *know* that John was in fact the very same person to which she was referring by "he." Fine: the claim is that a normal English speaker knows that you aren't normally supposed to utter (9c) or (9d) knowing that he = John. The "he" is somehow "marked" for non-identity for nouns in further subordinate clauses.

13 See Chomsky (1995b:71) for a more recent, and more technical statement of the constraint.

14 Similar anecdotes are reported in Lightfoot (1982).

15 I leave open the option of "whom" which is dying out in many dialects of English. Incidentally, not all English speakers (e.g. Australians) report being averse to (10d). Note, however, that all that is needed for the point here is *some* decided reluctance among *some* of us to it.

16 Kluender and Kutas (1993), Neville *et al*. (1991) all cited in Pinker (1994:309, 441).

17 Skinner (1950) actually claims at one point that *theory* in general is not an appropriate goal of psychology; that should be confined instead merely to the prediction and manipulation of behavior.

18 We'll return to the topic in discussing the role of idealization in psychology in §10.3.

19 This nice example is due to Ziff (1967/1971), who uses it to demonstrate the arbitrary disparity that can exist between the meaning of a sentence and the intentions with which it may be uttered.

20 Hint: "police" is both a noun and a verb, and English permits "that" to be deleted before subordinate clauses: so (13) could be a version of "Police (that police police) police. . . ." Still harder cases can be produced by considering internal nestings of relative clauses: "police (that) police (that) police police police police police (that) police (that) police police police." It is presumably still another language independent feature of human information processing that we find such internal nestings so difficult.

21 There are obviously other constraints on performance besides mortality: interest, attention, size, and structure of short-term memory. Precisely which things to count as part of grammatical competence and which as interfering performance constraints is a question part and parcel of a complete theory of the mind.

22 For those who nevertheless demur from believing in "infinite capacities," Fodor (1987:149ff) notes a cousin property, "systematicity," which here might be expressed thus: a person understands a sentence p iff she can understand any permissible grammatical permutation of p (for example, someone understands "Romeo loves Juliet or Gladys" iff she understands, e.g. "Gladys loves Juliet or Romeo" and "Juliet loves Romeo or Gladys)." We'll discuss this property as a property of thought in §8.8 below.

23 Not that, apart from use by human beings, there is anything the least bit "natural" about human languages. Indeed, as linguists can show, they are actually quite peculiar and inefficient in a surprising number of ways (why shouldn't we allow "wanna" in (10d)? We would all know precisely what is meant). They seem simply to be natural *for us* (or anyway for kids).

24 For further dramatic evidence of poverty and corruption of stimulus arguments, see Pinker's (1994:271–3) discussion of Stromswold's (1990) analysis of speech errors in pre-schoolers.

25 Which, again, is not to say that "is green" is in any way "natural" apart from our predilections. Indeed, the physics of color perception suggests it isn't.

26 I leave aside his quite unrelated (but also quite impressive) writings on politics and American foreign policy.

27 See Wynn 1992b (and, indeed, the other contributors to *Mind and Language* 7(4)/ 1992) for further discussion.

28   Consider another problem: why don't children think that "duck" refers to the *pictures* of ducks by means of which the term is usually introduced? Evidently, they have some grasp of the concept of *representation*. Given the notorious problems of providing an analysis of intentional notions, it would appear that at least *that* concept must be innate. For more on this and related topics see the anthology of Whiten (1991), and Mehler and Dupoux (1994) for a recent review of infant cognition generally.

29   The traditional problem with this claim is how to account for the tremendous amount of knowledge gained about the world through mathematics, knowledge of which does not seem to be justified by experience. Chomsky in this respect plays Kant to Skinner's Hume, although note that none of Chomsky's arguments actually bear on any issues of any sort of *knowledge, a priori*, innate or otherwise; something like mere *belief* (or, as Chomsky himself sometimes puts it, "cognizing") would suffice.

30   To a limited extent Quine (1973:16) can be regarded as addressing this problem. Noticing the divergence between "perceptual" and "receptual" similarity, he proposes defining the former in terms of the latter via the Law of Effect. This will work, however, only so long as he can rely on a physical description of the relevant classes of responses and reinforcements, which, as we have seen, there is no reason to think are any better off than are the relevant classes of stimuli.

31   I suspect this fact is not accidental, but a consequence of the kind of causal universe we inhabit, i.e. one of local causal interaction. Support for this speculation – entering the difficult debate regarding action at a distance – is fortunately just a little outside the scope of present ambitions.

32   Fodor (1986b) tried to make a similar point by appealing to the notion of a "non-projectible property," presumably like "grue" (see 4.2.4 above), arguing that only a creature with a mind would detect it. But this won't suffice. Simply connect a timer to some detectors of blue and green frequencies and you've got yourself a mind-less grue-detector. I'm indebted to Fodor nonetheless for raising the issue.

33   For example, "and" can be mirrored by an "and-gate," or a device that emits a signal iff it receives two signals; "not" by a "not-gate" which emits a signal iff it receives no signal (since all truth-functions can be constructed from these two, a physical device could be constructed to mirror any truth-function).

34   I oversimplify somewhat: Logical Positivists availed themselves of quantifiers and even modal operators, but often without fully realizing the complexities they introduce. Also, neither the empiricists nor the positivists probably thought in terms of transducible properties, although transducibilty might be a good answer to the otherwise puzzling question about just which "sensory" properties were basic and why.

35   Dennett once pointed out how indispensable "folk psychology" is to driving, and how (more) terrified one might be of driving on city streets if one wasn't confident there were psychologically normal human beings behind the wheels.

36   For example, the explanatory sketch Pinker (1994:317–22) provides of the operation of a language module doesn't obviously involve serious mentalism: a network of simple "and" and "not" gates might suffice (cf. n 33).

37   The actual role of "rules," as opposed to "principles and parameters" as an explanation of grammatical competence varies in the development of generative grammars; see, for

example, Chomsky (1995:24–5). Note, however, that, although principles and parameters may require less in the way of representation of any rules themselves, they do not in the least diminish the role of structural representations of the sentences of the natural language themselves.

5

Mentalism: Pre-Functionalist Approaches

With a general idea of some of the important explanatory work mental terms and concepts are supposed to play, we shall now consider plausible strategies for analyzing them, along the general lines for analyzing explanatory terms sketched in §1.5.2 above.

The two main traditional approaches to the analysis of mental terms and concepts have been *introspective* and *behavioral*. The introspective approach will be discussed in §5.1. It suffers from several problems, notably the "problem of application" (§5.1.1) and the "problem of other minds" (§5.1.2). These led a number of philosophers to propose abandoning what they regarded as an excessively "referential" conception of the semantics of mental terms (§5.1.2), endorsing a view I call "irreferentialism" (§5.2). Recalling the distinctions between kinds of mental phenomena we surveyed earlier (§1.1), this view can be applied with different degrees of plausibility to singular sensation terms (§5.2.1), sensation predicates (§5.2.2), propositional attitude terms (§5.2.3), and propositional content expressions (§5.2.4).

Whatever the merits of these different applications, irreferentialism is a *negative* doctrine. What do irreferentialists recommend as a *positive* view? Here, approaches notoriously diverge, but by far the most influential positive proposal was *analytical behaviorism* ("ABism," §5.3). This form of behaviorism needs to be sharply distinguished from the *Radical Behaviorism* ("RBism") discussed in the last chapter. This latter doctrine, recall, was a specific scientific proposal about the explanation of human and animal behavior. ABism is not that kind of explanatory hypothesis. Rather, it's a claim about the *semantics*, or *meaning*, or *analysis* of mental terms (ABists did not usually distinguish between these latter options). Strictly speaking, an RBist needn't care about ABism any more than a physicist need care about the analysis of religious language; and, conversely, an ABist, like some theists, could remain entirely agnostic about the correct scientific account of behavior. But that didn't prevent some authors, e.g. Skinner (1953), from endorsing both views.

ABism, itself, met with a number of problems that occasioned a re-casting of its main idea into what has come to be called, broadly speaking, "functionalist" proposals. Although initially these seemed only a technical modification of ABism, they turn out to have resources that allow us to go well beyond both ABism and many other traditional proposals, in ways that we'll consider at length in chapter 6.

5.1   Introspectivism

Probably the suggestion that leaps first to most people's minds in trying to analyze a mental term or concept is that its meaning is provided by the introspectible mental item to which it refers. Such a view would seem to be lurking in Locke when he writes:

> The other fountain from which experience furnisheth the understanding with *ideas* is the *perception of the operations of our own minds* within us, as it is employed about the ideas it has got; which operations, when the soul comes to reflect on and consider, do furnish the understanding with another set of *ideas*, which could not be had from things without. And such are *perception, thinking, doubting, believing, reasoning, knowing, willing, and all the different actings of our own minds*.   (1690/1977:II§4; see also §7–8)

To know what it is to perceive, think, doubt, or believe it is enough to "look inside" and acquaint oneself with these mental processes directly.[1] Although few philosophers today would subscribe to the view so expressed (Locke's diverse uses of his "idea" idea are legend), there lingers in the works of many philosophers a conviction that something essential about mental concepts is to be had from first-person acquaintance. Perhaps most prominently, John Searle writes:

> Because mental phenomena are essentially connected with consciousness, and because consciousness is essentially subjective, it follows that the ontology of the mental is essentially a first-person ontology. . . . [T]he first person point of view is primary. . . . [W]hat we are trying to get at when we study other people is precisely the first-person point of view.   (1992:20)

And, in considering various philosophical proposals, he constantly admonishes his readers to "remember to take the first-person point of view."[2]

There are a good number of problems raised by introspectivist proposals. In the first place, as a number of writers (e.g. Harman 1990, Dretske 1995) have stressed, a great deal of what passes for introspection of one's "inner" experience consists of reports about how the *outer* world seems: we don't so much report on the features of the "inner movie" as upon what that movie *represents* (e.g. that *barns* seem red, *the sky* a dome). Painters have to work hard to distinguish their judgments about the *actual* color of a red barn at sunset – it's *red*, of course! – from the colors that it *appears* to have in the waning light.

When we do bring ourselves to focus upon what seem to be features of our inner experience itself, then, aside from easy cases of gross sensory and emotional reports ("I'm having an orange after-image, and feel terrible"), introspection can be a pretty tricky business. Speaking for myself, when I try it at all carefully, I'm overwhelmed by a complex mosaic of (as I'm inclined to say) thoughts, judgments, fantasies, longings, feelings, sensations, twinges, vague impressions, ineffable qualities, rapidly telescoping thoughts about thoughts about . . . thoughts about all these things, and a gnawing sense that I'm still leaving a lot out (for one thing, it all goes by so quickly). Learning to think clearly about what would even *count* as a single element in that mosaic, much less learning to distinguish introspectively between one such element and another, is a pretty daunting business. Continuing with the exercise of the painter: how do I tell when I've really distinguished the *apparent* colors something has from what I *believe* are the colors that things of that sort standardly appear to have (say, at dusk)? How do I distinguish my actual sensations from my imaginings of them (are the latter "just fainter" as Hume maintained? Is a vivid imagining a sensation?)? Is an *imagined image* of a tiger really very like *seeing a tiger*? Imagine one: then ask how many stripes it has; *remember* a tiger you've seen; can you do any better? Do you introspect a determinate answer in either case – or even a judgment that it is indeterminate? What is it like to introspect a judgment? Sensations don't seem to accompany knowing where your feet are, or afford a way of distinguishing the thought that 3 and 3 are 6, from the thought that 5 and 5 are 10. Are feelings like happiness and grief just certain sorts of sensation? Could the pleasure of listening to a Bach fugue be produced merely by eating parsley? Is the cheerfulness of cheerful thoughts part of the thought, or something separate?[3] How are we even to tell when we are answering these questions correctly? Perhaps they are correct whenever they seem correct, so that contrary ones could be correct at different times. But then how do I settle the uncertainties I've just expressed? – or, on such occasions as this, do I simply have an indeterminate mental life? But then how am I supposed to access my mental life as it really is? What on earth are we talking about? However one may be inclined to answer these questions, the actual results of (broadly speaking) introspectivist disciplines – such as Wundtian psychology and Husserlian phenomenology[4] – have seemed mixed at best: neither have seemed reliable or fruitful ways of getting a clear idea of psychological realities, much less the meanings of mental terms.

Two problems with introspection bear special mention, if only to see how introspective results, no matter how refined, would probably not provide us generally with the analysis of mental terms and concepts that we are seeking.

5.1.1   The problem of application

A central theme running throughout the work of Ryle (1949) and the later Wittgenstein (1953, 1967, 1980-I, 1980-II) is that the deliverances of introspection are neither necessary nor sufficient for the application of most mental concepts. Wittgenstein's discussion is particularly compelling in this regard, since it is based not upon a scientistic disdain for introspection, but actually upon an often exquisite sensitivity to it, and to the nuances of mental talk.[5]

We've already touched upon one of Wittgenstein's worries in this regard in considering (§3.1.2) the "Kripkenstein" problem of distinguishing someone *adding* from someone *quadding*,[6] i.e. whether someone is following the rule:

(R1)   For every pair of numbers you're presented, provide the *sum* of those numbers;

or the rule:

(R2)   For every pair of numbers you're presented, provide the *sum* of these numbers, unless you're presented 68 and 57, in which case provide 5.

Now, as we saw, *Kripkenstein* thinks no purely *descriptive* account of what a person does can settle the issue: we need to appeal to some normative consideration. *Wittgenstein's* own attack is, arguably, only against an introspectivist solution, and is worth pursuing here a little further.[7]

Introspection doesn't seem adequate to settle the question, since rules (R1) and (R2) apply to an infinity of cases that obviously can't be surveyed introspectively. As Wittgenstein mocks the introspectivist:

> Your idea was that that act of meaning the order had in its own way already traversed all those steps: that, when you meant it, your mind as it were flew ahead and took all the steps before you physically arrived at this or that one.   (1953:§188)

But perhaps some other sort of introspectible event could help? One of the important themes running through much of Wittgenstein's later work is his insight that no such event would suffice, that *any kind of symbolic state always stands in need of an interpretation*. Thus, many might think a mental image might help: but for any image there will always be the issue of how the image is to be *applied*, or *projected* onto reality:

> Suppose that a picture does come before your mind when you hear the word "cube", say, the drawing of a cube. In what sense can this picture fit or fail to fit a use of the

138

word "cube"? – Perhaps you say: "It's quite simple; – if that picture occurs to me and I point to a triangular prism for instance, and say it is a cube, then this use of the word doesn't fit the picture." – But doesn't it fit? I have purposely so chosen the example that it is quite easy to imagine a *method of projection* according to which the picture does fit after all. . . .

I see a picture; it represents an old man walking up a steep path leaning on a stick. – How? Might it not have looked just the same had be been sliding downhill in the position? (1953:§139)

Perhaps intending one rule rather than another is just some idiosyncratic feeling, or *quale*? No, insists Wittgenstein, meaning is not any sort of purely *internal* event:

If God had looked into our minds he would not have been able to see there whom we were speaking of. . . . Meaning it is not a process which accompanies a word. For no *process* could have the consequences of meaning. (1953:217–18)

A little more mundanely, Kripkenstein writes:

Why not argue that "meaning addition by 'plus'" denotes an irreducible experience, with its own special *quale*, known directly to each of us by introspection?. . . . Well, suppose I do in fact feel a certain headache with a very special quality whenever I think of the "+" sign. How on earth would this headache help me figure out whether I ought to answer "125" or "5" when asked about "68+57"?. . . . The idea that each of my inner states – including, presumably, meaning what I do by "plus" – has its special discernible quality like a headache or tickle . . . is indeed one of the corner-stones of classical empiricism. Cornerstone it may be, but it is very hard to see how the alleged introspectible *quale* could be relevant to the problem at hand. (1982:41–2)

Indeed, two people might happen to have the same feeling with regard to following different rules; and they might have different feelings with regard to following the same rule (think of how some mathematicians "think spatially," others "algebraically").[8]

Perhaps we know what rule we're following somehow "directly," and not on the basis of any feeling or sensation. In terms of a metaphor that recurs in the history of philosophy, we might just "grasp" the rule, in the way that Platonists sometimes think that we just "grasp" numbers, concepts, and other universals. Quite apart from the somewhat mystical air of such a suggestion (it seems to many of its critics just short of appeals to revelation), this seems merely to give the question another name: the question can as well be asked, what makes it true that a person *grasps* one rule or meaning rather than another?

5.1.2   *The problem of other minds*

There is a potentially more serious problem with introspectivism: recalling the problem of "privacy" discussed in §2.5.4, if the meaning of mental terms is exhausted by their reference to introspectible objects like ideas and sensations, how do we know that anybody else in the world has them? Or that they have the same ones? Maybe you see green where I see red, you feel elated where I feel depressed, you have beliefs where I have desires (remember, we're supposing it's the introspectible feeling alone that exhausts the concepts; we're not also insisting that they be grounded in some physical property). Insofar as there seems to be at least no straightforward way of settling such matters, leaving the meanings of our mental (and many other) words to the items of introspection would seem to leave our mental talk a shambles. How could we communicate or begin to discuss any of these issues in a public language?[9]

Such worries are, of course, very like the skeptical worries that have haunted philosophy from early on: worries about whether all our experience is a dream, or the effect of some demon or scientist manipulating our brains. In an exasperated effort to banish such worries, and to provide a theory of meaning that would make science in general possible, the Logical Positivists of the 1920s developed a general *verifiability theory of meaning*, according to which the meaning of a claim is constituted by the conditions that could be marshalled to verify (and/or falsify) it. Hypotheses like that of the possibility of our lives being a dream, or other people having unknowably different mental lives were to be ruled out as "meaningless" if there really were in fact no evidence in principle that could make a difference to their truth or falsity. (For readers unacquainted with this theory, I provide a brief discussion of it and its main problems in §5.4 at the end of this chapter.) Thus they developed "phenomenalist" analyses of our claims about the external world whereby claims about external material objects were logically complex claims about sense experience; and "(Analytical) Behaviorist" ("ABist") analyses of our claims about the mind, according to which claims about minds were logically complex claims about people's dispositions to observable behavior.[10]

Although Wittgenstein was initially drawn to quite extreme verificationist proposals,[11] he, and then also Gilbert Ryle (1949), developed what might be regarded as an intermediate proposal about mental terms that I shall call "irreferentialism." Although it can pave the way for analytical behaviorism – it is essentially one way of inscribing the negative side of the same coin – it is quite independent of it, and deserves discussion in its own right.

5.2   Irreferentialism

Irreferentialism is the view that mental terms don't *refer*, but serve some other linguistic function. It is partly motivated by the rule-following issue, where introspectible items simply fail to do the work we're inclined to ask of them. Indeed, a novel suggestion that emerges from both the work of Wittgenstein (1953) and Ryle (1949)[12] is the idea that the traditional philosophical problems about the mind arise from certain misconceptions about the general nature of our "inner lives." Especially when we start doing philosophy, we tend to think about the phenomena that we introspect in our "inner mental worlds" too much on the model of the objects in the familiar "outer" one:

> something that we see and the other does not . . . something that exists within us and which we become aware of by looking into ourselves. And now psychology is the theory of this inner thing.   (Wittgenstein 1980-I:§692)

They thought that the temptation to this analogy arose, in part, from an excessively referential conception of the functioning of our mental vocabulary: we think that words like "belief," "thought," "sensation" refer to "inner," "private" objects, in the way that words like "cat" and "rock" refer to outer, public ones ("we have a substantive and think that something must correspond to it"; Wittgenstein 1958:1). We have already considered Wittgenstein's skepticism about introspectible objects serving as a basis for rule following. More generally, both he and Ryle thought they could avoid a great many traditional philosophical problems about the mind by resisting the temptation to suppose that mental terms function to refer to anything at all (at any rate, in anything like the way "cat" refers to cats). It's not, as the eliminativist would have it, that they don't *happen* to refer to anything; they don't even *purport* to refer to anything. This is the claim of Irreferentialism.[13]

This view is perhaps best known from Ryle's (1949:p. 15ff) attack on the idea of the "ghost in the machine," which he believes arose out of a failure to appreciate the non-referential functions of mental terms: a mind is not some sort of *thing* that *could* be a ghost; rather all mental talk should really be understood as talk about dispositions to behave in certain ways, which is what leads him (although not Wittgenstein) to the ABism that we will discuss in §5.3. For Wittgenstein, irreferentialism is a piece of his approach to semantics generally, captured in his famous slogan, "the meaning of a word is its use in the language" (1953:§43). Throughout the *Philosophical Investigations* he tries to show that the meanings of philosophically troublesome words are to be understood not by trying to understand what they *refer* to, but by examining the role the words play in various "language games" and "forms of life" in which people ordinarily participate. Once we appreciate the facts of ordinary use, philosophical problems should cease to arise. Thus, in a much quoted example, he writes:

> How does the philosophical problem about mental processes and states arise? – The first step is the one that altogether escapes notice. We talk of processes and states and leave their nature undecided. Sometimes perhaps we shall know more about them –

141

we think. But that is just what commits us to a particular way of looking at the matter. For we have a definite concept of what it means to know a process better. (The decisive move in the conjuring trick has been made, and it was the very one that we thought quite innocent.) – And now the analogy which was to make us understand our thoughts falls to pieces. So we have to deny the yet uncomprehended process in the yet unexplored medium. And now it looks as if we had denied mental processes. And naturally we don't want to deny them. (1953:§308; see also §571 and 1980-I:§292)

It is this irreferentialism that is of a piece with the antipathy we noted early on (introduction §2) that Ryle, Wittgenstein, and many of their followers feel towards a scientific psychology, particularly any one that suggests a "promise of hidden discoveries yet to be made of the hidden causes of our actions and reactions" (Ryle 1949:325).

Some irreferential suggestions are fairly truistic. Certainly many terms in language have meaning other than by functioning to refer to anything: logical particles ("or," "not"), quantifiers ("all," "some"), grammatical symbols (commas and questions marks), provide obvious examples. But even noun phrases may play some other role. "The average American family" does not merely fail to refer to a real family; it doesn't even *purport* to, which is why sentences like "The average American family has 3.2 children" can be true without there being any family with only a fifth of a child.

Quine's definition of a predicate that we provided early on (§1.1.1) affords a convenient way of dealing with the issue here: we replace only those portions of a sentence by variables that we need to license inferences to quantificational claims like "there exists an x such that . . . x . . .". Here Quine's advice is: "where it doesn't itch, don't scratch" (1960:160), a variant of Occam's razor, "Don't multiply entities beyond necessity." In particular, don't make a portion of a sentence accessible to quantification if you could get by without it. In keeping with our insistence on the primacy of explanation, those portions of the sentences of our theories we should make available to quantification depends in the end upon what *explanatory role* the resulting predicates and the objects in their extensions need to play.[14] If we think about the inferences we want to draw about the children of the average family, we obviously want to resort to a predicate like "$x = y/z$," where the values of "y" and "z" will be the number of children and families and x will then be the ratio between them.

Other examples are subtler, and a little harder to establish. Consider rainbows. It can seem natural enough to think of rainbows as things existing in the world independently of us, some of them seen by many different people at once. But is there really ever a single rainbow we all see, say, looking west on a rainy day? Think of the actual physics of a rainbow: it's the refraction of light through raindrops, a slightly different angle of refraction for different wave lengths of light. Do any of us ever see exactly the same refraction? Well, any two of us usually stand in significantly different angles to the drops, and so see light refracted from not only different drops, but slightly different regions of the sky. Perhaps with a good deal of complicated logical construction one could find some peculiar physical entity that is *the rainbow* we all (say, a whole city of people) see when we marvel at a particularly vivid one, but this would seem pretty artificial. And it would seem worse than artificial to insist that there really *are* such objects as rainbows, but they aren't *physical* objects, embracing some extravagant "dualism" (or perhaps "n-alism"?) about them. All this is needless metaphysics. Better simply to treat "rainbow" as a non-referential bit of language: "We all saw a marvelous rainbow in the sky tonight" can be true without there actually existing an x such that x is a marvelous rainbow and for each of us, $y_1, y_2, \ldots, y_n, y_1$ saw x and y_2 saw x, $\ldots$, y_n saw x. Better to talk just about how things *look* to a typical observer looking in a certain direction on a rainy day, and not indulge in gratuitous metaphysics (cf. Dennett 1969:9).

One might wonder what the difference is between *irreferentialism* about some term and *eliminativism* about whatever the term could be taken to describe: don't they really amount to the same thing? Very nearly; and many of the arguments raised for or against one position could equally well be taken to be arguments for or against the other. However, an interesting difference between them is that, unlike the eliminativist, *the irreferentialist avoids denying hosts of ordinary assertions that, but for the puzzles produced on philosophical reflection, seem entirely unproblematic.* Take the innocuous case of "rainbows." The eliminativist, construing "rainbow" as referential, has to deny such commonplaces as "Rainbows are coloured," on pain of the sort of Leibniz Law difficulties discussed above. But the irreferentialist has no such need. Since he doesn't think "rainbow" even *purports* to refer to anything at all, those difficulties can't arise: if there's no reference, there's no genuine *cross-reference* to worry about, much less any co-referential terms to substitute. The irreferentialist has no need to deny that rainbows are coloured, any more than he need deny, for fear of a fractional child, that the average American family has 1.2 of them. As Wittgenstein put it in an otherwise paradoxical passage with regard to pain: it "is not a *something*, but not a *nothing* either!. . . . If I speak of a fiction, then it is of a *grammatical* fiction" (1953:§294– 307). Construing philosophically troublesome entities as "grammatical fictions" was one among many ways in which he thought "philosophy . . . leaves everything as it is" (1953:§124). At least it needn't disrupt our ordinary claims about rainbows, or, returning to the case that most concerned him, about mental processes ("and naturally," he concludes in the above quote, "we don't want to deny them").[15]

Irreferentialism about mental terms is defensible to different degrees, depending largely on which of the major categories of mental phenomena (§1.1) is being considered. It has been specifically defended with regard to phenomenal objects and properties, propositional attitudes, and propositional contents. The explanatory demands being different in each case, they need to be discussed separately. Of course, since we haven't even begun even to sketch a plausible psychological theory, we are in no position to appreciate anything like the full explanatory demands of a serious psychology. But we can note cases in which irreferentialism seems an interesting option.

§5.2.1 *Phenomenal singular terms and their objects*

With regard to mental talk, irreferentialism is most plausible with respect to what I have called "singular sensation terms": the terms that at least superficially appear to refer to "phenomenal objects" such as pains, tickles, tingles, after-images, and visual and auditory images conjured up in one's imagination. One simple suggestion, mentioned in passing in Smart (1962/1991, see also Nagel 1965/1971:section 2), is to claim that, when we speak of such things, what we are really doing is merely *classifying* our *experiences* in a certain way. The *experience* of a green after-image is real enough; but that can be true without there existing, somehow in addition to that experience, *the green after-image* itself, some sort of special green patch mysteriously inlaid in your head (and even more mysteriously invisible to everyone but the haver of it!). Sometimes, after all, the particle "of" doesn't link genuinely referential expressions: something can be a picture of a unicorn without there actually existing any unicorn it is a picture of; something can be the story of Santa Claus without there being any Santa Claus it is a story of. The "of" here, and the noun phrase that follows it, are merely a way of *classifying* the picture or story, in particular in terms merely of the "meaning," what is sometimes called the *intentional content* of the noun phrase ("what it's about"), whether or not that content happens actually to succeed in referring to something in the real world ("picture of" and "story of" are, in the terms of §2.5.6, "referentially opaque"). Such intentional, or "classificatory" uses of "of" might be less misleadingly (if more awkwardly) expressed using a paraphrase suggested by Nelson Goodman (1968:§5), which, instead of speaking of "pictures or stories of x," speaks of "φ-pictures" ("unicorn-pictures" or "(Santa Claus coming down the chimney)-stories").[16] So the irreferentialist suggestion can be taken to be that we should understand "experiences of after-images" and "experiences of pains" as "after-image experiences" and "pain experiences."[17] (We'll return to this suggestion in §11.6 below.)

This is not say that all uses of "of" ought to be treated this way. Some uses seem not merely (if at all) classificatory, but genuinely relational, as in "a *photograph* of a horse." Presumably, a photograph couldn't be a genuine photograph of a horse unless *an actual horse* had stood in a certain causal relation to its production (it's for this reason that you can't have a genuine photo of a unicorn). But note that the relational and classificatory "of"s can pull here in different directions: a photograph (causally) of Bill Clinton taken from a mile off (in which he appears as a

144

speck) might bear so few of his characteristic features so as not to be classified as a Clinton photograph.

So why should we take the "of" of "experience of . . ." as merely classificatory? Recalling Quine's admonition to scratch only where it itches, the burden would seem to be on the *referentialist* to say why we should construe it otherwise. We need to ask: what *explanatory work might after-images themselves perform apart from after-image experiences, or pains apart from pain experiences?*

It might be thought that what we introspect requires positing after-images as objects. After all, how are we to account for the sometimes extremely vivid images many of us seem to experience? It does seem very hard to deny that *they* are real. But this reaction ignores the logic of the classificatory "of": a story of Santa Claus can be ever so vivid without there being a real Santa Claus to back it up. All that need be true is that the story have a certain *intentional content*, viz. the content, whatever it is, that makes it a vivid Santa Claus story (maybe graphic descriptions of him slithering down sooty chimneys in his red suit). Similarly, all that need be true of an experience of an image of a deep green forest is that the experience have a certain content, to a first approximation[18] of the content [deep green forest] (I use square-brackets here to distinguish the intensional object – in general the intentional content – from the deep green forests themselves.)

There is a way that some philosophers have tried to preserve the ontology of phenomenal objects, without embracing Cartesian dualism, and this is by speaking of them as "intentional-objects." This can be regarded as simply a convenient and picturesque way of speaking about the ingredients (whatever they may be) of intentional contents: thus, we might speak of the intentional-object, [Santa Claus] being an ingredient of the propositional content [Santa Claus doesn't exist]. And some philosophers who adopt this strategy are happy to regard intentional objects as genuine objects – not, of course, as *causally* efficacious objects in space and time, but as another kind of abstract object, perhaps "possible" or "impossible" objects, somewhat akin to numbers, serving as ingredients in the contents of propositional attitudes (see, for example, Lycan 1987). Many philosophers are loathe to so regard them unless forced, and not feeling forced, I therefore hyphenate "intentional-objects" to emphasize what will be crucial to our discussion: *that intentional objects may turn out not to be real objects at all* (just as phony abalone isn't abalone and decoy ducks aren't ducks). Thus, when someone thinks that there couldn't be a largest prime number, the content of their thought may well involve the intentional-object [largest prime]; but arguably *there is no such object* (indeed, didn't Euclid prove it was *impossible* for there to be one?)[19] Similarly, when you're having a green after-image, there is, if you like to speak this way, the intentional-object [green after-image]; this intentional-object is part of the intentional content, or the means of classifying your experience. But that's all it is: a part of a means of classification of experience, not a description of peculiar objects that are somehow being experienced. There is no *object* having the properties of a green after-image that is part of the causal order of any world, neither in your brain, nor in some ghostly dualistic world bearing any real causal relations to your brain.

5.2.2 *Phenomenal predicates and their properties*

There are, I think, few these days who actually do insist that phenomenal singular terms must be treated referentially. The situation is less clear, however, when it comes to phenomenal predicates, the predicates we regularly employ to convey, as we might so easily put it, the "phenomenal properties" of our experience, e.g. "phenomenal green," distinct from the corresponding properties in the external world, such as the greenness of the grass itself. There might not be a mental *patch* there when I experience a green image, but it's harder to resist the idea that there is *some* kind of *greenness*.

A large part of the problem here derives from the much greater unclarity surrounding the ontology of properties as contrasted with objects. There is simply no settled view on precisely what properties are and how we know about them (what's been known for some time as the "problem of universals" cf. §1.1.1 above). For one thing, many philosophers think that properties, unlike objects, can exist "uninstantiated" (for example, the property of *being a winged horse*). Given the classificatory proposal of the preceding section, a lot would depend on whether properties enter into the specification of contents, a question about which there continue to be quite complex disagreements.

However, with all those qualifications in mind, there is the interesting irreferentialist suggestion that, just as phenomenal objects are intentional-objects, so are phenomenal properties intentional-properties. Harman (1990) recently writes, for example:

> When you see a tree, you do not experience any features as intrinsic features of your experience. Look at a tree and try to turn your attention to intrinsic features of your visual experience. I predict you will find that the only features there to turn your attention to will be features of the presented tree, including relational features of the tree "from here." (1990:39)

Similarly, a searing pain running up and down one's leg is not something that is intrinsically searing or running up and down one's leg, but simply an experience that may be classified by its intentional content [searing pain running up and down one's leg] (cf. p. 41). As Harman nicely emphasizes, they are "properties of a represented object," not "properties of a representation of that object" (p. 35). Or, as I prefer to put it, our apparent "descriptions" of our experiences are better regarded as *expressions* of them.

Many people who are happy to deny the existence of phenomenal objects are still inclined to feel that this treatment of phenomenal properties leaves something out, something crucial to the nature of our experience. We will return to this issue in §11.5, where we'll develop what I hope will be an important motivation for the view, as well as some further distinctions within it.

5.2.3 *Propositional attitude terms and their states*

As was evident in the passages we've already cited, Wittgenstein does not confine his irreferentialism merely to phenomenal object terms and predicates, but extends it to mental language generally. Indeed, as the quotations I cited in the introduction (§2) show, Wittgenstein's (as well as Ryle's) assault on internal mental explanations of intelligent behavior is relentless: he continually attacks appeals to internal attitude states that are standardly invoked to explain, for example, vision (1967:§614; 1980-I:§918), color perception (1978:37–40), reading (1953:§160), language processing (1953:§1), understanding other people (1967:§220), aesthetic reactions (1966:17–20), and animal thought (1953:§25, 1967:§117, 1980-II:§192).[20]

The problem with these attacks, however, is that they don't address the issue we have identified as the central issue in the philosophy of mind, the *explanation* of mental phenomena. It may be that no explanation requires positing phenomenal objects and properties, but is it really plausible to think that propositional attitude states are dispensable?

Consider the Standardized Regularities discussed in chapter 3, and the rough "folk psychological" explanation we sketched of them (§4.4): the subjects of the tests saw and understood the instructions on the question sheet; preferred to make some money; believed that the way to do so was to provide correct answers, etc. Is it at all plausible to suppose that that explanation could succeed if the terms we used – "perceive," "understand," "prefer," "believe," "reason," "represent" – *didn't* refer to actual states of the subjects? If the explanation is in fact on the right track, then it would certainly seem as if, for example, the subjects' *understanding* of the instructions was brought about by their *seeing* the sheet, which in turn was caused by light from the sheet striking their eyes; and, unless the blackening of the appropriate boxes was entirely *accidental*, the actions involved must have have been caused by *decisions* to blacken just those boxes and were brought about in turn by their *reasoning* in a certain way. How could all these things begin to be true unless the italicized expressions referred to real events with causal powers?

Notice that the situation here is quite different from the situation with regard to phenomenal objects. We are *not* in the position of seriously referring to attitude states and objects merely on the basis of the kind of vivid, reified introspections that can lead us to think we are referring to, for example, *pains* and *after-images*. There it seemed pretty easy to conceive of an explanation that didn't require referentiality.[21] But with regard to talk of attitudes, it is not only introspection that invites reference, but rather the need to explain otherwise inexplicable regularities.[22] In any case, the crucial question an irreferentialist needs to address is how the usual mentalistic theory-sketch could begin to be *causally explanatory* if its terms did not refer to internal processes of thinking and decision-making as causes of the explained behavior.

Wittgenstein, himself, was apparently entirely prepared to discover that the order we perceive in intelligent behavior just emerges from no underlying regularities at all:

> if I talk or write, there is, I assume, a system of impulses going out from my brain and correlated with my spoken or written thoughts. But why should the *system* continue further in the direction of the centre? Why should this order not proceed, so to speak, out of chaos? (1967:§608, see also 1980:I-903)[23]

Now, perhaps the Standardized Regularities are just an artifact merely of the environment of the tests and the previous lives of the students. That, in a way, is just the claim of the RBism of chapter 4: what brings about the convergence in the answers is a common pattern of reinforcements in the subjects' pasts. We have seen, however, that this claim seems to be deeply mistaken. So Wittgenstein is either relying on a deeply mistaken theory of human and animal behavior, or he owes us another account.[24] Otherwise, he would seem to be in the position of those tobacco lobbyists who keep insisting that the correlations between smoking and lung cancer have nothing to do with what's in cigarettes (cf. §10.3.4).

In any case, even if the folk psychological explanation of those and so many other regularities isn't true, surely it's a perfectly intelligible and serious *candidate*. If it is, then it is hard to see why we shouldn't regard the attitude terms it employs as perfectly referential – even should they fail in the end to actually succeed in referring, as the eliminativist claims.

5.2.4 *Propositional content expressions and their propositions*

As we noted in §1.1, common attitude terms, like "belief" and "desire", are ambiguous between referring to the attitude *state itself* (e.g. the *belief* that p, in contrast to the *wish* that p), and referring to the *content* of the attitude (the belief *that p*, in contrast to the belief *that q*), that would appear to be referred to by the sentence complement (e.g. the "that . . ." or "to . . ." clause) following the attitude verb. We certainly seem ordinarily to treat these contents as objects in the world. For example, we talk as though we can count them: we say of someone that "she believes many things," that, indeed, "many of the things she believes are believed by everyone else," and, if asked to give examples of such things, we would refer to them with typical sentence complements: what she and everyone else believes is *that Columbus discovered America, that 9 + 9 = 18*, and *that everyone is only out for themselves* are "three of her beliefs." So we do at least appear to speak referentially, not only of the attitude states themselves, but of their contents as well. But do we really need to take such referentiality seriously?

Neither Wittgenstein nor Ryle, themselves, seem to have been particularly exercised by this specific issue. But it has been enormously controversial in American philosophy, at least since Quine (1953c) raised doubts about the notions of analyticity, synonymy, meaning, and – to use a term around which much of this specific controversy has turned – "propositions." Propositions, as opposed to mere *sentences,* are supposed by many to be the natural objects of the *soi-disant* "propositional attitudes." After all, two mono-linguals who speak different languages can nevertheless have *the very same* beliefs and desires (i.e. with the same contents): a German who knows no Basque and a Basque who knows no German can still both think that snow is white. A proposition is not identical to a sentence, but is *expressed* by it: the same proposition is expressed by all sentences that are *synonymous* with one another, i.e. they have the *same meaning,* the biconditional (". . . iff ____") linking them being *analytic.*

Skeptical about a satisfactory account of these latter notions, Quine (1960:216) proposed a "fusion" view of attitudes: treat the attitude term and its sentence complement as one long predicate, e.g. "x believes-that-Columbus-discovered-America-in-1492." That is: don't treat the complement as referential, but as simply a piece of a predicate that begins with the verb.

There is no way to do justice to the complexities of Quine's skepticism about propositions here.[25] Some of the issues as they impinge on our discussion will be treated in chapter 9. But many of them don't really matter here, since for present purposes we could take *contents* to be the content expressions – the very words – themselves, and so not commit ourselves to propositions.[26] All that is important here is to notice that the specific irreferential *fusion* proposal about content expressions would seem to fall prey to similar arguments that we have just considered with regard to attitude *state* terms. Just as we need to refer to attitude states in explaining the Standardized Regularities, so it would appear that we need to refer to the contents of those states, whatever they might ultimately be construed to be. There had better be *something* that will serve to ground the kinds of laws and generalizations that appear to be true and explanatory of much animal behavior. As we argued in §4.4, what seems to explain such behavior is at least something very like desires for certain things like food and water, and beliefs about where such things are to be found. Presumably there is some law roughly of the form ⌜If an animal desires that p and thinks that the best available way of securing that p is to perform act A, then, *ceteris paribus*, it performs A.⌝ Such humdrum generalizations clearly treat the sentence complement position as open to quantification and thereby as referential. Consequently, the verbs must be taken to express relations to some sorts of objects (or, if you like, properties) to which those sentence complements refer.[27]

It is worth making this point vivid with some examples. Suppose that on a standardized test, people are presented with typical problems such as:

I.   Suppose Peter has three pigs in a pen and two pigs in his truck, and he puts the pigs in his truck into the pen. How many pigs will then be in the pen?
     (a) 32; (b) 23; (c) 1; (d) 5; (e) 6

II. Suppose Gladys has three keys in her left hand and two keys in her right, and she places all the keys in an empty basket. How many keys will then be in the basket?
     (a) 32; (b) 23; (c) 1; (d) 5; (e) 6

Obviously, a statistically significant number of people would blacken box (d) in case I and box (d) in case II. And the obvious reason is that, at least for some range of cases, most people are competent at basic arithmetic. But how are we to capture this competence in a way that explains their providing these answers? Pending some alternative account, it would certainly appear that we need to refer not only to their having certain thought *states*, but to the specific contents of those thoughts. It is *inter alia* because, for any number of kinds of things, they think that three of the kind added to two of the kind yields five of the kind.

How could these explanations be captured by a fusion view? For lack of a way of referring to and then generalizing over expressions of content, psychology would have to enumerate all the examples *one by one*: people who think the pigs description will select I (d); people who think the keys description will select II (d); and so forth for *every instance* of this sort of question. *For, on the fusion view, the belief that 3 pigs and 2 pigs yield 5 pigs is as unrelated to the belief that 3 keys and 2 keys yield 5 keys as it is to the belief that ostriches have feathers*: the "that . . ." clauses don't pick anything out, but only serve to create more and more internally unrelated predicates. It would be *entirely accidental* that anyone that provides the right answer in the one case would provide it another – or that one gets the same results administering such questions in French. Of course, there may well be limits to how diverse or complicated the cases could be; but there's no question that there is *some* generality, a generality having to do with a certain arithmetic content. The fusion proposal prevents us from even *expressing* such generalizations.

Another way to appreciate the need to refer to causally efficacious contents is to consider Dretske's (1988) "soprano problem": a soprano's high-pitched singing can break glass, can cause musicians to swoon, and can inform someone about a new turn in the operatic plot. The first it does presumably by virtue of its purely *physical* properties; the second perhaps because of its purely *musical* ones; but the third it would need to do because of its *content*. How else can we explain listeners' changed understanding of the plot – not to mention their surprise or amusement about the turn of events – without supposing it was because her singing expressed a specific content? Or, to repeat a question we asked earlier: how can we explain the effectiveness of a joke without referring to its meaning? Perhaps there is a story

– Quine no doubt trusts to RBism to tell it – but on the face of it our talk of contents seems as fully referential as any.

5.3   Analytical Behaviorism

As I've said, irreferentialism is an essentially negative thesis about the analysis of mental terms. Understandably, many people might want to hear something more positive: if the analysis of mental terms doesn't involve the postulation of mental entities, what does it involve? Particularly for Wittgenstein and his followers this question (like, in their view, most philosophical questions) was the wrong one to ask: it exhibited a somehow inappropriate "craving for generality" (1958:17) about the nature of thought and language. That may in the end be so, but one would like to see him and his followers give a systematic account more of a try. The use of mental language doesn't seem entirely capricious and chaotic, and, if it isn't, it's not unreasonable at least to ask what the principles might be that guide its use.[28]

Ryle and others did propose a more positive approach, which emerged as the doctrine of *Analytical Behaviorism ("ABism")*. The general idea is that claims about the mind should be understood as equivalent to various sorts of *dispositional* or *conditional* claims about how an agent would behave *if* she were in such and such circumstances, on the model of dispositional claims elsewhere: "Salt is soluble" presumably means something like, "If salt is put into water in certain normal conditions, then it dissolves"; "Glass is fragile," something like "If struck in normal circumstances, it breaks." This was the way that, as we noted in §4.1.5, many RBists expected that what mentalisms they did introduce could be in principle eliminated by definition in purely physical terms.

Spelling out the appropriate dispositions in the case of mental terms was none too easy, certainly not as easy as with standard dispositions like fragility, solubility, or being a deadly poison. Ryle was never quite precise, but offered a strategy, exemplified by the following characterization of belief:

> [T]o believe that the ice is dangerously thin is to be unhesitant in telling oneself and others that it is thin, in acquiescing in other people's assertions to that effect, in objecting to statements to the contrary, in drawing consequences from the original proposition, and so forth.   (Ryle 1949:134–5)

Besides being a little loose, one problem with many of Ryle's proposals, as with some of Skinner's attempts to replace mental vocabulary (§4.1.5), is that they presuppose the very mentalisms that they are trying to explain. A particular physical noise produced by someone's vocal chords counts as "unhesitant[ly] telling oneself and others" something, or "acquiescing," "objecting," or "drawing consequences" *only if it is produced by certain intentions – indeed, intentions to express one's beliefs!* The behaviors Ryle is appealing are characteristically *actions*, not the "colorless movements" that Hull realized were crucial to the eliminativist program of RBism.[29]

Rather more precise proposals were indeed offered by RBists, not for mental terms generally, but to legitimate what mentalisms they found themselves driven to use. A well-known example was Tolman's attempted definition of "the rat expects food at location L":

> When we assert that a rat expects food at location L, what we assert is that *if* (1) he is deprived of food, (2) he has been trained on path P, (3) he is now put on path P, (4) path P is now blocked, and (5) there are other paths which lead away from path P, one of which points directly to location L, *then* he will run down the path which points to location L. When we assert that he does *not* expect food at location L, what we assert is that, under the same conditions, he will *not* run down the path which points directly to L. (Tolman et al. 1930, quoted in Taylor 1964:79)

Perhaps one of the most famous behavioristic analyses is that of "intelligence" proposed by Alan Turing, the so-called "Turing Test" of whether a computer should be counted as intelligent. To put it briefly, a computer was to be regarded as intelligent if a person communicating with it merely by teletype couldn't distinguish its responses from those of a normal human being (the idea was that we should control for the biases introduced by intellectually irrelevant issues such as human appearance). Note that this is an especially restrictive behavioral test, restricting the range of relevant behaviors to merely teletype exchanges.[30]

Although ABism was partly inspired by irreferentialism, and was often expressed in irreferential forms, it needn't be so committed. It all depends upon how one thinks of dispositional terms. If one thinks of them instrumentally, as merely pieces of "inference tickets" (licensing certain inferences), as Ryle (1949:chapter 5) did, then, to be sure, they needn't be taken to be any more referential than any other mere "instrument" of science. If, on the other hand, one is "realistic" about them, believing that their truth requires a "categorical basis" – in the way that salt's solubility consists in its having certain valence properties[31] – then they do refer: they refer to the internal states of brains, viz. those states of the body in which the causal basis of the disposition inheres.

Both for historical but also (as we shall see in §7.2.4) for recent purposes, it is important to appreciate some of the intuitive attractions of ABism. In the first place, given our almost complete lack of any *direct* knowledge of the neurophysiology of the brain, it's true that we ordinarily don't seem to be relying on it in applying mental terms. Indeed, we seem to be prepared to discover most anything about the *physical aetiology* of mental life: witness the remarks of Wittgenstein that we discussed in §5.2.3 regarding how the perceived order in our behavior "might proceed, so to speak, out of chaos" (1967:§608). Or, in a famous comparison of language learners with elephantine bushes, Quine wrote:

Different persons growing up in the same language are like different bushes trimmed and trained to take the shape of identical elephants. The anatomical detail of twigs and branches will fulfill the elephantine form differently from bush to bush, but the overall outward results are the same. (1960:8)

A standard thought experiment that can appear to clinch the case for ABism is to imagine opening up the heads of familiar people around you and discovering that they were empty, or full of sawdust; or perhaps multivarious: a brain here, sawdust there, wires and glass in the case of the people down the street. Would you conclude that they really didn't have any of the mental states you had previously supposed them to have? (We'll return to such questions in considering refined versions of them in §6.4.)

However, for every thought experiment arguing *for* ABism, there are compelling ones *against* it as well. Consider not only people with sawdust heads, but people who turn out to be robots cleverly controlled by radio waves produced by some ingenious scientists at MIT: such creatures would seem to have no more of a mental life than do marionettes. Or imagine someone whose motor cortex has been irreparably damaged, so that he is paralyzed or flails helplessly about: if we are not allowed to let our analyses mention anything about the inner aetiology of behavior, then the fact that such a case might be due merely to damage in the motor cortex can't be allowed to be relevant. But then, lacking *any* of the behavioral dispositions associated with mental states, the poor fellow would have to be counted as lacking *any* of those mental states themselves!

These examples are examples involving the ascription of *any* mental terms. When we consider specific mental terms, behavioral analyses begin to seem even more implausible. Putnam (1963/1975a) imagined a race of "Super-Spartans" who, as matter of training and principle, refuse to flinch or complain in response to even the most excruciating pain, and are inarticulate about an enormous range of their psychological repertoire. Surely it's *possible* that they have, by and large, the full range of psychological states of the more expressive and articulate. Conversely, there could be a society of talented actors who, throughout their ordinary life, feign a wide variety of emotional responses that they really never experience (like some people in our society who sometimes admit they are "entirely dead inside.") In general, it appears one could have the behavior without the mental states; and, conversely, one could have the states without the behavior.

Note that the Turing Test is especially problematic in this respect, since it is confined merely to verbal (worse, pure teletype) behavior: there's not even a requirement that the machine respond appropriately to *non-verbal* stimuli (e.g. naming objects presented to it)! As Block (1981b) pointed out in his thought-experiment regarding what has come to called a "Blockhead," a machine could pass such a purely verbal test merely by looking up and executing a correct teletype response from a vast look-up table: whenever it's presented with one conversational move, it searches its memory for at least one appropriate conversational riposte.[32] Intelligence would seem to depend not on behavior alone, but upon *the way* that that behavior is produced: accessing vast look-up tables no more displays intelligence than a schoolboy who, looking up the answers in the back of the book, displays an understanding of algebra.

Thus, intuitions can go different ways. As Dennett (1991a:282) has rightly emphasized, "intuition pumps" (as he calls the systematic use of them) *alone* don't tell us a great deal. What is important is to consider the *explanation* of the intuitions: it's in view of *it* that we may find reason to accept or reject a particular analysis (cf. §1.5.2 above). We've already seen some sources of pro-behaviorist intuitions: exasperation with unknowable facts about the mental lives of others – and sometimes even oneself (we'll discuss some other sources later (§7.2.4, §11.7.3). The *anti*-behaviorist intuitions have at least two simple and vivid sources: (1) *the patent fact that the relation between (most) mental states and behavior is wholly contingent* (cf. Strawson 1994:§2.5), and (2) *the fact that for many mental phenomena (e.g. thinking, experiencing genuine emotions), it's not the behavior that's important but the processes that may or may not produce the behavior.* Some people express their love with a subtle smile, others with a monstrous hug; sometimes courage is manifested by doing battle; other times by restraint; some people manifest their desires by trying to satisfy them; others by restraining themselves and looking glum; some express their beliefs by uttering sentences in Swahili, others by uttering Dutch; and some simply "can't find the words at all." On a moment's reflection, it can seem incredible that anyone is expected to find any analytic connection between a particular mental state and some specific behavior.

These facts are what lay behind a technical difficulty noticed by Roderick Chisholm (1957):[33] every effort to define most mental states by behavior seems to require citation of other mental states. Typically, *any particular mental state causes a particular behavior only in conjunction with (an often large number of) other mental states.*[34] Beliefs, hopes, expectations issue in behavior only in conjunction with (at least) desires; desires issue in behavior only in conjunction with (at least) beliefs and expectations. In Tolman's above proposed definition of "a rat expects food at location L", defining a rat's *expectation* that there's food at L in terms of his moving towards it, works only if the rat *wants* food; and the rat's *wanting* food can be defined in terms of its moving towards L only if it *expects* there's food at L. Insofar as this is true, the prospects of a definition of a *single* informational or *single* directional state in terms of behavior seem dim.[35]

These particular observations of Chisholm, however, aren't quite as devastating to ABism as they might initially appear. For it turns out to be technically open to the ABist to propose defining *all mental terms simultaneously* (which is why Chisholm's objection is sometimes taken to be *merely* technical).[36] This is *one* idea behind "functionalist" approaches to the analysis of mental terms. Only in the context of considering them will we able to assess more seriously the real issues involved in the ABist proposal.

Before leaving ABism, however, I want to spend a brief interlude discussing one of its general philosophical sources, the verificationist theory of meaning. This is important not only for understanding ABism, but, as we'll soon see, for understanding a great many more recent discussions. Indeed, although I've marked the next section as optional – one could pass on directly to the discussion of functionalism without loss of continuity – in some ways the verificationist theory of meaning continues to exert enormous influence in not only philosophy in general, but specifically in the philosophy of mind and in experimental psychological research. Acquiring some familiarity with its lures and pitfalls is indispensable to understanding a good number of on-going debates (see, for example, §7.2.4 and §9.1.2 below).

5.4* Verificationism

As I already mentioned (§5.1.2), verificationism was an attempt to rid our thought of hypotheses that, while they seemed initially intelligible, were thought impossible to settle in principle: for example, the hypothesis that all life was but a dream, or that everything in the universe had suddenly doubled in size. It has been most recently defended by Dennett (1991a), who presents himself as an "Urbane," as opposed to a presumably vulgar, "Village" verificationist, anxious to save us from "epiphenomenalism, zombies, conscious teddy bears, self-conscious spiders" (p. 461) – i.e. precisely the things from which verificationists – Urbane, Village, or otherwise – have always been trying to save us. In this section I'll just address Verificationism generally, raising what have seemed to many people to be overwhelming objections against most any form of it. Later in §7.2.4, I'll argue that Dennett's specific version of the view – what I call "Superficialism" – is indeed open to precisely these objections.

Generally, the verificationist strategy is to identify the meaning of an hypothesis with the evidence that could be adduced for or against it, the conditions of its verification or falsification. For example, claims about something's being an *acid* might be defined in terms of its turning litmus paper red. Or claims about the existence of material objects were to be analyzed as logical construction of claims about those sense experiences that we ordinarily take to confirm such claims (e.g. that we would have certain experiences of color, shape, resistance to touch, etc.). The principle has its source in the empiricism we discussed at the end of chapter 4. Indeed, it was advanced by Logical Positivists (sometimes aptly called "logical empiricists") as a way of spelling out the empiricist slogan "no idea without a corresponding impression" with the resources of modern logic.

There is no need here to settle the quite *general* issue of whether any meaningful sentence must ultimately be verifiable, except to note two general difficulties that arise at least for the specific formulations on which both ABists and some functionalists have relied: (1) the difficulty of specifying the principle in some non-vacuous way; and (2) the problem of specifying a *specific* verification condition as the meaning of a claim, a problem that emerges from the distinction between *nature* and *evidence*, and from the related phenomenon of *confirmation holism*.

To appreciate the first difficulty, consider the myriad *prima facie* counterexamples with which the principle must somehow contend: moral and aesthetic discourse, unprovable mathematical conjectures, or just ordinary claims about the past: all those pens, umbrellas, dinosaurs, and maybe even events before the Big Bang that have vanished without a trace. Of course, in some of these latter cases – e.g. the lost umbrellas and dinosaurs – the verificationist could claim that, although we mightn't be able *practically* to verify their existence, we certainly could do so "in principle". We certainly know what *would* count as evidence of them: for example, if we had been around several million years ago and lived to tell; if there had been good movie cameras rolling for millions of years at all the relevant spots; if we could just go back in time . . . ; in general, if only our epistemic access were in fact better than it is, we could surely verify all manner of conjecture. But some of these are very big "if"s, and it's by no means clear that there's a principled way of letting in the lost umbrellas, dinosaurs, and events before the Big Bang that would exclude any of the cases that worried people.[37] After all, if we can help ourselves to counterfactuals about our going back in time to check things out, why not help oneself to ones about some oracle or an omniscient God that could just tell us for *any* sentence – even ones about ethics, mathematics, or even people's "private" mental lives – whether it was true or false? Are we supposed to limit what is meaningful to just those counterfactuals that could be somehow grounded in *existing* science? But then how is it we are able to coherently wonder, in advance of settling our science, whether a particular claim is verifiable or not?

This difficulty of saying exactly what "verifiable in principle" itself actually comes to, would seem to be hopelessly compounded when we consider *indirect* means of verification. Initially, what people tend to consider in applying such a principle are fairly obvious, *direct* ways in which an hypothesis can be verified, dismissing as "meaningless" ones for which no such way can be conceived. However, in case after case, what initially passes as a statement immune to *direct* verification turns out, with a little imagination, to be verifiable by *indirect, theoretic* means. To take a famous example, consider the statement that "All processes in the universe have stopped for one hour": someone might wonder what it could mean to say *this*, and be right to think that there is no *direct* way to verify such a claim.[38] But, as Sydney Shoemaker (1969/1984) nicely pointed out, claims that may fail of *direct* verification can sometimes be verified *in*directly. Shoemaker imagines with

156

regard to the universally stalled processes, for example, that the universe consisted of three regions in each of which all processes periodically "freeze" for a year at intervals of, respectively, three, four, and five years. Since the periods don't coincide, it would be possible for scientists in each region to learn about the periodicities in the others. But then they could also conclude that processes in *all* regions stopped for a year, every year that was the product of those intervals, i.e. every 60 years: thus, there could be good evidence to conclude that every 60 years all of the processes in the universe stopped for one hour (Shoemaker 1969/ 1984:55–6). With a little bit of theoretic imagination we can see past what seemed initially to be unthinkable.

Once we appreciate how indirect verification can be, it is difficult to see what constraints verificationism may pose on any hypotheses: who can say that, with a little more imagination, we mightn't find some way of indirectly verifying *any* claim whatsoever? For all we know, with a little Shoemakerian imagination, there would be some way of verifying even "The Absolute enters into, but is itself incapable of evolution and progress" – the example, selected "at random" from Bradley's *Appearance and Reality*, that Ayer (1934/1952:36) holds up to his verificationist ridicule (indeed, one would have thought that the method of random selection of a sentence from a text was not the best way of guarding against such a possibility).

The second, deeper problem with verificationism is that, even were a satisfactory formulation found, and were it established that every meaning*ful* hypothesis had to satisfy it, still we wouldn't have established the much stronger claim that *the meaning of* an hypothesis *consists* in some specific method of verification. If meaning is supposed to perform the kind of "analytic" work that philosophers have traditionally required (see §1.5.1 above), verification conditions seem, by and large, unlikely candidates.

There are at least three reasons for this. In the first place, insofar as we are interested in discovering genuine analyses of phenomena (in the spirit of §1.5.1), the conditions we adduce as *evidence* for a phenomenon are seldom plausible candidates. Certainly, they are not plausible candidates for the *nature* of a phenomenon: how we *tell* what's what isn't the same issue as *what makes something the thing it is*. We may *tell* that something is water by checking whether it comes out of the kitchen tap, is odorless and tasteless, etc., but none of this begins to define the concept [water]: no one would think that something is water *by virtue of* those facts.[39] Most users of the term as it is meant in English know that the ways in which we happen to be acquainted with such things as water are by and large *accidental*; the features with which we're familiar are invariably *contingent* features of them. Most of us *know* this;[40] and that's why (as we noted in §1.5.2) we turn to experts to help us provide real and genuinely interesting definitions or analyses, and, as Putnam (1962/1975a) has observed, to *modify* the verification conditions for a claim as science progresses, at least sometimes without changing its meaning (consider merely the better tests we seek and sometimes find for diseases). Insofar as we expect a concept to play a serious explanatory role in some ultimate theory of the world, we have reason to doubt that its analysis would be captured by at least any verification conditions that accompanies our learning of the word.

But, secondly, whether or not we believe science is in the business of supplying analyses, it remains true that our beliefs about what confirms what are subject to continuous *revision*. The litmus tests of yesterday can be replaced by the more advanced spectroscopy of tomorrow. It would simply stultify empirical investigation to insist on tying a hypothesis to a particular test that happens to have been convenient today. Indeed, as Quine (1953c), has famously emphasized, in good science *any* belief can be revised in the light of experience should the resulting revision make for a better general theory of the world overall: thus did Darwin revise our beliefs about the nature of man, and Einstein our beliefs about the geometry of space. Verificationism would seem to invite dogmatism.

This latter observation of Quine's is connected with another of his doctrines, "confirmation holism," which raises a third serious problem with verificationist analyses: verification conditions can't, in general, be taken seriously in isolation from the rest of one's beliefs about the world. Our methods of testing hypotheses usually depend upon *complex interactions* between explanatorily interesting systems and observers.[41] To take an extreme example, think of the enormous complexity of a cyclotron, and of how the credibility of the evidence it provides about atomic structure depends upon a vast set of beliefs about its construction and operation, as well as elaborate assumptions about the laws and general conditions of the physical world; and the oddity, therefore, of claiming that it is a *defining condition of being an electron* that it have a certain effect in such a machine. (Suppose just *one* of those other beliefs and assumptions were wrong: should we conclude that there are no electrons?!) But even so humdrum a test as looking at a clock to see what time it is, if you think about the details, involves an enormously complicated set of assumptions about time, mechanical systems, lighting conditions, the reliability of one's visual system, and so on. Moreover, there's no reason to suppose that these background assumptions against which a particular test is to be taken seriously don't contain expressions – about material objects, other elementary particles, causation, space, and time – that are every bit as problematic as those in the claim for which the test condition was supposed to be the analysis.[42] As Quine (1953c) put it, "our claims about the world are confirmed not individually but only as a corporate body" (p. 41). Consequently, selecting some subset of those conditions as *the meaning* (much less the constitutive analysis) of claims about electrons, or about the time of day, would seem arbitrary and philosophically otiose.[43]

Essentially, confirmation holism is what's lying behind the apparently merely technical point of Chisholm that we discussed at the end of the last section. Just as electrons don't eventuate in cyclotron results in isolation of plenty of other physical forces, so beliefs don't result in specific behavior without desires, nor desires without beliefs (and, in both cases, without a lot of other conditions of psychology and physiology as well). Consequently, the prospects of defining one mental state in terms of behavior in isolation from others is hopeless.

However, as I said, Chisholm's specific technical objection has a technical solution, viz. functionalism. After we've set out the functionalist approach in general, we'll see how verificationism and the essential impulse of ABism can still play a role – but also how they can be avoided (§7.2.4).

Notes

1 It's not clear that Locke or anyone actually would have thought of the ideas resulting from this inner perception as providing *analyses* of mental terms or concepts, or merely thought that this was simply the source of our ideas, or whether there is for him or other empiricists a real distinction between these two.

2 Searle expects such introspective appeals to perform substantial philosophical work, for example in solving some of Quine's problems (Searle 1987). For similar appeals to introspection see Bealer (1984:328) and Strawson (1994:§6.6).

3 Wittgenstein is terrifically good at evoking the complexities one can encounter in careful introspection. Some representative examples from his *Zettel* (1967:§484–504):

> Is it hair-splitting to say: – joy, enjoyment, delight, are not sensations? – Let us at least ask ourselves: How much analogy is there between delight and what we call, for example, "sensation"? . . .
>
> "I feel great joy" – Where? – that sounds like nonsense. And yet one does say "I feel a joyful agitation in my breast." – But why is joy not localized? Is it because it is distributed over the whole body? Even where the feeling that arouses joy is localized, joy is not: if for example we rejoice in the smell of a flower. . . .
>
> "Horrible fear": is it the *sensations* that are so . . . horrible?
>
> Love is not a feeling. Love is put to the test, pain not. One does not say: "That was not true pain, or it would not have gone off so quickly."

(Readers unacquainted with Wittgenstein's writings should be cautioned about their fragmentary and often aphoristic style, which, while often quite irritating, doesn't prevent them from being sometimes unusually insightful.)

4 Phenomenologists are frequently anxious to distinguish themselves from Wundtian introspectionists, and there certainly are important differences between them. As I'm using "introspection" – for first-person reflections as opposed to essentially "third-person" investigations – these differences aren't important here.

5 Another philosopher who directs philosophical attention to the nuances of ordinary mental talk is J.L. Austin (1956/1964), but on issues less central to the concerns of the present book.

6   Wittgenstein (1953:§185) himself imagines a pupil responding to a teacher's order "Add 2" by (as we would say) adding 2 up to 1000, but then proceeding thereafter to write "1004, 1008, 1012 . . .". The question is: what determines that one rather than another continuation was intended by the teacher? Kripke changed the example to the one I am using, but the reader should bear in mind that there is a great deal of controversy about whether Wittgenstein himself would endorse all of Kripke's interpretation. I confine myself here only to the (I believe) relatively uncontroversial points Wittgenstein makes about introspectible states. For further discussion of this issue, see Kripke (1982) and Holzman and Leich (1981). We will deal with Kripke's own discussion of the so-called "Kripkenstein problem" in §10.3.

7   Wittgenstein (1953:§243ff) presented his discussion in the course of developing what has come to be called his "private language argument," or an argument to the effect that there couldn't be a language that was in principle comprehensible to only one person, by virtue, essentially, of referring to internal sensory states of which only an agent himself could possibly be aware.

8   See Wittgenstein (1953:§143,185ff) for further discussion. We'll return to the debate between "internalist" and "externalist" theories of meaning in chapter 9.

9   In his famous "private language argument," Wittgenstein (1953:§243ff) claims that such a language would be impossible. For critical discussion see Thomson (1964) and Chihara and Fodor (1965).

10 I leave aside the interesting question about how one might endorse *both* phenomenalism and behaviorism: which has priority, claims about the behavior of external objects, or claims about sense experience?

11 See Coffa (1991:chapter 7, especially pp. 249–52) and Monk (1990:287–8). There are those (e.g. Chihara and Fodor 1965) who think that he never really abandoned them, but only made them somewhat weaker and vaguer (see §5.3 below). But there is (to put it mildly) considerable scholarly disagreement over this point, as over most anything Wittgenstein had to say.

12 Although their views significantly overlap on these topics, I will treat Wittgenstein as the paradigm irreferentialist and Ryle as an ABist (which Wittgenstein clearly wasn't).

13 To avoid repeating qualifications that are not crucial to the present discussion, I shall use "refer" to mean the relation that holds, for example, between "cats" and cats, "stones" and stones, whatever that relation is; for it is *that* relation that Wittgenstein and Ryle are denying obtains between, for example, "pains" and pains. Both of them could allow – Wittgenstein (1967:§244) clearly does – that the ordinary word "refer" might be used without a commitment to *that* relation, and that there is, of course, a perfectly innocuous sense of "refer" in which "pain" refers to pains (this sense might, for example, be simply a way of expressing intentional content, the sense in which, of course, "Santa Claus" refers to Santa Claus).

14 See Quine's (1953d) "criterion of ontological commitment." I should point out that, in pursuing this Quinian and explanatory strategy for determining referentiality, I am pretty surely departing from the kind of mere reflection on ordinary use on which Wittgenstein or Ryle relied. This is of a piece with the general approach to the

analysis of explanatory terms and concepts that I recommended in §1.5.2, which they would surely have rejected.

15 Irreferential, as opposed to eliminativist, approaches have been applied elsewhere: for example, in (meta-)ethics, it emerges as "emotivism": the proper understanding of ethical talk is not as descriptive of real properties and relations in the world, but as expressive of certain of our feelings. The ultimate success of such approaches may depend upon deeper investigations of linguistic structure than Wittgenstein anticipated.

16 The "φ" is what is sometimes called a "dummy" variable, just standing in place of different phrases that can occur at that position, but *not* open to quantification (i.e. to inferences to "there exists an x such that . . . x . . .".) Thus, one might speaking of "either φ or it is not the case that φ" constructions in English, where what could go in the place marked by φ is just some or other presumably non-referential English sentence. What presumably could go in place of φ in "φ – story" is any noun phrase.

17 To my mind a more awkward and problematic proposal for the same purpose is the "adverbial" account, which treats "Jim is having an image of a red rose" as "Jim is being appeared to red rosily" (see Chisholm 1957 and Tye 1984, 1989, and 1995:74 for discussion of this proposal and its several technical difficulties).

18 There are, to be sure, problems in specifying the content of a particular experience. As we will see in chapter 9, there are problems in specifying the content of anything! We will consider how to specify the contents of sensory experience further in §11.5.

19 I say "arguably," since, also arguably for some, there *is* the intentional object, [*the largest prime number*] – but *it* isn't the same as *the largest prime number* itself. I leave to defenders of such objects the specification of the relation between these two different "objects," and what seem to me the needless circumlocutions such talk seems inevitably to involve. See, for example, Lycan (1987).

20 Lest there be any doubt, there is the following explicit statement:

> Misleading parallel: psychology treats of processes in the psychical sphere, as does physics in the physical. Seeing, hearing, thinking, willing, are not the subject of psychology in the same sense as that in which the movements of bodies, the phenomena of electricity etc., are the subject of physics. You can see this from the fact that the physicist sees, hears, thinks about, and informs us of these phenomena, and the psychologist observes the external reactions (the behavior) of the subject. (Wittgenstein 1953:§571; see also 1980-I:§292)

I discuss this and the other mentioned passages at greater length in Rey (1994).

21 Although, given the extreme generality of Wittgenstein's irreferentialism, he probably wouldn't accept our account, referring as it does to (φ-)*experiences*.

22 Someone might argue that, just as there are no pains over and above pain experiences, so there are no understandings or reasonings over and above *experiences* of understandings or reasonings. But this seems psychologically dubious: it certainly doesn't seem to be a person's *experience* of reasoning that leads them to their decisions – *that* experience might actually interfere with the reasoning, in the way that self-

consciousness of motor movements can interfere with the execution of those movements. It is the *reasoning* itself, whether or not it was experienced, that seems to be crucial.

23   In a passage frequently cited (by friend and foe), he compares the situation of thought to what he apparently was also prepared to discover even in botany:

> The case would be like the following – certain kinds of plants multiply by seed, so that a seed always produces a plant of the same kind as that from which it was produced – but nothing in the seed corresponds to the plant which comes from it; so that it is impossible to infer the properties or structure of the plant from those of the seed that it comes out of – this can only be done from the history of the seed. So an organism might come into being even out of something quite amorphous, as it were causelessly; and there is no reason why this should not really hold for our thoughts, and hence for our talking and writing.   Wittgenstein (1967:§608, see also 1980:I-903)

I gather from biologists that this is a pretty unlikely possibility, one that would render the common forms of instances of the same species across different environments something of a miracle.

24   That something like RBism is often lurking in the background of Wittgenstein's thought is suggested by the not infrequent appeals he makes to "training" to explain various regularities in human behavior, and language acquisition in particular: see, for example, 1953:§5–6, 86, 185, 630; 1980-I:§131; 1980-II:§6, 139, 327, 413; 1967:§318, 419. But it would have gone deeply against his grain to endorse RBism explicitly. More likely, he'd prefer simply to "just leave explaining alone" (1967:§614; see also 1980-I:§918).

25   See Quine (1960:§42–4) for an excellent, seminal survey and discussion of many of the basic issues.

26   Quine (1960:§44), himself, entertains this possibility in his survey of different positions. Davidson (1968/1984) develops this suggestion in an ingenious way: treat the "that" that follows the attitude verb as a demonstrative with an implied colon, so that what is referred to by the demonstrative is the sentence that follows. Thus, "Galileo believes that the earth moves" is to be understood as: "Galileo believes that: *the earth moves.*"

27   Scheffler (1963:I,8) seems to have been one of the first to discuss the issue in this way. For further arguments see Fodor (1978/1981).

28   There does appear to be a suggestion in Wittgenstein of some kind of semantic account of mental terms in his distinction between "criteria" vs. mere "symptoms" for their application. But it is notoriously difficult to set out this distinction in a satisfactory way (see Albritton (1959/1968) for a meticulous, if inconclusive discussion). Sometimes "criteria" seem to be defining conditions, as at 1958:24–5, 1987:§438, where he even seems to have in mind the kind of empirically revisable definitions we discussed in §1.5.2; in which case his view would seem to collapse to the ABism we are about to discuss. But sometimes they seem to be something weaker, for example, some sort of strong *prima facie* evidence, as when he suggests at 1953:§354 that water falling from the sky is a criterion, but not defining of rain, or,

presumably, when he suggests that "holding your cheek" is a criterion of "toothache" (1958:24). In this case, he would seem to be interested only in an *epistemic* issue of how we could *justify* our application of a term, not in the metaphysically constitutive issue that concerns us here (in virtue of what is a pain a pain?). See Rey (1996a) for discussion of the tensions involved in such Wittgensteinian appeals to "criteria."

29 Indeed, recall that it was to avoid this almost ubiquitous problem of citing non-tendentious behavioral evidence that I appealed to the Standardized Regularities in challenging eliminativism.

30 This "Turing *Test*" of intelligence is not to be confused with the very different "(Church)-Turing Thesis" about the computability of any function by a Turing Machine that we will discuss in §6.2. The tremendous importance of this *latter* thesis has led to excessive importance being attached to the test, which has confused a number of discussions, for example, Searle's "Chinese Room" (see §10.2 below).

31 As in Armstrong (1968:86) and Quine (1969a). The common example of solubility can be misleading, suggesting a *common* categorical basis in all instances of the disposition. The bases could vary from case to case, as they obviously do in the case of being a poison.

32 Pretty simple machines can get fairly good at this: witness the results of a number of actual Turing Tests that have been run (see e.g. Allen 1994). But, of course, this may be as much due to the (if you think about it, perfectly understandable) gullibility of the judges as to the intelligence of the machine. But how are we to control for that? We can't have the judges, themselves, be *too* intelligent, so that they might be able to tell from various features in, for example, the timing of responses whether they were dealing with a machine or not. The test seems a pretty poor test by anyone's standards, and it remains an interesting question in the psychology of philosophy why it has been taken so seriously (one source may be simply the well-deserved luster in this area of Turing's name).

33 He advances this observation as an instance of "Brentano's thesis" (see §1.2 above).

34 There are possible exceptions: intentions to perform basic actions (actions, like batting an eye, that are performed not by performing any other action).

35 In a related vein, Quine (1960:chapter 2) argues on behalf of his famous "thesis of the indeterminacy of translation" that there is no way to define the *contents* of propositional attitudes in behavioral terms: all the behavioral evidence in the world is equally compatible with the claim that a person is thinking of rabbithood, or of temporal slices of rabbits, or of the world's mass totality of rabbit, as of rabbits construed individually. He thinks of the thesis as being of a piece with Chisholm's claim and Brentano's thesis (1960:221).

36 Searle (1992:34) dismisses the point as merely technical. That it can have non-technical consequences will emerge in chapter 7 below.

37 Witness the problems contemporary verificationists like Dummett (1975, 1976) have with the meaningfulness of assertions about the remote past.

38 Shoemaker (1969/1984:49) claims that it seemed so to Aristotle, Hume, and McTaggart, among others.

39 Sometimes people are taken in here by an unfortunate ambiguity in the use of the word "determine": what *determines* what something is needn't coincide with how *we determine* what it is. The latter is, in the jargon of philosophy, an *epistemological* question

(a question about how we know something), the former *metaphysical* (a question about what the world is really like, whether we know it or not). Indeed, as Jerry Fodor once quipped: verificationism is the plan to buy some epistemology by selling off some metaphysics, a plan many view as a bad bargain.

40 Quite apart from endorsing Kripke's (1972) specific conclusions, consider how *intuitively* vivid is his discussion of cases like "gold."

41 This fact certainly makes plausible the original version of confirmation holism, confined, as it originally was by Duhem (1906/1964), to causal claims about the world. Whether it makes plausible Quine's extension of it to include logic and mathematics has been disputed (e.g. by Vuilleman 1986 and Rey 1993d).

42 For example, as Quine (1953c:39–40) pointed out, Carnap's efforts to analyze material object claims in terms of sense-experience failed to eliminate a crucial *spatial* predicate "x is at position y."

43 Quine (1953c), himself, regards this as a reason to give up on a theory of sentence and word meaning. There could be other responses – for example, abandoning verificationism! – some of which we will discuss in the latter parts of chapter 7.

6

Functionalism: Commonalities

The basic idea of functionalism is simple enough. Many things in the world are what they are, not particularly by virtue of what they're *made of*, but by virtue of what *function*, or role, they serve in some sort of system. For example, whether or not something is *money* depends not on what it's *made of* – gold, silver, paper, or even just electrical signals stored in the right places in a bank's computer will do – but on the specific *role* it plays in the exchange of commodities in a market. Something's being a *carburetor* depends largely upon whether it mixes oxygen and fuel and feeds it to the cylinders in an internal combustion engine, irrespective of the materials of which it's made. Something's being a *heart* depends in part upon its serving in a certain way to pump blood, even if, in these days of ever more sophisticated surgery, artificial hearts might be made of ever more diverse synthetic materials.

This basic idea, however, can be spelled out in surprisingly diverse ways. Consequently, functionalism should be regarded not so much as a particular *view* as a general *strategy* for analyzing mental phenomena. Indeed, because it has been something like the prevailing orthodoxy in philosophy of mind for the last thirty years or so, there has emerged a complexity of different versions of it, a complexity that will be reflected a little in the complexity of the next two chapters. In this chapter, I'll lay out some general ideas shared by all versions of functionalism: in §6.1, I'll introduce the basic idea, presenting in §6.2 a particularly important instance of it, the definition of a Turing Machine State, and in §6.3 the basic formal procedure, called ramsification, that provides a canonical form for functional definitions. In §6.4 I will draw out some of the interesting consequences of this analytic strategy, particularly its sanctioning of the different explanatory level(s) on which a psychology is likely to be defined. The next chapter will be devoted to considering different ways in which the strategy has been pursued.

6.1   The Basic Idea

The main advantage of any functionalist analysis is that it permits the simultaneous definition of a whole slew of terms at once. This can seem like merely a technical trick, merely allowing a reply to the circularity problem raised against ABism at the end of the last chapter. Although functionalism could be seen in this way as merely an amendment of ABism, it is important to see that it offers a great deal more than that. In particular, it has the resources to accommodate what we saw were two salient facts about many mental phenomena: that there is no direct tie between most mental states and specific behaviors, and that *how* behavior is produced is usually more important to the identity of a mental phenomenon than the specific behavior that is produced. It is thus able to capture a more traditional conception of the mind than ABism seemed to permit, but without some of the dualistic commitments associated with that traditional conception.

Although money, carburetors, and hearts are some of the standard sort of examples of functional phenomena, they are also examples of two other kinds of phenomena that are difficult to separate from functionality: being an *artifact*, and being a *biological* kind. Whether or not something is a specific sort of artifact – for example, a piece of money or a carburetor – may depend sometimes not upon what role it in fact plays, but upon what role its creators *intended* it to play (worthless money can still be money, a broken carburetor can still be a carburetor); and something's being of a certain biological kind may depend in part on its evolutionary history, even if it now fails to play any role at all (useless wisdom teeth are still teeth). We'll return to these issues in discussing teleo-functionalism (§7.2.3). But, in order temporarily to sidestep the further difficulties they raise, it's worth finding an example not confounded by them. Fortunately, there is one that also happens to possess a number of important properties that turn out to be of special interest for the philosophy of mind, namely the example of a *Turing Machine State*.

6.2   Turing Machines

The idea of a Turing Machine is perhaps one of the dozen deepest ideas of the century: it is one of the seminal ideas for the development of the modern computer, and, as we shall see, it is a crucial inspiration for the computational-representational theory of mind that we shall pursue in later chapters. It was conceived by the British mathematician, Alan Turing (1912–52), in order to characterize the nature of computation in general. Turing Machines are not actual concrete (or metal or plastic) machines,[1] but rather the specifications of highly idealized machines, just as the lines and triangles of the geometer are often not lines or triangles found in real space, but ideal ones. But, as in these geometric cases, although a Turing Machine can be defined purely mathematically, it helps

166

in thinking about one to imagine some physical device that "realizes" the specification, i.e. proceeds according to the specific steps.

A Turing Machine consists of a potentially infinitely long *tape* that is divided into individual *cells* that are read by a *scanner-printer* (I'll call it "a scanner" for short) and a finite set of *Machine States* (I shall refer to them as "TM states"), each of which determines what the scanner is to do when it reads a given input in a cell. In each of the cells on the tape there appears a symbol from some finite alphabet. At each stage of the machine's operation, the scanner *reads* a symbol that appears in a given cell, and, per the instructions specified by the specific TM state the machine happens to be in, it *erases* it, *prints* the same or a different symbol in its place, *moves* one cell left or right, and *enters* a new TM state or halts.

A crucial point that will figure in later discussions: the "instructions" specified by the TM states are not instructions the *machine* is necessarily equipped in any sense to "understand." Of course, we human beings could *follow* the instructions by understanding them. But the instructions are deliberately specified in such a simple way that it is perfectly clear how an actual machine in space and time could be constructed whose motions were caused to proceed *in accordance with* the instructions, but *without any understanding* of them whatsoever. Such simple and unambiguous instructions are called "algorithms." Machines *obey* their machine table algorithms without *following* them.[2] It is the possibility of specifying such mechanical algorithms for a wide variety of problems that inspired the construction of modern day computers, and suggested how at least some intelligent processes that require minds could be "reduced" to sequences of essentially unintelligent processes that do not.

By way of illustration, consider the specification of an extremely simple Turing Machine that can *add* any two numbers that are presented to it in *unary* notation (n series of strokes representing the number n) on the input portion of its tape. One needs, first, to specify an alphabet of symbols that a physical device could discriminate. In this case:

The TM Adder alphabet: 0, 1, and *

We will understand the number n to be represented by a series of contiguous cells on the tape filled with n "1"s, each such representation being separated by a "0." The "*"s indicate the ends of the input, the right "*" indicating also the beginning of the output. We will presume the machine is arranged so that the cursor is initially placed one cell to the right of the initial input.

The TM Adder's Tape with Cursor in standard initial state before receiving input:

*	1	1	1	0	1	1	0	*	0	0	0	0	0	0	0	0	0	0	0

input section · · · · · · · · · · · · · · · · output section

167

We now specify the TM states. I place them in a box, since they provide precisely the details that distinguish one Turing Machine from another (the rest of the apparatus is shared by all such machines). For ease in understanding the specific states, I have indicated their intuitive purpose to the right, but outside of the box: it is important to realize that the operation of the machine in no way depends upon *its* in any way appreciating this intuitive purpose. The machine is to be understood as operating precisely according to rules specified in the box below.[3]

The TM States of an Adder:

				go to	
state:	input:	print:	move:	state:	intuitive purpose:
S1	0	0	L	S1	Proceed to the left, passing by any
	1	0	R	S2	"0"s and staying in S1, until you
	*	*	R	H	find a "1." This you should change to a "0," and then proceed to the right, entering S2. When, however, you find a "*," halt!
S2	0	0	R	S2	Pass by all "1"s and "0"s, staying
	1	1	R	S2	in S2, until you reach a "*" (the
	*	*	R	S3	beginning of output), which you should leave as is: continue to the right, but then enter S3;
S3	0	1	L	S4	Pass by any "1"s, staying in S3;
	1	1	R	S3	but when you find a "0," change it
	*	*	L	S4	to a "1," go left and enter S4. Should you find a "*" (which you won't, if the tape is laid out correctly) leave it and also enter S4;
S4	0	0	L	S4	Pass by all "0"s and "1"s,
	1	1	L	S4	proceeding left and staying in S4;
	*	*	L	S1	when you find a "*," leave it, proceed left again and enter S1 (i.e. the initial state).

"H" designates the "Halt" state: the machine ceases its activity.

I've phrased the intuitive purposes colloquially to ease understanding. Each line of the instructions specified in the box should more literally be read as a

168

conditional, or "If . . . then . . ." claim. For example, the first two lines should be literally understood as:

> If the machine is in state S1 and its cursor reads a 0 on the tape, then it erases it, prints a 0, moves one cell to the L, and enters state S1;

> If the machine is in state S1 and its cursor reads a 1 on the tape, then it erases it, prints a 0, moves one cell to the R, and enters state S2.

It is worth following the machine through one "cycle" of its operation, seeing how, by repetitions of this cycle, it could add any two numbers. This adder works about as simply as any adder could: it is constructed (or "programmed") simply to recopy on the output side all the strokes representing the two (or more) input strings, but without the "0" that separates them. Thus, if the input are n strokes (representing the number n), and m strokes (representing the number m), the output will consist of (n + m) strokes (representing the number n + m). This is not intended to be a particularly subtle machine: the aim of the discussion at this point is precisely *not* to be subtle, but to describe processes that are so simple that an actual machine could obviously execute them.

We assume the scanner is always set to begin in state S1 in the above initial position (just left of the right "*"). In that position, given now the specific input of two and three strokes on the tape, it reads a "0" and then, per the instructions of S1, it writes a "0," moves one cell to the left, and stays in state S1. The situation now looks like this:

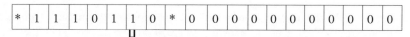

Here the scanner, still in S1, reads a "1," and per S1 instructions, erases it and writes a "0," moves one cell right, and goes into S2. The situation now looks like this:

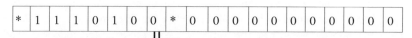

Being in S2 and reading a "0," the scanner is supposed to leave it alone (i.e. erase it and write it again) and move again one cell to the right, staying in S2:

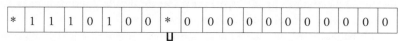

In S2, if the scanner reads a "*," it's supposed to leave it and merely move again to the right, but go into S3:

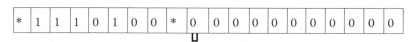

169

In S3, if it reads a "0," it's supposed to change it to a "1," move *left* one cell, and go into S4. (Had it read a "1," it would have ignored it, passing over all such "1"s until it found a "0." This is what it will do, of course, on subsequent cycles, copying more and more of the "1"s it encounters as input.) The situation now looks like this:

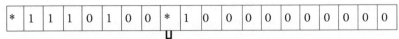

If the scanner were to encounter a "1" while in S4, it would pass over it, moving left until it encountered a "*." But this time, it encounters the "*" right away; and so, per S4 instructions, it leaves it alone, moves one cell to the left, and returns to state S1. It is now in the initial position, ready to proceed through another cycle of copying any "1"s it encounters as input:

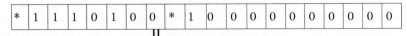

After proceeding through four more cycles like this, erasing "1"s in the input, and writing them as output (not counting [reading the "0" separating the two inputs and passing on] as a cycle), it will finally encounter the leftmost "*" while in S1. This will cause the machine to halt, and the final situation will look like this:

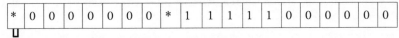

Comparing the initial configuration with the one in which the machine halts, we can now read off the tape the startling fact that $111 + 11 = 11111$ (i.e. the expression in unary arithmetic of the fact that $3 + 2 = 5$).

This is by no means the only Turing Machine adder we might have specified. A more complicated one might obey the familiar rules (or "algorithm") we all learned in school for doing sums on pairs of Arabic numerals. Here the alphabet would have to be increased to include the other Arabic numerals, 2, . . . , 9, and the machine would sum first the "units" place of the pair, and then the "tens" place, and then the "hundreds," and so forth, in such a fashion that in each case in which that sum is greater than nine, it would then "carry" the excess, increasing the sum of the next pair by *one*. I spare the reader the details of the many more TM states specifying such an adder would require.

This painfully tedious method of computation is interesting for the following reason. Turing, and independently Alonzo Church (1903–96), formulated a bold hypothesis:[4]

The Church–Turing Thesis: *any* intuitively computable function is computable by some or other Turing Machine.

Unlike many other *theorems* about Turing Machines that can be proved in logic and mathematics, this "thesis" is not susceptible to *proof*: it is a thesis about an *intuitive* notion, "intuitive computability," claiming that the technically defined notion, *Turing computability*, can be captured by it. Indeed, since obviously the operation of any Turing Machine involves intuitive computations, one might go so far as to say that the thesis provides an *analysis* of the intuitive concept of computation. It could be regarded as a paradigm of a kind of philosophical thesis, proposing an analysis of an obscure notion in terms of notions less obscure. And it seems to be an extremely good one: although many have tried, no one has succeeded in finding a counterexample to it; and it is one of the fundamental ideas that drives the development of ever more elaborate computer programs, which at a certain level of abstraction can be regarded as specifications of ever more elaborate Turing Machines designed to compute wider and wider varieties of functions.[5]

A derivative notion that is of almost equal importance to that of a Turing Machine is that of a *Universal Turing Machine*. To understand what it does, it is important to understand one other lovely insight of Turing's, viz., that *the instructions specifying the TM states of a Turing Machine can themselves be encoded in a fashion scannable by a Turing Machine.*[6] There are a number of ways of doing this. The simplest for our purposes consists in taking the alphabet for the code to comprise simply the symbols we used inside the box to specify the instructions (I add an additional punctuation symbol, the dash "-," to help separate groupings):

*,L,R,S,H,-,0,1,2,3,4,5,6,7,8,9

(I include all the standard Arabic numerals for the naming of indefinite numbers of different TM states). We could now specify our little Turing adder as simply one long sequence of these symbols separated by "-"s, in the order in which they are written in the table (double dashes separate the descriptions of entire states; triple dashes mark the endpoints of the whole coded description):[7]

− --S1-0-0-L-S1-1-0-R-S2-*-*-R-H--S2-0-0-R-S2-1-1-R-S2-*-*-R-S3--S3-
0-1-L-S4-1-1-R-S3-*-*-L-S4--S4-0-0-L-S4-1-1-L-S4-*-*-L-S1-- −

A Universal Turing Machine is a Turing Machine with a specific set of TM states that enable it, when presented a coded description (such as the above) of the TM states of *any* other Turing Machine, to compute what *that* machine *would* compute, were it to operate on the input that then follows its coded description.[8] Thus, if the above sequence of symbols were printed on the input portion of a Universal Turing Machine, and that sequence were followed by the pair of three and two "1"s that were provided on the input to our adder, the Universal Machine would compute precisely what our adder computed, and five "1"s would appear on the output portion of its tape. And if we were to encode the more elaborate TM states of the

171

alternative adder that obeys our grammar school algorithm and feed *that* code to the machine, the Universal Machine would produce as output the sums of whatever pairs of numbers *that* adder might be supplied.

A Universal Turing Machine is in this way something like a Universal Mimic: it can mimic what any other Turing Machine can do. Most all the machines we popularly call "computers" can be regarded as realizations of Universal Turing Machines[9]: the "programs" that you insert into them are coded descriptions of Turing Machines that can compute specific functions (e.g. for arithmetic, balancing a budget, or word-processing); the "documents," along with the data entered by key-strokes, are the input to *those* (coded) machines. The computer as a whole then performs computations on the "documents" and key-strokes according to the coded instructions it reads in the "programs" that it was supplied. Thus, a Universal Turing Machine not only *obeys* its basic "universal" algorithm, it also obeys the algorithms of the machines it emulates. But this it does by *following* the supplied *representations* of these latter algorithms. Small wonder that such an exploitation of representation should strike many as a promising model for the mind.

6.3   Ramsification

In an influential article, Putnam (1960/1975) noted some analogies between TM states and mental states, analogies that have proved fruitful in a number of ways. One important analogy was that TM states also exhibited Chisholm's problem about individual behavioral definability: just as belief can't be defined in terms of behavior without mention of desire, nor a desire without a belief, so can one TM state not be defined merely in terms of the output it provides given certain input, but typically must include mention of other TM states. If we look at the TM states that define our adder, for example, we see that the instructions that constitute state S1 make reference to S1 and S2; those that define S2 make reference to S2 and S3; S3 to S3 and S4; and S4 to S4 and S1. Indeed, since any Turing Machine will have a finite number of such states, such definitions will always involve circles of interdefined states. Why isn't this circle "vicious"? Well, in some sense it can't be a problem, since all the states taken together obviously do provide an illuminating specification of a computer. But one might wonder what is going on here: how are such definitions possible?

David Lewis (1972/1980) answered this question in a lucid rendition of an idea of Frank Ramsey (1903–30), defining what has come to be called a "(Lewis)-Ramsey sentence." He asks us to consider, first, how we might introduce certain characters in a story:

> A, B and C conspired to meet Mr. Body. Seventeen years ago, in the gold fields of Uganda, A was Body's partner. . . . Last week B and C conferred in a bar. . . .

Tuesday at 11:17, B went to the attic and set a time bomb. . . . Seventeen minutes later, A met C in the billiard room. . . . Just when the bomb went off in the attic, A fired three shots into the study.   (1972/1980:208)

Suppose one wanted to know *who* A, B, and C *were*. Well, given that the story is not intended to be about anyone any of us know, they are "defined" entirely in terms of just this story; the story says (*inter alia*) that there were these three people related in the way it specifies. So far as any distinctive meanings of terms are concerned, there would seem to be nothing more to them than that. The story "*implicitly* defines" who these figures are largely in terms of what they *do* to each other and other things, i.e. in terms of the relationships between them and other things.[10]

To make this perfectly clear, Lewis provides the following general recipe, sometimes called "ramsification," for introducing *any* "new" theoretic terms, or "t-terms," that one wanted to define by means of logic and whatever one took to be antecedently understood "o(ld)" terms[11] (I simplify his treatment slightly):

Ramsification as a Procedure for Defining a Term

(i)   Consider the theory M in which the t- and o- terms appear. Enrich this theory so that you are satisfied that it includes every claim you regard as constitutive of the application of any of the t-terms (ignoring for a moment the problem of circularities that we are addressing);

(ii)   Form a (typically quite long) conjunction, C_M, of all those sentences of theory M containing at least all that M claims with the t terms, $t_1, t_2, \ldots, t_n$, a sentence that we will represent as:

$$C_M(t_1, t_2, \ldots, t_n)$$

(iii)   Replace each t-term, $t_1, t_2, \ldots, t_n$, that appears in C by, respectively, the variables $x_1, \ldots, x_n$, thus forming the predicate:

$$C_M(x_1, x_2, \ldots, x_n)$$

(iv)   Since M was supposed to contain every claim that was constitutive for the application of any of the t-terms, we can suppose that this predicate, "$C_M(x_1, x_2, \ldots, x_n)$" is uniquely satisfied, i.e., that only things that are $t_1, \ldots, t_n$ will satisfy it. So we can write:

$$(\exists! x_1) \ldots (\exists! x_n) \, C_M(x_1 \ldots x_n)$$

(where "$(\exists! x)$" means "There is exactly one thing x such that"). This is "the Ramsey sentence for theory M."[12]

(v)   Now, for each term, t_i, introduced by the theory, you may provide a *functional definition* of t_i, by dropping its existential quantifier, and claiming:

$$t_i = \text{the } x_i \text{ such that } (\exists!x_1) \ldots (\exists!x_{i-1})(\exists!x_{i+1})(\exists!x_n)(\ C_M(x_1 \ldots x_i \ldots x_n))$$

Applying this procedure to the terms introduced in the tale of Mr Body: we suppose, by step (i), that the story exhausts what it is to be any of the individuals A, B, and C; we conjoin all those sentences and replace those names by variables; we form the Ramsey sentence, and then extract, one by one, each of those variables and define the original name in terms of the the rest of the sentence that remains. This just captures the reasonable intuition that, after all, the person A *just is* the person who conspired with some other unique y and z . . . and satisfied the rest of the things said about him or her and y and z in the story.

In a more theoretic vein, we might apply it to defining our little Turing Machine adder as follows: we take the machine table and presume that it says all there is to be said about states S1 through S4. Recall that each line of that table is a conditional, saying what the machine is to do if it receives a certain input. We form the long conjunction of all those conditionals – call it C_{TM}, and think of it as:

$$C_{TM}(S1,S2,S3,S4)$$

where "S1", . . . , "S4" are the t-terms we want to define. What we do now is to replace all occurences of "S1" through "S4" by the variables x_1 through x_4, and, since it's patent that all and only things that satisfy C_{TM} are the states S1 through S4,[13] we can claim:

$$(\exists!x_1)(\exists!x_2)(\exists!x_3)(\exists!x_4)C_{TM}(x_1,x_2,x_3,x_4)$$

This puts us in a position to define any one of the states S1 through S4, individually. For example:

$$S1 = \text{the } x_1 \text{ such that } (\exists!x_2)(\exists!x_3)(\exists!x_4)\ C_{TM}(x_1,x_2,x_3,x_4)$$
$$S3 = \text{the } x_3 \text{ such that } (\exists!x_1)(\exists!x_2)(\exists!x_4)\ C_{TM}(x_1,x_2,x_3,x_4)$$

Spelling out these clauses completely would, of course, require spelling out the long conjunction, $C_{TM}(x_1,x_2,x_3,x_4)$, i.e. spelling out all the lines in the Machine table. Here's how, for example, it would go in the case of S3:

$S3 = $ the x_3 such that there are unique states x_1, x_2, and x_4 such that:

If the machine is in state x_1 and its cursor reads a 0 on the tape, then it erases it, prints a 0, moves one cell to the **L**, and enters state x_1; and

If the machine is in state x_1 and its cursor reads a 1 on the tape, then it erases it, prints a 0, moves one cell to the **R**, and enters state x_2; and . . .

[and so forth through all the lines of the machine table until]

If the machine is in state x_4 and its cursor reads a * on the tape, then it erases it, prints a *, moves one cell to the **L** and returns to x_1.

Similar clauses would specify each of the other states, S1, S2, and S4. In providing them, we would certainly seem to have provided the clearest possible analysis of what it is to be one of these TM states. It is entirely by virtue of this story being true that those states are the states they are. Thus, there is no problem of vicious circularity in having to define a whole set of mutually dependent states (and/or concepts of them) at once.

6.3.1 Structure and the problem of uniqueness

Ramsification, so defined, is quite abstract and can be applied to most any story or theory in any domain. Its interest lies mostly in its capacity to capture phenomena whose nature depends upon their participation in a *structure* or *organization* or (where the o-terms include "x causes y") their role in a *causal network*. It seems a natural way to handle many of the terms of the functionalist's standard examples: money, markets, commodities, capital in economics; carburetors, distributors, camshafts, differentials in auto mechanics; valves, veins, hearts in biology. Some have argued that it might even be applicable to the basic terms of physics: certainly if one wanted to acquire a grasp of what on earth terms like "spin," "charm," "color," and "quarks" mean in physics it would appear one could do no better than to consult the physical theory in which these terms appear and presume that these theories implicitly define them (we'll return to this example in a moment).

It is, of course, this possibility of capturing causal structure that makes ramsification important for the functionalist about the mind. For, it is in this way that the functionalist hopes to capture the fact dismissed by the ABist, that *how* behavior is produced is often as important as the behavior itself (recall the Super-Spartans of §5.3, whose impassivity may be indistinguishable from that of some-one who feels nothing, but may for all that have all sorts of intense feelings). Ramsification is promising here: witness the way it can distinguish our simple unary adder from the more complicated one that obeys our grammar school algorithm. The two machines are input-output equivalent,[14] but, given the differ-ences in their machine tables (the set of their TM states), they are quite different machines. In particular, someone who is a functionalist about the mind is someone who looks to ramsification to provide the constitutive analysis of mental states by *its ability to specify those states in terms of the causal relations among them*. Different causal relations among those states distinguish different mental states that may nevertheless be behaviorally indistinguishable.

175

That this latter condition amounts to a serious constraint on permissible ramsifications can be brought out by considering a way in which ramsification might fail. Ned Block (1978/1980) has pointed out that there may be cases in which no amount of mere description of the causal role something plays seems adequate to capture our concept of it. He cites what was apparently at one time a serious possibility entertained in physics that electrons and positrons obey precisely the same laws, and that the *only* reason we would have to distinguish the one kind of particle from the other is that they annihilate each other on contact.[15] No story we could supply at stage (i) of ramsification would seem to be adequate; consequently, we couldn't construct a Ramsey sentence that would *uniquely* specify the kind of object we want to define. It would appear that there was some essential "thisness" (what people sometimes call a "quiddity") that distinguished electrons from positrons in a way that couldn't be captured merely by the stories about the relations they bear among themselves and to other things, and so couldn't be captured by ramsification alone. They are the sorts of things that might be captured only by some kind of *demonstrative*: "the particle that is involved in *this* reaction" (pointing to the result of some experiment).

Of course, one might ask, why not include demonstratives like "this" and "that" in the stage (i) stories? I think both friend and foe of the functionalist strategy would agree that this would violate its spirit. It would involve an appeal to something other than the mere (causal) relationships between things. Indeed, the role could be entirely accidental to the individual so demonstrated. *"This* president" (said, pointing to Clinton) refers to someone who presumably only *happens* to be president: it is no part of the analysis of what it is to be a president that it be Clinton, or what it is to be Clinton, that he is a president (*being Clinton* would indeed seem a paradigm of a *non-functional* property).[16] Of course, there could be mixed cases: perhaps an electron *is* something that necessarily obeys such and such laws *and* is the thing involved in *this* interaction. As we'll see, many philosophers think that this situation arises precisely in the case of qualitative experience – say, of the taste of pineapple – which they think therefore resists a purely functional analysis although it may enjoy one partially (see §7.2.1). For these reasons, I shall regard it as definitional of at least *pure functionalist proposals* that they do *not* include demonstratives, and that they confine the constitutive stories about mental phenomena to *causal relations among them*.

6.4 Multiple-Realizability and Levels of Explanation

If the above ramsification strategy were to succeed for the mental, then, *strictly speaking*, it affords a way of providing physical definitions of mental phenomena.[17] In particular, if, as a physicalist, one restricted the acceptable o-terms to only those of the physical sciences, then each mental predicate (together with all the others) could be defined by a logical apparatus applied in the end to only physical predicates. By far, most functionalists have been physicalists and have happily anticipated such definitions.[18]

However, this way of putting the matter would obscure an important fact about the way such a definition needs to be applied. One might theoretically define, say, water as "H_2O" and quite satisfactorily replace all occurrences of the word "water" by "H_2O." However, a ramsification especially of a fairly complex theory with many interrelated predicates requires that in applying any one of the predicates, one needs to be prepared to apply a number (maybe all) of the others. Unlike the case of "water," one can't just replace talk of "belief" or "desire" say, by talk of certain chemicals in the brain. To understand what it is *to be* a belief,[19] one has to understand its relations, for example, to desire, perception, reasoning, action: in terms of a Lewis-Ramsey sentence, *one needs to attend to all those other existentially bound variables that also occur within it*! In particular, one has to *apply* the theory, and in doing so, one needs to abstract from everything except the causal relations that are specified in the ramsification. The fact that ramsification can be expressed without introducing into one's antecedent (presumably physical) theory of the world any new *primitive* notions, is a welcome metaphysical afterthought, especially when we try to fit this complicated theory into a more general account of the world; but, in an important way, it is powerless to avoid the mentalistic conceptions that it defines.

This point is vividly illustrated by a related feature of functionalism that has occasioned much discussion, namely *multiple realizability*: functionally defined systems abstract away from most physical properties and so can be realized in an indefinite variety of physical substances. Using ramsification, one can describe a causal organization *without committing oneself to specific features of the realization of that organization*, i.e. all the *other*, often physical properties that aren't mentioned in the Ramsey sentence.[20] Again, the example of the Turing Machine is paradigmatic: our little adder could be realized by any number of physically different mechanisms. Turing Machine states can be realized in transistors, in electron tubes, in silicon, even in a system consisting of people placing pebbles on toilet paper squares (Weizenbaum 1976).[21] Standard computer programs like Lotus or WordPerfect can be run on very different kinds of machines (e.g. Macs, PCs, mainframes), with often physically different parts playing the same functional role in the program. Similarly, political and economic institutions can be realized by different people and physical things: different people with different physical properties can be senators or capitalists; arbitrarily different physical substances can serve as money, capital, banks, industry.[22] All that is important is that the specific patterns of causal relations be preserved.

By virtue of this multiple-realizability, functionalism with regard to the mind has *three* important consequences, one largely philosophical, one practical, and one methodological. The philosophical consequence consists in its capturing at least

177

some of the intuitions that we observed motivated ABism: that we are prepared to find most anything inside people's heads. On the face of it, it doesn't seem to matter to the analysis of mental phenomena whether someone had a carbon based brain, or (as some have imagined) a silicon based one, as in the skulls of creatures we might find on Mars. For those with hankerings for a hereafter, even the minds of ghosts, gods, and angels stand a chance: so far at least as functionalism is concerned, all that would be needed is that the functional organization of a mind be realized in whatever non-physical substances such possibilities involve (ghosts and angels have to see and think *somehow*!). (We may ultimately want to place limits on this liberality; see §7.2.1 and §11.7.2).

A more practical and maybe even attractive consequence of multiple realizability is that it *permits the possibility in principle of prosthetic replacement* of dysfunctional parts of the brain. It's virtually a truism these days that the chemistry of our brain is often not optimal: depression, violence, schizophrenia, and attention disorders seem to be due, in part, to various imbalances in hormones and neuroregulators. Now if someone's mental life depended upon a person's being made of the specific chemicals nature has provided, it would appear that all we could do is perhaps change the balance in these chemicals. But, if a person's mind is multiply realizable, then it becomes a serious option to search for chemicals that would play the same role in the healthy mind's organization, but without the deleterious effects. At least such possibilities are not ruled out *necessarily*, as they would seem to be in any theory that too closely analyzed a mental state as involving a particular *substance* (whether it be physical or dualistic!).

But perhaps the most important consequence of functionalism is a methodological one: it permits a level of psychological explanation that is relatively autonomous from the physical level, an autonomy it can enjoy without for a moment denying the reality or ultimate metaphysical importance of the physical level. There are widely prevalent views that psychology is only serious science when it is physiological, an attitude that can and does have significant consequences for the kind of research that is actually pursued in psychology departments. If functionalism is correct, and the mental does form an explanatory organizational level specified in terms of causal relations among a family of states, then studying merely the physiology of those states in the absence of that organization would be explanatorily inadequate. Indeed, it would often be irrelevant, rather like studying the chemistry of money to learn about business cycles; or of ink to understand Shakespeare; or, to return to our computer analogy, studying the physics of transistors to learn how a word processing program works. Many computer programmers have a profound understanding of the algorithms for computing certain functions without having a clue about the electrical properties of the machine on which those algorithms might be run. Similarly, it may shed rather little light on the organization of the mind to learn about merely the physical properties of the brain.

178

Some philosophers (e.g. Kim 1993) have balked at this proliferation of levels, arguing that if we have any reason to think there is a law at a "functional" level, then we have reason to think there is a law at a lower, ultimately basically physical level from which the functional law can be derived. However, if one bears in mind that some functional kinds (e.g. certain sorts of computers, certain sorts of economies) may well be defined merely in terms of elaborate causal relations between states, with only modest constraints on any other properties that these states may possess, then it is hard to see how there could be any unified lower level physical law that would serve. That certain causal relations happen to converge in certain situations in such a way as to give rise to the higher-level laws might well be a complete *accident* from the point of view of any lower level laws: it just so happens that certain functionally definable structures arise from carbon molecules under such and such conditions, from silicon molecules under such and such *very different* conditions, and from doubtless an indefinite number of different kinds of things under an indefinite number of other kinds of conditions. What the functional level allows us to do is to unify these sundry accounts of different substances in different conditions under a single set of explanatory laws.

A logical distinction of Quine's (1953c), between the "ontology" and the "ideology" of a theory, may be useful here. The *ontology* of a theory is the set of things that must exist for the theory to be true (see §1.11 above); its *ideology* is the set of the theory's *predicates* (the ontology is ordinarily a set of worldly things; the ideology a set of words). Now, as Quine nicely points out, two theories may share an ontology without sharing their ideology: they may describe *the same set of things* (or one theory may describe a subset of the things described by the other), but they may do so using predicates that radically cross-classify. To take a homely example, consider some theory, H, about *houses* (which might state generalizations about the kinds of houses to be found in different places). The ontology of this theory is presumably a subset of the ontology of a complete physical theory, P: every house, after all, is some or other physical thing. But the sets of physical things picked out by the ideology of H – for example, by the predicate "x is a house" – may not be a set picked out by any of the usual predicates in the ideology of P. After all, different houses may be made out of arbitrarily different physical substances (straw, wood, bricks, ice, . . .), obeying different physical laws. Houses, that is, are *multiply realized*. To appreciate the generalizations of theory H it will be essential to think of those sundry physical things as captured by the ideology of H, not P. But, of course, one can do this without denying that houses are, indeed, just physical things. Or, to put the point in terms of the type/token distinction we discussed briefly in §2.4, which has become popular in discussing the mind: every *token* house is a *token* physical object, but the *type* house (i.e. the set of house tokens) may not be identical to any natural *type* of physical theory.

To put an otherwise confusing redundancy of terminology to good use: one might say that functionalism invites us to agree to *materialism* about the ultimate *primitives* in the world, while rejecting *physicalism* about the possible levels of explanation. All that exists may well be matter in motion, and perhaps any property of it can be defined à la ramsification in whatever terms are required for the physical explanation of that motion. However, some explanatory levels can abstract from the physical properties that figure in that ultimate explanation: they can isolate certain patterns of causal relations across physically heterogeneous domains. Appreciation of this fact may go some way towards allaying fears people often have about "materialism," that it somehow renders mental phenomena "nothing but" certain physical phenomena. There may be, *ontologically*, nothing but matter in motion; but there may be no end to the elaborate organizations and, consequently, the *ideological* descriptions of it that a full understanding of reality would need to appreciate.

Having said all this, it should be emphasized that the "autonomy" of the mental could be exaggerated. For one thing, nothing that has been said so far commits us to only *one* level of explanation different from physiology. David Marr (1982), for example, distinguished three levels of explanation that were relevant to understanding vision: a purely *input/out* level,[23] at which we simply describe the input and the output of the visual system; an *algorithmic* level at which we describe the procedures (like those of a Turing Machine) that are responsible for computing the output from the input, and an *implementation* level, at which we describe how the physical hardware of the brain actually executes the algorithm. Peacocke (1986) has plausibly argued for further intermediary levels between those; and Lycan (1987) has rightly pointed out that, quite independently of any commitment to the mental, similar functionally defined levels occur in, for example, biology, physiology, and chemistry:

> *Cells* – to take a rather conspicuously functional term(!) – are constituted of co-operating teams of smaller elements including membrane, nucleus, mitochondria, and the like: these items are themselves *systems* of yet smaller, still cooperating constituents. . . . *Neurons* are cells, comprised of *somata* containing a nucleus and protoplasm, and fibers attached to these somata, which fibers have rather dramatically isolable functions.   (pp. 38–9)

Moreover, it's not at all clear that our ordinary mental talk is confined to any one level. As Dennett (1971/1978) has rightly emphasized, when things don't work quite according to rule at one level, it is reasonable to look to other levels for the explanation. Thus, do we sometimes look to neurophysiology for explanations of mental illness. But the point needn't be confined to breakdowns.[24] Patricia Churchland (1986) rightly points to a number of illuminating researches into, for example, the neurophysiology of memory (pp. 359–60), and discusses in detail work on gaze control (p. 433ff) and attention fixation (p. 474ff). It is not hard to think of other examples: the detailed, idiosyncratic structure of the eye as an explanation of features of color experience (Why three primary colors? Why complementary colored after-images?); the release of endorphins as a result of receiving "tender loving care"; the roles of neurotransmitters in emotions (Why do we have the peculiar experiences of *humor, fear, grief*?)[25] Given that there is every reason to think that human beings are not ideally designed, but are a hodgepodge of some very arbitrary evolutionary accidents, it would be astonishing if there were a sharp line between features of our psychology and features of our specific neural realization, or that all mental properties were to be defined at the same level of explanation. So it seems extremely unlikely that psychology stands a chance of being "completely autonomous" of physiology or other natural sciences in the way that is sometimes claimed.[26]

But everything depends here on the details; in particular, on the details of the story one provides at the initial stage of ramsification. Having set out the common core of functionalist views, we now turn to the different kinds of stories different functionalists tell.

Notes

1 In order to avoid the misleading construction, "concrete machine," I will refer to machines that are located in space and time as "actual" ones, not meaning to prejudice the (for our purposes irrelevant) issues of the reality of ideal or abstract machines that may or may not have any realizations in space and time.

2 I will try to keep to this usage: planets and people *obey*, for example, Newton's Laws, but only people ordinarily obey algorithms by *following* them (*pace* Fodor 1991c:225 who mysteriously excludes people as serving as parts of computers). At least one difference between the two is that following an algorithm, unlike mere obedience to it, requires a *representation* of it. Neither the planets nor people nor simple Turing Machines do this with respect to their basic instructions (we will see, though, that *some* Turing Machines – e.g. Universal ones – obey some algorithms by following representations of them).

3 Strictly speaking, what's specified in the box is a "finite state automaton" which becomes a Turing Machine when supplied with a source of input on the (potentially) infinite tape.

4 Church actually proposed it about a different sort of computational tool, the "primitive recursive functions." However, once it was proved that this class and the class of functions computable by Turing machines were identical, the two theses were joined. Sometimes, though, one reads of "Church's thesis" or "Turing's Thesis" mentioned separately.

   However, it is absolutely crucial to distinguish between this deep and important *thesis*, from the far less interesting, and, as we saw (§5.3), fairly implausible "Turing *Test*" for intelligence (whereby a machine was counted as intelligent if its teletype responses were indistinguishable from a normal person).

5 The word "function" gets used for many different purposes. In mathematics it is used in a way only distantly related to the use in this chapter, viz., for ordered n-tuples, such that for every initial n-1 elements, there is a unique n-th element, for example, for each column of figures, there is a unique *sum* and a unique *product* that is "a function" of those figures (Skinner used to call *his* RBism "functional analysis," since it tried to show that behavior is a function, in this sense, of stimulus history). The Church-Turing Thesis is that if such ordered n-tuples can computed in any way at all, they can be computed by some Turing Machine.

6 Turing was especially talented in thinking about codes. During World War II, it was his work that was chiefly responsible for the de-coding of German war messages. See Hodges (1983) for an excellent biography.

7 Strictly, this codes the finite state automaton that comprises a Turing Machine when combined with the tape (see note 2). Incidentally, a more standard method of coding is not alphabetical but numerical. For example, along the lines of the actual method used in present day computers, each of the symbols in the alphabet can be associated with a binary number of four digits: *: 0000, L: 0001, R: 0010, S: 0011, H: 0100, -: 0101, 0: 0111, 1: 0111, . . . 9: 1111. If a machine was constructed of parts that admitted of two states, e.g. on/off, it is not hard to see how it could be constructed to be sensitive to such a code.

8 There are an infinite number of possible Universal Turing Machines, some of them surprisingly simple to specify. See Minsky (1967) for examples.

9 Well, not quite: given the eventual heat death of the universe, they presumably all access only a finite tape. But it's still pretty long. Note that the "tape" can come in many forms: not only the data from the keyboard, but data from floppy disks, compact disks, modems, infra-red sensors. . . .

10 Whether this counts as genuine *definition*, as Lewis seems to presume, is an issue to which we'll return shortly (§7.1.1).

11 By labeling them "o-" and "t-" terms, Lewis slyly echoes the more usual, but troublesome distinction between "observational" and "theoretic" terms, which can be regarded as simply an instance of, respectively, "o-" and "t-" terms.

12 I have actually defined what Lewis (1972/1980) calls a "modified Ramsey sentence," since Ramsey sentences don't always include the claim on uniqueness (demanded by the "(∃!)." We'll discuss this crucial commitment shortly.

13 This does require the assumption that the variables here are ranging over *state types* as opposed to tokens (see §2.4), which the reader should take as read. With a bit more trouble, one could have them range over state tokens.

14 In the interests of familiarity, I described the grammar school adder as operating on Arabic numerals. Strictly, to render this machine behaviorally equivalent to the unary adder, we would need to append to its states some further states that convert those Arabic numerals to unary ones (thus, writing "1" for "1," "11" for "2," "111" for "3," etc.). (Easy, but worthwhile exercise to the reader unfamiliar with Turing Machines: specify a Turing Machine that effects such a conversion.)

15 Something like this was apparently believed to be true in physics ca. 1975, but has since been superceded. But the point remains as at least an important epistemic possibility. For the question is how to define concepts that allow for such possibilities.

16 There are some who might deny this. The reader wanting to understand the full

metaphysical issues surrounding functionalism and quiddities may want to pursue the recent discussions of "(anti-)haecceitism" in for example, Kaplan (1975).

17 There are subtle issues that there is not space to pursue about how precisely to think of the metaphysics of functional *properties*. One standard way is to regard them as *second-order* properties: i.e. properties of things having some or other first-order (physical) properties that allow the role to be realized. Thus, the property of being a carburetor is the property of something's having some property or other that causes the fuel and the oxygen to be fed to the cylinders (see Block (1978/1980) for discussion). I, myself, am dissatisfied with this approach (what do we say if the fundamental properties of physics turn out to be functional?), but have no better proposal that would surmount the numerous technical problems in this area. However, note that even such second-order properties are definable using no more than physical terms (and a logic for second-order property definitions).

18 But note that functionalism could be entertained by a dualist, who posited some further non-physical phenomena – say, some ghostly ectoplasm – as the stuff that sustains the defining causal interactions with the physical; or by someone who thought that irreducibly sociological or biological predicates ought to be included among the non-mental predicates of the physical theory.

19 By "understanding" here, I don't mean in order to have the concept at all; rather, in order to appreciate the nature of the phenomenon it picks out.

20 This is particularly obvious if one thinks of a functional property as a second-order property (see note 17 above): the property of having some or other first-order physical property clearly mentions no specific physical properties at all; it just quantifies over them.

21 We'll discuss in chapter 7 further constraints on what would count as a realization of a functional organization.

22 Note that English words for functional kinds are mercilessly ambiguous between referring to the *kind* ("Money makes the world go round") and to the *realizer* of the kind ("Keep your hands off that money!").

23 Marr calls this a "functional" level, but enough uses here of this promiscuous word!

24 Indeed: what counts as a "breakdown"? Is susceptibility to the gambler's fallacy a "breakdown"? How about love, fear, or panic?

25 I discuss the significance of this work in Rey (1980c), although see below (§11.5) for some retraction.

26 In the way, for example, that Quine (1960:221) in the passage we quoted in §1.2.3 famously defines the issue between himself and Brentano.

7

Functionalism: Differences

In this chapter, we will consider the differences among ways in which the functionalist strategy has been pursued. As is not unusual in philosophy, these include not only different kinds of specific functional stories one might tell, but also different *meta*-approaches for deciding *between* those different kinds of stories. I'll deal with these latter first (§7.1), distinguishing "folk" functionalism (§7.1.1) from *a priori* functionalism (§7.1.2), and both of those from the psycho-functionalism that I will endorse (§7.1.3). With that meta-approach in hand, I will then consider four different kinds of functionalist stories (§7.2): "input/output" vs. what I call "anchored" functionalisms (§7.2.1); holistic vs. molecular functionalism (§7.2.2); teleo-functionalism (§7.2.3), and what I call "superficialism" (§7.2.4). Towards minimizing the commitments of mentalism, I will then defend mentalism as a theory – the so-called "theory theory" (§7.3) – for which I will propose a "Modest Mentalism" – a distally anchored, molecularist view – as a framework for understanding the computational/representational theory of the remainder of the book.

7.1 Different Meta-Approaches to Constitutive Stories

The project of presenting a constitutive story of the mind that, through ramsification, could provide a basis for defining mental terms is not likely to be easy. Constitutive stories of even the standard functionalist examples of carburetors and hearts are probably not as available as they initially seem (just how much of the story about internal combustion or biology need we tell?); and there can be little doubt that spelling out the relevant organization of the mind is a lot more complicated and a lot less well understood.

There have been three broad approaches to the problem, one based entirely on

184

folk beliefs; one based on traditional philosophical analysis; and one that looks, at least in part, to the development of an adequate empirical psychology.

7.1.1   Folk functionalism

In the same article in which he proposed the above procedure for ramsification, Lewis (1972/80) proposed an approach to finding the right story that has come to known as commonsense or *"folk functionalism"*:[1]

> Think of commonsense psychology as a term-introducing scientific theory, though one invented long before there was any institution as professional science. Collect all the platitudes you can think of regarding the causal relations of mental states, sensory stimuli, and motor responses. . . . Add also all the platitudes to the effect that one mental state falls under another "toothache is a kind of pain" and the like. . . . Include only platitudes which are common knowledge among us – everyone knows them, everyone knows that everyone else knows them, and so on. For the meanings of our words are common knowledge, and I am going to claim that the names of mental states derive their meaning from these platitudes. (1972/1980:212)

Note that this is an *approach* to telling the relevant story, not the story itself.[2]

The attraction of this view is that it affords a simple answer to the question of how we understand the meanings of our ordinary mental words: we understand them exactly as well as we understand the platitudes. Moreover, the skeptical possibilities that led people to ABism seem also to be met, but without the drawbacks of that view. For example, the possibility of behavioral "zombies" (creatures that behave normally, but without an inner life) would seem to be at least greatly reduced, since to have an "inner mental life" is just to satisfy the platitudes, and (the assumption might be uncritically made) there is no more problem about ascertaining this in other people's cases than in one's own. Jackson and Pettit (1993) have even recruited the view to answer the eliminativist about beliefs and desires: if we restrict the commonplaces to ones "not open to serious doubt," then, they conclude, "there can be no doubt that there is commonplace belief and . . . desire" (p. 303).

However, it is important to note that, aside from the suggestion of some general classificatory examples like "toothache is a pain," it's not entirely obvious just what might get included among the platitudes. For starters, there's the problem of what to do about eliminativists and other philosophers who might well render the "common knowledge" virtually null (eliminativists don't think there are any beliefs or desires; and neither they nor epiphenomenalists think any mental states cause *anything* at all!) But if one were to rule out anyone who's thought about philosophy, the "common knowledge" might get pretty wild: overwhelming numbers of the population take for granted beliefs about dualism, the immor-

185

tality of the soul, a will that is free from causal determination, the essential privacy of the mind that – to put it mildly – might well be mistaken. On a less metaphysical level, consider traditional platitudes about human egoism, women's subservience, or the sickness of homosexuality: is all manner of pop psychology to be enshrined as *analytic*? Certainly this would put a crimp in the style of those who doubt some of it.[3] (Moreover, as Lewis states the view, should any *one* of these "commonsense platitudes" turn out to be seriously mistaken, *no* mental terms would apply whatsoever! We'll return to this holism issue shortly (§7.2.2).[4]

Part of the problem here is that the folk, themselves, don't regard just anything they all happen to know (or believe; and believe that everyone else believes) as being genuinely definitional. Although they know that people typically say "ow!" when they're in pain, they also know that this is an entirely contingent fact, and that it could change: as we noted in criticizing ABism, there could be races of Super-Spartans who don't express their feelings about anything much at all. Surely the folk, on a moment's reflection, would realize that most commonplaces serve merely as "reference fixers": descriptions that fix what we are talking *about* when we use our mental terms, that distinguish what we are talking about from contextual rivals, but are not intended to serve as anything like constitutive analyses (see §1.5 above).[5] Resting the analysis of the mental on folk platitudes alone doesn't allow for the folk's own views about the analysis of their own terms.[6]

But what *do* the folk regard as definitional? Presumably this question really is: what is definitional, or genuinely analytic for the folk – and the rest of us? This is, of course, the question with which we (and lots of other philosophy) started (cf. §1.5.1).

7.1.2 A priori *functionalism*

According to *a priori* functionalism, the correct story to submit to ramsification is to be found by the traditional *a priori* methods of philosophical analysis. Its most influential proponent has been Sydney Shoemaker (1984), and he defends the position in a series of papers of great richness and sophistication.[7] Although he never actually provides examples of specific analyses, he suggests how they would go:

> The analytic functionalist seeks to extract his definition from a "theory" consisting of analytic or conceptual truths about the relations of mental states to inputs, outputs and other mental states. (1984:272)

an approach that is to be contrasted with Lewis':

> David Lewis is often classified as an analytic functionalist. But Lewis characterizes the theory from which functional definitions are to be derived as consisting of

186

"commonsense platitudes" about the mind – and while he suggests that at least some of these have the flavor of analyticity about them, it is no by means clear that he wants to include only those platitudes that could be claimed to be analytic. . . . Assuming that our "common-sense platitudes" are synthetic, if one of them should turn out to be contradicted by scientific findings we presumably would not want to include it in the theory to which the Ramsey-Lewis technique is to be applied; we do not want to define our mental terms in terms of a *false* theory. (1984:273)

We discussed the traditional methods of analysis briefly in §1.5.1. And while these may be fruitful in providing some constraints on the application of our terms and concepts, at least in the case of explanatorily interesting ones, we noted that at least the folk frequently "defer to experts." They know they don't know about the nature of things, and wonder what the proper constitutive analysis might be. This would seem overwhelmingly true in the case of mental terms, where most of us are obviously at sea in trying even to begin to define them. At best, what would seem to be available from *a priori* analysis would be some rough constraints that merely "fix the reference" of mental terms. If this is true, then of course the analyses provided by the folk are not themselves complete functional analyses. They will have an indexical element in them, and that, as we already noted, seems to be incompatible with the aim of the functionalist strategy.

The only way functionalism could be saved in this case, would be if the kind picked out by the indexical were in fact a functional kind. But to determine what kind that is, we would need the aid of an *empirical* psychological theory: the analysis of mental phenomena may be no more a fit topic of purely *a priori* investigation than is the analysis of physical phenomena. The functionalism that emerges from this strategy is called "psycho-functionalism."

7.1.3 *Psycho-functionalism*[8]

Psycho-functionalism is the view that the story about the mind that will provide the basis for analysis by ramsification will be the one provided (at least in part) by a theoretical psychology. Its main motivation is the idea I urged in §1.5.2 that explanatory concepts are likely to be best defined in terms of conditions initially hidden to us about the character of the relevant explanatory theory. As one of its foremost proponents, William Lycan (1988), put it:

As in Putnam's examples of "water", "tiger" and so on . . . the ordinary word "belief" (qua theoretical term of folk psychology) points dimly towards a natural kind that we have not yet fully grasped and that only a mature psychology will reveal. (1988:32)

Psychology is not different from any other science in exploiting terms whose proper definition will only emerge from an adequate theory of the phenomena that are ordinarily picked out by what are often only accidental traits.[9]

Or is it? In a recent book, Colin McGinn (1991:132ff) resists psycho-functionalism (what he calls "Strong Scientific Realism" (about the mind)), pointing out that the multiple realizability emphasized by functionalism rules out the kind of hidden essences one finds in, for example, the cases of "water" and "gold" emphasized by Putnam and Kripke: it is the *substance that realizes* a certain role that has the relevant hidden essence in these cases, not the role itself.[10] Similarly, Jackson and Pettit (1993) claim:

> it would be a mistake to hold that "believer" tags the kind: warmblooded, car-bon based creature. Silicon-based, cold-blooded Vesuvians might have had beliefs. (1993:304)

These objections, however, overlook the variety of different phenomena that mental terms can be taken to ordinarily "tag." The psycho-functionalist is not concerned with cases in which mental terms might be used to tag *occupiers* of a functional role, any more than an economist trying to understand the nature of money would be interested in uses of "money" merely to tag a particular currency ("Pass me the money on the table"). Terms used to tag an occupier of a role can also be used to tag *the role itself* ("Money is whatever is used as a medium of ex-change . . ."). It is an accident of the history of the "deferential" move in semantics, evident in the above quote from Lycan, that the paradigm examples were species and substance terms like "tiger," "water," and "gold," where this particular ambiguity doesn't so obviously arise. This has led many authors to suppose that psycho-functionalism is committed to the analyses of mental terms proceeding in strict analogy with such terms. But the examples are slightly misleading; the analogy must be understood more abstractly.

Consider the standard functionalist examples of automotive and biological kinds. Certainly it is possible to run the same appeals to explanation that I argued motivate deference in the chemical cases. Thus, "carburetor" might have been introduced to someone as a term for a certain part of an engine, without them having the slightest idea what it does: it's just that odd looking thing to one side of the distributor. They can then ask what a carburetor really is: what constitutes being a carburetor. And here, surely, a functional specification is at least partly appropriate; and on the basis of it many things that didn't look at all like the original carburetor are included. The term "carburetor" tagged a *functional kind*. Similarly, "eye" names a biological functional kind, even if it was introduced merely by reference to a certain shaped organ in the face, which is why the peculiar little colored patches that speckle the interiors of (large) clams count as genuine eyes, but not the shapes that decorate the feathers of a peacock.

According to the psycho-functionalist, what has been tagged by, for example, "belief" is not a *biological* kind, but rather a *psychological* kind, and psychological kinds are individuated not by either their substance or their origin (as in the case of "water" or "tiger") but rather *a specific functional role*.[11] To put it another way: there is nothing in psycho-functionalism that requires the hidden essences to be, so to say, "vertical," as they happen to be in the case of substance terms like "water" or "gold," where the essence is provided by underlying *internal* features of the referent. There might well be hidden, "horizontal" essences, as is likely in cases like "battery," "capitalist," "ecological niche," or "spleen," where the essence is provided by the *external relations* the referent bears to other things, often (as, in the case of functional definitions) at the same explanatory level.

7.1.4   Some constraints on thought experiments

Jackson and Pettit (1993:304) do go on to consider whether "belief" might pick out "a distinctive style of information processing" (which was Lycan's psychological speculation), but worry that:

> it would be unduly chauvinistic to insist that in order to count as a believer a creature must solve the informational processing problems a world sets its inhabitants in the same general way that we do, or in anything like the way we do. Monocular silicon-based Vesuvians would no doubt process information about the location of objects around them . . . very differently from the way we binocular carbon-based Earthians do, but any science-fiction buff knows that our concept of belief does not thereby preclude the Vesuvians from having beliefs, say, about the location of objects around them.   (1993:304–5)

Leaving aside for a moment the unfortunate vagaries of the phrase "information processing" (which applies at a multitude of different theoretical levels), it's instructive to become clear about what precisely "any science-fiction buffs knows." Is it really true, as this passage and our earlier intuitions on behalf of ABism suggest, that it really makes no difference to our mental concepts what goes on at *any* psychological level that might be hidden in the brain?

Take as an extreme case, that of finding that many otherwise ordinary people's skulls are empty, or filled with oatmeal: would that be a reason to think that they didn't have minds? The *psycho-functionalist* needn't think so, for a very simple reason: it's open to him to presume that these creatures' minds are *realized otherwise than the way they happen to be in the cases that we have so far examined*. There are a number of ways this might be true: for starters, notice that if it were revealed that some behaviorally normal person had *nothing* inside his skull, that would simply be a reason for thinking it wasn't his brain that was responsible for his behavior at all. Indeed, if we had nothing inside *our own*, that would be a reason for thinking that we are as mistaken as past philosophers have been about what played the role of the "organ of thought" (Aristotle believed it was the heart; Descartes that it involved some special substance that only interacted with the brain in the pineal gland).

The mere "logical possibility" – and here, not even clearly a quantum possibility! – of bizarrely headed Vesuvians need not *per se* deter us from defining psychological states in terms of ordinarily hidden cognitive structure. Indeed, Vesuvians might differ from humans at *many* different levels of description: substance, physical arrangement of their "nervous system," input systems, monocular vs. binocular vision, even at many levels of "information processing." The question is *whether they differ at the level at which a mature psychology will define psychological phenomena*.

Consider a nice example of Donald Davidson's (1973/1979) in which he rightly observes that whether an act was intentional (in the sense of deliberate) depends upon the *way* in which a reason brings about an act:

> A climber might want to rid himself of the weight and danger of holding another man on a rope, and he might know that by loosening his hold on the rope he could rid himself of the weight and danger. This belief and want might so unnerve him as to cause him to loosen his hold, and yet it might be the case that he never *chose* to loosen his hold, nor did he do it intentionally. (1973/1979:79)

Davidson (pp. 80–1), himself, despairs of spelling out the appropriate way that would distinguish genuine intentional action from the behavior of the climber, and we might well agree with him that there is no *a priori* way of doing so. But why shouldn't this be precisely the sort of distinction one might expect of a mature psychology, just as (to return to the examples of Putnam we discussed in §1.5.2) distinctions among diseases is what one expects of medicine and biology? If it is, then it could well turn out that some people who let go of ropes in such circumstances are doing it deliberately, and others aren't; and perhaps the psychology of the normal actions of Vesuvians is, despite commonsense appearances, more like the latter, so that it could turn out that none of their actions are actually *deliberate* as many of ours are: the distinction just doesn't apply to them (just as it may not apply to many animals).

A deference to hidden essences can, I think, be detected in many other mental phenomena. Ask yourself, for example, whether dreams should be counted as *conscious* experiences; whether we make genuine *decisions* in them; whether, when driving an automobile engaged in lively conversation, one is conscious of the details of the road; or what it takes to be courageous rather than foolhardy, "weak" vs. "strong" willed, self-deceptive vs. simply forgetful. Does your mastery of commonplaces really determine the correct answer (or even whether the answer is indeterminate)? These cases would seem to exhibit even more dramatically what Grice (1965:463), anticipating Putnam (1975b; see §1.5.2 above), claimed about *perception*, that our analysis "leaves a blank space to be filled in by the specialist."

Ironically enough, when we turn to the folk for definitions, they turn to the scientists: the folk seem to *know they don't know* how properly to define mental phenomena (whether concepts or properties).

In sum, in seriously assessing science-fiction cases that appear to undermine psycho-functionalism, an unusual number of intellectual controls need to be exercised: one needs to (a) measure them against the demands of specific mentalistic concepts, (b) imagine plausible definitions of those concepts that might issue from a mature psychology, (c) control for the possibility of unusual realizations, and (d) consider whether the possibility would be sufficiently serious to undermine a mature psychology. Psycho-functionalism would seem a not unreasonable approach to the analysis of mental terms, pending the provision of examples that satisfy all these constraints.[12]

7.2   Different Functionalist Stories

There is a surprising variety of different kinds of specific stories functionalists tell, a variety that, we'll see, is crucial to defending the strategy against objections too often directed to only one species of it. Most of these stories will be of interest only to a psycho-functionalist, although we'll see that some might be told by the folk functionalist, depending upon the platitudes on which the folk as matter of fact manage to agree.

7.2.1   *Input/output vs. anchored functionalism*

An issue that is left entirely unspecified in the above ramsification procedure is precisely what "old" terms – in our case, what non-mental terms – are to be included in the M story provided at stage (i). There are a variety of further constraints different functionalists have proposed.

The form of functionalism that one finds most cited in the literature is what might be called "Input/Output" (or "I/O") functionalism. This would model the analyses of mental states closely on the model of the analyses of TM states, which as the above examples make clear, are individuated *merely by inputs, outputs, and their relations to other states*.[13] In the case of the analysis of any particular mental state, this would mean that the ramsification would mention nothing but patterns of afferent and efferent electrical signals, and relations among them and other mental states.

I/O functionalism can actually be understood in two ways, depending upon a crucial issue of how one specifies what counts as "inputs" and "outputs." As Block (1978/1980) has rightly pointed out, this can be done at various levels of abstraction, and it's not clear what principles ought to constrain us. At one extreme of abstraction, one might define inputs and outputs merely as further states to be included in the ramsification: an input is just whatever causes the system to enter certain states that produce certain outputs and further states in a specific pattern, and output is just what is caused by those states when they've been effected by a certain input in that pattern. The resulting I/O functionalism would be maximally abstract: one would have described simply an abstract causal structure that need not have any specific ties to the material world. We might call this "abstract I/O functionalism" (Block calls attention to some disturbing risks of such abstractness that we'll discuss in §9.3). Alternatively, one might refer to the particular patterns of firings of afferent (input) and efferent (output) *nerve* ends that are peculiar to human beings – risking here, though, confining mental states only to creatures that actually have nerve ends like ours.

As austere as either version of I/O functionalism might be, they do have resources to capture a great deal that can seem crucial to mental phenomena. For example, someone might argue that all that is essential to thought is reasoning, and that all that is essential to reasoning is computation. If so, then it would appear that all that is essential to thought might be captured merely by Turing Machines, or, at any rate, that mental states need involve no more than inputs and outputs and the causal relations that define TM states.

Although one can appreciate this general reason for restricting functional definitions in this way, it is worth noting that nothing about ramsification or even a commitment to the above computational suggestion, requires it. While causal relations between states may capture *certain* central features of thought, one might well not regard them as sufficient by themselves. For starters, mental states have *meaning* or *content*, and it is not at all obvious that this is captured by relations among states alone.

One might regard this issue as another aspect of properly characterizing "inputs" and "outputs." One strategy is simply to presume that certain *semantic* or *content* relations might be specified *independently* of the specification of a mind. Some aspects of *meaning* conceivably could be defined prior to *mentality*.[14] If this were possible, one might then plausibly confine "inputs" and "outputs" to only *symbols*, i.e. states that in fact enjoyed the content properties specified by that semantic theory. After all, Turing Machines themselves are understood in something like this way: Turing simply *presumes* the inputs and outputs are, for example, *numerals* that *represent* numbers; or (in the case of a Universal Machine) strings of letters that *represent* a Turing Machine. And, as we'll see, many people who take seriously a computational theory of the mind, presume the contents of the states depend upon the relations that features or states of the brain bear to phenomena in the external world.

Alternatively, one might think that the theory of meaning can't be specified independently of a theory of mind. In this case, either one would provide a way of specifying meaning entirely by means of internal relations among the states (sometimes called a "conceptual role semantics") or, if one thought that any real

192

symbols still had to be related to an external environment, one might expand the functional definition to include reference to phenomena in the external world. This gives rise to what Block (1978/1980) calls "long-armed functionalism": the "inputs" and "outputs" are not confined to "proximal" stimuli at the surface of the body of the mental agent, but in terms of the *distal*, often stable causes of those proximal stimuli – e.g. shapes, objects, people, properties in the external world – and the worldly effects of those efferent discharges: the motion of arms and legs and lips, the uttering of sentences, the pressing of buttons, the destruction of empires. Philosophers inclined to see minds as necessarily embedded in an environment might be inclined towards functional defintions of this sort.[15]

There are other quite plausible constraints on functional specification. *Thinking*, after all, is a *process* taking place in real time. For a system to have a thought, it shouldn't be enough merely for a system to satisfy a conditional concerning what it *would* do were it presented with certain inputs; what is at least equally important is what it is *in fact* doing at a particular time: i.e. it had better be *performing* the requisite computations (and perhaps to actually have a thought is to enjoy a stage in such a real process, a stage that wouldn't count as a thought were it separated from this process).

Not only must many mental processes take place in time, but arguably many of them had better take place at a certain *rate* and in elaborate conjunction with certain other processes: someone doesn't ordinarily count as *intelligent* if it takes him hours (or years!) to perform the computations that would take a normal child only a few minutes. And, whatever else appreciating a work of art or a piece of music may involve, it arguably involves appreciating a whole lot of inputs "at once": certain states need to be run "in parallel."[16]

Still further constraints can be imagined. A folk functionalist might well observe that, although the folk may not know anything very specific about the brain, it's surely a platitude that all mental things they've ever encountered are biologically *alive*.[17] So *some* general physiological constraints might conceivably be introduced on the states; such views might be called "physiofunctionalist."[18] A number of philosophers (Block 1978/1980, Shoemaker 1981/1984) have supposed that certain features of qualitative experience may essentially involve such physiological constraints. The problem, of course, is to provide a principled reason for including any specific physiological properties. But this is a piece of the general problem that we haven't yet pretended to solve, of saying precisely which story of the mind we should accept. But since the causal relations among the states might still play a significant role in identifying particular states – belief and desire, for example, might still need to be defined by their joint relation to action – such views would still seem to count as functionalist.

I call all these various supplementations to pure I/O functionalism various forms of "anchored" functionalisms: states are partly individuated by input and output and relations among themselves, but *also* by relations to certain non-functional, non-mental features, like timing or certain content relations to other phenomena, or simply certain physiological properties that realize the I/O states (I'll sometimes include reference to specific sorts of anchors – e.g. distal, environmental ones for semantics; physiological ones for qualitative states – in identifying an anchoring theory). In terms of the ramsification procedure, one is simply including these features as "old" terms that may be included in specifying the relations among the defined mental states.

7.2.2   Holistic vs. molecular (and homuncular) functionalism

The very advantage ramsification affords of defining a set of terms at once, if not handled carefully, can also be a trap: terms defined together fall together. If *any* clause of the M-story provided at stage (i) of the ramsification were to turn out to be false, then the entire Ramsey sentence is false, and *none* of the terms defined by it apply to *anything*! For example, suppose we wondered whether some actual computer was in state S1 of our unary adder. Well, a machine couldn't be in state S1 unless, when it read a 1 it went into state S2; and it couldn't be in S2 unless when it read a *, it went into S3, . . . and so forth, around the states.

Lewis' commonsense proposal seems to fall into just this trap. As stated, the view entails that *the applicability of any one mental predicate depends upon the applicability of all the others*. Consequently, should *some* platitudes of folk psychology turn out to be false, either of people generally or of some creatures that happen to lack some of the capacities that people possess, then *no mental terms would refer* to states of those systems: the Ramsey sentence, $(\exists!x_1) \ldots (\exists!x_n)C_M (x_1 \ldots x_n)$, (where C_M is the conjunction of platitudes) would be false of them, and so, for each mental term, t_i, of folk psychology, there simply would not exist "the x_i such that $(\exists!x_1) \ldots (\exists!x_{i1})(\exists!x_{i+1})(\exists!x_n)(C_M(x_1 \ldots x_i \ldots x_n))$"! But surely people or animals who fail to satisfy *some* folk terms shouldn't thereby fail to satisfy *all* of them: e.g. people who can't feel pain, or psychopaths who don't form the usual personal attachments, can surely have beliefs and desires and other perceptions. Moreover, it's surely not implausible that *some* platitudes about some portion of the mind – say, about egoism, sexuality, unconscious motivation, empiricism, dualism, will turn out to be quite seriously mistaken, and so undermine any reasonable notion of even approximate truth.[19]

A more plausible alternative is to use ramsification not all at once, but bit by bit, defining small *clusters* of mental terms in relative isolation from one another. Thus, the terms clustering around an account of perception ("stimulation," "appearance," "belief") might be interdefined independently of the terms clustering around action ("intention," "decision"). Some of the molecules may form a hierarchy: perhaps belief and desire ought to be defined together; and then, having so defined desire, we might proceed to define perception partly in terms of belief, intention partly in terms of desire; hope in terms of both . . . and so forth, in such

194

a way that, although a failure at the bottom of such a hierarchy could vitiate the rest of it (so that something without beliefs couldn't have intentions), a failure at the top could leave the lower and cousin terms intact (so that something that didn't form intentions might still have beliefs; or someone centrally paralyzed could still have perceptions, and someone congenitally blind could still be capable of making decisions).[20] Note that, to return to the functionalist's standard analogies, this strategy would be by no means peculiar to the mind: one would sensibly be a molecular functionalist about the parts of automobiles or, in biology, the parts of bodies (the parts of the transmission will be definable independently of the parts of the brakes, the parts of the digestive system independently of the heart). A hierarchical, molecular functionalism seems to be a general strategy for understanding nature at any number of different levels of organization at which interesting law-like generalizations occur.

Many psychological theories – not to mention popular thought – are molecular in a very particular way: they posit further *personal agencies* as functional molecules constitutive of a normal human being. Thus, there is Freudian talk of the struggles between ego, id, and superego; Plato's conception of a person as a kind of republic writ small; and even talk in cognitive science about sub-routines being executed by certain processors following certain instructions. This sort of molecular functionalism has been endorsed by Lycan (1987:40–1) as "Homuncular Functionalism" (or "Homuncularism").

A common worry about homuncular theories, raised most famously by Ryle (1949), is that explaining people's behavior by appeal to further people inside them invites an infinite regress that can't be explanatory. Although initially plausible, and perhaps damaging to theories like Freud's, Fodor (1968) and others[21] have pointed out that the regress isn't infinite if eventually the homunculi get so stupid they can obviously be replaced by a machine. If, for example, the innermost homunculi in such an explanation are agents that behave like the scanners in a Turing Machine, then they can be "discharged" simply by imagining some mechanical device that could be sensitive to printed characters on a tape, and move left or right accordingly (we'll see how this is precisely the strategy of the computational theory of mind discussed in the next chapter).

One philosophically important consequence of molecular functionalism is that it finally affords us the possibility of completely freeing the identification of a psychological state from any tight connection with behavior. It's perfectly open to the molecularist to suppose, quite along the lines of ordinary thought, that few (if any) of the states of subsystems of the mind are actually defined in terms of actual behavior. For example, the output of a perceptual system would presumably not have anything to do with muscular contractions, but with input to some reasoning sub-system; the output of a reasoning system with input to a decision making sub-system; and even a decision-making system might only issue in abstract efferent commands to a motor sub-system that might then execute those efferent commands in ways not entirely specified by the other sub-systems – or it might be unable to execute these commands at all! Thus, a person might have perfectly normal perceptions and even processes of rational thought, even though they might be paralyzed; or perhaps simply unable to "make up their mind" about what to do.[22] In line with one of the main objections we raised against ABism, the relation of most psychological states and specific behaviors can be entirely *contingent*.

7.2.3   Teleo-functionalism

One might, however, wonder what entitles functionalists to think that "functions" (or roles) are real features of the world. Doesn't something serve a function only relative to the interests of someone who uses it for a certain purpose? A metal bar, for example, is an axle – and two metal bars are a broken axle – given that the bar(s) was intended by the automaker to play a certain role. Searle concludes from this that no talk of function is legitimate apart from assumptions about the intentions of an agent:

> The so-called "functional level" is not a separate level at all, but simply one of the causal levels *described in terms of our interests*. . . . [W]hen we say that the heart functions to pump blood, the only facts in question are that the heart does, in fact, pump blood [and] that fact is important to us. . . . If the only thing that interested us about the heart was that it made a thumping noise . . . we would have a com- pletely different conception of its "functioning".   (1992:237–8)

Searle is right to call attention to an issue here that has not always received in the philosophy of mind the attention it deserves.[23] After all, if Searle were right, functionalism would presuppose and so could not explain mentality. However, there has in fact been substantial discussion of the issue in the philosophy of biology, an area quite independent of the mind where talk of function seems to play an important explanatory role. One fairly compelling line of argument suggests that something plays a certain functional role insofar as it was *selected* to do so. In the case of an artifact, it was the artifactor who selected certain things to play certain roles; and, perhaps, if God created living things, the roles their parts play would be determined by Her intentions. Darwin, however, taught us that the selection process need not be intentional. It could be "natural": out of a randomly generated pool of genetic possibilities in a certain environment, certain species are more fit for replication than others and so are selected *by virtue of possessing certain traits*. A number of philosophers have argued that such a process of selection not only legitimizes speaking of these latter traits as serving a function in the survival and replication of the species, but that a great deal of actual physiological tax- onomy presupposes that it does.[24] Thus, a particular bodily organ is a heart insofar as it originated in a process whereby it was selected to play that role: thus a defective heart is still a heart. Some of these philosophers would go on to argue in a similar vein that nothing really is a realization of a Turing Machine state unless its being so is based either in an intentional or natural selection process.

There is no need to enter into the details of this important discussion here (we shall return to it only briefly in considering teleosemantic theories of meaning in §9.2.3), much less settle whether all talk of function does rely in this way upon some process of selection.[25] It is enough to see the room for the view, and the resulting evolutionary restrictions someone convinced of it might want to place on functional analyses of mental phenomena. Functionalist views so restricted are what are called "teleo-fuctionalist" views (where the "telos" is the end, either natural or intentional, for which a trait is selected).

7.2.4 *Superficialism*

"An inner process stands in need of outward criteria," declared Wittgenstein (1953:§580), and (as we've seen, introduction §2, §5.3) he inveighed against those who supposed that psychology was about something "hidden," somehow literally "inside" one's mind or brain. The motto could be taken as an expression of ABism: an inner process must be *defined* in terms of observable, external behavior. But it can also be taken in a weaker way: it could mean merely that for every mental process there is *some or other* piece of outward behavior that would, in a particular context, be criterial (or decisive) of its presence.[26] One needn't insist that it be the *same* piece of behavior in every context. Thus, sometimes pain may be indicated by screams, another by biting one's lip, still another by someone's simply saying (again in the right circumstances) "It will soon abate." Although this weaker reading would deprive us of the behavioral analyses promised by ABism, many philosophers think that it is a reasonable constraint on any functionalist analyses. Thus, Dennett, although clearly not an ABist, recently writes:

> I unhesitatingly endorse the claim that necessarily, if two organisms are behaviorally exactly alike, they are psychologically exactly alike.   (1993:922)

I call this weaker form "superficialism."[27]

The main motive for superficialism is one natural understanding of the "folk functionalism" we discussed above, particularly an understanding of it rooted in the verificationism we discussed at the end of chapter 5. To relieve anxieties about skeptical possibilities – e.g. that other people are "mere automatons" lacking any conscious life – philosophers want to tie the constitutive conditions of a concept to its evidential ones. Dennett (1991a) has been explicit in endorsing the view for precisely these sorts of reasons:

> Philosophers have recently managed to convince themselves – and many an innocent bystander – that verificationism is *always* a sin. . . . [But] it is time for the pendulum

to swing back. . . . I am ready to come out of the closet as some sort of verificationist, but not please, a Village Verificationist; let's all be *Urbane* Verificationists. (1991a:461)

His worry is the standard one:

[I]f we are not urbane verificationists, we will end up tolerating all sorts of nonsense: epiphenomenalism, zombies, indistinguishable inverted spectra, conscious teddy bears, self-conscious spiders. (1991a:461)

Dennett never exactly defines "urbane verificationism," but that it qualifies as superficialist emerges from the way in which he deploys it. For example, in the same book he writes:

Suppose something happened in my presence, but left its trace on me for only "a millionth of a second". . . . Whatever could it mean to say that I was, however briefly and ineffectually, conscious of it? (1991a:132)
"Just because you can't tell, by your preferred ways, whether or not you *were* conscious of x, doesn't mean you *weren't*. Maybe you *were* conscious of it but just can't find any evidence for it!" Does anyone, on reflection, really want to say that? (1991a:133, italics mine)

Indeed, he concludes:

There is no reality of conscious experience independent of the effects of various vehicles of content on subsequent action (and hence, of course, on memory). (1991a:132)

Now, what's important here is not the question whether there actually *is*, for example, a conscious event of a millionth of a second, but whether Dennett's reflections here establish that it's absurd to think so. At first blush, he would appear to be falling into the worst excesses of verificationism: it's not the least bit absurd to suppose that many, even the vast majority of conscious experiences vanish without a trace – along with all countless pencils, umbrellas, once-mighty empires and pre-historic birds, and cups of coffee (*most* things vanish without any known trace; certainly most mental episodes do!). However, even were Dennett to avoid this excess (say, by appeal to "possible traces"), he would still seem to be falling afoul of precisely the moral of the Shoemaker example of stalled time, supposing that because there is no obvious *direct* verification of a claim, there could be no verification whatsoever.

A second thought, however, needs to be considered: that there are certain concepts whose meaning *is* somehow exhausted by certain direct verifications. Although I don't really want to defend this view here, it's important to appreciate its plausibility. Consider an ordinary concept like [extremely poisonous]: presumably this means something like "would cause severe illness or death if ingested by a normal human being." One, indeed, might take severe illness or death regularly following ingestion to be be pretty good (*prima facie*, defeasible) evidence that something was poisonous.[28] Could something be poisonous that didn't pass this test (it *never* caused illness or death upon being ingested)? Perhaps; but it does strain one's intuitions to think so.[29] It would seem to be part and parcel of the very concept [poisonous] that this couldn't happen.

I think Dennett thinks mental concepts ought to be regarded in this way; their application cannot completely transcend all the *ordinary* evidence we adduce for them. Indeed, Dennett (1995b) agrees with my characterization of him as a "superficialist," quoting with approval Quine's quotation of a motto of the Sherwin-Williams paint company, "Save the surface and you save all" (1995b:530). He in turn characterizes the psycho-functionalism I defend as "hysterical realism, an attempt to turn the nominal essences of science into real essences" (p. 535). Mental concepts are not like the natural kind concept [water], but rather like the more plausibly superficial kind, [dust] (which presumably does not have any sort of hidden essence):

> The question then that divides Rey and me might seem to be: Are the concepts of folk psychology like the concept of dust or like the concept of water? . . . I think we already know enough about many of them to know that even though they may aspire to name natural kinds (unlike the concept dust) they aren't good enough to succeed. (1995b:536).

But why think this? Dennett does go on to admit that "this is a difference of opinion arising from different readings of the empirical facts," and, in a revealing passage a few pages earlier, compares our present situation in psychology with the situation of Einstein in physics, despairing of drawing a distinction between a gravitational field and an accelerated frame of reference (p. 532).

However, surely if there's anything clear about our present situation in psychology it is that it's decidedly *not* remotely like the position of Einstein in relation to the physics of 1900. The (albeit mistaken) physics of 1900 was a well-worked out, well-confirmed, mature theory of the world that allowed Einstein to say with real empirical authority that certain distinctions had no basis in reality. Psychology may not still be in its infancy; but with such massive conceptual and experimental problems of the sort we have been discussing in this book, the best that could be claimed for it is an extremely awkward early adolescence. In any case, we are certainly in no position to say with anything like Einstein's authority that certain folk distinctions correspond to no real distinctions in the world. To the contrary, unlike explanations appealing to such genuinely superficial phenomena like poisons and dust – or Sherwin-Williams' paint – folk psychological explanations do seem as though they are on to something; indeed, as we observed at the end of chapter 4, they seem like the only explanation of a variety of phenomena that we can seriously imagine (we will return to other aspects of "hysterical realism" in §10.3.4).

I suspect what drives Dennett and others to superficialism is not any illusion about the maturity of current psychology, but, rather, more traditional assumptions about our grasp of mental (and perhaps any)[30] concepts. Superficialism has the advantage of not only promising a possible answer to the problem of other minds, but also of answering the otherwise puzzling question of what the meanings of mental terms might be, and how anyone could possibly grasp them. Here it might be thought that superficialism is supported by folk functionalism, which analyzes mental terms by appeal to what folk users of them can be presumed to know. But, as we saw, there is reason to doubt that it is supportable in this way: as the examples of intentional action, courage, self-deception, and even being conscious were intended to show, commonsense acknowledges its own limitations and defers to science about the meanings of many mental terms.[31]

Indeed, despite the pull of superficialism, some of our ordinary mental concepts do seem to rely on the existence of facts that may not be available on the surface. Consider the nice case Dennett (1988a, 1991a:395–6) himself discusses of the adult beer-drinker who wonders whether in coming to like it since childhood, it's his *experiences* or his *preferences* that have changed. The wonder seems perfectly intelligible, yet it can certainly seem obscure what further considerations should settle the matter: it's not implausible to suppose that mere introspective memory or present behavioral discriminations wouldn't suffice. Indeed, let us suppose with Dennett that all of the behavioral and introspective data are compatible with either hypothesis.[32] Dennett concludes:

> So if a beer drinker . . . says that what he is referring to is "*the way the beer tastes to me right now*," he is definitely kidding himself if he thinks he can *thereby* refer to a quale of his acquaintance, a subjective state that is independent of his changing reactive attitudes. (1991a:396)

But now suppose it turns out that children have more taste buds than adults. One might have independent evidence that both children and adults have the same *preferences* for bitter titillation, but that consequently children reach a painful threshold sooner with the same quantity of a bitter substance. It *tastes* differently, since, arguably, more intense sensation is caused by their tongues and/or gustation sub-systems. Why couldn't the beer drinker's references to his taste sensations be vindicatable in just this way? When he talks about the "taste of beer," as opposed to his preferences regarding it, why couldn't he be taken to be referring to the output of his gustation module, if there is one? However, in such a case he would be doing so in a way that transcends strictly superficial, i.e. mere introspective and behavioral, evidence. That is, our ordinary distinction between *perception* and *preference* would seem to depend upon there being principled distinctions hidden away in our nervous systems that are not perhaps even in principle superficially available.[33]

Similar cases could be made for the other phenomena mentioned in our discussion of folk functionalism, e.g. whether drivers engrossed in conversation are or aren't conscious of the road; whether dreams are conscious; whether we make decisions in dreams. Although it's *possible* that there could be surface phenomena that would decide these issues, it's hard to see why there *must* be. To the extent that *this* also is common knowledge among the folk, the folk are, I submit, not only psycho-functionalists, but non-superficialist ones at that. In any case, I shall take for granted non-superficialist psycho-functionalism for the remainder of this book.

7.3   Towards Minimizing Commitments

7.3.1   The theory theory

Mentalism, as it is ordinarily employed, does not appear to be a theory. Our understanding of ourselves and others as mental beings seems so automatic that it seems odd to compare it with what is usually the self-conscious activity of scientific speculation. Indeed, there has recently arisen considerable controversy regarding the actual processes people exploit in understanding one another: whether they do so by deploying what strikes many people as a cumbersome inferential apparatus (the "theory theory"), or rather run "simulations" of, for example, what *they* would do if they were in the other people's shoes (the "simulation theory").[34] *This* debate, however, needn't concern us here. For we need to be concerned at this point not with the *processing* question about how people *do* manage to understand one another and deploy folk psychological concepts, but rather with the *justificatory* question about how whatever mentalistic theory and concepts they do deploy could be defended (so as, *inter alia*, to meet the eliminativist challenge).[35]

But, if mentalism is a theory, where are the laws? Certainly it cannot boast any very precise ones. Mentalism, at this point, should be regarded not as a full-blown theory, but (as in the case of most developing sciences) a "theory sketch" (Hempel 1965). In a quite useful analogy, Lycan (1993) compares our epistemic situation with respect to the mind to that of aliens who couldn't look inside an automobile, but who could observe its external behavior. What could they infer about an automobiles's internal structure? Probably quite a bit. They could make quite plausible inferences from the complex behavior of automobiles to systems for steering, braking, ignition, gear transmission, and so forth. *However, it's only as they succeeded in correctly isolating these relevant sub-systems that they could hope to specify laws about how those sub-systems worked, and then how their interaction eventuated in the observable external behavior*. Indeed, there might well *not* be very good laws about the behavior of the car as a whole. Similarly, there might not be many deep laws of human *behavior*; the seriously explanatory laws will be about various sub-phenomena: sub-systems, sub-capacities, "competencies," to recall Chomsky's characterization of the subject matter of linguistics (§4.2.1 above).

Critics of mentalistic explanation often complain that plausible laws of the mind are so loose as to be circular: people may do what they most prefer; but that is only because what they most prefer is determined only by what in fact they do. As Skinner was fond of pointing out, practical explanation begins to look like the "dormitive virtue" explanations ridiculed by Molière.[36] Quite apart from the point just considered – that actual *behavior* is the wrong place to look for laws; what laws of decision making there might be will be about some sub-system of the mind – such a conception in any case ignores the substantial intricacy of mental ascriptions. A serious account of practical reasoning, for example, would consist of laws relating innumerable *instances* of beliefs, preferences, and acts, each instance providing independent evidence for the others: a belief may combine with other preferences to rationalize and explain one array of acts; and a preference may combine with other beliefs to rationalize and explain another array. *Wanting water* explains why if I think there's some to the left, I turn left, and why, if I think there's some to the right, I turn right. *Believing there's some to the right* explains why, if I want some, I turn right, and, if I want to avoid some, I turn elsewhere. As more beliefs and preferences are added, there are more and more possible combinations with consequences that admit of independent test. Furthermore, this network involves not only practical, but also other forms of (deductive, inductive/abductive)[37] reasoning whose execution in varying degrees (particularly insofar as such processes are genuinely causal) is open to still further independent test. And the entire network is further constrained by the innumerable true generalizations of plausible psychological research: generalizations about, for example, attention, gaze-fixation, startle, fear, memory, the effects of various drugs, and so forth; i.e. it will be constrained by the actual habits, needs, and physiology of the organism under various actual and counter-factual conditions. If one seriously bears in mind all these constraints, far from being circular, it is hard to formulate laws of practical reason that have a chance of being *true* – but, then, who said psychology should be easy?

In a related vein, it is sometimes protested that these laws can't be "empirical," that these generalizations are constitutive of the use of the mental terms and so are "analytic." Consequently, they cannot serve as the proper domain of a science, which strives to discover new, "contingent" laws. However, even if some of the generalizations – such as those involving deductive or practical reason – were to emerge from the above complexity as somehow constitutive of the meaning of the constituent terms, that shouldn't count against them. In the first place, theoretical roles of this sort may provide the basis for defining theoretical terms in general, precisely as we have seen that ramsification allows. Science may well consist in the imposition of these idealized generalizations upon a complicated world. If this is true, then it would not be surprising to find that, as Cummins (1983) has emphasized, a good part of the interest of psychology, as of many other scientific projects, consists not so much in the discovery of new laws, as in analyses of complicated cases to see how old laws apply.

So mental concepts might well be defended as pieces of a theory. But what sort of theory? Do the data of chapters 3 and 4 commit us to all the traditional claims about the mind that have given rise to all the problems of chapter 2? Are full-blown ordinary *belief*, *desire*, and *sensory experience* necessary? Is *free will* or *consciousness* necessary?

7.3.2   Modest Mentalism

Towards answering these questions, I want to propose a modest mentalistic explanatory structure that needn't at this stage be committed to answering these difficult questions one way or the other. To be as neutral as possible, I will simply refer to the broad distinction among propositional attiudes that I introduced in §1.1.2: the "informational" attitudes (which merely represent the world being a certain way) and the "directional" ones (which direct the agent towards or away from the world being a certain way). "Modest Mentalism" can be defined as follows:

1   stimuli cause informational states (perception)
2   some informational states are retained (memory)
3   informational states combine sometimes in rational patterns to produce other informational states (thought, reasoning)
4   informational states combine sometimes in rational patterns with (perhaps some pre-existing) directional states to produce further directional states and actions (decision making, action, approach, avoidance)
5   stimuli are caused by distal phenomena that provide many of the informational states with their meaning or content
6   systems organized according to 1–6 have been either naturally or intentional selected for being so.

These conditions are not intended to be an analysis of any mental phenomena.[38] In keeping with psycho-functionalism, we may leave that to a better theory than anyone yet has, and with it the difficult questions of whether, for example, a system could have informational without any directional states, perception without thought or thought without perception, or whether it would be possible for a being that hadn't been selected to be enjoying a completely hallucinatory mental life somewhere in a vat. All that is claimed for Modest Mentalism is that it provides a plausible framework in which we may begin to explain the non-question begging evidence that we adduced for the mind in chapters 3 and 4. It seems to provide the core of what is at issue in the debate over eliminativism. If nothing were to satisfy it, it would be unclear what explanatory point there would be to talk of minds at all. Moreover, it captures a very great deal of the structure of ordinary "folk psychology": I submit that it is the core of what many authors regard as mentalistic explanation: what Weber (1922/1978) regarded as "Verstehen" or empathic explanation; what Dennett (1971/1978) regards as constitutive of the "intentional stance;" what Freudians seem to be appealing to in deepening our understanding of people's neurotic behavior. It certainly includes the structure of the plausible explanatory sketch we provided (§4.4) of what we have been taking to be the crucial evidence for mentalism, viz. the Standardized Regularities: stimuli from the question sheet cause the agent to enter various informational states regarding the instructions on the test; some of these states are retained and combine in rational patterns to produce other informational states, some of which ultimately combine with directional states concerning making a little money, and cause the subjects to move their hands in such a way that certain squares in the answer sheet get filled with graphite. It is the task of a cognitive psychology to spell out precisely what the informational and directional states need to be like in order to explain the specific patterns of graphite that are observed. Once we have that account we will be in a position to ask to what extent the states such a psychology specifies correspond to ordinary concepts like [perceive], [believe], [desire], [intend], [conscious], [free]. It is at least some of this task that the Computational/Representational Theory of Thought begins to perform, as we shall see in the remainder of this book.

Notes

1 There are some terminological headaches here. Lewis proposes ramsification of commonplaces as an account of the "meaning" of mental terms. However, for reasons that will emerge in this section, many would agree with Shoemaker (1984:273) that, insofar as this view doesn't distinguish between *a priori* and merely empirical commonplaces, it needs to be distinguished from the more traditional "analytic" or what I, after Block (1980a:271), call "a priori" functionalism which would, and which I will discuss in the next section. Folk functionalism is associated also with David Armstrong (1968), Colin McGinn (1991), and Jackson and Pettit (1993).

2 Lewis (1994:416) is explicit about this: "I offer not analyses, but a recipe for analyses."

3 Perhaps in this enlightened age, there couldn't be consensus about these now controversial matters. Fine: consider the commonsense mental platitudes of a century or two ago: or the platitudes that no one has yet bothered to examine. The same problem would arise for the stray philosophers and social critics who, then or now, might try to question them.

4   Lewis (1994) recently has retreated from "gathering platitudes" to "a theory: folk psychology [that] is common knowledge among us . . . tacit, as our grammatical knowledge is" (p. 416). Unfortunately, he is not more explicit. It's hard to see how it would avoid some of the deeply rooted, quite general metaphysical and sociological prejudices I have mentioned. But, if it's really to be modeled on the kind of tacit grammars postulated by someone like Chomsky, it would be impossible at this point to know what it might contain. At best, the view ought to be treated as a version of the "a priori functionalism" to be considered next.

5   Indeed, the original little detective story by which Lewis introduced his method that we quoted suggests as much, since it would be odd to claim that the story actually provides an *analysis* of the proper names (or their referents): it seems perfectly reasonable to say, "But A, B, and C might *not* have done any of the things you say they did" (which might arise equally for fictional as for real characters). Cf. in this connection Kripke's (1972) arguments against descriptional theories of the meanings of proper names.

6   Another potential difficulty that is a little hard to assess without more specific examples than Lewis provides is the problem of the "old terms" permitted at stage (i) of ramsification: which "old terms" are essential to the grasp of a mental concept. Folk platitudes will doubtless mention all manner of accidental facts about people – e.g. that (to take an example from Lewis 1994:417) they sometimes kick balls – that surely are not essential to grasping the meaning of most mental terms.

7   Indeed, for a deeper understanding of some of the metaphysical issues surrounding functionalism (and for still further distinctions) that space has mercifully forced me to ignore, the reader couldn't do better than to study his articles in detail.

8   The term is due to Block (1978/1980).

9   Psycho-functionalism is also advocated by Tye (1992:p. 165 n. 7, p. 167 n. 9).

10 McGinn raises other more idiosyncratic objections to psycho-functionalism that I address in Rey (1993b).

11 Some confusion was likely engendered by some of the original discussion of "tags," "rigid designators," and "reference fixers" in Kripke (1972), where the concern was largely with proper names, which name *individual occupiers* of variable roles, as in "Benjamin Franklin, the inventor of bifocals." I see no reason why "kind" terms can't name whatever sort of kind one "happens" to be interested in.

12 Shoemaker (1984:281) also opposes psycho-functionalism by a thought experiment involving Martians whose internal workings satisfy the claims of the best psychology of humans available up to 1985, but differs along lines discovered thereafter. He claims that excluding these Martians from having mental states because of their failure to satisfy the latter lines would be "obviously wrong" and unduly "chauvinist." Here, too, everything depends upon the details, in particular, for example, of how much of the "blank spaces" the folk left to be filled in by the specialist were in fact filled in by 1985.

13 Putnam (1960/1975a) seems actually to propose identifying mental states with Turing Machine states, a fairly implausible proposal that is roundly criticized by Block and Fodor (1972).

14 For example, many "co-variational," or "locking" theories offer theories of meaning of this sort; see §7.2.2.

15 There is a long tradition of such suggestions, beginning at least with Hegel, and flowering most prominently in the work of Heidegger (1924/1962). Recent Anglo-American defenses of it can be found in Dreyfus (1972/1979), and particularly in the semantical views of Putnam (1975b) and Burge (1979, 1986) (§7.2.2).

16 Of course, there are "parallel" computers, that can run several sequences of instructions simultaneously: the point here is merely that to insist on such a "computational architecture" is to insist on a feature that is not always definable merely in terms of inputs, outputs, and causal relations to other states alone. Timing relations might enter essentially into distinguishing them from a purely serial machine that was computing the same algorithm (imagine a batch of serial computers each devoted to different parts of a problem that could, in principle, be solved either serially or in parallel).

17 The platitudes here may, however, prove very difficult to sort out: "alive" would seem to be synonymous with "not dead," but when people look forward to "life after death," they are presumably not anticipating a blatant contradiction; "alive" there seems to be simply synonymous with "conscious."

18 The term is Block's (1978/1980). Note that one of the foremost functionalists, Shoemaker (1984) has expressed views that are partly physiofunctionalist, insofar, for example, as he is inclined to identify the actual qualities of experience with properties of the brain.

19 Lewis does note the difficulty, but considers only *slight* errors, which allows him to talk about "approximately" true. He might further avail himself of some logical complexity – say, conjoining conjunctions of disjunctions of commonplaces (a move Ned Block claims to have heard Lewis propose) – but this would require a considerable amount of careful analysis, which it is doubtful the folk have carefully thought through.

20 For illuminating discussion of the role of hierarchies in functional analysis; see Cummins (1983), as well as Neander (1995).

21 Lycan (1987:39) points out that this strategy appears also in Attneave (1960). See also Dennett (1978e).

22 See Damasio (1994: chapter 3) for a particularly striking case of just such a person.

23 Although see Lycan (1981), Cummins (1983).

24 See, for example, Wright (1973), Millikan (1984), Papineau (1987), Sober (1985), Neander (1991).

25 For a challenge to this latter claim, see Bigelow and Pargetter (1987).

26 Given Wittgenstein's general aversion to traditional philosophical analysis, the latter reading is probably all that he intended. But, as so often with Wittgenstein's text, there would be problems in sustaining this interpretation.

27 Another term for a related view as it arises in more purely psychological research is "methodological behaviorism," or the view that all *evidence* for cognitive states must be overtly behavioral. Note that this is a form of behaviorism distinct both from RBism (since it fully allows for the existence of mental states) and from ABism (since it makes no claim about the analysis of mental states).

28 Why the qualifications? Imagine that a wicked scientist has arranged for anyone who drinks milk to be killed by a laser shortly thereafter. Such a case would not make *milk itself* poisonous (although, of course, you'd be well advised not to drink any).

29 I suspect the same intuitions could be elicited for most any ordinary dispositional term, e.g. "fragile," "water soluble."

30 Interestingly, in the passages immediately following the above comparison of the mental to dust, Dennett proceeds to question the legitimacy of hidden essence views even of water (p. 536).

31 Another reason for distinguishing them is that "external behavior" may also exceed commonsense knowledge in surprising ways: arguably, differences in response time, galvanic skin response, magnetic resonance, which are all detectable from outside the skull, would seem to count as "behavior" (unless "behavior" is restricted to *far less* than the folk know, e.g. to only input-ouput relations, as in I/O functionalism). So superficialism, strictly speaking, comes to the view that there could be no inner process that eluded all *possible* extra-cranial evidence. So stated, it does seem a fairly arbitrary view, dependent upon quite contingent facts about relations between the insides and outsides of skulls. I suspect that what Dennett actually endorses is a combination of folk and superficialist functionalism, but he nowhere addresses the issue explicitly.

32 At least for the sake of argument. Actually, I think it's no easier to imagine the resources here than in the more general case of *any* possible evidence.

33 See Fodor (1983:76–7) for particularly subtle empirical evidence for hypotheses of this very sort with regard to perception of phonemes. Perhaps this sort of line commits us to what Dennett calls the "bizarre category of the objectively subjective" (1991a:132), but it looks like we were already so committed in even beginning to wonder about the taste of beer.

34 Proponents of the theory theory include Churchland (1981), Stich (1984), and Gopnik (1994); of the simulation account, Gordon (1986) and Goldman (1986).

35 Note that, *pace* Goldman (1992), the present project is not committed to satisfactory analyses of concepts actually entering into anyone's ordinary mental processing (cf. Rey 1992).

36 In his "La Maladie Imaginaire," Molière has a charlatan doctor explain that the reason certain potions put people to sleep is that they possess "dormitive virtue" – supposedly a paradigm of a vacuous explanation. Note, however, that it is not altogether clear precisely wherein the problem of dormative virtue explanations is supposed to lie. After all, something's *being a sleeping pill* can be explanatory of why it put someone to sleep (it wasn't an accident, an allergic reaction, something that had been combined with the pill . . .). Presumably the vice of dormitive virtue is not its "*virtue,*" but just the fact that it's not very deep: it doesn't explain much *else.* So perhaps the criticism of mentalism here is simply that its particular predicates do not enter into interesting explanations. But that of course remains to be seen.

37 We'll discuss these forms of reasoning in §8.3.

38 I was so tempted in Rey (1994b) in defining "minimal mentalism." I'm indebted to Ned Block for restraining me in this regard.

8
CRTT: Computation
(Meeting Descartes' Challenge)

Our Modest Mentalism (MM) might be found to be a little abstract and vague. Although we mentioned ordinary mental states like belief and desire as examples of informational and directional states, we're still a long way from adequately defining them, much less meeting the serious challenges raised by Descartes and Brentano about the possibility of a physical object possessing any mental properties at all. Why think a mere physical object could possess the informational and directional states that make it possible for people (recalling Descartes' words in §1.2) "to act in all the contingencies of life in the way in which our reason makes us act"? In this chapter, I want to begin to fill out MM with an account, the Computational-Representational Theory of Thought (CRTT), that promises both to unify a great deal of psychological research and to meet some of the challenges raised by the dualist.[1]

As its name suggests, CRTT has two components: a *computational* component that focuses upon computations defined over syntactically specified representations in a special language, and a *representational* (or meaning, or "content") component, that focuses upon how those syntactically specified representations do in fact have specific meanings. The syntactic component will be the topic of the present chapter, which we shall see *abstracts away* from any meaning those representations might possess. The representational component will be the topic of chapter 9. It should be stressed from the start that this division is a *purely expository device*: the different problems raised by the two components simply require separate expository treatment. This does not for a moment entail that they are *analytically* independent: it may well be that computations can only be defined over things, like syntactic representations, that do in fact possess semantic interpretations; and it may well be (what I, myself, believe to be true) that an adequate semantic theory will need to appeal to computational relations over syntactic representations. As we observed in discussing ramsification of functionalist theories, the various parts of a theory may ultimately need to be *defined* together – but they still might need to be *explained* separately.

CRTT claims, of course, that the mind is a specific sort of computer – but, note, not just *any* sort of computer, or any computer whose behavior seems intelligent. It is a computer that functions in a specific sort of way that will be sketched in this chapter and ultimately specified by an adequate cognitive psychology. But *caveat emptor*: although the general structure of MM could be realized on most existing computers, the *details* of that structure that permit us (or even most animals) "to act in all the contingencies of life in the way in which our reason enables us to act" turn out to be extremely hard to specify. We seem to be extremely clever computers – or at least very clever for the circumstances in which evolution molded us. Although I shall argue that we do have serious reason to think that both Descartes' and Brentano's challenges *can* eventually be met, *they haven't been met to date, and there are good reasons to think they will not be met in the near future.* There are still extremely deep problems regarding the specific computations involved merely in navigating an ordinary environment, or grasping even the most commonplace of our ordinary concepts, like [table], [cat], [cause], [person]. The prospect of creating genuine *artificial intelligence* comparable to that of even a spider or a rat is staggeringly far off, far further off than the naive initial predictions about such matters in the computer's early days might have led people to believe.[2] However, if the various conceptual difficulties discussed in chapter 2 could be met, and we could sketch how a physical account of how MM could *in principle* be provided, then these problems could be regarded as largely practical.

The situation to which we can aspire would be like that presently enjoyed by molecular biology: although the details of, for example, embryonic development are enormously complex and only understood in the most general ways, we have every reason to think the research program sound. The fantastic difficulties in actually specifying the mechanisms of the development of the heart or brain provide no reason whatsoever for supposing that embryonic development isn't a biochemical process. Just so, if the account to be sketched in the following chapters is largely correct, we will have no reason to suppose that at least a Modest Mind is not a physically explicable phenomenon.

8.1   Syntactic Computational Architecture

CRTT is a species of psycho-functionalism, in that it attempts to analyze propositional attitudes[3] in terms of internal relations, much as a biological theory provides a particular functional analysis of digestion. According to CRTT, the mind (and/or brain) is to be understood as a computer with a very specific structure, or "computational architecture." Specifying that architecture in adequate detail is the burden of CRTT.

Recall that, as we noted in §1.1, different propositional attitudes are distinguishable in at least two ways that are often blurred in ordinary talk: by their *contents* (expressed by the sentence complement, for example, the "that . . ." clause, that follows the attitude verb) and by the different *states*, consisting in the agent bearing one or another attitude relation to the same contents, e.g. *believing* vs. *hoping* that God exists. I argued in §5.2.3–.4 that both these attitude states and their contents must be treated as real, causally efficacious entities if mentalistic explanations are to succeed. This is precisely what CRTT does. It proposes to capture the attitude states by positing different relations borne by the agent to sentences in a special language, called the "language of thought" ("LOT"), in which the content of those states is expressed. These sentences are actually entokened in the brain, and are subject to certain causal processes. Both those processes and the different attitude relations are to be spelt out in terms of a computational model, and so are called "computational relations" (about which more shortly). The same LOT sentences with the same content can occur in different propositional attitudes: hoping, imagining, wishing, dreading, believing, and preferring that p consist in different computational relations to a sentence that expresses the proposition [that p]. For example, one can hope, imagine, wish, dread, believe, or prefer [that dinner will be served before midnight] by virtue of standing in different computational relations to an LOT sentence that expresses the content [Dinner is served at midnight]. Generally, and to a first approximation as a certain theoretical ideal, CRTT, then, is the claim:[4]

(CRTT) For any agent x, time t, and propositional attitude, A *that p*, there exists some computationally definable relation C_A such that:

x A's that p at t iff $(\exists \sigma)(xC_A\sigma,t$ & σ means that p)

For example, for the attitudes *occurrently judging that p* and *occurrently preferring that q* there would exist relations J and P that an agent, x, might bear to sentences in its LOT that express the propositions [p] and [q]:[5]

x occurently judges that p at t iff $(\exists \sigma)(xJ\sigma,t$ & σ means that p),

and

x occurently prefers that q at t iff $(\exists \tau)(xP\tau,t$ & τ means that q)

It is useful (but not essential) to think of the computational relations as involving the presence of representations in particular *addresses* that are accessible to some and not other operations. Hence one reads of sentences being stored in a "belief" or "judgment" or "volition box," all of which, understood literally, is patent nonsense in the case of the brain, but provides a useful metaphor for discussing what are otherwise very abstract computational relations.[6] Thus, we can imagine that the above J and P relations involve actually storing σ and τ at specific addresses that are accessed at appropriate times in the execution of certain processes. For example, occurrent judgment might be the output of perceptual and reasoning sub-systems that forms the input to a decision making sub-system. What CRTT proposes is that for every propositional attitude there is such a "computational" relation (i.e. one specifiable in terms of such states and causal transitions) that the agent of the attitude bears to sentences in its LOT.

Incidentally, just as talk of "boxes" mustn't be taken too literally, so, too, "sentences" entokened in the brain will not have all the features of sentences as they are inscribed on pages of books. Sentences, it must be remembered, are *highly abstract* objects that can be entokened in an endless variety of ways: as sound wave forms (in speech), as sequences of dots and dashes (Morse code), as sequences of electrically charged particles (on recording tape). It is presumably in something like the latter form that sentences would be entokened in the head.[7] Indeed, CRTT is best viewed as simply the claim that the brain has logically structured, causally efficacious states. While this hypothesis may conceivably be false, so stated it surely isn't *patently* absurd.

Another confusion to avoid is between the language in which the system's *thought contents will be expressed*, and whatever language might be used in specifying *the rules* for manipulating the expressions in that language. The latter stands to the former as, in logic, a "meta-language" stands to an "object-language": in a standard text on first-order logic, the object-language is the formal language being studied, and the meta-language is the language in which the rules for manipulating symbols in that formal language are expressed (e.g. *modus ponens* is a rule expressed *in English* for deriving sentences in a *formal language*). There might well be causally efficacious tokens of an LOT in a system, without there being similarly efficacious tokens of the *instructions* for manipulating them.[8]

What sort of computational relations might be appropriate for rational thought? In the next sections, I'll sketch the three main classes of rational relations that invite specific computational proposals. In order to provide a sense of how they could eventually be spelt out as a proposal about the structure of a mind, I will provide a toy example thereafter (§8.5).

8.2 The Paradigm Case: Syntactic Computations for Deduction

One of the chief inspirations for CRTT is the immense success in this century of work in formal logic. This work showed that the paradigmatic example of a rational process, deductive logic, can be *formalized*: that is to say, it can be characterized in terms of relations among *syntactically specified sentences* in a formal language that can receive a *systematic semantic interpretation*. In particular, building on the seminal work of Frege and Russell, Kurt Gödel (1930) showed in his "completeness theorem for first-order logic" that a certain set of syntactically specifiable rules was adequate to capture all first-order valid arguments:[9] that is, the rules could be specified entirely by reference to the *spelling* alone of the sentences in the formal language; no reference to any *semantic* properties (e.g. reference, truth, validity) was necessary, even though they could be shown to capture an important semantically specifiable set of sentences (viz. the valid arguments). In short, syntax could in this particular respect do some of the work of semantics. This was important since it seemed as if syntactic properties were a *lot clearer* and more manageable than the semantic ones by themselves (it is easier to check whether a certain argument has been *spelt* correctly than to survey *all* possible worlds or interpretations to see if there is one that makes the premises true and the conclusion false).

Now, ordinarily, sentences in logic are manipulated by people consciously following explicit rules that are defined over their syntactic form. However, the work of Alan Turing showed that any suitably specified formal process can be specified as a computational one; and that any computational process can be captured by a Turing Machine (§6.2). Since the processes of a Turing Machine are obviously realizable by a physical process, it followed that there could be a sequence of physical processes that realized any finite piece of deductive reasoning simply as a consequence of its physical organization. Consequently, the rules of logic could be *obeyed* not by virtue of someone *representing* and *following* them, but as a result of *the causal organization of the brain*; which is, of course, precisely how actual computers are constructed: they obey rules by virtue of the causal organization of their electronic hardware.[10]

Since one sometimes hears the complaint that this notion of "computation" is left dangerously vague (see, for example, Searle 1992:204–5), it is worth spelling out the notion precisely as it is employed by CRTT. In presenting his classic formulation of the view, Fodor (1975), for example, wrote:

> Every computational device is a complex system which changes physical state in some way determined by physical laws. It is feasible to think of such a system as a computer just insofar as it is possible to devise some mapping which pairs physical states of the device with formulae in a computing language in such a fashion as to preserve desired semantic relations among the formulae. For example, we may assign physical states of the machine to sentences in the language in such a way that if $S_1 \ldots S_n$ are machine states, and if $F_1 \ldots F_{n-1}$, F_n are the sentences paired with $S_1 \ldots S_{n-1}$, S_n, respectively, then the physical constitution of the machine is such that it will actually run through that sequence of states only if $F_1 \ldots F_{n-1}$ constitutes a proof of F_n. (1975:73)

To make his "example" more concrete, imagine that we built as literal an instantiation of a "Turing Machine" as possible,[11] and that its physical states were so constituted as to realize the machine table for executing the logical operation of *modus ponens* in a standard formalization of the predicate calculus.[12] It's not hard to imagine how such a machine would operate. Input sentences in the formal language would be printed, say, in patterns of charged particles on a long piece of tape. The machine would be constructed in such a way that, whenever it encountered a pattern that entokened a syntactically specified sentence σ, and then another pattern that entokened any similarly specified sentence of the form "($\sigma \Rightarrow \tau$)", it would be caused to print out a pattern entokening τ by itself on the "output" portion of the tape. For example, if it encountered "Fa" and "Fa $\Rightarrow$ Gb" on the input portion, it would print out "Gb" on the output portion; and it would do so for any such physical patterns that entokened well-formed sentences in the language. In such a case, Fodor's characterization of an example of computation would be satisfied as follows: let S_1, S_2 be physical states of the machine that correspond to reading sentences "σ" and "($\sigma \Rightarrow \tau$)", and let S_3 correspond to the machine printing out "τ"; then the machine is so constructed that as a causal consequence of entering states S_1 and S_2, it will enter S_3. Thus, it will pass from S_1 and S_2 to S_3 if and only if the sentences corresponding to S_1 and S_2 constitute a proof of the sentence corresponding to S_3. The machine in this way "mimics" *modus ponens*. What Gödel and Turing showed is that such mimicry of logical operations by a series of physical states can be performed for at least all the operations of first-order deductive logic.

These insights of Gödel and Turing are what give rise to the explanatory division of labor that we have already noted at the beginning of this chapter. In the same way that Gödel and Turing prove their results by considering the syntactic properties of sentences in abstraction from their semantic interpretation, so is the first part of our discussion concerned with getting a grip on these *computational* relations that agents bear to syntactically specified LOT sentences in abstraction from what those sentences mean. Essentially, we are separating Descartes' and Brentano's challenges: the present computational discussion is an attempt to meet Descartes' challenge; the discussion of content in the next section is an attempt to meet Brentano's.

Unfortunately, this division of analytic labor has misled a number of philosophers into supposing that CRTT is a theory necessarily about meaningless symbols. Thus, Searle (1984) writes:

A digital computer, as defined, cannot have more than just formal symbols because the operation of the computer . . . is defined in terms of its ability to implement programs. And those programs are purely formally specifiable – that is, they have no semantic content. (1984:33)

213

And Dreyfus and Dreyfus (1986) claim:

> [L]ogicians such as Alan Turing were already accustomed to thinking of computers as devices for manipulating symbols according to exact rules. The symbols themselves don't mean anything. (1986:53)

Actually, as we noted in discussing Turing Machines in §6.2, this isn't quite true of Turing: the symbols of a Turing Machine tape are standardly taken to be *numerals* referring to *numbers*. However, this doesn't prevent Turing, or us, from *abstracting* from this fact in characterizing the operation of such a machine. Abstracting from an object's possession of a certain property for theoretical purposes doesn't entail that the object *doesn't in fact possess that property*: bachelors can be quite neurotic, despite the fact that this property isn't mentioned in the definition of "bachelor." Similarly, the above thesis about computation that we have just considered, that thinking can be characterized as a formal process defined over syntactically defined sentences, *does not for a moment entail that those sentences don't have lots of real and important semantic properties*, indeed, just the semantic properties that thought ordinarily seems to possess. Moreover, a *full* analysis of both computation and thought will plausibly involve reference to both syntax and semantics: i.e. to be a computation is to be a formal process defined over semantically valuable representations.

Once such formal deductive techniques are available, it becomes possible to formalize any theory expressible in the formal language and carefully examine its deductive consequences. A great deal of effort has been put into the formalization of arithmetic and other branches of mathematics, with the result, also proved by Gödel and Turing, that any computable function in arithmetic can also be computed mechanically, i.e. by a Turing Machine. So CRTT is spurred on by success not only in capturing logical deduction in the abstract, but also in capturing mathematical reasoning as well.[13]

8.3   Extensions to Induction and Abduction

Although deductive logic and arithmetic may be the very paradigms of reason, they are not the whole of it. Intelligent creatures must make *inductive inferences* from examined to unexamined cases, as we do when we generalize from some representative sample of a population of cases to the population as a whole. And especially intelligent creatures seem to make *abductive* ones as well, making what are called "inferences to the best explanation": they not only generalize beyond their finite data, but make extraordinary leaps to hypotheses that might refer to phenomena not remotely available in the data, but which provide the "best explanation" of it. Thus, citizens in the courtroom infer that Sikes is the murderer from the evidence of motives, fingerprints, and shoe impressions in the mud; and scientists in the laboratory infer the existence of the Big Bang from the patterns of electromagnetic radiation detectable in space. Neither induction nor abduction are deductive, since the conclusion reached in such cases is not *entailed* by the premises that support it; it's entirely possible for the premises (the claims regarding the sample or the evidence) to be true and the inferred conclusion to be false. But they certainly seem rational all the same: the premises are thought to make the conclusion at least "more likely."

Success in describing mechanical procedures for these sorts of inferences has not been as stunning as in the case of deduction. But there are promising strategies. Induction can be captured to some degree either by various species of statistical rules whereby hypotheses are generated directly from the data, or as, themselves, a species of abduction, in which the statistical properties of the whole population simply provide the best explanation of the statistical properties of the sample (the best explanation of why we have correlations between smoking and cancer in our sample of smokers is that there is indeed such a correlation in the population of smokers as a whole).

The general idea behind abduction is that one selects a hypothesis that explains one's data better than all other rival hypotheses. One possible mechanical realization of such a process in a perceptual case would be as follows:

(i)   the agent has available to herself a certain set of possible hypotheses H_1 through H_n, that she will seriously entertain about her present situation, to each of which she assigns a certain initial probability;

(ii)   She receives a set of perceptual stimuli P^*, which cause her to entertain H_1 through H_n one by one;

(iii)   For each hypothesis, H_i, she deduces some set S_i, of its likely stimulus consequences; i.e. she judges a set of hypotheticals of the form
        "If H_i, then I should be receiving stimuli S_i";

(iv)   Each set S_i is compared for correspondence with the original set P^*; i.e. for each P_i the agent judges a "degree of fit" between it and P^*, a basis for the computation then of the probability of the actual stimuli given the hypothesis.

(v)   That hypothesis is selected as a function of this degree of fit and the initial probabilities, i.e. whose overall probability, given the initial probability of the hypothesis, is greatest (or reaches a particular "satisfactory" value above a certain minimum).

Take for example the case of Sikes. If the hypotheses someone was considering were narrowed down to two, "Sikes alone did it" (with initial probability 0.8) and "Moriarty alone did it" (with initial probability 0.6), and the former fits the perceptual data (the fingerprints and shoe impressions) far better than the latter, we have every reason to convict Sikes. Of course, probabilities aren't always so nicely weighted, and don't always line up so easily: the "best fit" (or the probabilities of the hypotheses given the evidence) don't always correspond to the initial probabilities, and so one turns to probability theory (e.g. Bayes' theorem) to compute the functions appropriate for step (v).

But, in any case, the model is obviously a stupendous simplification of anything like ordinary abductive reasoning. Generalizing beyond the perceptual case would require specifying sets of judgments that would count as "data" with respect to some range of competing hypotheses being considered. Rendering such a process more realistic would involve adjusting for the varying degrees of confidence (or "degrees of belief") an agent might have about her estimates of the probabilities. And this is to say nothing about the complexities involved in specifying what determines the probabilities of the initial hypotheses in the first place; how the system is constrained so as to deduce a manageable set of relevant perceptual consequences; how "degrees of fit" are assessed; how memory is accessed to bring relevant data to bear on that assessment. These are among the hardest questions of continuing, sometimes very fruitful research in psychology, philosophy of science, and artificial intelligence.[14]

All that matters for purposes here is that such a process captures at least a simple core of abduction and that it is plausibly realizable by a machine. The model does capture a central idea of the standard "hypothetical deductive" model of scientific inference (where a hypothesis is to be assessed in terms of the predictive consequences that can be deduced from it), as well as Quine's insight that hypotheses are assessed by such global properties as simplicity, modesty, and conservativism (which presumably are ways of trying to begin to spell out the general idea of a "best fit").[15] The hope is that the process will be every bit as formalizable as the logic and arithmetic that it exploits in deducing consequences from hypotheses, and computing the relevant probability functions.

8.4 Practical Reason: Decision Theory

Creatures don't only reason about how the world is; they also reason about what they *ought to do*. Whether or not this is properly regarded as a species of *reason*, understood normatively and as continuous with the normative status of deduction, induction, and abduction, there can be little doubt that it is a *thought process* that needs to be *described* psychologically. Contemporary *decision theory* provides a framework for beginning to understand that process. For purposes here, something like the following description will serve as a good first-approximation:[16]

(i)   The agent judges herself to be in a certain situation S;
(ii)   She judges that a certain set of exclusive and exhaustive basic acts – A_1, A_2, ... A_n – are live options for her to perform in S;[17]
(iii)   She predicts the probable consequences, C_1, ... C_n, of performing each of A_1

216

through A_n; i.e. for each A_i, she judges a set of hypotheticals of the form: prob $(C_i/A_i) = r_i$ (i.e. "If I perform A_i, then the probability of C_i occurring $= p_i$");

(iv)   A preference ordering is assigned C_1 through C_n;

(v)   The agent selects one of the acts as a decision-theoretic function (e.g. maximize expected utility) of the probabilities of (iii) and the preference ordering of (iv).

To take a simple example, suppose someone is in a situation in which she can get money by pressing buttons: either by pressing only button-1 with her right index finger (action A_1), only button-2 with her left (action A_2), or both (A_3) or neither (A_4). And suppose she believes that the following are the probabilities of expected payoffs:

prob $(\$90./A_1) = 0.9$
prob $(\$80./A_2) = 0.8$
prob $(\$70./A_3) = 0.7$
prob $(\$60./A_4) = 0.6$

In such a case, she would have reason to perform action A_1. Of course, this sort of decision problem, in which the probabilities and the preferences line up neatly in the same order, is absurdly easy. Things are, alas, more difficult when the things you want more are harder to get than the things you want less. For such decisions, one needs to trade off preferences and probabilities in the kinds of ways studied by "expected utility theory." Here one assigns positive and negative numbers (for attractions and aversions) to one's preferences as well, and defines "utility" as the product of a preference and a probability assignment. Then one might perform the action that has the highest expected utility; or the action with the lowest risk (i.e. least negative utility); or perhaps one that only "satisfices" (has a "good enough" utility value, as in Slote 1989). There is no need here to decide among these and many other approaches to decision.

Indeed, as in the case of abduction, this is obviously a vast simplification of ordinary decision making. Most of us are certainly not aware of assigning numerical probabilities to the consequences of our acts; we often don't know how to compare consequences; we operate under time pressure and other sources of anxiety and don't keep all such reasoning fully in mind. And, of course, heaps of complexities go into clause (iv) whereby consequences are assessed. Moreover, typically, one reassesses one's options and preferences after a single round of such reasoning, and then performs the reasoning again, as in the familiar phenomenon of "sour grapes" cf. Elster 1983. We needn't delve into these complexities here. It's enough to suppose that the above process is *one* mechanical way that an agent could succeed in being practically rational.

8.5 A Toy Example: the COG Program

If mechanical theories of induction, abduction, and practical reason meet with the same success as deduction, then, of course, the possibility is raised of constructing a machine that could reason. In order to provide as vivid an account of CRTT as possible, it is worth working through a toy example of such a machine.

In understanding this example, it will, again, be important to bear in mind the separation of the *syntactic-computational* features of our account from the *semantic* ones. If one were really strict about the matter, one would set out the syntactic features, particularly the forms of the LOT sentences, without providing any clue as to their meaning, so insuring that no issue of semantics was being illicitly presupposed. However, such an exposition would be tiresome and practically unreadable. It will be far easier to treat the formally specified sentences in a way that will intuitively presuppose their natural interpretation (an account of which will be defended in the next chapter).[18] However, in order to keep things honest, I shall surround the relevant category of expression by pound brackets, "# . . . #" – e.g. "#sentences#," "#hypotheses#," "#axioms#," "#beliefs#." Strictly speaking, we should drop the brackets only after we've discussed in chapter 9 ways to invest the entities in the respective category with appropriate meanings. For now, the difference between an #*axiom*# and an *axiom* is merely that the latter, but not the former, is a syntactically specified object understood as possessing an interpretation that in turn is specified by an adequate semantic theory.

With this proviso in mind, consider the following (set of) program(s), which I shall call "COG," that I want to argue will be capable of computing syntactic functions for a Modest Mentalism. COG will essentially be a program for manipulating sentences of a fairly simple formal language, a logical language of the sort introduced in a symbolic logic text. Since we will be considering something that is supposed to be capable of at least some of the kinds of mental states humans can attain, we will imagine running COG on a machine equipped both with sensory transducers (a television camera, a microphone, heat and pressure sensors) as input devices, and a speaker, teletype, and mechanical arms as output executors.

COG itself will consist of the following:

(L) the alphabet, formation, and transformation rules for predicate logic. This is the system's "Language of Thought," which I shall call "COG-L."

(O) A set of observation sentences: i.e. a set of atomic sentences (and their negations) of COG-L that are released as a consequence of certain patterns of input from the transducers;

(A) a system of abductive logic, i.e. a library of #hypotheses# (a set of

218

sentences of COG-L), with a "reasonable" function for selecting among them on the basis of whatever observation sentences are triggered by transducer input;

(D)   the #axioms# for decision theory, with some set of basic #preference descriptions#, and a set of #basic act descriptions# (further atomic sentences and their negations in COG-L) that are capable of causing the execution of basic acts.

Intuitively, what COG is supposed to do is select #hypotheses# on the basis of its #observations#, and act on the basis of those #hypotheses# in a way that maximizes its expected utilities.[19] More specifically: the input supplied by the transducers would produce #observation sentences# whose presence would trigger the retrieval of #hypotheses# from the library of (A). Some of the #logical consequences# of the #hypotheses# that are also #observation sentences# would be deduced by the rules of (L) and compared with the original #observation sentences# from the transducers. #Hypotheses# would be selected whose #observation consequences# "best matched" the #observation sentences#. #Conditionals# of the form ⌜If B_i then prob(C_i)=j,⌝ where B is a basic act description and C a sentence in the set of #preference descriptions#, would be computed on the basis of the selected #hypotheses#. These #conditionals# in turn would serve as input to (D), where, on the basis of them, the given #preferences#, and the decision theoretic functions, a "most preferred" #basic act description# would be generated, and then executed by the speaker, teletype, and mechanical arms.

A flat-footed example of COG's operation might be the following. Imagine that COG has the #hypotheses# "$(\exists x)Sx,i,n$" and "$(\exists x)Cx,i,n$" stored in its library, and assigned the initial probabilities, 0.8 and 0.2, respectively.[20] Its transducers present it with some inputs that directly cause it to access its library, select one of the hypotheses and to deduce consequences regarding the character of the input to be expected. For simplicity in this case, we can even suppose that "templates" are stored in the machine, to be retrieved on such occasions as the present one when an input is to be classified.[21] The template is retrieved and compared with the pattern created by the input. A degree of fit is computed and stored. The same process is performed for the other hypothesis, and the hypothesis is stored in #memory# as a (e.g. Baysean) function of the initial probabilities and the highest degree of fit.

We then may suppose that the machine is capable of performing certain basic #actions#. That is, there are certain events in its executors that are nomologically related to certain computational events in (D): *ceteris paribus*, whenever certain syntactic expressions (so to say, commands) are the output of D, actions of the executors specific to that syntactic form are executed as a causal consequence. We may also suppose that (D) includes a set of basic preferences about the states that would result from the performance of an action. Thus, suppose that the machine, m, can push either button B_1 or B_2, and that if m were to push B_1 then with probability 0.9 any pattern on the screen in front of it will be *obliterated*, and if it were to push B_2 any such pattern will be *replicated*; and suppose it also has sentences in its #memory# that represent these latter facts. Again, for the sake of ease of reading, let us suppose the correct semantic theory tells us that "Ox,y,z" means "y obliterates x at time $(z+\in)$"; "Rx,y,z" means "y replicates x at time z," and "Py,w,z" means "y pushes w at time $z+\in$)" (where $\in$ is the appropriate interval for the execution of an action; and "Sx,y,z" and "Cx,y,z" are as defined in fn20). Let the machine's #preferences# be the sentences:

"(x)(y)(z)(Sx,y,z $\rightarrow$ Ox,y,z$+\in$)" and "(x)(y)(z)(Cx,y,x $\rightarrow$ Rx,y,z$+\in$)"

(That is, m #prefers# to obliterate squares and replicate circles.) And suppose that m has in its #memory#, the following sentences:

"(x)(y)(z)(Ox,y,z $\rightarrow$ Py,b_1,z$+\in$)" and "(x)(y)(z)(Rx,y,z$\rightarrow$ Py,b_2,z$+\in$)"

Imagine now that m is presented with a well-drawn square in front of its TV camera. It stores a representation of it, fetches one of the two hypotheses, generates a template and compares it with the representation, and computes a probability of that hypothesis being true, given that evidence. It then does the same for the other hypothesis. And it then compares the comparisons, and feeds one of the hypotheses into the decision theoretic sub-system, where, as a consequence of the above preferences, button B_1 gets pushed.

We now can return to the question we asked at the beginning of this chapter: what are the different relations between a person and a proposition that distinguish the different (propositional) attitudes the person might assume? In the COG program, we can define two relations, J and P, that seem to play something very like the ordinary role of judgment and preference as follows (we will return to the question whether J and P should serve as the analysis of the ordinary relations of judgment and preference in §9.5):

xJσ iff (σ is the output of (O), (L), (A), or its memory and the input to (D))

xPτ iff (τ is a #basic preference# in (D) or is a decision-theoretic result of computing a preference sentence on the basis of #basic preferences# and #beliefs#).

In terms of the picture of internal "addresses" or "boxes," the J addresses might be identified as the ones that collect the outputs of the abductive program, (A), that serve as the inputs to the decision theoretic program (D); and the P addresses might be identified as the ones which cause a certain basic action description to be generated, given the contents of the J addresses and a particular decision theoretic function (note the necessity of defining all of the relevant notions at once, à la functionalism).

8.6   Free Will

If the above accounts provide at least possible computational explanations of both theoretical and practical reasoning, then there is no need to settle here the issue of "free will" that we raised in §2.5.2. "Reason" could apparently get along without it. As our toy example shows, something that operated according to the procedures sketched could behave quite rationally; and there seems to be no in principle reason to suppose that much of the intelligent behavior of people and many animals doesn't proceed essentially by such procedures.

But, of course, there are the cases of indecision, both practical and intellectual, when we seem torn between options. There's Sartre's (1973) young man choosing between joining the resistance or taking care of his mother, and there's just someone puzzling about what to do in the face of an argument that challenges some cherished belief. Here, though, one should bear in mind that hard cases make bad law. Although it may be difficult to see how the above models are to be applied to such cases, this is no more reason to despair here than in the case, say, of applying the laws of physics to the complexities of ocean waves. It's not easy, but why think it's *impossible?* What one needs is an argument that shows that these or other cases couldn't possibly be explained by models of the above sort.

Of course, there have been famous arguments to show that no such mechanical processes could explain a perfectly "free will," which, arguably, is incompatible with the workings of any deterministic (and, also arguably, any indeterministic!) universe. But what is needed are not merely arguments that show that *if there were free will* (of the requisite sort), then computational accounts of mind would be inadequate; what is needed is *(non-tendentious!)* evidence that *there actually exists such free will* in the first place. What evidence is there that anyone ever acts in a way that cannot in principle be explained, if not by the above computational models, then by some (quantum-)mechanical process?[22] Indeed, as we noted in §3.1.1, there is "no causal break" in the production of any event in either the brain or in a person's behavior. If there's no evidence of any mechanical break, why think there's a computational one?

8.7*   The Irrelevance of Gödel's Theorem

Invariably in philosophical discussions of whether the mind is a computer, an important theorem of Gödel's (1931/1970) is cited as showing that there is something that people can do that is not possible for any machine.[23] There are a number of simple errors usually involved in this claim that are fairly quickly disposed of.

Simultaneous with the development of the powerful formal systems of modern logic there emerged a deepening insight into their surprising limitations. Much of this insight involved the construction of often paradoxical, "self-referential" claims or properties, claims or properties that seem in one way or another to "refer to themselves," often with absurd and unacceptable consequences. A common reaction to such paradoxes is to suppose that they show there is something illegitimate about self-reference, that there is something generally paradoxical and impossible about *anything* – a claim, a property, and particularly a mind – referring to itself. It is worth indicating how the actual results in logic show precisely the contrary; that self-reference is a relatively trivial, and in any case a quite essential and important feature of most interesting formal systems.

An attraction of modern symbolic logic is that it affords a systematic way of talking about arithmetic, i.e. the theory of natural numbers. Indeed, logic and set theory were initially developed by Frege and Russell with the hope – or program, called "logicism" – that all the truths of arithmetic could be shown to be truths of set theory which in turn were thought to be (contrary to Kant) truths of logic. Some progress had been made on this program by Giuseppe Peano (1858–1932), who (ca. 1880) provided some plausible axioms for arithmetic, the so-called "Peano axioms" (these include such basic assertions about numbers as that 0 is a number, and that every number has a successor). Frege showed how to express these axioms in logic and set theory. Gödel (1931/1970), however, showed in his (in)famous proof of the essential incompleteness of *any* theory of arithmetic, that at least one ambition of the logicist project could never be fulfilled. He proved that absolutely no set of axioms could ever capture all the truths of arithmetic. Any set of axioms strong enough to capture the ordinary operations of multiplication and exponentiation could always be shown to be inadequate: either they are *incomplete*, failing to prove something that's true, or they are *inconsistent*, proving a contradiction. So as to make its irrelevance to the philosophy of mind clear, it's worth setting out the essential moves of his proof.

Gödel first shows how to code arbitrary strings of symbols into numbers, which, as the code numbers of expressions are called "Gödel numbers." He then goes on to show how *each of the rules of the syntax of a formal language*, and *each of the rules of inference* can be matched by an arithmetically defined operation on exponents on those numbers. As a result, the set of *well-formed formulae* of the language can be shown to correspond to a certain set of numbers that can be defined merely in terms of standard arithmetic overations. The axioms of arithmetic correspond to a subset of those numbers. And similarly the set of *theorems of L and of arithmetic itself* can be shown to correspond to another set of numbers also defined in terms of arithmetic (this "mirroring" of logic by arithmetic is comparable to the similarly impressive feat, performed by Descartes, of showing, through the use of "Cartesian coordinates," how geometry and algebra "mirrored" one another).

Having defined in arithmetic a class of numbers, A, that turn out to be the Gödel numbers of theorems of arithmetic, Gödel now constructs an interesting sentence of arithmetic (again, purely in terms of multiplication, etc.), which says of a certain number that it is not in the class A: i.e.:

$-Ag$

where g can be shown to be the Gödel number of that very sentence, i.e.:

$g = G\#("-Ag")!$

Following out Gödel's coding, what this sentence says is: "g is not a number that is a Gödel number of a theorem of arithmetic." In slightly rougher translation, what it says is "I'm not provable."

Once this sentence is constructed (again, in pure arithmetic), the rest of the argument is fairly straightforward. Suppose "$-Ag$" is false. If it's false, then, by the coding, g *is* a G# of a theorem of arithmetic. So "$-Ag$" is a theorem. But if "$-Ag$" is a theorem, then, by the interpretation of "A" (the set of all and only those sentences that are theorems of arithmetic) and the same coding of "g" (= the G# of "$-Ag$"), "Ag" *is* a theorem. So both "Ag" and "$-Ag$" are theorems, in which case arithmetic is patently inconsistent. So suppose instead that "$-Ag$" is true. Then, by the coding, "$-Ag$" is not a theorem. So there is at least one truth that arithmetic fails to prove, and so arithmetic is incomplete. Since "$-Ag$" is either false or true, arithmetic is either inconsistent or incomplete. Q.E.D.

Now it can certainly appear as though the very production of the proof by a human being shows that the mind couldn't be a machine. For it would appear that for any given machine that purports to replicate someone's psychology, there would be at least one sentence – namely, the appropriate Gödel sentence as constructed above – that the person could somehow know to be true, but which the machine couldn't know, because it couldn't prove it.

There are a lot of fallacies in arguments of this sort: for starters, who ever said that all that a machine could ever know was what it could *prove*? As our above discussion makes explicit, machines deal also in inductions and abductions which are notoriously non-deductive processes. Secondly, the impossibility being claimed is not one that should be pictured as a kind of *physical* impossibility, like, say, the impossibility of exceeding the speed of light. It's not as though, as the machine approached the proof of the appropriate "$-Ag$," time and space would begin to warp in some way. To the contrary, the machine could well *prove* the undecidable sentence, printing it out as a consequence of its deductive procedures. The only problem is that, if it did prove it, *it could also in time prove its negation.*

223

Indeed, it might prove them both in an easy day's work. It would simply then have contradicted itself. No big deal; people and probably quite a few machines do it all the time. Indeed, the most fundamental error in trying to derive anti-mechanist conclusions from Gödel's theorem consists in ignoring its essentially *disjunctive* character: to repeat, Gödel's theorem states that *either* arithmetic is incomplete, *or* it's inconsistent. All we are entitled to say on the basis of this theorem is that there is a sentence that a person could know to be true that a purported mechanical emulation of her couldn't prove *only if* that person could also know that the theory she is using to know it is itself *consistent*. But how is she to know *that*? By Gödel's Second Theorem (a direct consequence of the Incompleteness Theorem), any system strong enough to express arithmetic cannot prove its own consistency, on pain of being *in*consistent. And in an inconsistent system, *anything* can be proven – small comfort to those claiming that a person could prove something that a (consistent?) machine couldn't. But how else is someone to know that her theory is consistent? Being inconsistent is, after all, a non-obvious property (it's not as though we – or the machine – would *explode* if we proved "p&-p"). Indeed, it is well known that contradictions can pop up as consequences of the most intuitively plausible assumptions.[24] So, pending some way for a person to establish her own consistency without at the same time violating it, it is not at all a consequence of Gödel's Theorem that there's something a person could know that a given mechanical simulation couldn't prove. There are certainly things that no machine can do – for example, prove all the truths of arithmetic without contradicting itself. But it remains to be shown that any person can do them either.

8.8 Bridging Explanatory Gaps: CRTT vs. Radical Connectionism

It will help clarify the commitments of CRTT by contrasting it with its chief rival, the so-called "radical connectionist" (what I shall call "RCON") models of cognition.[25] They are to be distinguished from what might be called "liberal" connectionist ('LCON') models, whose proponents regard them as merely possible implementations of "classical" models such as CRTT.[26] There is no reason for us to consider LCON models at all – they simply are not addressed to questions at any of the levels of the present discussion.

But nor need we consider RCON models in detail either.[27] As I emphasized in §1.2, the concern here is not with a theory of *actual* human psychological processing, but with meeting the philosophical challenges to a *possible* naturalistic account of it. If CRTT can be defended as such an account then this philosophical aim will have been satisfied. That there might also be *another* such account is no argument that CRTT doesn't suffice as one. If both accounts were possible, there would, of course, arise the interesting question which was true of people – and even whether one was true of some and the other of others. This is a question I suspect we can leave to that very far off date when both theories are shown to be, in fact, genuinely explanatorily adequate.

Some light, however, can be shed on some of the important issues that divide RCON from CRTT by considering what our project here *does* require, namely the ways in which CRTT *promises* to be explanatorily adequate, ways in which it could in principle bridge the "explanatory gaps" mentioned in §1.2. We can compare these ways with the prospects of RCON, and so appreciate some of the outstanding issues that divide the two views.

First, a brief account of RCON. In a useful introduction to the subject, Bechtel and Abrahamsen (1991) characterize (what amounts to) RCON thus:

> Connectionism can be distinguished from the traditional symbolic paradigm by the fact that it does not construe cognition as involving symbol manipulation. It offers a radically different conception of the basic processing system of the mind/brain. This conception is inspired by our knowledge of the nervous system. The basic idea is that there is a network of elementary *units* or nodes, each of which has some degree of *activation*. These units are *connected* to each other so that active units excite or inhibit other units. The network is a *dynamical system* which, once supplied with

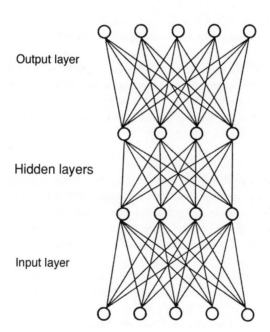

Figure 8.1   A Simple Connectionist Network (from Dinsmore 1992:9).

initial input, spreads excitations and inhibitions among its units. In some types of networks this process does not stop until a *stable state* is achieved. (1991:2)

The following is a simple schematic example of such a network:

Each node is assigned a particular number, corresponding to its level of activation (say, between -1 and $+1$), and each branch is assigned a number corresponding to its "weight" (between -1 and $+1$), or the degree to which the output of a node at one end of the branch (the "parent") can affect the activation of the node at the other (the "child"). If weight of a branch is positive the activation of the parent node will *raise* the activation of the child node (an "excitatory connection"); if it is negative, it will *lower* it (an "inhibitory connection"). In a process called "back propagation," the weights of the "hidden nodes" are gradually readjusted as the system emits certain values from the output nodes in response to new values provided at the input ones, and receives further "tutorial" signals indicating the degree to which the pattern of its output matched some preset values (corresponding to some target pattern to be "matched"). According to RCON, it is this way that our nervous systems "adapt" our minds to our environments and we come to exhibit what psychological regularities there are to be observed.[28]

Churchland (1995:79–82) describes a well-known example of such a network operating in response to sonar echos from underwater rocks and mines. Initially the weights and activation levels are set randomly, but then, as echo patterns are fed into the input nodes, the excitation spreads through the network, and the output nodes are caused to fire in certain patterns. These patterns are compared with some ideal set of values, an error value is computed, and the weights of the branches are modified according to various rules (say, altering the weights one at a time from left to right). The network's success in distinguishing rocks from mines consists in its "settling down" over many, many such "trials," into certain weight and activation assignments, until its output values consistently match the preset ones.

Indeed, such systems seem well suited to perform the kinds of massively parallel, rapid statistical analyses that seem to characterize much human pattern recognition and feature detection. As Churchland (1995) nicely explains, many recognition tasks consist in having to compare a great many features of a novel stimulus against stored representations of previous stimuli, checking for a best fit. Detecting statistical trends in clusterings of n properties among previously encountered stimuli can be viewed as the task of mapping areas of a n-dimension vector space, each dimension representing the possible values of a certain property, each vector representing the possession of a property to a specific degree. Garrison Cottrell (1991) has achieved some excellent successes in getting machines to "recognize faces."[29] As Churchland rightly emphasizes, such processes are a way of capturing the "holism" of pattern recognition stressed by many critics of CRTT, (e.g. Dreyfus 1972/1979, Dreyfus and Dreyfus 1986:28).[30] Churchland (1995) discusses a variety of cognitive phenomena amenable to such treatment, for example: sensory coding (pp. 22–6), stereoscopic vision (pp. 57–79), facial recognition (pp. 27–51), speech perception (pp. 84–91), sensori-motor coordination (pp. 91–6), recognition of emotional states (p. 125), and "inductive inference" (pp. 54–5).

Moreover, as connectionists generally (e.g. Smolensky 1988a) stress, RCON has a number of empirically confirmed advantages over "classical symbol manipulation" programs like CRTT and COG. They cite some general problems AI researchers have confronted with programs of the latter sort: they are "brittle" and "impractical," they fail to capture the extraordinary swiftness of perception and thought, they fail to perform "gracefully" in degraded circumstances.[31] All of these problems would be greatly reduced by an RCON program.

Of course, so characterized, it is not clear that there is any real conflict between the two approaches. After all, a connectionist network could simply supplement CRTT. Or, along the lines of LCON, it could provide one way that CRTT could be realized or "implemented": both descriptions would be true of people, but simply at different explanatory levels, much as neurophysiology, chemistry, and physics provide equally true descriptions at further, different levels. In a fashion familiar from discussions of functional organization (§6.4), each level would be important to capturing generalizations lost at another. Such would be the place of LCON, and as such they might excite little more than the interests of cognitive engineers.

The crucial feature that distinguishes RCON from LCON and CRTT models is the claim that *there is no causally efficacious constituent structure to the mental representations that play a role in the processing.* Thus, where a Classical, CRTT model postulates computations over data structures like those of the predicate calculus ("Rab," "(∃x)(Fx v Gx)"), where the constituents (such as "R," "a," "b," "∃") are themselves causally efficacious entities, an RCON model treats all representations pretty much *atomically*: there are simply solitary nodes representing objects or properties ("features"), none of them functioning causally as logical operators. A network simply responds to a feature, or statistical function of features without exploiting logico-syntactic structure.

In assessing the debate between RCON and CRTT it's crucial to note that these claims put RCON in a riskier, asymmetric position with respect to CRTT: CRTT can cheerfully allow connectionist processes as LCON implementations; but RCON has to show that there is *no* aspect of mentation that requires CRTT states. A negative existential of that sort is difficult for any theory. It is particularly difficult for RCON, given the strong *prima facie* evidence that can be adduced for at least *some* phenomena requiring CRTT.

In particular, the availability of causally efficacious constituent structure allows CRTT to explain a range of phenomena that present serious difficulties for RCON.

227

Many of these phenomena we have already encountered in earlier chapters as presenting one or another problem or explanatory gap; some of them are amplifications of further subtleties in those phenomena. If CRTT does in fact explain these phenomena, then, I submit, we will have begun to bridge those explanatory gaps, since, if CRTT is correct, then there is upward necessitation from natural facts about the world to CRTT descriptions. We can then consider the prospects of RCON fulfilling a similar promise.

At this point in the discussion, there are seven such phenomena (we will consider several more in chapters 9 and 11):

(1)   The Propositional Structure of Attitudes
(2)   The Productivity of Attitudes
(3)   The Systematicity of Attitudes
(4)   Rational Relations among Attitudes
(5)   Irrational Relations and Errors among Attitudes
(6)   The Multiple Roles of Attitudes
(7)   The Causal Efficacy of Attitudes

I will discuss each in turn.

(1)   the propositional structure of attitudes: as noted above, the notion of a propositional structure is crucial to a realist conception of attitudes. What is it to be such a structure? Russell (1903:§54) struggled valiantly over this problem when he worried about what he called "the unity of the proposition," or how to distinguish a proposition from a mere list, e.g. how to distinguish between the *meaningful sentence* "Socrates is bald" and the *co-referential* list of words "Socrates, being, bald"; or between the list "Romeo, love, Juliet" and the meaningful sentences, "Romeo loves Juliet" and "Juliet loves Romeo"; or between thinking that someone loves everyone and that everyone is loved by someone or other. These differences are essential to the function of a proposition or mental state expressing some *judgment* or representing some possible state of affairs, a function that cannot be performed by mere lists or sets of associations.

CRTT captures this distinction by defining different *computational roles* for different sorts of symbols – predicates, singular terms, variables, quantifiers – to play. Thus, "aRb" is subject to different computations than "bRa," as is "Someone loves everyone" vs. "everyone loves someone."[32] As in Wittgenstein's *Tractatus* (which was in part a reply to Russell's struggles), it is the *relations* among the symbols that constitute the sentential facts capable of representing the possible facts to which thought has access.[33]

Since all the nodes in a connectionist network play an identical type of role, RCON approaches have a serious *prima facie* difficulty with any such distinction. There is little room for the different kinds of relations provided by the different kinds of symbols, and so no basis for the requisite propositional structure. Lists or associations like "Socrates baldness" and "Romeo Juliet love" would seem to be all that a network could ground.[34]

(2) *the productivity of attitudes*: in the same sense that human languages are productive (§4.2.3), people seem to be able to think a potential infinitude of thoughts. That is, to a first approximation, for any agent x, attitude A and content p, and where L(p,q) is any permissible construction out of the logical components of p and q:

productivity: if (x can A p & x can A q), then x can A L(p,q)

The potential infinity arises because the principle is clearly recursive: if x can think, as a result of previous applications of the law, [Sam is fat or Beth is tall] and [Gwen is smart only if Bill is short], then, by a further application, x could think [(Sam is fat or Beth is tall) iff (Gwen is smart only if Bill is short)]; and then so on for further combinations of that and other content, and for other logical operators.

As we also noted in discussing Chomsky's similar claims, many people balk at what can seem like the extravagant idealizations. Is it really true that there is no limit to the complexity of thoughts we can entertain? How about a thought with a logical structure of a quadrillion logical constants? Surely there are limits on our lifetimes, memories, and interests in understanding. But notice we *can* easily understand *some* such constructions: if we knew that the thought consisted in a conjunction or disjunction of [snow is white] iterated a quadrillion times, then the thought would be equivalent to the thought [snow is white] by itself. Perhaps, however, this would not involve thinking the quadrillion iterations themselves. But we would need a complicated explanation to rule out thinking such thoughts in this indirect way (as might occur in a logical proof). A reasonable claim of a psychologist is that, per our discussion of idealization in the previous section, such idealization carves our mind at natural joints, leaving the limitations to interference from these other natural features (memory, mortality), just as a biologist might (or might not) claim that, *ceteris paribus*, animals are immortal, and not genetically programmed to die.

Nevertheless, for those who are wary of such idealizations to potential infinities, Fodor (1987:147ff) offered a related, more finite property.

(3) *the systematicity of attitudes*: people can think contents in ways that are systematically related: e.g. if someone can think that [Romeo loves Juliet], she can also think that [Juliet loves Romeo], if she can think [If Romeo loves Juliet then Juliet loves Romeo], then she can also think that [if Romeo loves Juliet then Juliet loves Romeo], and so forth for all permissible patterns of logical construction i.e.:

systematicity: if x can A p then x can A L(p)

(where "A" is any attitude verb, and "L(p)" is any logical permutation of the logico-syntactic parts of p).

Note that such systematicity is not limited merely to linguistic creatures: animals that can discriminate one set of directions seem to be able to discriminate any permutation of them (recall that rats that learned a maze could more easily learn its mirror image).

Symbolic approaches capture these kinds of differences by supposing the agent stands in sufficiently rich computational relations to a productive language system: since the constituents of the language are available to the system in order for it to think any one thought, they are available to think logical permutations of those constituents. Insofar as RCON models do not make the constituents of thoughts available, it would be entirely *accidental* that a system that could think one thought could similarly think the related logical permutations.[35]

Some writers (e.g. Sterelny 1990) have suggested that systematicity could simply be a *collection* of separate capacities, one for each particular concept (property, relation, logical operator). It's important to note that systematicity runs deeper than that. If you pay someone enough, they will symbolize *most any* relation among n things by a capital letter followed by n lower case variables: they are able, that is, to generalize *across* all such concepts, a feat that would be difficult to explain were (apparent?) systematicity simply a result of a collection of separate capacities.[36]

A crucial point is sometimes lost in the discussion of this issue. It isn't enough merely that a connectionist network produce systematic relations *inter alia*. After all, a monkey randomly typing on a typewriter forever is eventually bound to produce L(p) iff it produces p. What is required is an explanation of systematicity that shows why people are *biased* towards systematic thought: they produce it, but not just *any* pattern of thought. It is this that CRTT can explain, but an RCON network could not, at least not without further assumptions not motivated by the brain's architecture (this point applies, *mutatis mutandis*, to all of the other explanatory issues we're discussing).

(4) rational relations among attitudes: many of peoples' attitudes seem at least *sometimes* related in rational ways: e.g. there's a deductive relation between a person's belief that there is an infinitude of primes and her belief in the steps of Euclid's proof; some kind of inductive relation between her belief that smoking causes cancer and her belief in various statistical studies and theories of cancer; some kind of "practical syllogism" involved in her belief that smoking causes cancer, her desire not to die, and her deciding not to smoke. These relations typically involve relations among constituents of different attitudes: practical reasoning works by beliefs about means having constituents that *overlap* desires for

certain ends (my thinking there's water to the left combines with my desire for water through the constituent [water]).

CRTT captures these relations by postulating logically constructive abilities among the computational abilities of the brain: the brain can actually construct a complex logical formula, such as "$(\exists x)(y)(Rxy \Rightarrow Ryx)$," and this opens the possibility of capturing rational relations by supplying suitable objects – formally specific sentences – in which rational relations are standardly expressed, along the lines we discussed above.[37] RCON models, lacking the Classical constituent structure of sentences, obviously have difficulties capturing such rationality.

(5) irrational relations and errors among attitudes: irrationality is as every bit in need of content ascription as rationality. Moreover, much of it seems to be *structure sensitive*: fallacies in reasoning sometimes seem due to formal confusions of negations, antecedents and consequents, necessary with sufficient conditions, scopes of operators (e.g. confusing "Everyone strives for an end" with "There's an end for which everyone strives"). Obviously any theory that is committed to the existence of causally efficacious logical structures stands a better chance of explaining these patterns than one that doesn't.

CRTT captures these irrationalities by supplying appropriate objects and plausible computational errors for explaining such mistakes: for example, computing errors in dealing with repeated symbols and syntactically similar forms (e.g. nested negations, scope ambiguities), or in placement of lexical items in given syntactic slots; assumptions treating infinite on the model of finite cases; representing reasons with the same symbols as those for causes. By contrast, it would be entirely fortuitous for a connectionist model to predict, for example, scope ambiguities that, per (1), it would even have trouble expressing.

Interestingly, connectionist networks do offer a promise for accounting for some forms of irrationality. Thus, as Wason and Johnson-Laird (1972) and Kahneman et al. (1982), have shown, people are biased towards positive instances in confirming hypotheses, ignore background frequencies in assessing probabilities, and are liable to gambler fallacies. Tversky (1977) argues that this is due to the primacy of prototypical forms of reasoning. Considered as a phenomenon in isolation from the other issues, such mistakes lend themselves to treatment by a connectionist network. However, as is often disregarded in the prototype literature (e.g. Rosch 1973 and Smith and Medin 1981), such phenomena by no means exhaust people's competence with concepts. Indeed, there is the important phenomenon of conceptual stability, to which we will return in §9.4.

(6) the multiple roles of attitudes: different attitudes can be directed on the same thoughts. People often *wish* for the *very same condition* that they *believe* does not presently obtain; they often come to *think* that what they previously only *feared*, e.g. that Sam (but not Mark) might come to dinner. CRTT captures this by

different computational relations (to a first approximation, one for each attitude) to the same internal representation. RCON would seem to be committed to positing a different set of excitations for each thought.

Indeed, without these multiple roles, it's utterly unclear why one should regard a system as genuinely having attitudes at all. Again, why think with Tienson (1987:11) that, just because a connectionist system has networks whose activation co-varies with being Penelope and being English, that it *believes* anything? Belief is ordinarily supposed to be a state that interacts with, for example, desires, fears, hopes in rather specific ways, none of which seem capturable by RCON.

(7) the causal efficacy of attitudes: the above rational, irrational, and multiple-role patterns of thought seem sometimes to involve *causal* relations among attitudes, not only "(ir)rationalizing" but also *causally explaining* changes of state and behavior. That is to say, there is a *non-accidental* relation between the antecedent and consequent states.

CRTT permits this possibility by supposing that tokens of sentences that are objects of attitudes are physically entokened in the nervous systems of the agents, and that, moreover, there are laws connecting the various states *by virtue of their syntactic and semantic constituents*. Thus, there are both laws relating states by virtue of their *content* (e.g. "People who think they're getting tender, loving care release more endorphins") and laws relating states by virtue of their *constituent form* (e.g. "For any thoughts P and Q, reasonings involving [P and Q] are easier than reasonings involving [−(−P v −Q)]"). But lack of constituent causality is, of course, how Smolensky (1988a) proudly distinguishes RCON from CRTT, which consequently, deprives RCON of any account of the causal efficacy of structured thoughts (see Rey 1990 and 1995a for further discussion).

Of course, perhaps there will emerge proposals showing how RCON can accommodate all of these phenomena just as easily as CRTT does. All to the good: that would simply show that there were *two* ways of meeting Descartes' and Brentano's challenges about the possibility of a naturalistic theory of mind. For our purposes, however, one will do; and I hope some of the discussion of this chapter has provided reason to think that we do have such a one.

Alternatively, a defender of RCON might deny that the above phenomena are genuine. This has been the strategy of many, who have claimed, for example, that productivity and systematicity are not nearly as well established as defenders of CRTT make out (see van Gelder and Niklasson 1994). Sometimes RCON simply aligns itself with outright eliminativism about mental states or, at any rate, with denials of their causal efficacy (see Ramsey et al. 1990). Frequently it goes hand in hand with the interpretavism and Dennett's Patternalism that we discussed in §3.1.2, and/or the irreferentialism about ascriptions of propositional attitude that we discussed in §5.2.3: such ascriptions do not refer to causal states, but are ascribed as parts of whole, "normative" patterns. Indeed, RCON's conception of the mental is captured very well by some of the irreferentialist passages of the later Wittgenstein that we quoted earlier (§5.2.3). Just as Wittgenstein was prepared to find that the "system of impulses going out from my brain and correlated with my spoken or written thoughts . . . [mightn't] continue further in the direction of the centre," and might indeed, "proceed, so to speak, out of chaos" (1967:§608), an RCONist like Smolensky (1988a) is prepared to regard apparent regularities in our minds as merely "harmony maxima" induced in a chaotic system of neural connections by stabilities in the environment.[38]

We've already noted in §5.2.3 the implausibility of regarding attitude ascriptions as irreferential in the way that Wittgenstein proposed. I postpone replying fully to such interpretativist defenses of RCON until after we've considered the issues of semantics and normativity in chapters 9 and 10 on which those defenses rely (see §10.3.4).

Notes

1   The awkward phrase abbreviated by "CRTT" is my term for the view, although Loewer and I used in it in our (1992) introduction to the work of Fodor. Anticipations of different features of the view are to be found in Hobbes (1651/1965), Sellars (1956), and Harman (1972). My discussion is closest to Fodor's (1975, 1987), although it diverges from his views in the understanding of some of the semantic issues in chapter 9, and certainly with regard to the qualitative issues in chapter 11. See also Haugeland (1985) and Sterelny (1990) for helpful related expositions.

2   See Dreyfus (1972/1979) for a critique of the amazing optimism of early enthusiasts of artificial intelligence. Note that one can share Dreyfus' skepticism about such *naiveté* without agreeing to the arguments he believes can be raised against the program in principle. See §10.1.4 below.

3   In chapter 11, we'll consider ways in which it might be applied to other kinds of mental states, e.g. sensory experiences.

4   This formulation is due to Field (1978a). He is concerned there almost exclusively with the "means that" relation. I shall turn to that in chapter 9. Here I want to focus merely on the different computational relations. In anticipation of that later discussion (especially §9.3–.4), I should emphasize that the present distinctions are not intended to rule out the possibility that the computational relation may be a component of a full account of content.

5   We will be largely concerned with trying to analyze what are standardly called "occurrent" psychological states, such as *actively judging*; more dispositional ones, such as *belief*, would be analyzed as dispositions to enter certain active computational states; see, for example, Alston (1967) and Goldman (1970) for discussion.

6   Schiffer (1981), for example, considers the sentences being stored in what he calls a "Yes-Box."

7   See Stich (1983:35–8) for excellent expansion of this point.

8   Of course there could be: for any number of reasons it might be useful for a system to represent the rules that govern its own representations, in which case, the computer would not be obeying the rules by following them, but following them by obeying them!

9   This (1930) result of Gödel's is to be distinguished from his more famous (1931) proof of the essential *incompleteness* of arithmetic, to be discussed shortly (§8.7).

10 Readers impatient with the worry that all such talk will be non-explanatory of the mind because it will require an homunculus to follow the rules and read the symbols will have to wait until §10.1.3.

11 There are obvious limits to this: we couldn't supply it with a literally infinite tape. So let it be merely an indefinitely long one.

12 *Modus ponens* is the rule that permits derivation of a sentence "q" from sentences of the form "p" and "if p then q"; for example, "There are ducks in Ohio" from "There are ducks in Cincinnati" and "If there are ducks in Cincinnati then there are ducks in Ohio."

13 This, unfortunately, does not show that arithmetic is *complete*; for what Gödel (1931) showed is that there are uncomputable functions in arithmetic; see §8.7 for a brief discussion of this issue and how, popular reports to the contrary, it *doesn't* show that human reasoning transcends that of any machine.

14 There is a wealth of material on the topic; see Thagard (1988) and Josephson and Josephson (eds 1994) for treatments not far from the approach sketched here.

15 See his (1955/1976), but also the introductory freshman text, Quine and Ullian (1970/78).

16 I provide a variant of the model presented by Fodor (1975:28–9).

17 A "basic act" is an act whose performance doesn't involve the performance of any other act (see Danto 1963, and Goldman 1970). Thus, *wriggling one's right big toe* is a basic act for most of us, while *wriggling one's ears* is not (I have to use my hands). I'm presuming that sometimes *not wriggling one's right big toe* also counts as a basic act, but nothing depends upon deciding on these details here.

18 Just as, in reasonable expositions of first-order logic, the syntactically defined formalism is set out with an eye to its intended interpretation: e.g. "⇔" is better called "the biconditional" than merely "the double arrow."

19 That is, this is the intended interpretation of the program. But, to reiterate what has already been emphasized, we will not have a right to that interpretation until a semantics is specified.

20 To aid in reading, we may think of these sentences as saying, respectively, "There's a square in front of me now" and "There's a circle in front of me now," bearing in mind that these translations into English are inessential to the (understanding of the) operation of COG.

21 It is worth comparing this process with the process Kant (1783/1968:B172ff) posited in his "schematism," whereby the concepts of the understanding were applied to sensible intuitions. Kant does claim that such applications require "mother wit," for the lack of which no philosophy could suffice. Although different – particularly highly theoretic – concepts will require more complex patterns of inference, there is no reason to suppose that such "mother wit" would not be capturable by essentially the process outlined here.

234

22   Or – if one resorts to the uncertainties of quantum mechanics – that any genuinely free
      action actually is due to those uncertainties. Note that, although the next click of a
      Geiger counter may be indeterminate in principle, this wouldn't seem to render the
      behavior of the Geiger counter a whit more "free" in the sense relevant to human
      action or moral responsibility. For further and insightful reflections on the probable
      incoherence of the demands we make on the relevant notion of freedom, see Galen
      Strawson (1987).

23   See, for example, Lucas (1961); Nagel and Newman (1958), Globus (1976), and, most
      recently, Penrose (1989, 1994). For more detailed discussion than is possible here see
      Lewis (1969, 1979b).

24   Russell's Paradox is a case in point: who would have thought there wasn't a set for
      every predicate?

25   Some main proponents are Tienson (1987), Smolensky (1988a,b), Ramsey et al.
      (1990), and Cummins and Schwarz (1987).

26   By which I mean to include what Bechtel and Abrahamson (1991:238) call
      "compatibilist" models, such as those of Touretsky and Hinton (1985).

27   There are good summaries available: see Bechtel and Abrahamson (1991), Clark
      (1989).

28   That is, RCONists not only claim that they can explain everything explainable by
      CRTT, but sometimes that many of the things claimed to be explained by CRTT are
      not genuine phenomena, notably systematicity and productivity of thought: either the
      phenomena is denied outright, as in van Gelder and Niklasson (1994), or is regarded
      as only an "approximation," as in Smolensky (1988a).

29   To use the words that both Cottrell (1991) and Churchland (1995:38–55) use to
      describe what the machines are doing. One might wonder whether merely being able
      to distinguish typical faces amounts to *recognizing faces*, since recognizing would seem
      to imply *cognizing*, which in turn would suggest that the machine has the concept
      [face]. But what's the argument for *that*? It's surely not enough that the machine can
      discriminate typical faces, any more than it's enough to have the concept [bird] merely
      that could discriminate typical birds. We'll return to this issue shortly (§8.8). See also
      Rey (1983, 1985).

30   Actually, Dreyfus and Dreyfus (1986) present a special problem in this regard, since
      they want to insist that holistic pattern recognition involves "no decomposition into
      features" (p. 28), which presumably would rule out even connectionist proposals such
      as Churchland's. However, they provide no clue as to how pattern recognition,
      especially non-local, non-physical properties (cf. §4.3 above) could otherwise possibly
      be explained.

31   McLaughlin (forthcoming) points out, however, that a number of studies comparing
      classical and connectionist models don't bear these charges out.

32   Cf. Fodor and Pylyshyn's (1988:23ff) discussion of the distinction between "John
      loves Sally and Bill hates Mary" and "John hates Mary and Bill loves Sally."

33   Distinguishing propositions from lists was one of the central issues addressed by the
      early Wittgenstein (1920/1961). What distinguishes "aRb" from "bRa" is obviously
      not that their constituents name different things, but that these constituents enter
      into different relations with each other, the predicate and (in this case) the order
      performing the function of actually creating that relation (this is, I think, the central

point of his unjustly maligned "picture theory of language," see 1920/1961:§3.142–.1432). Indeed, the young Wittgenstein presumed there was a *language* of thought. In a letter (Aug 19, 1919) to Russell he writes, "I don't know *what* the constituents of a thought are but I know *that* it must have such constituents which correspond to the words of language. Again the kind of relation the constituents of the thought and of the pictured fact is irrelevant. It would be a matter of psychology to find out" Wittgenstein (1979:130). Another important anticipation is in Kant (1781/1968:A100ff) where, against associationist sense-data theories – so like connectionist networks – Kant argues forcefully for the need of rule-governed "syntheses" of the manifold.

34 *Pace* Tienson (1987:11), we have no basis for saying of a system that merely has states that co-vary with being Penelope and being English that it "believes *Penelope is English*" (emphasis reversed).

35 See Fodor (1987), Fodor & Pylyshyn (1988), and Fodor and McLaughlin (1990) for rich discussion of this issue.

36 See, for example, Smolensky's (1988a) treatment of [coffee], which would be different when extracted from [coffee cup], [coffee can], or [coffee tree].

37 They are so standardly expressed this way that arguably logical relations are partly *constituted* by logico-syntactic relations. If this is true, then it affords a basis for a not merely empirical argument for CRTT that I explore in Rey (1995a).

38 I discuss this hypothesis in relation to Wittgenstein in Rey (1991b). See Pinker and Mehler (1988) for serious empirical doubts about it.

9

CRTT: Representation[1]
(Meeting Brentano's Challenge)

The issues surrounding "content" and "semantics" are some of the most complex, vexed, and interesting in the whole of philosophy. It would be preposterous to try to summarize the mountains of material written on the subject, or even do justice to the views that pertain to the specific issues confronting CRTT. The best that can be done here is to provide a geography of some of the main approaches to the problem, indicating their prospects and some of the problems they still face.

As I (and most of its adherents) think of it, CRTT is intended to serve as a fully *realistic* theory about propositional attitude states: it is an attempt to provide an account of how creatures for example, genuinely believe the specific contents they seem to believe, and how believing those contents can help explain their behavior. Consequently, we will not be concerned in this section with the large number of semantic views that do not treat claims about meaning realistically. For example, we won't consider at this point Dennett's or Davidson's interpretavist semantics, or Stich's (1983) "syntactic theory of mind," according to which only the syntactic architecture of CRTT is required for psychology; claims about content are indeterminate, to be settled only pragmatically.[2]

One cautionary note in thinking about semantics for any "computer" model of the mind: what we popularly call computers are *artifacts*, things intentionally made by people with certain purposes. Now, it's a basic fact about any artifact that its creator gets to determine a great deal about it: something's a *doorstop* if someone uses it, thinking of it that way; some symbol in a code means what it does if it was devised by someone with that idea in mind, no matter how poorly it may perform as one. In the case of assigning meaning to states of a computer, this fact plays an especially prominent role: *the states of artifactual computers usually have what meaning they have entirely by virtue of the intentions of their creators and/or programmers.* They have what meaning they have rather in the way that words in books do.

But, of course, if CRTT were correct, then the semantics of *some* computers, e.g. animal brains, isn't determined in any such fashion: animals aren't anyone's artifacts.[3] In so using an artifact as a model for a non-artifactual natural object, CRTT is, of course, no worse off than a biology that treats kidneys as *filters* and hearts as *pumps*. Presumably, hearts and kidneys are so characterized not because biologists believe they are artifacts, but because so characterizing them has some explanatory point. Just so: characterizing the brain as a computer with semantic states is an explanatory proposal freed from the conventions surrounding artifacts.

9.1 Internalist Theories

One of the most natural ideas about meaning is that it is some sort of introspectible idea inside one's mind and/or head, what (after Quine 1968:278) we shall call the "idea idea." We already encountered a simple version of it in §5.1.1; it is worth considering more sophisticated versions.

9.1.1 Images and stereotypes

Historically, an appealing idea has been that mental representations are images.[4] The idea is that imagistic representation is somehow unproblematic: an image represents what it resembles. Thus, a green triangle image is supposed to represent a green triangle because it resembles one. As appealing as this idea has been, it is obvious that it won't get us very far with semantics generally. No one expects to find entities that are actually triangular and green in the brains of people who think about green triangles. Perhaps talk of resemblance is just a way of talking about a correspondence between features of neural events and real world properties, but then the problem is the problem of specifying why one correspondence rather than another provides the correct interpretation (cf. §5.1.1 above). In any case, even if some mental representations can be usefully thought of as images, it is extremely implausible that *all*, or even a significant proportion of LOT representations can be. Images simply don't combine to produce *logically complex* images. What image, for example, could represent a *negative* fact, as in the thought that there are *no* green triangles? A green triangle with a line through it? How is that to be distinguished from a (unnegated) image of a triangle with a black cane laid across it? What image could hope to represent a complex definition involving abstract concepts, such as "(x)(x is a US citizen iff (x is either (i) born on US soil, (ii) naturalized, or (iii) the offspring of US citizens))," or "A prime number is one not divisible by any other numbers than itself and 1?" While imagistic representations might well play some role in some cognitive processes, they simply seem inadequate for any serious logical thought. Sentences seem to be the only physically realizable objects that begin to have anything like the requisite expressive potential.[5]

238

9.1.2   Conceptual roles

One kind of proposal that naturally emerges from functionalist accounts of mental states is a view that is also motivated by Wittgenstein's (1953:§43) famous dictum that "the meaning of a word is its use." This is the view that the meaning of a LOT expression is determined by its conceptual role.[6] There are various versions of "conceptual role semantics" in the field.[7] Most of them characterize an expression's conceptual role in terms of its evidentiary and other logical connections to other expressions, connections that Fodor (1987) called "epistemic liaisons." Thus, the meaning of "human being" might be the associations, implications, and evidentiary connections someone's beliefs about human beings would have with others of her beliefs (e.g. if something's human, it's animal; speaks language; eats; dies, etc.).

Conceptual role theories of meaning are most plausible for the logical connectives. For example, a certain expression "#" might plausibly mean "and" in virtue of the fact that thinking "P#Q" tends to cause thinking P and thinking Q, which in turn tends to cause thinking "P#Q."[8] However, extending the account even to other logical particles is notoriously fraught with difficulties. Consider just "or" and disputes about the law of excluded middle: do the different parties to the dispute mean something different by "or"? How then are they actually disagreeing? As one moves away from purely logical cases, the problem seems daunting: which liaisons are crucial to "human" or "animal"? In any event, no one has actually constructed an adequate conceptual role theory that specifies exactly how conceptual role in general determines meaning in a way that is applicable across different individuals. Many philosophers are skeptical that any such account is possible.[9]

There are a number of reasons for skepticism. One problem, raised by Fodor and LePore (1992), is that, on the face of it, conceptual roles don't seem *compositional* in the way that content ought to be. The content [brown cow] ought, after all, to be some kind of compositional function of the content [brown] and the content [cow]. However, it's not at all clear that the conceptual role of [brown cow] is a compositional function of the role of [brown] and the role of [cow]: there may well be inferences that are peculiar to brown cows that are not shared by brown things or cows alone (e.g. only brown cows live in Guam).

Perhaps the suggestion is to limit the relevant content determining conceptual roles to certain definitive inferences. This isn't an entirely new idea: recall our discussion in §5.4 of the verification theory of meaning. That was certainly an attempt to spell out the meaning of a concept in terms of epistemic liaisons, specifically those liaisons with ultimately the sensory evidence that would confirm or disconfirm its application. As we saw, however, there are serious difficulties with such a proposal. For purposes here, the most serious are Quine's observations about revisability and confirmation holism: how can we single out certain epistemic liaisons as constitutive of meaning if any of them are revisable and play their epistemic role only in conjunction with all other such liaisons? Quine marshals these observations on behalf of his general skepticism about there being *any* satisfactory way to distinguish what's essential to the meaning of a concept. This is his highly influential attack on the "analytic"/"synthetic" distinction, or the distinction between claims "true by virtue of meaning" vs. those true by virtue of the way the world happens to be.

These problems seem particularly acute for psychology in view of the fact that we seem to encounter people who we have every reason to suppose *possess* a concept but nevertheless seem capable of entertaining arbitrary beliefs involving it. With a little imagination, and for any apparently analytic claim, it seems always possible to construct a story whereby someone (particularly a philosopher) denies that claim while still seeming to possess the relevant concepts, simply by having a sufficiently bizarre theory about the world. Thus, some creationists seem to be denying that humans are animals; some nominalists, that numbers are abstract; and some idealists, that tables are material objects.[10] There would seem to be no epistemic liaison so secure that, with a little ancillary theory, someone couldn't break it and yet still be competent with the relevant concept. So how could some epistemic liaison provide the meaning of a concept?[11]

These observations about revisability and *confirmation* holism have led many advocates of a conceptual role semantics to the desperate measure of *semantic* holism: *all* of a term's epistemic liaisons are constitutive of its meaning.[12] This view has some serious drawbacks. Note first of all that a*ny* change in *any* belief in an individual would be a change in the contents of *all* beliefs: if p changes, then its immediate liaisons, $q_1, \ldots, q_n$ are changed; if they are changed, all *their* liaisons are changed as well; and so on, through the whole of the web of a person's beliefs. Similarly, *any* difference in *any* belief *between* different individuals would be a change in *all* of their beliefs. This would have such startling consequences as: (1) no normal person gaining new beliefs as she peers at the world around her could ever *remember anything* (after all, those new beliefs would change the contents of all old states); (2) one couldn't hope to find new evidence for or against a belief, since the discovery of the evidence would change its liaisons and thus its content; (3) it would be a cosmic coincidence if two people ever shared a belief, since to agree on *anything* they'd have to agree on absolutely *everything*, which (given just their different positions in the world) would be virtually impossible. All this would severely cripple generalization in psychology. Short of cosmic coincidence, generalizations of the form "If anyone thinks/desires that p, then . . ." involving any specific p would apply to only a *single* individual at a *single* time: one couldn't say, for example, that 3-year-olds have trouble with the concept [belief], since no two of them would share it! Semantic holism would seem to be tantamount to the defeat of any serious cognitive psychology.[13]

9.1.3   A general problem for any purely internalist theory

A problem with any purely internalist theory emerges from considering the observations of Kripke (1972/1980), Putnam (1975b), and Burge (1979) regarding the ways in which the meanings of many terms depend crucially upon the environment of the agent. Putnam famously imagines a planet called "Twin Earth" that is exactly like Earth in every respect (including history) except for having a superficially similar chemical, XYZ, everywhere that the earth has H_2O. He claims that, since in fact water *is* H_2O, there is no water on Twin Earth. Now consider some Earthling adult Sophie, who knows no chemical theory, and her "twin," Twin-Sophie, on Twin-Earth, and suppose (along the improbable lines of the story) that they are molecule-for-molecule duplicates of each other.[14] Certainly, there would seem to be no "internal" psychological differences between them. And yet, if XYZ is not genuine water, then Sophie and Twin-Sophie are not referring to the same substance when they use the word "water." If meaning is what determines extension, then, as Putnam (1975b:227) pithily put it, "cut the pie any way you like, 'meanings' just ain't in the head!"[15]

Indeed, whatever one thinks of Putnam's cases, still a further problem can be raised in terms of a general question for any theory that takes thought to be formal symbol manipulation: according to the Löwenheim-Skolem theorem, it's always possible to provide incompatible interpretations of a formal theory on which all its theorems remain *true* (indeed, any true theory about anything could be interpreted to be simply about *numbers*). Moreover, if we relax the requirement of truth, there are obviously even further possible interpretations: one could just let the terms and predicates refer to most anything! Now, it's not clear that programming a computer to manipulate formally specified symbols provides any constraints that will rule out these competing interpretations. Indeed, a computer could use "the same program" one day to play chess, the next to fight a war (after all, the situations and strategies could turn out to be perfectly isomorphic).[16] It would seem that something *external* to the language, program, and computer must determine the meaning of at least some terms in any language.[17]

9.2   Externalist Theories

Interestingly enough, the suggestion that meaning might be something external seems to be every bit as natural as the idea that it's internal. At any rate, besides the "idea idea," one of the oldest theories of meaning is what is sometimes called the "'Fido'/Fido theory," according to which the meaning of a representation is the object for which it stands. Obviously, so stated, the theory is false (for starters, there's the problem of names like "Zeus" that don't succeed in referring to anything). However, as in the case of the "idea idea," there are sophisticated versions of it. There are at least three main types of such "externalist" theories that have been proposed: those that appeal to the *actual* causal history of a representation; those that appeal to *co-variational* relations between a representation and phenomena in the world; and *"teleo-semantic"* theories that appeal to evolutionary selectional processes. We will examine each in turn.

9.2.1   Historical causal theories

Critics of internalist semantics proposed an alternative semantic "picture" whereby the reference of a token term is determined by the causal relations it bears to other tokens and ultimately to individuals or kinds.[18] Although the picture was originally proposed with regard to terms in a natural language, many of its morals carry over to terms in an LOT. An early effort to account for this aspect of meaning involved considering *actual* causal chains linking a speaker's use of a particular word to users of that word to dub the thing (object, substance, kind) to which the speaker thereby refers. Kripke (1972) and Putnam (1975b) vividly argued for such an account of proper names and for natural kind terms (cf. §1.5.2 above). Thus, Kripke argued that what determines the reference of a name like "Aristotle" is not any of the common beliefs associated with the name, which he claimed could all turn out to be false, but rather a chain of uses of the name that extends from present uses all the way back to Aristotle's original dubbing with the name. Similarly, Putnam (1975b) argued that "water" refers to H_2O by virtue of causal chains extending from present uses back to early dubbing uses of it that were in fact dubbings of the substance H_2O (although, of course, the original users of the word didn't know this). Moreover, since they are causally connected to different substances, our earthling English speaker thereby refers to H_2O, while her twin refers to XYZ.

Although many philosophers are persuaded that actual causal histories have some role to play in a theory of reference, it is widely thought that such histories are not in themselves sufficient for a satisfactory theory, since at every stage of such causal chains there are events (such as *ostensions, dubbings, communications, understandings*) that require intentional characterization.[19] For example, it requires that the original dubber had one thing rather than another in mind on the occasion of the dubbing. What in Aristotle's parent's brain determined that it was the *infant*, Aristotle, and not the kind *human being*, or *animal*, or just his nose, or a temporal stage of him that got dubbed? All these things, after all, are equally in the path described by the dubber's ostending finger. (This is the "qua" problem, discussed at length in Devitt and Sterelny 1987.)

Historical causal theories took *proper names* as their prime examples, extending the treatment to *natural kind* and to some artifactual *terms*. The problems just raised seem to require a more general account of the meaning of *predicates* generally.

9.2.2 Co-variational locking theories

A natural answer to the question of what a dubber dubbed might be: whatever kind of thing she would *discriminate* as that thing; that is, whatever she would apply the term to, as opposed to everything she wouldn't. Along these lines, a number of philosophers have considered ways in which states involving token expressions might have, in addition to *actual* causal histories, certain *counterfactual* dispositional properties to co-vary with certain phenomena in the world. The suggestion has its origin in the "natural sign" theories of Peirce (1897–1906/ 1931) and Morris (1946/1955), and was incorporated into behavioristic theories of meaning such as one finds in Skinner (1957) and Quine (1960). Of course, the versions of the theory that interest us here will be ones that take this behavioristic proposal partly "inside" an agent, permitting internal symbols to be one of the co-variants. The idea essential to this approach is that intentional meaning is treated as a species of "information," or so-called "natural" meaning, the kind of meaning that is said to obtain between dark clouds and rain, red spots and measles, expansions of mercury in a thermometer and ambient temperature.[20] One event naturally means another if there is a causal law connecting them, or, to put it in Dretske's (1981) terms, the one event carries "information" about the other. A sentence, on this view, means what it carries information about: the sentence "it's raining" means that it's raining, since it carries the information (causally co-varies) with the fact that it's raining.[21]

Nevertheless, so stated, the view is open to several immediate objections. Any such naturalistic theory needs to say what's *special* about meaning. As Antony and Levine (1991) have emphasized, buying meaning too cheaply from nature runs the risk of "pan-semanticism": almost everything would mean something, since almost everything is reliably caused by *something*. So there must be some further condition. In particular, *most* tokenings of sentences (whether in English or LOT) are produced in the *absence* of the conditions that they nevertheless mean: "That's a horse" can be uttered on a dark night in the presence of a cow, or just idly in the presence of anything. Fodor (1987) calls these latter usages "wild"; the property whereby tokens of symbols can mean things that aren't on occasion their actual cause he calls "robustness."

The problem for any co-variational theory is to account for robustness. In doing so it needs to solve what has come to be called the "disjunction" problem: given that among the causes of a symbol's tokenings, there are both meaning-forming and wild causes, what distinguishes them? In particular, what makes it true that some symbol "F" means [horse] and not [horse or cow on a dark night], or [horse or cow on a dark night or w_2 or w_3 or . . .] (where each w_i is one of the purportedly "wild" causes)? This problem is, of course, of a piece with the "Kripkenstein" problem that we discussed in §3.1.2, where the problem was to distinguish someone who has *added* 57 and 63 and obtained 5 as an "error" from someone who is computing a different function, "quaddition" which is identical to addition except for the case of 57 and 63. Note that, contrary to the appearance of these examples, disjunctive concepts need not be at all unnatural: [sibling] might well be understood to be [brother or sister], [US Citizen] as [native born or naturalized]. So the possibility being raised could be regarded as an entirely real one.

Several proposals have been advanced for handling the disjunction problem. They have in common trying to constrain the occasions on which the nomic connection is meaning-forming.

9.2.2.1 Ideal co-variation   A natural suggestion regarding meaning-forming conditions is that they are in some sense "optimal" conditions, conditions that obtain when nothing is interfering with the belief formation system. One of the first such theories was that of Stampe (1977), which was taken up by Stalnaker (1984) and independently proposed (and then later rejected) by Fodor (1980/ 1990, 1987).[22] The attraction of such a theory lies in its capturing the idea that two individuals *meaning* the same thing by some symbol consists in their agreeing about what it would apply to, were *everything else* about the world known. Their disagreements are to be explained as due to their limited epistemic positions and reasoning capacities, which interfere with their being as omniscient as the right conditions for agreement would require. Insisting on such distinctions is like insisting on a distinction between guided missiles that end up at a certain location because that's where they were aimed, from those that, aimed elsewhere, ended up there because of an error in navigation. Wherever they happen to end up, the missiles are "locked onto" a certain destination. Terms have a certain meaning by virtue of being "locked onto" a certain phenomenon in the world.

Such theories in this way suggest a means of isolating an interesting *semantic stability* from issues of *epistemic* differences. In particular, a co-variation theory allows us to capture what in the world an agent is "getting at" in her use of a symbol, isolating that from her relative epistemic success or failure in reaching it. It provides a basis for beginning to predict how an agent will react to further evidence and argument, enabling us to distinguish cases alterable by such processes from those not so alterable, cases in which one needs to get the agent to deploy a different concept and "to think of the phenomenon differently."

Although such theories might not be obviously *false*, they do seem to be subject to a number of difficulties, the chief one consisting of the circularity that seems unavoidable in specifying the optimal conditions: it would appear that those conditions cannot be specified without employing the very intentional idiom the theory is supposed to explain (see Fodor 1987:104–6, and Loewer 1987). For example, it is difficult to see how to rule out the interference of other intentional states – e.g. the aforementioned "bizarre" theories that are the bane of conceptual role accounts – or the cooperation of certain intentional states, such as "attending," "thinking of," "wanting to get things right," or merely the effects of "ignorance."

In order to avoid these problems Fodor (1987, 1990) went on to propose another kind of co-variation, what has come to be known as the "asymmetric dependency" relation. Although it makes no explicit appeal to ideal epistemic conditions, much of its motivation can be appreciated by thinking of the ideal co-variational theory in the background.

9.2.2.2 *Fodor's asymmetric dependencies*

According to the ideal co-variational theory, under epistemically ideal conditions, tokenings of a predicate co-vary with the property it expresses. But, of course, tokens of it may also be produced by many properties it doesn't express: tokens might be produced by things errone-ously taken to have the property, by things associated with the property, by mere thoughts about the property, etc. Now, one way to understand the asymmetric dependency theory is first to notice that, plausibly, all these latter cases depend upon the ideal case, but not vice versa: the wild tokenings depend upon the ideal ones, but the ideal ones don't depend upon the wild ones (getting things wrong depends upon getting things right in a way that getting things right doesn't depend upon getting things wrong).[23] Thus, the property HORSE causes "cow" tokenings because some horses (for example, those at the far end of the meadow) look like cows, and, under ideal circumstances, COW causes "cow" tokenings. If COW didn't cause "cow"s then those horses wouldn't cause them either. But COW causing (under ideal circumstances) "cow" tokenings presumably doesn't depend upon HORSE doing so: people's eyes could improve without that disrupt-ing the fact that cow causes "cow"s. MILK causes "cow" because seeing some milk causes one to think "milk," and this reminds one of where milk comes from, which, under ideal conditions, would be the sort of thing that causes "cow" tokenings.

A useful analogy might be made with the phenomenon of imprinting:[24] gos-lings are evidently born with a disposition to become bonded to the first animal they encounter. But this disposition causes goslings to imprint on different animals in different niches. Moreover, once the imprinting occurs, mis-ident-ifications of an animal as the imprintee depend upon the (original) correct identi-fications, but not *vice versa*. One can imagine there being a variety of different imprinting mechanisms in an animal: one for its prime caretaker, another for its home, another for certain foods, and so forth. In a way, concepts, on the present proposal, can be regarded as an elaborate expansion of such imprinting dispositions.[25]

So formulated, of course, the account still mentions ideal conditions, and these Fodor has conceded cannot be specified non-circularly. His further interesting, indeed, audacious suggestion is, however, that mention of the ideal conditions here is entirely inessential: the structure of asymmetric causal dependency alone, abstracted from any specific conditions or causal chains, will do all the required work!

245

The asymmetric dependency theory does seem to accord well with the original externalist intuitions urged by Putnam. It seems to have the consequence that Sophie's and Twin-Sophie's LOT tokens of "water" refer to different substances. Sophie's tokens nomically co-vary with H_2O while her twin's co-vary with XYZ. Although, for both, there are law-like connections between H_2O and "water" and XYZ and "water," the dependency relations are reversed. Sophie's XYZ-"water" connections depend on her H_2O – "water" connections since, if the former were broken (e.g. Sophie discovers how to detect XYZ) the latter would remain intact but not *vice versa*. The situation is reversed for Twin-Sophie.

Although the theory is quite elegant, and seems to account quite intuitively for some cases, it seems not yet to have inspired a great many adherents. Numerous counterexamples have been raised, to which Fodor has offered numerous replies (see e.g. Fodor 1990, 1991a). One problem noted by many is that, in its effort to provide an account of meaning entirely independent of any mention of mentality, it risks what I call "gratuitous lockings," lockings brought about the physics of the world that have no cognitive significance for the agent. For example, electrical stimulation by a poking neurosurgeon, or by cosmic rays, causing tokenings of a mental symbol in one set of circumstances (e.g. when potassium levels were high) might depend upon their lawfully causing those tokenings under other circumstances (e.g. when sodium levels were low), but not *vice versa*: would a mental symbol really have thèse further phenomena as *meanings*? Fodor has replied to many of these objections with considerable, if not always entirely convincing ingenuity.[26] However, what's needed is not only to rule out cases one by one, but some *positive* reason to believe one *always* could; a reason, not for thinking that semantic relations may exhibit asymmetric dependencies, which many might agree that they do, but rather for thinking that they can do this without mention of any mental condition. Given the explanatory work content ascriptions are supposed to do, it would seem surprising were this possible. Until this issue is addressed, mere acrobatics with the examples doesn't reassure.

We shall discuss some further inadequacies of Fodor's account when we consider problems for purely externalist theories generally (§9.2.4). Before that, one last important class of externalist theories needs to be mentioned.

9.2.3   Teleo-semantic theories[27]

As a piece of the general teleo-semantic approach to the mind that we discussed in §7.2.3, Millikan (1984), Papineau (1987), Dretske (1988), Neander (1991), and Godfrey-Smith (1994, 1996) have been working on a general account of meaning that is based upon the role mental states play in a biological account of the evolution and life of an organism. On this view, beliefs (and other intentional states) possess certain information-carrying functions, even if there are no conditions under which they presently carry out such functions. These functions,

246

determined by natural selection, fix the belief's intentional content. Thus, a frog's tokening "F" whenever a black speck crosses its retinal field might be interpreted as meaning [fly], since it is *flies* that are responsible for the survival of frogs (cf. Lettvin et al. 1951).[28] Such teleological ideas can be combined with co-variational approaches: thus, Dretske (1988) proposes treating meaning as the "recruitment" of a co-variation between an internal state and a worldly phenomenon on behalf of some adaptive response; the fact of the co-variation itself (say, between a state of the frog and the motion of a fly) is an explanatorily significant cause of the frog's shooting out its tongue at such nutritious prey.

All such teleo-semantic approaches face some general problems. A worry that has been much discussed about "selectionist" theories in general is that they are "Panglossian,"[29] assuming that all useful traits were evolutionarily selected. In an influential article, the biologists Gould and Lewontin (1979) point out that many desirable traits of animals may not have been themselves selected, but are rather by-products of other traits that were, much as the lovely "spandrels of St Marco" (triangular areas created by multiple gothic arches in the church of St Marco in Venice) were an unintended consequence of intentionally produced arches. Critics of teleo-semantics, like Fodor (1987, 1991a), argue that we have no reason to think that large parts of thought and language, and their meaning, are not spandrels or other unselected effects, and so of no help in determining semantic content.

One kind of spandrel effect that Fodor (1990:71ff) thinks would be fatal to teleosemantics would be the presence of a property that happened to co-vary with a supposed semantic property in the evolutionarily relevant circumstances. Thus, suppose that BEING A FLY happened to co-vary in the relevant historical swamps with BEING A SMALL, MOVING BLACK BUG (all and only the flies in the neighborhood are small, moving black bugs). On what basis can the teleosemanticist claim that the frog's "F" tokens mean [fly] rather than [small, moving black bug]? Or, by a similar argument, [the best frog food], [source of vitamin v], [fly or beebee], [fly or unicorn]? Should frogs in those circumstances have been sensitive to *these*, or to any other indefinitely many such locally co-variant properties, they would have survived just as well. As Fodor (1990) puts it, " 'Erst kommt das Fressen, dann kommt die Morale.' *Darwin cares how many flies you eat, but not what description you eat them under*" (p. 73).

Neander (1995) provides a two-part response to this problem. First, along with other teleo-semanticists (e.g. Millikan 1991), she cites an important distinction of Sober (1985) between selection *of* and selection *for*: hearts pump the blood, normally (let as assume), iff they make pumping sounds; but it was presumably their pumping, not their thumping that led to the proliferation of certain genes. Although there was selection *of* both traits, only pumping was selected *for*. In this way, Neander argues, teleo-semantics need only look at those properties that cause tokenings that were *in fact causally responsible* in this way for the proliferation of the underlying genes. "F" tokens in the frog were presumably not selected *for* respond- ing to FLY OR BEEBEE or FLY OR UNICORN, and so do not have those properties as their content (even if there was selection *of* both of them). Secondly, where more than one property is causally relevant (as both FLY, and SMALL, MOVING BLACK DOT arguably are), she draws further distinctions among the causal dependencies between the properties: e.g. it is *by* reacting to small, moving dots that the frog detects flies, and not *vice versa*. (Millikan 1991:161–3 proposes a similar account, but privileges different properties.)

However, in addition to spandrel problems, there is also the problem that *properties of thought and language seem to outstrip any pressures from natural selection.* Insofar, for example, as many of our concepts involve commitments to full, potentially infinite universal quantifications, it is difficult to see how they, as opposed to more modest finite cousins, could have been selected by a finite history: how can we possibly have a concept of number allowing for infinite instances, when selection could have gotten by just as well with a concept allowing for only some large finite number? How can we have a concept of infinite time, if selection would have done as well with merely a concept of large finite intervals? As Peacocke (1992) points out:

> The truth (if they are true) of the commitments of a content that have no causal impact on the thinker remain unabsorbed into its content on the teleological theory as currently formulated. They do not contribute in the appropriate way to the explanation of the survival of the mechanisms and of members of the species. We should perhaps recall that in the case of unrestricted universal generalizations over space and time, these commitments will include those about objects outside the thinker's light cone, objects that could not have any causal impact upon him. (1992:131)

Another worry for teleo-semantics is the possibility of a "swampman" (Davidson 1987). Imagine that one day by a swamp a normal human being is struck by lightning, and a few seconds later lightning strikes the swamp, and out of it appears an atom-for-atom duplicate of that person. This duplicate doesn't have any of the evolutionary history of the original human being; therefore, on a teleo-semantic view, it wouldn't have *any* of its intentional states. But it would certainly *appear* to have those states: indeed, it would certainly appear to behave, talk, interact with others, be subject to the same psychological laws and generali- zations, as the original human being. Wouldn't it be not only arbitrary, but seriously unjust, not to think of it as every bit as much an intentional creature as the original?[30]

But perhaps the most serious worry about such teleo-semantic approaches to content is that, given the vicissitudes of natural selection, the wrong contents might get assigned to psychological states. Pietroski (1992) imagines a case in which an animal gets attracted by red flowers on high hills, and so avoids predators in the low lying valleys. The teleo-semanticist would appear to be committed to claiming that the state of responding to the red flowers actually has something like the content [avoid predator] – even if the animal could never actually recognize a predator when face to face with it!

In response to many of these difficulties, Sterelny (1990) and Neander (1995) propose restricting the teleo-semantic story merely to the conceptual "primitives" of the system, and suppose the bulk of a person's concepts are obtained through construction. They would have to identify such primitives, show that indeed they were selected, and then provide such constructions. As we noted in discussing verificationism (§5.4), such construction programs have not fared well in the past. But perhaps not all the moves in this difficult area have yet been made.

9.2.4* General problems with purely externalist accounts

A familiar difficulty that arises for any pure externalist account is the problem we noticed early on in discussing properties (§1.1.1) and intentionality (§2.5.6): that the distinctions of the mind seem to outrun the distinctions that the external world independently provides. Sometimes we are interested not only in what worldly phenomena, if any, an agent is getting at, but *what way of thinking of that phenomenon* she is trying to get at as well; and we have no reason to think that the world is sufficiently rich in phenomena independently of our minds to distinguish among them. Indeed, externalist accounts run not only into standard difficulties of intensionality, or distinctions among concepts (such as [renate] and [cordate]) that *happen* in the real world to be co-extensive, but into difficulties of "hyper-intensionality": distinguishing among *necessarily co-instantiated concepts*, i.e. concepts that are instantiated in all the same possible worlds and/or counterfactual situations.

There are two kinds of such co-instantiated concepts: those expressed by *necessarily co-extensive* terms, such as "triangle" and "trilateral,"[31] "eucalyptus" and "gum tree," "circle" and "point equidistant locus of co-planar points" (whatever satisfies one in each of these pairs necessarily satisfies the other); and what might be called the *necessarily co-divided* ones that we mentioned briefly in §2.1, such as "rabbit," vs. "undetached rabbit parts," vs. "temporal stage of a rabbit"[32] (*different* things satisfy each of these three expressions, but whenever an agent is presented with something that satisfies one of them she's presented with something that satisfies the others).

Consider in this connection the phenomenon of "subception," whereby many animals are able to recognize groups of things of certain (usually modest) cardinality (Gallistel 1990:chapter 10). Take a pigeon that has been trained to peck at "three-membered patterns." Along the lines of a pure co-variation theory, we can suppose that one of these animals actually does have an internal symbol that bears some co-variational or selection relation to, say, the property of triplicity: for any sortal property, F-ness, that it can otherwise discriminate, it can also discriminate 3F-ness. Now, does this animal plausibly have the same concept [three] that I have? There's this reason to think not: the concept I (and most of us) have is a concept controlled by general principles, e.g. Peano's axioms for arithmetic (e.g. zero is a number; every number has a successor), whereby we can be led by reasonings into understanding a potential infinity of complex arithmetic truths. As Gallistel remarks:

> To discriminate on the basis of numerosity is not, however, to have a concept of number, if by "having a concept of number" we mean that an animal is capable of manipulating [numerical representations] in accord with the relational and combinatorial operations of arithmetic. (1990:348)

Humans who can actually reason arithmetically have what might be called the concept [Peano-three]. [Peano-three] and [subcept-three] certainly pick out the same worldly phenomenon; for a symbol to lock onto the one is for it to lock onto the other. But there is good reason for distinguishing them from a psychological point of view: the cognitive manipulations for the one are not the same as for the other – no amount of argument or reasoning would get a pigeon to realize that 27 is the cube of 3: the bird just doesn't have a symbol controlled by the relevant rules. Indeed, it may well be that normal human beings have both concepts, and that it's informative to learn that subcept-three = Peano-three.[33]

A particularly crucial set of cases of necessarily co-instantiated concepts are the *necessarily uninstantiated* ones: e.g. [largest prime], [round-square]. Now, one way to think of dealing with such cases is to try dealing with them as logically complex: so [largest prime] would actually involve a logically complex construction about of symbols meaning [large] and [prime].[34] However, there seem to be plenty of non-complex cases. Saul Kripke (1972), for example, has argued that unicorns could not *possibly* exist – they were an effort to refer which, since it in fact failed, couldn't possibly succeed with the same meaning. And in a related vein, others have argued that nothing could *possibly* satisfy [miracle], [magic], [monster], [free will], or [soul].[35] Perhaps some of these cases are spurious. But all that is needed are two. What is a pure external theory to say of *them*? That the concepts, since they are locked onto the same (viz. *no*) property in the world, are one and the same?

Still another problem for a pure co-variation theory is presented by concepts involving varying degrees of *normativity*, very often a quite obvious *moral* normativity. *Pace* Dennett, we need not think of ordinary mentalistic concepts like [belief]. Rather there are what have come to be called "response-dependent" concepts like [shameful], [tragic], [funny], [bizarre]: although it's not clear that possession of these concepts actually requires any specific behavioral response in a person, it's hard to see how they don't require some appreciation of certain conceptual connections, e.g. between being funny and being an occasion for laughter, being tragic and an occasion for tears. But quite apart from the intuitive connections that would seem to be required in such cases, there is the crucial point that *the same normative concept can cause its possessors to lock onto different phenomena.* After all, it is a commonplace that different people find different things funny, shameful, tragic, bizarre; and this is not in all cases plausibly due to differences in their epistemic position. You and I may disagree about what's funny, well, just *simpliciter*, perhaps as a result of simply very brute differences between out nervous systems: you may simply have a different threshold for, say, gallows or toilet humor. Consequently, there is no reason to expect convergence even under ideal circumstances; nor consequently any reason to think that a purely externalist theory like Fodor's could account for what is the nonetheless patent fact that you and I could perfectly well share the concept [funny] (or, *mutatis mutandis*, [shameful], [tragic], [bizarre]).

For all these reasons it would seem that any co-variational theory will need to be supplemented by some facts about a term's inferential role: "triangle" bears a direct relation to "angle" that "trilateral" lacks; "undetached proper rabbit part," but not "rabbit" play different roles in mereological inferences;[36] and [free will], but not [unicorn], is tied to impossible claims about spontaneity and moral responsibility; [funny] is tied to laughter.

In any case, for all the interest of externalist intuitions, there seems to be *something* to the "idea idea;" there seems to be *something* semantic "in the head." Indeed, it's hard to resist thinking that there is some important "internalist," or "narrow" sense of content that allows that Sophie and Twin-Sophie have the very same thoughts, thoughts with the very same content. Wouldn't the same intentional explanations be at some important level true of each of them? Both, for example, would think that what rained from heaven also filled the seas, would reach for what they each called "water" when they were thirsty, and would have the same illusions "as of water" on distant hot asphalt.[37] Doesn't psychology need a notion of "narrow" content, the kind of content *common* to Sophie and Twin-Sophie to capture such generalizations?

9.3   Two Factor Theorists: Narrow and Wide Content

Philosophers have disagreed over whether intentional psychology requires a notion of narrow content, over whether it's a coherent notion at all, and, if there is a notion, how precisely to characterize it. Many of the original proponents of "wide" content – Putnam (1975b, 1988), Burge (1979, 1986) – think that psychology can get on quite well with wide notions. Burge (1986), in particular, has argued that psychological explanations, such as Marr's (1982) theory of vision, actually presuppose wide content. I won't enter this debate here, except to sketch the possibility of such a mixed view, what might be called the " 'Fido'/fido idea idea," but is more usually called a "two factor theory."

One suggestion might be to allow the *representational vehicle* – the very sentence in the language of thought – itself to be a component of content. This suggestion seems a natural way of distinguishing necessarily co-instantiated concepts that, so to say, have different logical structure. Thus, the thought that water is wet is distinct from the thought that H_2O is wet by virtue of the fact that the content of the one thought involves a logically complex expression, "H_2O," that the other doesn't; thoughts about equi*angular* triangles involve different representational constructions than thoughts about equi*lateral* ones.

However, such a suggestion by itself is unlikely to suffice for all the cases: after all, there can be logically simple expressions – names, simple predicates – that are necessarily co-extensive ("Mark Twain," "Sam Clemens"; "eucalyptus," "gum tree"), and, although they might be associated with different contents *within* the mind of a single person, it doesn't seem as though they should always express different contents *across* people. Indeed, surely different people could have the same thought about Sam Clemens or gum trees without the vehicles of thought being actually *spelt* the same! Intuitively, all that would seem to matter is that the *role* of the vehicles in their thought be the same. Consequently, some two-factor theorists (e.g. Loar (1981), Block (1986)) suggest that the narrow component be identified with a term's conceptual role, along the lines – but also subject to the difficulties – sketched in §9.2.

Another suggestion is to identify the narrow content with a *rule* in the head that – along the lines of Grice (1965) and Putnam (1975a) – may leave some sort of "blank space to be filled in by the specialist," a kind of indexical element that permits a full semantic content to be determined by the context with which the agent interacts, much as the semantics of indexical terms like "I," "now," "this," and "that" do (cf. Kaplan 1979). White (1982) and Fodor (1987) develop this strategy, generally identifying the narrow content of an LOT expression with a function (in the set theoretic sense) that maps a context onto a broad content. For example, the narrow content of Sophie and Twin-Sophie's "water" is the function that maps Sophie's context onto H_2O and her twin's context onto XYZ. When Sophie utters "Water is wet," she thereby expresses the content [H_2O is wet], while when Twin-Sophie utters it she expresses the content [XYZ is wet]. Two symbols have the same narrow content just in case they serve to compute the same such function: it is this that is shared by Sophie and her twin.

Whether narrow content defined so abstractly could actually perform any serious work in psychological theory is as yet not entirely clear. Block (1991) complains that it would render the narrow content of all kind terms *identical* – e.g. "the stuff around here that the experts will tell us about" – but others, e.g. Bealer (1987) and Rey (1993d) argue that, while the narrow contents of many kind terms might be unilluminating in this way, the narrow contents of many other, more traditional philosophical terms – e.g. "justice," "rights," "person," "coercion" might be significantly more substantial, and of interest to both philosophy and psychology. In any case, we'll see in chapter 11 that appealing to some sort of narrow content either the vehicle, its conceptual role, a rule, or a function may afford a way for CRTT to capture both subjectivity and qualitative states. So a two-factor theory, at least in the case of *some* terms, is not an option that a CRTT theorist ought lightly to dismiss.

Where does all this leave the issue of content? Although the above discussion is far from conclusive, it should be clear that Brentano's challenge is far weaker than it originally seemed to be. There are lots of resources here, both in terms of various kinds of co-variation and in terms of details of internal computational roles. Given at least the appropriateness of each of various approaches as at least *partial* replies to the challenge, the burden would seem to be shifted to the defenders of Brentano to show that no combination of them could possibly succeed.

9.4   Further, Semantic Arguments for CRTT vs. RCON

Supposing some combination of the above semantic proposals were to succeed, two further phenomena on behalf of a CRTT model could be added to the list we began at the end of the last chapter. Again, these are not only phenomena that CRTT can explain rather naturally; they are phenomena that present serious *prima facie* difficulties for Radical Connectionism. The phenomena are: the stability of concepts, and the hyper-intensionality of attitudes.

(1)   the stability of concepts: influenced by a famous passage of Wittgenstein (1953:§66–7), many philosophers and psychologists have become attracted to what has come to be called a "prototype" theory of concepts, according to which whether something satisfies a concept, {F}, is not a matter of it satisfying some "classical definition" of F, but rather in how similar it is in certain respects to a prototypical (or stereotypical) example of F. Thus, people can be shown to be faster in judging robins, rather than penguins, to be birds.[38] One important fact to note against this trend, however, is that, at least in the case of most adult human beings, subjects' grasp of concepts is not confined to the particular instances (paradigms, or prototypes) of them that they may have encountered. As we have noticed in a number of connections (§§1.5.2, §4.3, §5.4), especially explanatorily interesting concepts are more stable than that, both across people and within a given person. People typically are able to *transcend* the stereotypes and resemblances that they may nevertheless exploit in *accessing* the concepts for which such

stereotypes seem to serve merely as *addresses*. Thus, people readily recognize the possibility of *non-typical* cases (penguins are perfectly good birds), *fraudulent* cases (toy birds are not), certain *possibilities and not others* (paralyzed birds but not inanimate ones), and engage in classical conceptual combination (a tropical bird is a bird that lives in the tropics, not one that somehow combines what is typical of bird with what is typical of tropical).[39]

CRTT can capture this stability by supposing concepts are captured by general rules, and not merely by networks of association (cf. §4.3 above). [Penguins are birds] can be firmly believed by a CRTT system, even if it hesitates slightly in assenting. Where we have a unified concept, RCON approaches seem to predict radically different ones, dependent entirely on the instances to which the agent has been exposed.

Notice that Churchland's (1995) optimism about the capacity of connectionist networks in this regard is quite unfounded. In the middle of his discussion of different cases of recognition by vector coding, he effortlessly alludes to "the emergence of categories" (p. 49) and "concepts" (pp. 50, 83, 90–1), but nowhere offers any semantic theory that begins to justify the content ascriptions he takes for granted in each case. *Perhaps* sensory concepts are plausibly treated as merely recognitional capacities: but, as we saw in discussing the problems with pure semantic externalism (§9.2.4), more abstract concepts plausibly bring with them certain other commitments: certainly it isn't enough for having the concept of [sadness] that a system merely be able to discriminate characteristically sad faces, with, as Churchland insouciantly adds:

> no conception of what sorts of causal antecedents typically *produce* the principal emotions, and no conception of what *effects* these emotions have on the on-going cognitive, social and physical behaviors of the people who come to have them. (1995:127)

If the system really has no such conceptions, what on earth justifies claiming that it's *sadness* it's recognizing?! In any case, it wouldn't nearly even discriminate what we discriminate when we discriminate (with, say, maximal information) sadness, since it would founder in any untypical case. Indeed, it would seem to be merely a recognizer of certain physical patterns, which, *pace* traditional empiricist reductionism (§4.3 and §5.4), cannot themselves be identified with the property of [sadness] itself. In short, *vector coding may well be an efficient means of quick categorization for a system that already possesses a concept of the category; it cannot without further argument serve as the basis for that possession.* Consequently, a problem for RCON is to provide an account of such concepts.

(2) the hyper-intensionality of attitudes: we've actually already discussed this phenomenon in discussing ways in which CRTT might exploit a "two-factor" semantic theory to accommodate the problems confronting any purely externalist

semantics (§9.2.4–9.3): attitude contexts are not only intensional in not allowing substitutions of necessarily co-referential terms; they are *hyper*-intensional, not even allowing the substitution of (apparently) co-intensional terms! There is, after all, a difference between thinking that a square lies in a circle and thinking that a square lies within a locus of co-planar points equidistant from a given point; there's even a difference between thinking London is beautiful and that Londres is (see Loar 1987). [40] Minds exceed the abilities of mere detectors: a mind can piece together constituents to form a complex concept for a property that might also be detected by a logically simple state. This is presumably the way in which we got theoretical insight into the phenomena we otherwise detect with simple concepts, e.g. geometrical shapes, colors, species, substances. Chisholm (1956:510) and Searle (1992), in his discussion of "aspectual shape," go so far as to suggest that such phenomena of non-substitutability are actually *constitutive* of the mental (and/or the ascription thereof). [41]

As we noted (§9.3), CRTT can distinguish these attitudes by distinguishing syntactically between different, even co-intensional symbolic structures – and/or the roles, rules, or functions that govern them – to which an agent can be related. [42] By contrast, RCON *seems confined to a merely externalist semantics,* lacking the resources of inferential rules for distinguishing between nomologically co-referential or co-intensional concepts (§9.2.4). Nodes, or networks of nodes, might be caused by, or co-vary with some phenomenon, but indifferently to the "aspect" of that phenomenon, e.g. [water] vs. [H$_2$O], [Mark Twain] vs. [Sam Clemens], [circle] vs. [locus of point-equidistant points]. Consequently they would seem bereft of any means to make such distinctions.

9.5   Status of the CRTT

This concludes my sketch of the basic ideas of CRTT and how it hopes to meet Descartes' and Brentano's challenges. Recall that those challenges involved claiming that it was *impossible* to provide a physical account of rationality and intentionality. If CRTT is coherent, those challenges have been met: for CRTT presents at least a *possible* story about how such a physical account might go, how, indeed, a mere material object could manage to think rationally about the world. There is no need to present the theory at this point as the gospel truth about people's mental lives, but only as at least *one* possible, coherent story about how they could be explained. [43]

Of course, someone might protest that although CRTT provides an explanatory framework for much animal behavior, there is no reason to suppose that it comes anywhere near capturing ordinary folk mentalistic notions. Although proof in these matters is difficult to come by, the chief reason for thinking that CRTT offers a way of beginning to capture, for example, judgment and preference is that it would certainly appear as though the J and P relations (§8.5), when considered not merely according to their definition in terms of computational and syntactic properties, but as relations to semantically valuable (e.g. true or false) sentences, *perform the essential explanatory work that judgment and preference are supposed to perform.* Of course, it is only a beginning; CRTT is the broadest sketch of a theory of the mind. For a psycho-functionalist, a full analysis of these and other mental phenomena await a much richer development of the theory. The claim here is only that CRTT is on the right track, and that ultimately we will be in the position of Turing regarding the notion of computation, and will be able to ask rhetorically: what else is needed?

Well, many might claim right now that *consciousness* is needed. This claim is so persistent, in even recent work, that it requires some separate discussion.

9.6   Is Consciousness Necessary for a Mental State?

Many people have no trouble with explanations that advert to unconscious processes. They certainly don't seem to be merely a passing fashion of cognitive science: Whyte (1967:186) surveys appeals appeals to unconscious processes in such diverse authors as Cudworth, Leibniz, Hamann, Carus, Schelling, Schopenhauer, Fechner, and Nietzsche. But, in any case, Freudian explanations that advert to unconscious desires and even Chomskian explanations that advert to unconscious rules seem to many people to be immensely intuitive. But a number of recent philosophers have objected to such postulations. Searle (1992) and Galen Strawson (1994) have wanted to insist that it is some sort of conceptual truth that mental states involve at least a disposition to have certain experiences. Searle (1992), for example, defends what he calls his "connection principle":

> We understand the notion of an unconscious mental state only as a possible content of consciousness, only as the sort of thing that, though not conscious, and perhaps impossible to bring to consciousness for various reasons, nonetheless is the *sort of thing* that could be or could have been conscious . . . all unconscious states are in principle accessible to consciousness. (1992:155–6)

and claims that he "cannot find or invent a coherent interpretation of" Freud's postulation that "our unconscious mental states exist both as unconscious and as occurrent intrinsic intentional states even when unconscious" (p. 168).

The most that Searle will allow in the way of unconscious mental states are (defeasible) *dispositions* to cause conscious ones: a person couldn't believe that p unless she were disposed, *ceteris paribus*, to consciously think that p at the time(s) that she believes it (cf. 1992:161).[44] There is no fact about something's being an intentional state apart from such a disposition, any more than there is a fact about something's being a poison apart from its (*ceteris paribus*) causing someone to die:

The overall picture that emerges is this. There is nothing going on in my brain but neurophysiological processes, some conscious, some unconscious. Of the unconscious neurophysiological processes, some are mental, some are not. The difference between them is . . . that the mental processes are candidates for consciousness, because they are capable of causing conscious states. But that's all. . . . What in my brain is my "mental life"? Just two things: conscious states and those neurophysiological states and processes that – given the right circumstances – are capable of generating conscious states. (1992:161–2)

Strawson (1994) goes even further and claims that "there are, strictly speaking, no dispositional nonexperiential mental phenomena" (p. 167)! He compares a nonexperiential brain to a CD recording of a Beethoven quartet that is not currently being played, and which could be used either to produce a genuine acoustical event on a CD player, or a light show on some other device:

As it sits there, a physical object with a complex structure, the CD is not *intrinsically* musically contentful. It is no more intrinsically musically contentful than it is light-pattern contentful. Nor are our brains intrinsically mentally contentful . . . when considered as physical systems in which no experiential processes are going on. (1994:166)

Strawson does not pretend to be offering an *argument* for this claim: "it is only an intuition, but it has a natural place in a discussion of the word 'mental'" (p. 167).

However, what tells against Strawson's intuition is the patent intelligibility and, indeed, *need* of the postulation of unconscious states having genuine causal/ explanatory powers. Freudian postulations of unconscious motives, for example, are interesting because they explain certain *content-sensitive* behaviors, like slips of the tongue or various sexual behaviors. Weiskrantz's postulation of "blindsight" explains his patients' ability to perform better than chance at picking out stimuli of which they are unaware. Or, to take an example from our discussion of Chomsky in §4.2, it is only by supposing that there are unconscious representations of the syntactic structure of English sentences that we can explain an auditor's displacement of "clicks" to grammatical boundaries. The crucial difference between Strawson's example of the unplayed CD and the unconscious brain is that, whereas the *musical* properties of the unplayed CD are indeed at that time causally inert, the *intentional content properties of these unconscious mental states are not*. Strawson's strictures, and Searle's confinement of the mental to conscious dispositions seem gratuitous. They fly in the face of genuine explanatory needs of psychology. And that, I submit, is enough to capture the conceptual point of the present chapter: that these are *possible* needs that could be raised by the *possible* data of, for example, Freud, Weiskrantz, or Garrett is enough to establish that mental states of the sort they postulate are at least *intelligible*.

Of course, we could merely give Strawson and Searle the ordinary words and simply invent new ones that correspond to the CRTT notions, but without any presumption of consciousness. It would be like arguing with some pre-Galilean who thought the word "mass" could only refer to terrestial phenomena: fine; we just invent a new word "schmass" that is exactly like "mass" except that it drops the assumption of terrestiality. Similarly, a CRTT theorist could agree to prefix all his uses of ordinary mental expressions by "schma-belief," "schma-desire," etc. But, what would be the point? If the same explanatory work would be performed by the "schma" idioms as by the non-schma-ed, the new idioms may as well take over.

Searle, however, does makes a claim that takes the argument beyond a merely verbal issue. He challenges CRTT even as an account of the modest mentalism that I claimed was required to explain the Standardized Regularities. For he claims that no account lacking consciousness can account for "aspectual shape" (1992:156–61, 169–72). This is his term for the phenomena of intensionality, or the ability of the mind to distinguish among even necessarily co-extensive concepts, such as [water] and [H_2O]. Indeed, on this basis he even goes so far as to claim that we "can't make [Freud's] account of the unconscious consistent with what we know about the brain" (1992:169). In particular, he asks:

> how can the nonconscious neurophysiology have aspectual shape and subjectivity right then and there? (1992:169)

Now, as we have seen, CRTT explicitly addresses Searle's skepticism: a propositional attitude is a relation between an agent and a sentence that expresses a certain external content. Many different sentences may express the same such content: "water is wet," "H_2O is wet" express the same external content, but the thoughts involving them are distinguished by virtue of the different sentences in their LOT that express them.[45]

Searle is also worried, however, about "subjectivity," as we saw Nagel and Jackson and others to be (§2.6). Now there's no question that there is a phenomenon here to be explained, one to which we will turn in the next chapter. However, no argument has yet been produced that shows that *that* phenomenon is essential to mentality. It may be a feature of some, but certainly not necessarily *all* possible mental systems. Many animals might satisfy Modest Mentalism by satisfying CRTT alone.

Moreover, a number of philosophers think that CRTT could be easily supplemented so that it captured even subjectivity as well. But this is the topic of the last chapter. For now, it is enough to see that there is no reason to claim that consciousness is essential to the kinds of explanatory mental states captured by CRTT.

We turn now to some general objections that have been raised against the possibility of CRTT.

Notes

1 This chapter is essentially an expansion, with some revisions, of §III of Loewer and Rey (1992a).

2 We will return to Dennett's rejection of CRTT's realism in §10.3.2. Another approach I shall not consider is that of Robert Cummins (1989), who, although he feels he has a "transcendental argument" (p. 105) for supposing some particular interpretation of a brain is the correct one, provides no clear indication of how it would be determined.

3 I leave aside the fanciful theological speculation, which I doubt even the most ardent Creationist believes, that human beings are actually computational *artifacts* of God, who, as our programmer, is thereby the source of our intentionality. Even in such a case, of course, there would be the problem of the semantics of God's states, which, if the CRTT is correct, would leave us in the same position for them that I take us to be in here with respect to people and animals.

4 Aristotle and Locke both seem to have had versions of imagistic views. See Cummins (1989) for useful discussion.

5 For further discussion of a limited role images may play in thought, see e.g. Kosslyn (1980), Rey (1980a), Pylyshyn (1981), Block (1981a) and Tye (1991). Lewis (1994) suggests maps as a general medium for thought, citing Ramsey's remark that beliefs are "maps by which we steer," but provides no indication of how they would suffice for logically complex thoughts, or how Ramsey's remark is anything but a useful metaphor. Sowa (1984:§4.2) develops some elegant suggestions of Peirce (1897–1906/1960), exploiting graphs to represent first-order logic. However, although imagistic information is usefully exploited in such a system, logico-syntactic symbols (especially for negation) also seem essential. In Rey (1995a), I venture the following speculation: any notation adequate to express all the thoughts expressible by first-order logic must employ *some* system that allows iterations of logical operators (quantifiers, connectives) and referential devices (predicates, variables, names).

6 There are also "long armed" conceptual role theories which include an expression's epistemic relations to distal stimuli in an expression's conceptual role, see Harman (1982) and Block (1986). I ignore this possibility here as it straddles the distinction between internalist and externalist theories, without constituting a substantively different possibility from those I shall consider.

7 See, for example, Grice and Strawson (1956), Field (1977), Loar (1981), LePore and Loewer (1987), Block (1986). Although he doesn't put the issues in these terms, Jackendoff's (1987, 1989) proposals could be regarded as theories of this sort as well.

8 Peacocke (1992) offers this as one of his parade examples for his own (in part) conceptual role account, according to which a symbol, "#" means "and" iff its user feels

"primitively compelled" to make the transition from "p#q" to "p" and to "q." See Rey (1996) for doubts that this will suffice.

9   Thus, Grice and Strawson (1956) and Field (1977) propose a confirmation theory of meaning, but one that, as Field readily acknowledges, is not applicable intersubjectively.

10 Fodor (1987:125) cites the example of Berkeley who thought chairs were "ideas," and asks: "which are we to say he lacked, the concept MENTAL or the concept CHAIR?." Burge (1978) also explores ways in which it seems reasonable to suppose people could make errors about analyticities: e.g. mistakenly thinking a fortnight is ten days.

11 A solution I have proposed (Rey 1994a) to at least this latter problem of the wayward-ness of belief is to retreat from *belief* states to *sub-belief* (what Stich 1983 has called "sub-doxastic") states. Such states could involve rules that control the deployment of predicates, but which are not readily available to introspection or even verbal dispo-sitions. They may control the deployment of mentalese symbols – and words in natural language – rather in the way rules of grammar control judgments of grammaticality, without the agent being aware of them; indeed, as in the case of grammars, they might even consciously contradict them, as presumably Berkeley did when he denied that objects exist independently of us. However, I spare the reader a full defense of this strategy here.

12 Various versions of this view can be found in Quine (1960), Churchland (1979), Davidson (1984), and Block (1986). See Fodor and LePore (1992) for discussion.

13 Indeed, a thorough-going conceptual role semantics arguably imperils claims of objectivity and realism in general, as in Kuhn (1962). Bilgrami (1992) tries to show how both psychology and objectivity might survive such holism.

14 Barring differences in H_2O and XYZ. This was an unfortunate artifact of Putnam's original example. There are many other, less far-fetched, but less famous examples in Burge (1979) and in Stich (1983).

15 Some have taken this claim to be incompatible with the claim that meanings are *represented* in the head. Thus, Jackendoff (1987) writes, "meanings must be finitely representable and stored in a brain. . . . This rules out any sort of "extensional" theory of meaning in which, for instance, the meaning of "dog" is taken to be the set of all dogs: there are no dogs in the mind, only at best dog-representations" (p. 126). This last, of course, is true but is not being denied by any extensionalist, who is free to regard extensional meanings as either properties of those representations or (as in the cases Putnam is discussing) as relations those representations bear to external objects. See Rey (1995c) for discussion.

16 Nothing about the strings of code or internal states of the machine would *determine* that the machine was running a program about chess and not a war. See Fodor (1981b), Rey (1980d), Fodor and Pylyshyn (1981:207), Stich (1983:108), and Baker (1987:57) for discussion. It is this fact that exercises Searle (1980a, 1984) in his rejection of computational theories. As should be clear from the present discussion, this is hardly an issue that computationalists haven't faced. I'll address Searle's worries in this regard in §10.2.

17 Devitt (1991) emphasizes the non-syntactic character of inputs and outputs as a possible source of semantic constraints.

18   See Kripke (1972) and Devitt (1981) for developments of this view. For simplicity here, I include Burge's (1979) emphasis upon the social context of the agent as a species of historical causal chains, although Burge, himself, is not committed to the role of society being causal.

19   Kripke (1972) was under no illusion here, not regarding the "alternative picture" he drew as any sort or "theory." Much of the problem here comes to the "qua" problem raised by one of the historical theory's most ardent defenders, Devitt (1981), and by Devitt and Sterelny (1987:§4.4).

20   Grice (1957) distinguished "natural" "meaning-n" from "non-natural" "meaning-nn." Co-variational views in general attempt to construct the latter as a species of the former.

21   For simplicity at this point in an introductory discussion, I will restrict the examples merely to such "objectless" predication's of the form "It's F-ing" (as in "It's raining," "It's snowing"), where, moreover, we can regard the relata of laws to be properties, not individual things: thus, it's not the *horses* but *the property of being a horse* that is the relevant cause of a tokening of "It's H-ing" (the view has problems enough with examples of this sort). Moreover, in being couched in terms of properties, this account has certain further attractive features, affording a way of accounting for the meanings even of predicates that express un-instantiated properties, such as [unicorn]. There can be a law linking "unicorn" to the property of being a unicorn, even if there are no unicorns (in the same way there can be ideal gas laws even though there are no ideal gases).

22   Fodor (1980/1990) proposed his version of the theory in the widely circulated *paper* called "Psychosemantics," which was published *after* the *book* – Fodor (1987) – of the same title in which he *rejects* any such theory. The oddity of the dates is due to the fact that a number of people *liked* the theory more than Fodor did, and urged that it be published even after his rejection of it.

23   As emphasized in Fodor (1987:109), the dependence here is intended to be *synchronic*, not *diachronic*. An example of the sort of dependence Fodor has in mind is afforded by the behavior of sail boats: their moving into the wind depends upon Bernoulli's Principle, but that principle doesn't depend upon sail boats moving into the wind (since the effect will only be achieved given certain properties of wind, etc.).

24   This analogy arose in discussion with Michael Slote. It has the defect, which the reader should ignore, of making dependencies seem *diachronic*, whereas Fodor intends his to be read *synchronically*: i.e. it's an asymmetric causal dependence *at a time*.

25   Note that, in keeping with Fodor's more modest moments (e.g. Fodor 1987:124), we have confined the Asymmetric Dependency thesis to supplying only a *sufficient*, not a necessary physicalistic condition for predicate expression. He believes this is all that he is required to do, in order to meet Brentano's challenge. Fodor feels that, if there are no counterexamples to (M), then he has done all that he needs to do to show that, contrary to Brentano, certain physical arrangements are sufficient for intentionality. Cf. our discussion (§1.5.1) of how even partial constitutive analyses may be illuminating.

26   See Fodor (1987:chapter 4, 1990:100–19, and 1991a:255–77, 302–4).

27   Millikan's "teleo-functional" theories are to be distinguished from the kinds of theories Fodor (1987) calls "teleological," to be discussed in due course. The crucial

difference between them is that the former, but not the latter, are committed to claims about some form of co-variation.

28 There's actually not concurrence among teleo-semanticists about just what the content of the frog's thought is. Neander (1995) makes an excellent case for it being [black dot].

29 "Pangloss" is the character in Voltaire's *Candide* who insists upon interpreting all manner of disaster as showing that this is the best of all possible worlds. The argument against selectionism, incidentally, is not in the slightest an argument against evolutionary biology (much less for Creationism), but an argument *within* that disciple about the explanatory role selection plays. For a defense of selectionism in general along lines relevant to teleo-functionalism, see Dennett (1987:chapter 7 and 1995a).

30 Neander (forthcoming) argues, however, that "swampman" *intuitions alone* ought to carry no more weight against semantic proposals than "swampcow" intuitions ought to carry weight against evolutionary definitions of species in biology. However, few critics of teleo-semantics intend their argument to rest on swampman intuitions alone. Note that semantics is not in anything like the relatively stable state of biology.

31 If you find "triangle" vs. "trilateral" a little too fine for your taste, try "equiangular Euclidean triangle" vs. "equilateral Euclidean trilateral" – the terms that in high school you had to *prove* were indeed necessarily co-extensive.

32 Quine (1960:chapter 2) deserves credit for discovering this latter, distinctive category and the interesting puzzles to which it gives rise, even if it's not at all clear that he's entitled to derive from it his sweeping "thesis of the indeterminacy of translation." It should be regarded as a nice puzzle, a little like Zeno's paradoxes, which forces us to think more clearly about meaning, as Zeno forced us to think about motion.

33 A similar distinction could be drawn between a low-level sensory concept of redness and the more theoretically oriented one that Levine (1993) correctly notes many of us deploy.

34 Fodor (1990:101) speculates that all such cases could be handled in this way, but provides little in the way of reassurance.

35 Slote (1975) has argued that nothing could possibly satisfy our concept, [monster]: when "Nessie" of Loch Ness is ultimately captured, she'll quickly be dissected, analyzed, and classified by the techniques of natural science, after which she'll no longer be a "monster," but just another animal (for example, a wayward dinosaur). Spinoza, as well as Wittgenstein (1929/1968), made similar claims about [miracle], Putnam (in conversation) about [magic], and Galen Strawson (1987) about [free will].

36 This is not intended to be a full reply to Quine's (1960) interesting challenge; only an indication of where a reply, if any, is likely to be found.

37 It actually is quite difficult to state this point exactly, since for every "narrow" behavior ("reaching for what we each call 'water'") the internalist can argue is shared by twins, the externalist can cite a "wide" behavior that isn't (Sophie reaches for *water* where Twin-Sophie reaches for *XYZ*). This is the topic of an exchange between Burge (1986) and Fodor (1987:chapter 2 and 1991b), into the intricacies of which we needn't enter here.

38 See Rosch (1973) and Smith and Medin (1981). I criticize some of this work in Rey (1983b, 1985).

39 For discussion see Osherson and Smith (1981).

40　This last is the basis for the "paradox of analysis": how can an analysis of a term be informative, since, if successful, the analysis should be synonymous with the analysandum and so known trivially to every competent speaker. For rich discussion of this and the other examples, see Church (1946), Mates (1951), Burge (1978), Kripke (1979), Bealer (1982), and Salmon (1986:121–3).

41　It certainly does seem to be a deeply intrinsic feature of minds, even of, for example, omniscient ones. *Pace* Fodor (1994), it's not only ignorance that gives rise to opacity. "Belief" is simply not the best attitude to display this; consider "notice" or "desire": even an omniscient being could *notice* or *desire* that Oedipus be married to Jocasta, without *noticing* or *desiring* that the son of Jocasta be so married.

42　Searle (1992) does argue that only consciousness can distinguish aspectual shapes; but he provides no argument for this – or really for how consciousness helps – much less any indication of how the syntactic resources of CRTT are inadequate. I'll consider his view in detail shortly (§9.6).

43　Searle (1990b:639) misses this *modal* point in his reply to my defense of CRTT against his (1990a).

44　And presumably the conscious thought must have been brought about by the disposition in the right way (otherwise virtually any thought, no matter how deeply "unconscious" would count as conscious: all you have to do is think it!). Searle doesn't supply these other qualifications and the *ceteris paribus* clause, but it's clear from his subsequent discussion of apparent exceptions being due to "blockage of some sort" (p163) that he needs them. And there's no problem with such qualifications and clauses should there be reason to think them explanatorily interesting; see §10.3 below.

45　Perhaps "water is wet" vs. "H$_2$O is wet" are not Searle's best examples. He should rather have cited Quine's (1960) "gavagai" examples discussed earlier (§9.2.4). But then the burden would be on Searle (as it is on Quine) to show that no appeal to computational role would suffice to distinguish them. See Bealer (1984).

10

Replies to Common Objections

In this chapter I want to address a number of objections that have been raised against computational models like CRTT. Some of them are red herrings, based on relatively straightforward misunderstandings of just what CRTT claims; these I'll deal with briefly in §10.1. But some objections are more complex, involving a number of seductive intuitions and hidden presuppositions that will require some care to sort out. There are two main such objections: in §10.2 I will try to disentangle the several issues that are confounded in Searle's famous "Chinese Room" argument, and in §10.3 I will address some of the issues surrounding idealization that underlie claims about the "normativity" of the mental that we noted in §3.1.2.

10.1   Red Herrings

10.1.1   Introspection

An immediate reaction many people have to CRTT is to protest that this conflicts with their introspections. In the popular argot, while there may be "left-brained" people who "think in language," there are "right brained" people who think more "intuitively," imagistically and somatically.[1] Indeed, doesn't this latter phenomenology tell directly against CRTT?

CRTT is not committed to any particular claims about the character of introspection or phenomenology, which may well seem (as to many of us it does seem) not the least bit sentential or propositional.[2] As should be clear from our earlier discussion of phenomenal objects (§5.2.1 above), even the most intense eidetic imagery and visual hallucination is compatible with CRTT: all that need be true of such cases is that there are events with certain visual contents ("as if seeing a bright green bird hovering before me"). CRTT does need to *explain, inter*

264

alia our introspections, but that it may do without it being in the least introspectible *itself.*

In a related vein, CRTT is not committed to the language of thought being confined only to creatures that speak a *natural language*, much less to the Language of Thought actually *being* a natural language. This latter is a further hypothesis taken seriously by one of CRTT's earliest proponents, Harman (1972) (see also Devitt 1981); but it has also seemed to many others quite unlikely: natural languages, with all their ambiguities, seem an unpromising medium for *computation.*[3] In any case, they would be unavailable to infra-linguistic creatures, such as speechless chimpanzees, octopi, and human infants that may well be capable of the kinds of thought that CRTT explains (*pace* Patricia Churchland 1986:388).

10.1.2 Images and "mental models"

A deeper issue than phenomenology is sometimes at stake. A number of psychologists claim that there is substantial evidence for actual cognitive processing being non-sentential. Johnson-Laird (1983), for example, claims that CRTT models are incompatible with actual patterns in people's reasoning, which betray a reliance not on syntactic manipulations, but on what he calls "mental models." He writes:

> The models that people use to reason are more likely to resemble perception or conception of the events (from a God's-eye view) than a string of symbols directly corresponding to the linguistic form of the premises and then applying rules of inference to them in order to derive a conclusion. (1983:53–4)

Now, it's not altogether clear what contrast he intends to be drawing here: even if people don't ordinarily use the Frege/Russell predicate calculus in reasoning syllogistically, they presumably have to use *some* mechanical, representational medium when they "perceive or conceive" events, even "from a God's eye view." It may be true that it *seems* to a reasoner that she is surveying logical space somehow "directly," searching for counterexamples, just as it seems to many mathematicians that they are simply surveying the "world of numbers" and concepts (and to "naive realists" that they are "directly perceiving" the world around them). But surely this appearance can't be right: how on earth would such direct perception or conception work? How can a physical being *in space and time* do anything with abstract entities and possibilities *outside space and time* unless these things are physically represented?

Perhaps what is imagined are images, which *could* be physical, but still non-sentential representations. And there is indeed considerable evidence that suggests that people use imagistic representations in some cognitive processing, for example, in the intriguing "rotation" experiments that we discussed briefly in

§2.5.3; and perhaps in their exploitation of spatial analogies in thought and language generally (see, especially, Jackendoff 1987). It may well be that people often reason far more efficiently by exploiting a spatial-reasoning ability that happens to be especially well-developed in human beings and other navigating animals; and it may even also turn out that that module exploits imagistic representations, i.e. representations whose spatial properties and relations function to represent properties and relations of what the whole representation represents, in the way, for example, that relative distance between points on a map represents relative distance between the actual places represented.[4] There are puzzles about how they could be laid out and accessed in the brain. But they might themselves be *functionally* defined, as triptychs are even for the visual system: just as the different frames of a triptych are processed as being a single unified painting by our eyes, so might a highly distributed imagistic representation be processed as a unit by our brain.

It often isn't noticed that appealing to functional images alone won't explain much cognition.[5] Some further questions must be addressed, both in considering how a person *maps* a topic (say, the premises of a syllogism) onto the appropriate spatial relations, and how she understands the spatial relations in the first place. One circle, A, inside another, B, could represent that *A* has the property *B*, *A* is an element of *B*, or *A* is a subset of *B*. Moreover, the *transitive* relation [x is left of y] would seem to be *visually* indistinguishable from the *in*transitive [x is next to y]. In order to *understand* the images or other "mental models" one constructs, and especially their relevance to some originally non-spatial problem, one needs to have some way of *representing* the original and the relevant spatial properties and relations, and, again, images alone won't do. For the reasons we discussed in §9.1.1, only a system with something like the structure and expressive power of the predicate calculus stands a chance. Processing of images and "mental models" seems to require, and therefore is unlikely to replace, CRTT.

But, in any case, CRTT need not claim that *all* or even *most* ordinary mental activities involve sentential representations. CRTT is a claim about the *capacities* or, in Chomsky's phrase, *competencies* of a creature, not its *actual* activities or *performance* (see §4.2.2 above). People may well also exploit the resources of "images, prototypes, schemata, semantic frames, metaphors and metonymy" (Johnson 1993:152), some (although probably not all) of which may be represented non-sententially. Certainly much pattern recognition, statistical analysis and other mental processes could be performed by a connectionist – even "dynamical" – architecture (Churchland 1995, van Gelder and Niklasson 1994).[6] Perhaps people actually entertain thoughts requiring sentential structure very little of the time. To expand on Thoreau, people may ordinarily live lives of quiet desperation, routinely performing mindless connectionist tasks. CRTT needn't be in the least disturbed.

266

10.1.3   Homunculi objections

An extremely common objection not only to CRTT but to a very large class of psychological explanations is that they presuppose the very sorts of processes they purport to explain. In particular, a framework like CRTT, with its "computations" defined over a "language" all presuppose the existence of some further mental entity, a "little man," or "homunculus," who can *understand* the language and *execute* the instructions (see Wittgenstein (1953:§32) and Skinner (1963/ 1984:615)). Although this objection dominated some two or three decades of philosophy of mind,[7] it admits of a relatively straightforward reply. Insofar as such explanations involve appealing to "homunculi" (and not all of them by any means do), we need only require that in the long run the homunculi become so stupid they can be "replaced by a machine" (Dennett 1978e:80–1). Thus, a complicated algorithm for computing object distances from stereotypical data can be broken down into computational steps that can be broken down into further computational steps, . . . and so forth, until we arrive at basic steps that consist in, say, comparing the contents of two addresses for (type) identity. In short: what does the work of the homunculus is simply brute physical causation. We owe to Church and Turing the deep suggestion that any function computable at all is computable by operations that could be brute causal in this way (see §6.2 above).

Searle (1992:212–14) professes to be unsatisfied by this response. He is worried that, syntax is not "intrinsic to physics":

> Notions such as *computation, algorithm,* and *program do* not name intrinsic physical features *of systems.* . . . There is no way you could discover that something is intrinsically a digital computer because the characterization of it as a digital computer is always relative to an observer who assigns an interpretation to the purely physical features of the system. As applied to the language of thought hypothesis, this has the consequence that the thesis is incoherent.   (1992:210)

This argument is relying, however, upon some assumption to the effect that if a property is not "an intrinsic" physical property, then it must be an observer-relative one, an assumption it is difficult to see why anyone should accept: are familiar macro-properties of *being a heart, being a free market,* or (to take one of Searle's (1992:47) own examples!) *being a split-level ranch house*[8] really either "intrinsic" physical properties or observer-relative ones? But hearts – and even free-markets and ranch houses – could exist (even *as* hearts, markets, and houses) without observers, or even without anyone thinking of them in these ways: it's enough that they *function* as hearts, markets or houses; and, as we noted in §7.2.3, this they can do without any intentional selection: various forms of natural selection will suffice. Searle is quite right to note that in the case of *commercial* computers, "there is no homunculus problem, because each user is the homunculus" (p. 214). But not all computers are artifacts. We have reason to believe that there are non-artifactual computers to the extent that we have reason to think that positing computational processes is the best explanation of certain genuine regularities in the world. That, at any rate, is the burden of CRTT. It is no greater a burden than is borne by a biological explanation that also describes kidneys and heart in originally artifactual terms of "filters" and "pumps."

10.1.4   Actual and artificial intelligence

As I have already emphasized a number of times, the CRTT proposal that I have been considering – particularly the COG program of §8.5 – is motivated largely by a purely *philosophical* interest in meeting various philosophical challenges that have been raised against the possibility of a naturalistic account of the mind. It is an account designed in the first instance to answer certain very general, "How possibly?" questions (§1.2): how possibly a mere material object could think; how we could possibly explain thought as ultimately arising from purely material processes. CRTT could well serve this role without actual serving as an account of how anything actually *does* think. Of course, someone like Fodor (1975) does present it as a theory of actual thought, and I presented some reasons for understanding it in this way in §8.8. Moreover, as we noted in §9.5, it may ultimately serve as a framework for psychofunctionalist *analyses* of many mental phenomena, and so may turn out to be necessarily true.[9] But none of this is essential to its role in meeting Descartes' and Brentano's challenges. Claims about how *possibly* something *could* happen do not themselves entail claims about how it does *in fact* happen.

CRTT bears an even less direct relation to most current work in artificial intelligence. This field is in fact not particularly concerned with either philosophy *or* psychology: its aim is largely to build machines that manage to solve problems whose solution usually requires intelligence: problems presented by games, medical diagnosis, object detection, speech recognition and production. What is centrally important to this research are the *products* of such intelligence, not the *process* by which they are produced. Indeed, many researchers would be just as happy to dream up a process that was stupider than human or animal processing, if it turned out to be faster or more reliable (consider "brute force" game playing machines which simply search through the "trees" of possible moves at lightning speed, as in the case of the recent machine "Deep Blue" that vied for the world championship in chess).

Alan Turing's own measure for success in AI, his behavioristic "Turing Test," that we discussed earlier (§5.3), has tended to be the measure for much AI research. Here the concern is merely to fool normal human beings into thinking they are conversing (via teletype) with another human being. Needless to say, this could be – and has been! – accomplished without instilling in the machine anything but a bag of silly tricks.[10] As Fodor (1991) remarks in this connection:

> I don't think you do the science of complex phenomena by attempting to model gross observable variance. Physics, for example, is not the attempt to construct a machine that would be indistinguishable from the real world for the length of a conversation. We do not think of Disneyland as a major *scientific* achievement. (1991:279)

In any case, such initiation is neither necessary nor sufficient for a computational understanding of the mind (which is why the Turing Test is such an obviously poor test of intelligence).[11] CRTT, as a species of molecular functionalism (§7.2.2), is most naturally concerned with the characterization of *sub-systems* of the mind, not with actual behavior. The right way to produce genuine artificial *intelligence*, as opposed to merely fooling people, would be first to construct theories about human cognitive *competencies* – in perception, scientific reasoning, decision making, language comprehension and production. *Only then* should an attempt be made to integrate these systems into a system that might conceivably behave with anything like the sophistication of human beings in a natural environment.

Note, by the way, that CRTT does not entail that we are Turing Machines (i.e. that our psychology is best regarded as a realization of one). In arguing for its plausibility, I relied on Turing's work to establish that logical features are mechanically computable. However, a person could be a lot *less* than a Turing machine for that to be true (for example, there might be nomologically determined limitations on her memory); and, of course, she conceivably might even have access to a great deal *more*: perhaps some methods of computation of which such people as Penrose (1989:chapter 4) dream, when they dream that Gödel's theorem shows we aren't Turing machines (see §8.7 above). In any case, CRTT is certainly not committed to supposing that our mental architecture remotely resembles that of a Turing Machine, or a von Neumann architecture, or any deterministic or serial automaton. CRTT presents only a quite weak *constraint* on possible architectures, viz. that logico-syntactic properties be causally efficacious; and this is compatible with an indefinitely rich variety of architectures, for example, ones that might be implemented on connectionist or other massively parallel processors.

10.1.5   Nativism

As something of an historical accident, the CRTT hypothesis was first defended by Fodor in the same book in which he also defended a highly controversial thesis about *the innateness of all concepts*. That thesis originally stirred more controversy than did CRTT itself, much of which was further (and much more forcefully) addressed in Fodor (1981c). But it is entirely independent of it. It is certainly true that, for CRTT to be true, the brain would likely need to have a good deal of innate structure. But this fact shouldn't be controversial: we find quite elaborate innate structure in every other organ of the body. Whether this structure includes *conceptual* structure, and in particular *all* the conceptual structure that an animal would ever be capable of thinking, is a highly theoretic question depending upon far subtler issues about the nature of concepts, thinking, and learning than are the concern of CRTT by itself.[12] So worries about conceptual nativism, like those of Churchland (1986:389) and Putnam (1988), in no way tell against CRTT.

10.2   Searle's Worries About His "Chinese Room"

We have discussed at different points a number of attacks John Searle has made on CRTT-style theories, but we have yet to confront his most famous thought-experiment, his "Chinese Room" example, which he believes presents a decisive refutation of any such theory. In particular, he believes it refutes what he calls "Strong AI," or the view that "the appropriately programmed computer really *is* a mind in the sense that computers given the right programs can literally be said to *understand* and have other cognitive states" (Searle 1980a:417).[13] Although, for the reasons just mentioned, CRTT is not committed to much of what is presently regarded as "AI" research, it pretty clearly would be an equal target of Searle's attack. In order to restrain the already excessive neologisms introduced in this book, I will, however, treat Searle's attack as though it were simply on CRTT.

Briefly, we are to imagine someone entirely ignorant of Chinese being placed in a room with batches of Chinese characters and some rules in English for "correlating" them. These correlation rules specify which Chinese characters the person is to hand out of the room when further characters are handed in, in such a fashion that, were a normal Chinese speaker to view the subsequent exchange of characters from outside, she would find it indistinguishable from a normal Chinese conversation. Searle claims that the person in the room following such a program still doesn't understand a word of Chinese: he's just following rules relating one set of – for him – meaningless characters to another. Consequently, Searle concludes, no CRTT program can be sufficient for understanding Chinese, or any other natural language. Indeed:

> It is not because I am the instantiation of a computer program that I am able to understand English and have other forms of intentionality . . . , but as far as we know it is because I am a certain sort of organism with a certain biological (i.e. chemical and physical) structure. . . . Only something that had those causal powers could have that intentionality.   (Searle 1980a:422)

There can be no denying the charm and apparent elegance of the example. Certainly, as described, the person in the room doesn't understand Chinese.

270

Recalling, however, Dennett's cautions about "intuition pumps" (§5.3), we need to consider the best *explanation* of our verdicts here. In particular we need to diagnose precisely what features of the case are responsible for those verdicts, and whether they would remain the same *no matter what program* the person in the room was obeying. Once we do this, I think we will find that the power of Searle's example in fact derives largely from a surprising number of simultaneous confusions regarding the claims of CRTT.[14] In particular, Searle burdens CRTT with the Turing Test (§10.2.1), a thesis about the autonomy of language (§10.2.2) and a fallacy of division (§10.2.3), to none of which is it remotely committed.

10.2.1   *The Turing Test vs. the right program*

One of the difficulties in addressing Searle's argument is identifying its proper target. Many people have serious reservations about the specific work in AI that Searle has in mind, that of Abelson and Schank (see Schank 1984) on story understanding. Roughly, this work tries to capture story understanding by programming a machine to access a "script" about a typical situation described in the story, e.g. ordering a hamburger in a restaurant. Thus, in ordering a hamburger, one presumes it will be a certain size, will come on a bun with or without onions, and will be paid for at the conclusion of the meal. Abelson and Schank simply build in such "knowledge" as explicit information forming part of the relevant script.

Now, as indicated above, CRTT isn't committed for a moment to regarding those sorts of programs as remotely approximating any genuine understanding of stories, or any such "script" for Chinese conversations being adequate for an understanding of the language. We've already discussed the red herring of the "Turing Test" in discussing both analytical behaviorism (§5.2.3) and AI above (§10.1.4). The fact that the Chinese room and/or its occupant might put out Chinese symbols to Chinese symbol inputs in a way indistinguishable from the behavior of a normal Chinese speaker is entirely irrelevant to CRTT. The question for CRTT is rather: is what is happening *inside* the room *functionally equivalent* to what is happening inside a normal Chinese speaker? In particular, is it *"CRTT equivalent"* (i.e. is it a realization of the same CRTT organization)?

Of course, it isn't; not, anyway, as Searle describes it. In the first place, the only rules Searle permits himself to have in the room are ones "correlating" a minute class of normal inputs and outputs to an intelligent human being, viz. merely the symbols to a natural language. There are absolutely no rules whatsoever for telling the person what to do with inputs from any of the multitude of other programs that CRTT needs to posit to explain, for example, perception, belief fixation, problem solving, preference ordering, decision making, along even the relatively modest lines of our COG program of §8.5. All of these further processes are obviously intimately bound up with a normal Chinese speaker's use of Chinese:

271

after all, Chinese sentences are frequently uttered in response to non-sentential sensory input, typically only when the speaker has decided to express what she believes. Furthermore, her understanding of other peoples' sentences requires that she be at least sometimes prepared to react non-verbally to them in appropriate ways, e.g. passing the egg foo young when asked. Apart from the paltry Turing Test, the system as Searle has described it wouldn't even pass any reasonable *behavioral* test for understanding. So it's unlikely that the system is CRTT-equivalent to one.

10.2.2 The (non-)autonomy of language

Indeed, Searle's example burdens CRTT with a quite extreme view about the "autonomy" of language, a view that would allow that understanding a language need involve *only intra*-linguistic symbol manipulations. Perhaps Abelson and Schank, along with Turing, believe some such thesis, and it may lead them to make extravagant claims about the abilities of their programs. But there are certainly myriad reasons independent of this discussion to deny it. In any case, there is no reason to attach it to CRTT.

To put Searle's example even in the running as a possible counterexample to CRTT, we need to imagine the person in the room following rules that relate Chinese characters not only to one another, but also to the inputs and outputs of the *other* programs CRTT posits to account for the other mental processes of a normal Chinese speaker.[15] Moreover, if the claims of externalist semantics that we discussed in chapter 9 are right, there had better be connections between internal symbols and external phenomena. Just how many such *inter*-programmatic rules and extra-systematic relations a system must satisfy to qualify as understanding Chinese is open to standard debates in the philosophy of language. Arguably, understanding a language involves being able to relate the symbols of the language to at least *some* perceptions, beliefs, desires, and, as they used to say, "dispositions to behave," e.g. to utter "Squiggle squoggle" when you take yourself to have been asked the color of some snow that's been presented to your receptors. The most Searle allows in this regard is that some of the Chinese symbols issue, unbeknownst to the person in the room, from a television camera. There is no allowance whatsoever for the kind of discrimination, or ideal co-variation abilities that, as we discussed in §9.2.2, many have argued (independently of CRTT) are required for intrinsic content in any system whatsoever. In the specific case of understanding a natural language, many philosophers would even claim that you'd better have recursive rules of the form "σ is true iff p" for Chinese σ and (assuming for the moment with Searle that the rules are in English) English p: e.g. "'Squiggle squoggle' is true iff snow is white," "'Squiggle squoggle square' is true iff snow is not white," "'Squiggle squoggle spot swirl' is true iff snow is white and the USA is a paper tiger."[16] Indeed, I don't see why we oughtn't let CRTT lay its semantic cards right out, as it were, on the table, and include recursive rules of the form "σ *means* that p." Provided that the CRTT can specify algorithms for effectively computing such rules (and Searle surely can't be disputing *this* possibility; after all, recursive translation manuals are surely *possible* for *some* languages; why not Chinese?) such algorithms would just be more "program," and I should think CRTT should help itself to all it needs.

Someone, of course, might want to ask how it is that the person in the room can understand all these elaborate instructions written in *English*. English, here, is the system's *Language of Thought*, and the question how that language acquires any meaning is an important question, which we addressed in chapter 9.[17] But it is important to see that these are not the questions directly raised by Searle's *example* as he describes it. For Searle everywhere presupposes in his example that the person in the room understands *English*, and follows the rules accordingly. His claim is that no such set of rules would be adequate or even relevant to understanding *Chinese*. However, as we begin to fill out the program in the ways I have sketched, it becomes less and less clear that the person in the room need be quite as innocent of Chinese as Searle claims. The Chinese characters hardly need be the entirely "meaningless symbols" for that person that they were in Searle's example; for the person is now certainly *in a position* to determine *something* about what the symbols mean. What other *"causal powers of the brain"* besides abilities to obey evidential, assertability, truth conditional, and outright semantic rules of Chinese could he need? Does he need to secrete norepinepherine over them as well? Why in the world should *that* be necessary?

10.2.3 *Searle's own problem and his fallacy of division*

Notice that a puzzle arises here *even on Searle's own account*. The human being in Searle's Chinese room *does* presumably possess the requisite biological structure, yet, according to Searle, he *still* doesn't understand Chinese. *If neither the biology nor the program, alone or together, are sufficient, what more for Searle is needed?*[18] Well, I suppose that for Searle, as indeed for the functionalist, the biology somehow doesn't enter the picture in *the right way*. But what might the right way be?

Perhaps the problem is this. Even in the enriched program that I have described, the rules are still *outside the person* in the room: he has to look up the rules in a book. If that were all there were to understanding Chinese, then all of us could be said to understand all languages simply by virtue of the fact that we're all capable of looking up and following the rules that standard language instruction books provide. Something needs to be "internalized" in a way that the person in the room, even with all his biology, has failed to do. That person may be, as I said, "in a position" to understand Chinese; but he does seem to have to do something more to exploit that position and succeed in genuinely understanding it.

At this point, it's important to see that this problem really need not be of particular concern to CRTT. For it is not in the least committed to making rich psychological claims about *the person in the room*. *That* person corresponds not to the *whole* of the emulated Chinese speaker, but merely to that person's Central Processing Unit (her "CPU"). For our purposes, this can be abstractly regarded as a species of *Universal Turing Machine* (§6.2), designed to read and execute the coded descriptions of *other* Turing Machines that are themselves designed to compute specific functions (e.g. machines that execute the instructions, per above, for computing the syntax and semantics of Chinese symbols). Given my earlier remarks about the variety of sub-systems CRTT needs to posit for our different mental capacities, these coded descriptions of Turing Machines are presumably the output of still further Universal Turing Machines that realize those other sub-systems, particularly of those machines that realize the perceptual and belief fixation sub-systems. Thus, even on this preposterously abstract simplification of a person's psychology, the whole of the relevant portions of a Chinese Speaker system consists of a battery of nested Universal Turing Machines, many of them putting out descriptions of further Turing Machines to one particular Universal Turing Machine, the CPU, that plays the important role of deciding what finally gets said and done, when. CRTT no more needs or ought to ascribe any understanding of Chinese to this latter part of the entire system than we need or ought to ascribe the properties of the entire British Empire to Queen Victoria. Of course, it could turn out that Queen Victoria did have many properties of her empire; just so, were the role of a system's CPU played by a *person*, then, as I have indicated, that person would be in a position to acquire some of the properties of the system as a whole. But the point is that this acquisition is in no way required, and standardly does not occur. Indeed, were the CPU *required* to have the mental states that are ascribed to the system as a whole, we would seem to be confronted with the familiar regress of homunculi that we noted (in §10.1.3) approaches like CRTT are expressly designed to avoid.

This fallacy of division is, of course, precisely what was worrying several of Searle's original critics when they claimed that it is "the room," not the person within it, that is the relevant agent understanding Chinese. Searle's reply to this claim is telling. He proposes changing the example so that the person in the room *memorizes* the rules: now the "system" and the person are one, so there's no "division"; yet, claims Searle, there is still no understanding. But is this true? There we have our flesh and blood person, with as fully a biological brain as Searle would demand; he's now not merely following rules *reading* an external manual, but has, by memorizing them, *internalized* them. – And remember: they are not the mere "correlation" rules of the sort Searle provides, but full recursive grammatical and semantic rules of the sort that many philosophers of language would demand. – The person in the room has done all this and *still* he doesn't understand Chinese? What more could Searle conceivably want? Surely this sort of internalization is precisely what's *ordinarily* involved in understanding Chinese. When people want to learn to carry on a conversation in Beijing, what they generally do is to go and memorize a lot of vocabulary and rules of grammar. Perhaps if they only apply the rules *consciously*, taking hours to describe to themselves the squiggles and squoggles and to recollect which rules apply, then their understanding might be regarded as only marginal. But once they streamline the operation, applying the rules so quickly and unconsciously that they "hear through" the squiggles to their meaning (viz., the consequences in the rest of their thought) they understand Chinese as well as anyone. What's good enough for people in Beijing is surely good enough for the guy in the Chinese room. For CRTT, what Searle's proposal of memorization comes to is simply programming the CPU with the program of the entire system in such a fashion that they are functionally indistinguishable (notice, though, that strictly speaking, the room would still constitute a system were the person in it to revert to reading the external text). The AI-functionalist then goes on to point out that the flesh and blood clause is inessential: memorization of the rules is quite enough. To avoid the charge of a specious speciesism, Searle needs an argument now that it isn't.

I conclude that Searle's example is not an example that ought to cast any doubt on Strong AI. There is no reason to regard that view as committed to the Turing Test, to any thesis about the autonomy of language, nor to imputing to the agent's CPU what is properly only a property of the agent.

More recently, Searle (1992) has argued that even supposing there are algorithmic manipulations of syntax in a machine presupposes *someone else's* intentionality. We have dealt with this objection already (see §7.2.3 and §10.1.3 above). However, his inclination to see some sort of observer-relativity in computational and mentalistic ascriptions to machines, and (going beyond Searle) even to people, is widespread in contemporary philosophy, and deserves separate discussion. It arises particularly in relation to the supposed "normativity" of mental ascription that we discussed in §3.1.2, and the idealizations that they sometimes involve, to which we now turn.

10.3   Worries about Idealization

In §3.1.2 we considered "Kripkenstein's" (or Wittgenstein's 1953 as it struck Kripke 1982) worries about the normativity of the ascription of rules (adding vs. quadding), and related "interpretavist" views of Davidson and Dennett regarding the normativity of mental ascription generally. Speaking on behalf of this view, Dennett (1987:48–9), for example, claimed:

> As many philosophers have observed . . . a system's beliefs are those it ought to have given its perceptual capacities, its epistemic needs, and its biography . . . , [its]

> desires are those it ought to have given its biological needs and the most practicable
> means of satisfying them . . . [where] "ought to have" means "would have if it were
> ideally ensconced in its environmental niche." (1987:48–9)

and marshals such claims on behalf of his instrumentalist – what I called his
"Patternalist" – views regarding the mind that we discussed in §3.1.3, e.g. "the
decision to adopt the [intentional] strategy is pragmatic and not intrinsically right
or wrong" (1978a:7). If such claims about normativity and Patternalism were true,
CRTT would be in trouble: specifically, its claim to provide the real causal bases
in the physical world for contentful mental states would have to be abandoned.[19]
Dennett is not unaware of these consequences for CRTT, and has ridiculed its
defenders as "industrial strength" and "hysterical" realists (1995b:530). It's time
to examine whether there is any basis for such ridicule and the claims about
normativity and Patternalism on which they rest.

10.3.1 Normative vs. descriptive idealizations

Fortunately for CRTT – and psychology generally – there are a number of
problems with the arguments here. To begin with, appeals to "ideals" suffer from
a crucial ambiguity: there are genuinely *normative* ideals, such as one finds in ethics
and aesthetics, ideals of goodness and beauty which, though perhaps forever
uninstantiated in this dismal world, are the standards by which we judge things.
These are to be distinguished from *descriptive, explanatory idealizations*, which seem
to arise essentially *throughout the sciences*, mostly in the macro-ones, but quite
arguably even in the "academic physical ones:" there are, after all, Boyle's and
Kepler's Laws, Bernoulli's Principle, and even (short of the utopian grand unified
"Theory of Everything") the fundamental laws of electromagnetism and gravitation, which must idealize away from interactions among themselves.[20] On this
latter, descriptive reading, idealizations to rationality need make no more claim to
how people *ought* to speak, think, or act, than do Boyle's idealizations about gases
make some sort of moral claim about how gases morally *ought* to behave, or
Kepler's laws about how planets morally *ought* to move. Such idealizations are not
justified on any *normative* grounds other than the standard epistemic norms of *good
theory and explanation*. One idealization, like Boyle's or Bernoulli's or Kepler's, is
selected over another presumably because of its greater *explanatory power*: do the
book-keeping *this* way, claiming *this* to be a law and the rest to be noise or
interference, and you'll get a better explanation – objectively better, "carving
nature closer to her joints" – than if you do it otherwise: think of the planets as
moving in ellipses, with deviations due to interactions and interferences, and
you'll get a more correct theory than if you think of them of them as moving in
circles. As Chomsky (1995) notes, "idealization is a misleading term for the only
reasonable way to approach a grasp of reality" (p. 7).

In any event, however one thinks of the ultimate status of idealizations in science, Dennett has provided no reason to think that idealization in psychology is any worse off than the idealizations involved in the rest of science.[21]

10.3.2 *Dennett's specific idealizations*

Setting aside, then, this general confusion about the "normativity" of idealizations, we need to consider whether there is any specific normativity that arises in the mental case. Dennett and Davidson seem to think there is, and so we need to examine the explanatory adequacy of such idealizations.

At this early point in psychology, it would seem wildly premature to decide upon the appropriate idealizations for the field: think of the difficulties of picking the right idealizations in merely linguistics, not to mention the enormous difficulties in even framing genuinely descriptive criteria of inductive or practical rationality. In any case, it's difficult to see why we should accept the particular idealizations Dennett recommends: that, for example, even ideally, people believe what they ought – under deductive closure! (1978a:10–11)[22] – or desire what they need. Off hand, these particular idealizations seem about as likely as that the planets move in circles.

But, fine, appearances can be deceptive, and science can explain them away. Dennett, however, doesn't defend his idealizations along any empirically compelling lines, addressing *in detail* the experimental literature that raises problems for such claims.[23] Indeed, confronted with familiar experimental problems for his model (1987:52), he simply writes:

> I would insist, however, that all this empirically obtained lore is laid over a fundamental generative and normative framework that has the features I have described. (1987:54)

After all, "No other view of folk psychology . . . can explain the fact that we do so well explaining each other's behavior" (1987:51). This last, however, is a quite substantive claim for which he hasn't provided any serious empirical evidence, much less convincing philosophical argument. Surely we all the time make sense of one another without assuming anything remotely like deductive closure or a correspondence between wants and needs – to the contrary, we'd be positively *mystified* were either of these actually to be observed in someone (e.g. someone who immediately saw any consequence of Peano's axioms and was never so much as *tempted* by anything she didn't need!).

Indeed, an important point that Dennett oddly overlooks is that *many patterns of irrationality demand every bit as much intentionality as patterns of rationality*. Consider not merely Kahneman and Tversky's "deliberately [induced] situations that provoke irrational responses" (1987:52), but just any of the fallacies enumerated in any elementary logic text. One might wonder why they are *there*, as opposed to some neurophysiological manual (they are certainly not part of *logic*). The reason is clear: these are errors that often *appear* to be logical. As such, they are *intentionally comprehensible*, usually by virtue of their *content*. The fallacy of composition involves uncritically inferring properties of the whole from properties of the parts; the gambler, supposing that what's true of an infinite set is true of its large finite subsets; the genetic fallacy, confusing mere causes of a claim with its reasons.[24] These are no mere *mechanical* breakdowns, comprehensible only from some *non*-intentional stance; to the contrary, they are specific patterns in *contentful* thought that people find persistently compelling.[25] *Pace* Dennett (1987:87), they do not "defy description in ordinary terms of belief and desire." The intentional stance, far from being undermined by such cases, would seem to be required by them.

Along similar lines, Fodor (1981a:108) pointed out that in playing chess, for example, part and parcel of one's intentional stance may be the hypothesis that one's opponent is "a sucker for a knight fork." Dennett attempts to account for such meta-reasoning by claiming that:

> Being approximately rational, Black is not likely to notice threats that would take a great deal of time and effort to discover. . . . If Black is, as Fodor supposes, rather unlikely to notice the threat, it must be because the threat is somewhat distant in the search tree. (1987:80)

But what's the evidence that that is the right diagnosis? Why shouldn't the fork be "right in front of his nose," and White just knows he's bad at noticing patterns of that sort? In any case, Dennett is now modifying the claim of optimal rationality: it's no longer deductive closure, but something like optimal use of time and effort (we'll return shortly (§10.3.4) to the further interesting commitments of *that*); and we can ask once more, why on earth should we believe it – about *us*?!

10.3.3   *"Unrealistic" idealizations*

Dennett's extravagant idealizations have not gone unnoticed by his critics (see e.g. Stich 1984). However, sometimes they are rejected for wrong reasons, reasons that would undermine *any* "unrealistic" idealizations, even those that are arguably needed for CRTT. Thus, in an otherwise valuable study on the limits of rationality assumptions, Cherniak (1986) suggests that the problem with Dennett's idealization is simply *its statistical inapplicability*. Rightly emphasizing what he calls the "finitary predicament of having fixed limits on their cognitive capacities and the time available to them," he claims that "this is the 'cognitive friction' the idealizations overlook" (p. 8). Indeed:

Since any human being is in the finitary predicament, using a cognitive theory with [e.g. Dennett's] ideal rationality condition seems to amount to having very nearly no applicable theory at all. (Cherniak 1986:8)

And accompanying this view is the usual appeal to normativity: "The value of an idealization is always relative to a set of goals" (p. 8).

However, idealizations, sometimes preposterously remote from direct application to the observable world, seem to be the rule in most serious sciences, quite apart from any goals of an investigator (save truth). As the very example of *friction* shows, idealization is not a mere instrument.[26] It is irrelevant to the scientific purposes served by frictionless planes, perfect vacuums, or ideal gases whether or not there *actually are* instances of such things: in some cases, it actually may be a law that there *aren't*. Yet the idealizations are accepted as correct anyway. The relevant question would seem to be not, are these idealizations statistically plausible, but rather: do they partition reality at its joints? In particular: can the failures at the level of observation be explained as the consequence of independent interference?

The problem with the kind of ideal rationality conditions proposed by Dennett is not that they abstract too far from actual reasoning, but that independent evidence of human failures to abide by them is not plausibly available. Our failure to compute *all* the deductive consequences of our beliefs is not plausibly due merely to the fact that we haven't enough time. As Cherniak himself recognizes, deductive closure would simply not serve the purposes of an intelligent organism: only a "heuristic imbecile" (p. 11) would while away even its infinite lifetime deducing strings of conjunctions of its initial beliefs, or every sentence from a contradiction. The idealization simply seems false.

We needn't and don't idealize as extravagantly as Dennett supposes. This is not to suggest, however, that we don't or oughtn't idealize at all. As Cherniak himself emphasizes (pp. 55–7), we have abundant independent reason to distinguish short-term from long-term memory, and to presume a wide variety of heuristic constraints (pp. 11–15), in a way that permits us to recognize a corresponding variety of logical lapses. To consider one of his examples, someone may decide to illuminate the contents of a gasoline tank by holding a match, fully knowing, but not sufficiently "thinking" about the potential for explosion. To many, this might seem like a complete breakdown of rational idealizations of any sort, until we invoke an independently motivatable distinction between "storage" and on-line processing of thought contents.

Similarly, to return to the Kripkenstein puzzle: the obvious way to distinguish someone who is adding from someone who is quadding is to determine which idealization of the person's psychology is the right one. Is the person intending to add merely making a slip of the pen, or memory, or attention? Or are none of these

279

factors responsible, and the person *did* in fact fully intend the quadding result? What did they intend *ceteris paribus*?

Kripkenstein considers such an appeal to a *ceteris paribus* idealization, but, like Cherniak, rejects it because it seems too unrealistic:

> How in the world can I tell what would happen if my brain were stuffed with extra brain matter, or if my life were prolonged by some magic elixir? Surely such speculation should be left to science fiction writers and futurologists. We have no idea what the results of such experiments would be. (Kripke 1982:27)

What is puzzling about this worry is that, were it legitimate, *it would argue against almost every ceteris paribus law in every serious science*! Newton's laws that appeal to "frictionless planes," Boyle's Laws that appeal to perfectly elastic molecules and perfectly rigid containers, indeed, any laws that appealed to a "closed system," involve speculations about often nomologically impossible situations. Given the actual existence of the infinitely extending force fields of physics, such idealization requires supposing that *nothing* exists outside the system being considered. Surely that is every bit as much a piece of "science fiction" as our more modest speculations about the mind or brain.

The mistake consists in part in trying to make sense of idealizations as speculations about what would happen *if* the world were a certain way. As an alternative, Pietroski and Rey (1995) have developed in some detail a different suggestion: a *ceteris paribus* clause is a check written on the banks of independent theories, where apparent exceptions to the law are the result of independent interferences.[27] If that check can't be cashed, if the interference can't be independently identified, that is a reason for thinking the original law doesn't hold. Thus, if some quantity of gas seems to disobey Boyle's Laws, and there is no independent account of the elasticity of molecules or the rigidity of containers, or about the effect of comets passing near the container that would explain the failure, that is a good reason for thinking Boyle's Laws are false. Similarly then with mentalistic laws: if they fail even when we can't find any independent account of the specific failures, then that would be a good reason for thinking the purported laws are false.[28]

However, it is by no means a foregone conclusion that the particular systematizations of the mind that seem to be presupposed by much of our ordinary mental talk are in fact correct. Some of them – e.g. the popular division of the mind into such subsystems as "soul," "intellect," "will" – are probably quite mistaken. If certain RCON views are correct, then it may well be that even the idealizations we make to, for example, a logical and mathematical faculty are mistaken, and some of Kripkenstein's speculations could turn out to be true.[29] However, as we saw in §8.8, such views have yet to account for a wide variety of phenomena that seem clearly explained by CRTT.

10.3.4   Is CRTT's realism really hysterical?

I trust the discussion of the last few sections has shown that merely the presence in psychology of highly abstract idealizations doesn't in the least undermine CRTT's realistic claims about the causal efficacy of internal sentences. But perhaps realism about the mind is hysterical anyway.[30] I'd like to end this chapter by indicating some reasons for thinking this isn't so, that indeed we – and, indeed, interpretavists like Dennett and Davidson themselves – have plenty of reasons to think mental states are genuine, causally efficacious states of the sort postulated by CRTT.

Dennett, himself, at unguarded moments, betrays his own commitments to causal representations. Recall his reply to Fodor's observations about chess a few pages back:

> Being approximately rational, Black is not likely to notice threats that would take a great deal of time and effort to discover. . . . If Black is, as Fodor supposes, rather unlikely to notice the threat, it must be because the threat is somewhat distant in the search tree.   (1987:80).

Leave aside whether Dennett's diagnosis of Black's problem is correct. How are we to understand what Black needs to spend "a great deal of time and effort" doing? Evidently, whatever it is, it involves a "search tree" in which some branches are "somewhat distant." It is difficult to see how to make sense of this without supposing the agent is actually inspecting some sort of internal representation of a tree, inspection of which would have the consequences *in time and effort* that Dennett postulates. And what are the branches of such a tree? Presumably specifications of different moves in chess. But these are standardly represented by *sentences*. So reasoning in such cases must be *causal* and *sentential* after all![31]

Moreover, as Dennett elsewhere admits, we need to know how it is that beliefs can cause not only actions they normatively rationalize, but also "blushes, verbal slips, heart attacks, and the like" (1987:57). Davidson (1963/1980), too, rightly observed that we distinguish the *real* from *merely a rationalized* reason for an act – or a blush – by regarding the real reason as being the *genuine attitude that caused it*. If it was her discovery that *Sam Clemens* was married that caused his mistress tears (and, not, as she claimed at the time, merely his brusque manner), we need some means of distinguishing that cause from her knowing this all along about *Mark Twain*. CRTT, with its different internal representations of the same content, would seem to be precisely what Dennett and Davidson themselves need.[32]

In any case, realism about mental states would also seem to be what's needed to sort out the thorny issues of Freudian theory and "recovered memory" that we noted in the introduction (§4) have been touched by philosophical views. Consider again the claims of Nagel (1994a), which he acknowledges have their source in Davidson's interpretavism:

> Much of human mental life consists of complex events with multiple causes and background conditions that will never precisely recur. . . . That doesn't mean that explanation is impossible, only that it cannot be sought by the methods appropriate in particle physics, cancer research, or the study of reflexes. We may not be able to run controlled experiments, but we can still try to make internal sense of what people do, in light of their circumstances, relying on a general form of understanding that is supported by its usefulness in countless other cases. (1994a:35)

Note, first of all, the actual reason that Nagel adduces here for his view is quite irrelevant. The fact that individual mental events are unique is no reason to despair of the methods of science: *all* events are unique, from the Big Bang, to the disappearance of the dinosaurs, to the latest experiment in a linear accelerator. What science hopes to do is to explain some particular event in the light of laws that can be established independently through, *inter alia*, controlled experiments. As Gopnik's reply to Nagel that I quoted earlier rightly points out, this is precisely what is occurring in the debate about repressed memory.

But, in any event, interpretavism doesn't seem the right way to resolve the issue. Should we really decide whether adult disorders are the effects of repressed abuse just by "making internal sense" of people's behavior and what they say? A browse through the popular psychology section of any bookstore, or a sampling of any of a multitude of different psychotherapies, can provide a plethora of different accounts of a person's life that "make internal sense," some of which doubtless prove "useful in countless circumstances." Various religious stories say, about original sin, God's love and wrath and the need for atonement; or the effects of "bad karma" or the wrong "archetypes" – often seem to make much better "internal sense" of human misery than, say, a story about our biochemistry. And sometimes seriously believing these stories can make someone a lot happier. But, for all that, the religious stories might be false, the biochemical one true; or perhaps there really was abuse, the memories were repressed and they did in fact give rise to the adult disorders. It's very hard to see why we shouldn't at least *try* to establish which story is true using the usual methods employed in any other investigation of the world. Quite apart from the need for truth generally, claims in this particular area can have pretty serious consequences: unacknowledged abuse can occasion substantial mental grief; false accounts of abuse and its effects can result in appalling travesties of justice; and, in the long run, retreat to merely telling stories that "make internal sense" can undermine the seriousness with which therapists make their claims and others take them. If their claims aren't factual, why *shouldn't* they say whatever sells or fits their religion best? (But then why should the state or insurance companies pay?)

Doubtless in these "post modern," "deconstructive" days when it's fashionable to think that there's "nothing outside of texts,"[33] realism about *anything* strikes many as hysterical. But surely, amidst such madness, insisting on the reality of one's mind – or, anyway, of at least *some* explanatory mental states – may well be the only way not to lose it.

Notes

1 I don't mean to endorse this argot: the differences between the hemispheres are far more complex than it suggests (see Gleitman 1986:41–8).

2 Just for the record, my own phenomenology of thought is largely non-verbal, a hodge-podge of sensations, moods, images, a sure sense of north, and an endless repetition of certain bits of music.

3 Indeed, the very feature that Barwise and Perry (1983:5) perceptively praise about natural language, its "efficiency" – e.g. that a small stock of proper names are used with endless ambiguity; that a small set of demonstratives depend almost entirely on context for their reference – makes it utterly unreliable for computations.

4 I abbreviate here my discussion of Rey (1980a). Pylyshyn (1981), incidentally, shows how non-imagistic CRTT hypotheses are compatible with much of the purported imagistic data. See also Block (1981a) and Tye (1991) for discussion.

5 Note also that, even if there are functional images on which the brain computes, still there would be Leibniz Law difficulties with identifying them with the seeming objects of internal image experiences: a functional image in the brain of a green tomato is presumably not itself *green*, nor, as we plausibly allowed in allowing it to be distributed over the brain, are *its* parts actually contiguous, in the way that the tomato image certainly seems to be. The identification of the one sort of image with the other would need to deal with these difficulties.

6 Although it's interesting to note in this regard that the alleged superiority of connectionist over classical architectures has evidently been exaggerated. McLaughlin and Warfield (forthcoming) show that, for a large selection of well-known tasks, there is a classical machine comparable in efficiency to any connectionist one.

7 And surprisingly persists in some quarters: Goldfarb (1992:114–15), for example, ridicules cognitive scientific explanations, citing an account of absolute pitch that appeared to appeal to "mental tuning forks," a metaphor, he admits (p. 115) occurred (as did Skinner's homunculi) only in a popular presentation, not in the original research paper on which the article was based.

8 Indeed, there is more than a little tension between Searle's insistence on "intrinsic" physical properties to ground facts and his incredulity at what he takes to be (1992:47) a standard bad argument for eliminativism that bases itself on a premise that all real properties are physical properties.

9 Some of us – Maloney (1989), Davies (1991), Lycan (1993), and Rey (1995a) – have argued that CRTT is a theory about the structure of any possible thinking thing. And Fodor (1975:epigraph) notoriously claimed that CRTT was "the only president you've got." But sustaining these arguments is far beyond the needs of the present work.

10 See Weizenbaum's (1976) discussion of his ELIZA program, designed to emulate the reactions of a Rogerian psychotherapist. See also Allen (1994) regarding the results of an actual Turing Test.

11 Dreyfus (1972/1979) and Dreyfus and Dreyfus (1986) rightly chastise many computer scientists for making exaggerated claims about their programs, which are generally suitable only for what, from a normal human point of view, are extremely artificial environments in which the problems are artificially standardized. Dreyfus and Dreyfus think that these problems for programming intelligence constitute in principle arguments against the success of *any* computational/representational (or so-called "classical") program. These problems, however, show no such thing, any more than the failure of a physicist to mimic the motion of a leaf in the wind tells against the truth of proposed physical laws.

12 Roughly, Fodor (1975, 1981c) argues that since (1) learning is hypothesis confirmation, and (2) there are no serious "decompositions" of any substantial concepts into sensory ones, all concepts must be innate. A proponent of CRTT might deny either of these premises and/or the validity of the argument. *Pace* Patricia Churchland (1986:389), it's not enough merely to declare the conclusion absurd: given the uncertain status of empiricist claims about conceptual analysis (see §4.3 and §5.4 above), one is best advised to treat this, as so many other of one's folk opinions about the mind (see Introduction §2), as a highly theoretic matter awaiting far more evidence and argument than anyone has yet adduced.

13 In order to stay close to Searle's texts, I will continue to use use his expression "Strong AI." For purposes here CRTT can be regarded nearly enough as a species of Strong AI, even though, for the reasons discussed in §9.1.3 ff, many of its proponents would hardly regard the semantics of a system to be settled merely by an *internal* story, computational or otherwise. So "Strong AI" should be allowed to be supplemented with claims about the causal relations between the "room" and the world. (That Searle is not fazed by this modification is indicated by his response to it at 1980b:454).

14 I suspect that discussion of the example has persisted in the literature for so long in large part because his critics, correctly pointing to now this, now that, error, too often spend their time disagreeing among themselves about what the *real*, essential problem is. In my reply here I don't mean for a moment to downplay the correctness of a number of other commentators' objections, but only emphasize the importance of noticing the effect of several *simultaneous* errors in Searle's discussion.

15 This is the truth in the "Robot" reply made by several of the original commentators on Searle's article.

16 Along the lines of "disquotational" theories of truth discussed in §3.2.1 above. Alternatively, one might require biconditionals involving "warrantedly assertable" instead of "true"; I assume the differences are orthogonal to the present discussion.

17 Actually, recalling our discussion in §8.1, there are at least *three* languages that need to be distinguished in Searle's example: the *natural* language, in this case Chinese, that the system is attempting to *speak*; *the language of thought*, into which the system would be translating, and the *processing language*, the system's *meta-language* of thought, in

which the rules for effecting that translation would be expressed. This last language need not be represented, but only implemented in the system.

18   Well, perhaps what's needed is "the background" and "the network" (Searle 1992). By Searle's own admission, these notions are far from satisfactorily spelt out, but they amount, respectively, to the elaborate set of social practices in effect in a person's environment, and the vast set of beliefs a person has about those practices and many other matters. Searle nowhere provides a suggestion about why these things couldn't in principle be supplied to the "Chinese room" (as, respectively, the environment in which the interaction takes place, and lots of data-structures about that environment and many other matters).

19   Perhaps there could be fall-back positions to which it could retreat. Stich (1983), for example, defends merely a *syntactic* version of CRTT, treating the *semantic* issues of content as essentially pragmatic and interest-relative, well-nigh "normative" for all that the facts of computation establish. Such a position is a lot less than CRTT, or any psychology of *actual* minds, might reasonably settle for. Moreover, as Fodor (1987:166 n. 3, 1991a:311–12) emphasizes, it would miss a great many generalizations that seem naturally expressible only at the intentional level. Consequently, it is important to meet this supposed problem of normativity head-on.

20   See Cartwright (1983, 1989) for lively discussion of idealization in even fundamental physics. Cartwright does think that these idealizations show that "physics lies," and sometimes it would appear that this is what Dennett would like to say about the intentional stance. But it's not what he does say, which is not that that stance is merely *false*, but that there is "no fact of the matter"!

21   Notice one immense difference between normative and descriptive idealization: ethical and aesthetical ideals are not, *per se*, invoked in a *causal explanation* of anything. (Of course, a *belief* in or *desire* for the ideal may be: but, as powerful as the belief might be, the ideal itself may be forever uninstantiated and so causally impotent.) The factors postulated in descriptive idealizations, however, typically *are* causal: it was *because* the pressure increased, and, because ideally (or *ceteris paribus*), increases in pressure with constant volume *cause* increases in temperature, that the temperature increased.

22   Dennett does seem to retract this extreme view at 1987:94, claiming he really intends a *"flexible* line" between folk practice and overtly normative theory. But a page later he hedges it, claiming that "in the course of making [a] case for what we might call implication-insulated cognitive states, ... we must talk about what our agent 'pseudo-believes' and 'pseudo-knows,' [or] ... 'sub-doxastic states'" (1987:95). I, who see no such need, am therefore inclined to hold Dennett to the closure condition, as a condition on at least *full* belief.

23   Stich (1984) provides a useful discussion of much of this material in relation to Dennett.

24   These are, of course, rough diagnoses. I only want to bring out their probable semantic content; the details are surely much subtler than anyone presently knows.

25   Johnson-Laird's (1983) work is an example of an effort within intentional psychology to explain oddities in people's deductive reasoning. Notice, incidentally, *pace* Stich, the difficulty of capturing the generalizations about these fallacies without a *semantic*

level (even though, *pace* Johnson-Laird, they still may need to be *implemented* at an entirely syntactic level as well). Note, too, that, *pace* Stich, the errors we can understand in others need not be ones to which we are prey ourselves: I need not be prey to the "gambler" for a moment to recognize the (nevertheless fully semantic) pattern in others.

26   Except, of course, insofar as all scientific theories are instruments. Although I don't share this view, it is beyond the present scope to consider it. As I have stressed earlier, it will be enough for present purposes if psychology turns out to be no more problematic as a realistic and objective enterprise than any other science.

27   Pietroski and I actually present this condition as merely sufficient for saving a *ceteris paribus* law from *vacuity*. We acknowledge (§2.4) that proposed laws could be defective for many other reasons.

28   Davidson (1974/1980) quite rightly notices that the *ceteris paribus* clause involved, for example, in ascriptions of intention could never be entirely eliminated, since "there can be no finite list of things we think might prevent us from doing what we intend" (p. 94). Moreover, since the list would in any case involve non-mental conditions, the laws would be "heteronomic" giving rise to "the anomalousness of the mental," or the thesis that there are no mental laws at all (1970/1980:219–24). But this doesn't follow. Were scientific laws required to be always "homonomic," forming a closed system, there would be no science except the whole of physics (cf. Fodor 1975:9–26).

29   That is, it could turn out on those views that there is indeed no fact of the matter about whether someone means addition or quaddition by their use of "add." I am doubtful that what "fact of the matter" remains could be established by social practice in the fashion suggested by Kripke (1982) in the remainder of his discussion. But we need not settle that issue here.

30   Sometimes Dennett makes the issue seem as though the realist is committed to *every* question about the mind receiving a determinate answer. Such a view would indeed be hysterical, in psychology as in any other domain; and CRTT is no worse off here than any other theory. It can allow that there are hard cases – e.g. about whether someone in a delirium is actually thinking, whether it is determinate at every instant whether someone has a particular belief or desire – that may admit of only indeterminate answers (arguably, there really is no fact of the matter whether certain only half hirsute men are bald). See Rey (1995b:267–8) for discussion of this persistent red herring in Dennett's writings – and Dennett (1995a:531–2 and 1995b:37–9, 95, 201–2) for still further recurrences of it.

31   Which is not to say that *all* casual ascriptions of attitudes need to be regarded as referring to internal structures. Another chess example discussed by Dennett and Cummins (see Cummins 1986) involves a machine that's observed to "like to get its queen out early," although nothing inside the machine corresponds to such a sentence. But if nothing in the machine corresponds to such a structure, that's a reason for supposing that the ascription isn't *literally* true – or is just a way of metaphorically ascribing a desire, as one might the desire for oil to a car.

32   Louise Antony (1987, 1989) discusses some of the tensions between Davidson's causal and interpretavist views, also suggesting that he would appear to need CRTT to ground his claims about the causal efficacy of the mind.

33 "Il n'y a pas de hors texte," Dennett (1991a:411) approvingly quotes Lodge quoting Derrida. Dennett does hasten to add, "I wouldn't say there is *nothing* outside the text. There are, for instance, all the bookcases, buildings, bodies, bacteria . . ." (p. 411) – but, conspicuously, no mention of any mental states. See also his (1986) endorsement of Jaynes' (1976) notorious conflation of consciousness with people's *claims* about consciousness.

11

Further Capacities (Meeting Levine's Challenge)

The burden of the preceding three chapters has been to set out some basic features of the Computational/Representational Theory of Thought and to indicate some of the ways in which it might solve some of the main mind/body problems that have been with us since Descartes. In particular, I hope I have indicated at least some strategies by means of which it might eventually close the explanatory gaps Descartes and Brentano claimed existed between rationality, intentionality, and any physical phenomena.

There remains the gap with the qualitative, and many of the peculiar properties associated with it that we noted in chapter 2. Here, too, I think CRTT promises some progress, but there is no question that puzzles remain. In this concluding chapter I will consider ways in which CRTT might be extended to account for qualitative experience, an extension I will call "CRTQ."[1] Dealing with any of the problems it faces in adequate depth would require an entire book on its own.[2] In what follows, I will approach the qualitative fairly gingerly, discussing, first, ways in which CRTQ can handle "nested intentionality" (§11.1), first-person reflexive indexical thoughts (§11.2.1), and, towards capturing the distinction between the conscious and unconscious, a distinction between central and avowed attitudes (§11.2.2). With these in hand, I will then propose an account of conscious qualitative experience modeled on the treatment of indexical thoughts (§11.3). This account affords a way of dealing with a number of the arguments against materialism that we discussed in chapter 2, for example, the phenomena of privacy (§11.4.1), privileged access (§11.4.2), and knowledge of "what it's like" (§11.4.3). It does raise what can seem like a surprising issue about the *semantics* of experience – if experience involves referential devices, what do they refer to? (§11.5); but we'll see that that question can be settled by supposing that, while experience *seems* and maybe even *purports* to refer to certain phenomenal objects and properties (§11.6), it doesn't actually succeed in doing so. There is no need to postulate such phenomena and lots of reasons not to; merely the specific computational states and processes that constitute experience will suffice (§11.6.1). This also affords a concessive, but still materialist way of answering Kripke's version of the Cartesian argument regarding the essences of mental states (§11.6.2).

Alas, some problems remain (§11.7). It is hard to dismiss at least *the possibility* of functional isomorphs that might have different narrow intentional contents (say, complementary phenomenal colors) (§11.7.1). And then there is still the harder problem of the arbitrary realizability of functionally defined structures that is inherent in most any functionalist proposal (§11.7.2). But it is important to note that the problems here are not ones presented by the existence of any non-tendentious data. The former may have to do with only an epistemic possibility that is not metaphysically real. And the latter may have to do merely with the ineluctable biases we all seem to have to things that look and act like our conspecifics, and related moral, but non-explanatory demands we therefore place on mental phenomena (§11.7.3).

11.1   Nested Intentionality

Many people have pointed out that a distinguishing feature of much human reasoning is not only that humans have beliefs and desires about, for example, lions, tigers, bears, and the natural numbers, but also beliefs and desires *about beliefs and desires*. They enjoy what Dennett (1978a) calls "second-order intentionality," or, more generally, allowing attitudes about attitudes about attitudes, . . . indefinitely *"nested* intentionality." Frankfurt (1971), for example, has emphasized that what gives people's desires certain moral importance is the fact that they have desires about those desires. He distinguishes, for example, what he calls a "wanton" from a morally serious drug addict, by pointing out that the latter, but not the former, may have second-order desires to not act from the first-order desire for the addicting substance. Dennett (1978a) makes a good case for such nested intentionality being a necessary condition of genuine personhood.

Now, insofar as CRTT is able to capture intentional states with content at all, there should be no special problem about its capturing intentional states that happen to have intentional states themselves as their content. The details would depend, of course, on the details of one's theory of content, about which there is no need to decide here. By way of example, however, imagine that having the concept of belief involves mastering enough of, say, Dennett's "intentional stance," or the Modest Mentalism sketched earlier (§7.3.2), to understand how it figures in reasoning and combines with, for example, desires to explain the behavior of people and many animals. Thus, people who regularly and successfully predict others' behavior by this means would arguably have the concept of belief. Alternatively, they may need simply to be able to discriminate believers from non-believers, or have had this discrimination ability brought about by some selection process.[3]

11.2 Subjectivity

11.2.1 Essential indexicals

Nested intentionality brings us one step towards what many regard as a crucial feature of the human mind, its capacity for "self-consciousness."[4] This can seem a particularly unique, "subjective" feature of persons, that would seem to elude any "objective" account.

There are two ways to have thoughts about oneself, a "third-person" way, whereby one has thoughts about oneself in the same way that one has thoughts about anyone else: it just happens to be oneself that is the referent of the thought. Thus, I might consult a birth record and discover that the son of Noël Rey was born at 4:52; but I might note that fact without noting that "That's me! *I* was born at 4:52!" This latter sort of self-consciousness is, of course, what interests people concerned about "self-consciousness." This is "reflexive self-consciousness," ascriptions of it, "first-person reflexive ascriptions." It is sometimes distinguished by appending an asterisk to the relevant pronoun: thus, in the case of the birth records in which my discovery initially *lacks* the reflexive self-consciousness, people might say of me merely "He thinks he was born at 4:52"; but afterwards, when I gain it, they could now say, "He thinks he* was born at 4:52."[5]

CRTT affords a particularly easy way of capturing such thought. Recall the main thesis of CRTT that we discussed in §8.1:

(CRTT) For any agent x, time t, and propositional attitude, *A that p*, there exists some computationally definable relation C_A such that:

$$x \text{ A's that p at t iff } (\exists \sigma)(xC_A\sigma,t \ \& \ \sigma \text{ means that p})$$

Thus, in the case of the attitude *occurrently judging that snow is white*, the claim of CRTT is that there exists some computationally specifiable relation, J, that an agent, x, might bear to sentences in its LOT that express the proposition [Snow is white]; e.g. it might be the output of memory or a reasoning sub-system that is the input to a decision-making one (cf. §8.5; in general to make reference to simply the computational component of an attitude, I'll prefix the attitude word with "comp-": thus, I'll call the present relation, J, "comp-judging"). This thesis was the basis for our initially distinguishing the computational relation of an attitude from its semantic content.

But then we observed in §9.3 that, in order to distinguish among necessarily co-instantiated concepts, a full theory of the content of an attitude state might need to incorporate, in addition to the worldly phenomena a mental symbol might represent, also either the symbol itself, or the role, rule, or function that governed it. Whether or not such a "two factor" theory is workable for semantics generally, it does seem to hold a key to subjectivity.[6]

Let us suppose that, just as "I" is a singular term in English subject to familiar restrictions on its use (e.g. for speakers to refer to themselves), there is presumably a similarly restricted singular term in the LOT, except in this case the restrictions here concern not public use of a term, but instead its role in computation. Just as in English the speaker is supposed to use "I" only to refer to his or herself, in LOT the "system" uses a certain term to refer only to the receiver of present inputs, the instigator of outputs, and the subject of intervening mental states. Suppose the term were "i," and that the system uses "i" to record automatically that it had certain perceptions and judgments and preferences; and that *its behavior is crucially determined by just those attitudes that do have this "i" as their subject*: i.e. its actions are standardly caused by beliefs and preferences that are designated as belonging to "i." Merely my comp-judging the sentence "GR ought to get moving right now" won't be enough to get me moving; I've got to comp-judge "i had better get moving right now."

A little more exactly, the following might be the restrictions on such a "first-person reflexive term" ("FPRT"):

α is a FPRT for agent x iff:[7]

(I-1)   Whenever an input ϕ is received, x stores $\ulcorner \phi \alpha \urcorner$;

(I-2)   Whenever x is in a mental state M, x is prepared to comp-judge a predication $\ulcorner \phi \alpha \urcorner$ that (ordinarily) gets released only when x is in M;

(I-3)   All preference states, and all basic action descriptions in x's decision system that lead up to action in a standard decision theoretic way are states and descriptions whose subject is α.

For example, whenever a sound, s, is heard, the agent stores "i heard s"; whenever it wants or thinks something, p, she is prepared to judge "i want/think that p"; and her actions are based upon such attitudes that have "i" as their subject. These restrictions, themselves, need not be *thought* by the agent; it is enough that they are causally realized: the effect of receiving sensory input, entering a mental state and deciding upon a course of action, involves comp-judging certain sentences containing this restricted singular term, whose narrow meaning is provided by its playing this specific causal role.

Along the lines of the main thesis of CRTT, we could then characterize special "first-person reflexive" thoughts thus:

x judges he* is F iff $(\exists \alpha)(\exists \phi)\{\alpha$ is an FPRT for x & x comp-judges $\ulcorner \phi \alpha \urcorner$ & $\ulcorner \phi \alpha \urcorner$ means [Fx]}

For example:

GR judges he* was born at 4:52 iff $(\exists\alpha)(\exists\phi)\{\alpha$ is an FPRT for GR & GR comp-judges $\ulcorner\alpha$ is born at 4:52$\urcorner$ & $\ulcorner\phi\alpha\urcorner$ means [GR was born at 4:52]}

If "i" were indeed a FPRT, and I did comp-judge "i was born at 4:52", the content of which was indeed [GR was born at 4:52], then I did succeed in judging *that I* was born at 4:52*. It should be emphasized, however, that this characterization of first-person reflexive thought is not entailed by *CRTT* itself. This is the first of several extensions of CRTT that will comprise *CRTQ*, the CRTT-style account of qualitative states.

11.2.2 Central vs. avowed attitudes

It would be tempting to think that once a system possesses concepts for nested intentionality and has such a first-person reflexive term in its LOT, it would have all that's needed for self-consciousness. Rosenthal (1991), advocating a "Higher-Order Thought" ("HOT") theory of consciousness, proposes that it's all that would be needed for a state to be conscious, which he claims consists merely that state's being the object of a higher-order thought. Some might feel, however, that a further dimension is needed as well, since it seems hard to rule out the possibility of *un*conscious nested thoughts (as when neurotics suffer from unconscious fears of their own guilt-ridden impulses).[8]

We noted in §3.2.2 that people's actual mental states can sometimes diverge from their introspective reports of them. For example, people sometimes claim to be unaware of features of stimuli (e.g. the order of socks in an array, pupillary dilation) that demonstrably affect their choices; and often claim that features are affecting them that patently are not (e.g. different textures of the socks). Stich (1983) argues that cases in which there are demonstrable discrepancies between what is said and what is done lead to a breakdown of ordinary mentalistic ways of talk: "it is a fundamental tenet of folk psychology that *the very same* state which underlies the sincere assertion of 'p' also may lead to a variety of non-verbal behaviors" (p. 231). He cites the very experiments of Nisbett and Wilson that we discussed as showing that "*our* cognitive system keeps two sets of books," from which he concludes that "this is a finding for which folk psychology is radically unprepared; . . . under those circumstances I am strongly inclined to say that *there are no such things as beliefs*" (p. 231).

Stich supplies surprisingly little argument for this claim. Presumably he takes it to be a consequence of the close connection he feels between thought and (natural) language: "A belief that p is a belief-like state similar to the one which we would *normally express by uttering 'p'*" (p. 231; see also pp. 79–81). Others feel this connection: Davidson (1980:86) writes, "If someone who knows English says

292

honestly 'Snow is white', then he believes snow is white," and, elsewhere (1984:170) he rejects ascribing propositional attitudes to non-linguistic animals.

But is thought really so closely tied not merely to language, but to actual language *use*? It's hard to believe that animals don't have attitudes or that Nisbett and Wilson's own accounts of their results, viz. as showing there are *non-conscious* attitudes, are incoherent. What makes it so hard is that in both sorts of cases the attribution of attitudes has such *explanatory power*. *Pace* Malcolm (1972), attributing beliefs and preferences to a dog that, chasing a squirrel, barks up the wrong tree is not merely picturesque; it is explanatory precisely in the familiar mentalistic ways we've considered earlier (§4.4, §7.3.2, §9.6). We could, for example, systematically alter the direction of the dog's bark by altering (with decoy squirrels) his beliefs, or (with some well-placed bones) his preferences. Similarly, attributing non-conscious beliefs and preferences to the subjects in the self-attribution experiments often permits us to apply practical reason in a way that explains the results, and predicts how they would differ were those beliefs and preferences to differ. Many of these attributions may be false; but they certainly *make sense*. What attribution of non-conscious or non-verbalizable beliefs and preferences to people or animals does is to bring out the *explanatory* basis that I have been urging throughout this book is implicit in much of our ordinary ascriptions of attitudes: we are justified in attributing attitudes to creatures as part of an inference to the best explanation of their behavior and whatever else we know about them. Ordinarily, this explanatory basis may coincide, nearly enough, with the verbal basis so emphasized by Davidson and Stich. What the self-attribution experiments do is show how the two bases may diverge.

Having said all that, however, let me now take some of it back. The explanatory strategy I have endorsed can invite the assumption that the verbal basis, being merely one piece of the total evidential story, is entirely subordinate to the full explanatory basis. We are justified in taking a person's saying that p as evidence of her believing that p if and only if the best explanation of her so saying is her so believing. It is hard to take exception to this line if one thinks justification in general involves inference to the best explanation. But strict adherence to it in the case of attitude ascription raises certain difficulties, difficulties that I think provide reason to preserve something like the independent verbal basis that Davidson and Stich suggest.

Consider a participant in Hess' pupillary dilation experiment (in which men are shown to unwittingly prefer women's faces with dilated pupils): he could be moved by the results of the experiment and conclude on that basis that he, too, must have this non-conscious preference and so assert, "(I guess) I prefer faces with dilated pupils," much as someone in psychotherapy might acquiesce to the non-conscious motives ascribed to him by his therapist. But (as the optional use of "I guess" helps make explicit), his *report* of his beliefs or preferences in this way would have to be distinguished from *expressions* of them that he might produce using the very same words. These expressions would not be based upon his acceptance of the explanatory speculations, but would simply be a way of his saying, for example, that he prefers faces with dilated pupils. In the case of the educated neurotic, one wants to distinguish his acquiescence to the ascriptions from his genuinely *admitting* (with, say, the appropriate feelings and "commitment") the ascribed attitudes. In *reporting* a belief, a person makes a first-person attitude ascription from an unusual third-person point of view; *expressing* the belief, whether by saying "p" or "I believe that p," is usually done "directly," from the first-person.

When Stich thinks of a belief as a state that we would normally express by uttering "p," he would seem to be collapsing the third- to this first-person point of view, and with it the difference between reports and expressions. This may be why he finds so little room in his account for the purely explanatory basis suggested by the self-attribution experiments. There is this to be said, though, for taking a person's verbal expressions seriously: as a result of sincerely expressing, and so "committing" herself to certain beliefs and preferences, it would seem that she must *have* those beliefs and preferences, at least "at some level." Indeed, notice that for some purposes we would insist that she does: were she required in a law court to "swear to tell the truth," she wouldn't be swearing to make inferences to the best explanation of her behavior, but only to sincerely *express* "what she believes."[9]

Instead of trying to relieve this tension between the explanatory and verbal bases for ascriptions, perhaps we can simply learn to live with it. Taking seriously the "two sets of books" that Stich fears we keep, let us suppose that a person is a computer having (at least) two sets of addresses: the "central" set, a set of addresses that contains the contents of attitudes that enter into instances of practical reasoning that largely determine one's acts along the lines sketched in chapter 8; and the "avowal" set, a set of special addresses that specifically provides the contents for sincere assertions and other functions in which one is to be taken at one's word (testifying under oath, answering questions on examinations).[10] I shall say that a person *centrally believes* the contents of her central addresses, and that she *avowedly believes* or simply "avows" (explicitly or merely "inwardly"), the contents of her avowal addresses. Note that, on this usage, a person need not actually *say*, or even be easily disposed to *say*, what she may nevertheless avow: although the contents may be accessible for sincere assertion, there could be a number of inadequacies in the speech production system that prevent the contents actually being expressed, even under normal circumstances. Hence, inarticulate adults, pre-linguistic children and speechless animals can avow things.[11]

It should come as no surprise that I think of avowed beliefs (and other similarly expressible attitudes) as beginning to capture the phenomenon of conscious experience.[12] Indeed, it does seem to me that avowed first-person reflexive thoughts begin to capture some of the phenomena of "subjectivity" that have concerned philosophers. However, I don't want yet to press such a proposal. I've hardly

294

provided a satisfactory *definition* of the class of attitudes I have in mind (which, of course, is not surprising for a psychofunctionalist like myself, who expects such a definition to emerge only from a more detailed account of the mind than we presently possess); and I haven't said anything about the astonishing phenomenal world to which any such subjectivity seems to be subject.

11.3   Sensational Sentences

So what, finally, of phenomenal experience? An idea that a number of philosophers have independently developed is that it might be modeled (roughly) on the treatment we accorded first-person-reflexive terms: just as a first-person reflexive thought involves a term restricted to a certain computational role in a person's psychology, so do sensation experiences involve predicates also subject to certain restricted roles.[13] The idea here is that just as "I" thoughts provide a kind of special representation of thoughts about oneself, qualitative experience involves a special representation of thoughts either about the world or about certain of one's internal states (we shall discuss which shortly).

Towards making this idea more concrete, consider a "modular" account of sensory perception. Fodor (1983) and others have proposed that standard sensory experiences, e.g. of sight and sound, involve at least some specially dedicated *modules* that translate various kinds of physical disturbances into standard representations for the brain in a fashion that is rapid, automatic, involuntary, and largely protected from higher information processing (it is "informationally encapsulated"). The standard argument for the existence of such a module in the case of, for example, vision is the persistence of perceptual illusions even for people who know about them: no matter how often and carefully you measure the horizontal lines in the Müller-Lyer illusion (figure 11.1):

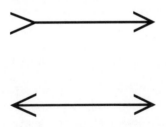

Figure 11.1   Müller-Lyer Illusion.

the top one continues to look longer than the bottom.

Now let us suppose that the output of such sensory modules are special predications subject to restrictions on the internal roles they play, just as first-person-reflexive terms are special singular terms subject to restrictions (I-1)–(I-3).

A first pass at these, what I shall call "S-restrictions" might be as follows (for simplicity, I shall assume that these predicates standardly enter into "object-less" predications, $\ulcorner It(\phi)s \urcorner$, on the model of the English "It rains'; recall also that "comp-X" refers to the computational relation underlying X-ing, in abstraction from its semantic content):

A sensory predication $\ulcorner It(\phi)s \urcorner$ is S-Res(tricted) iff:

(S-1)   it is the output of sensory modules and the input to the comp-thinking system, and can be comp-avowed, normally, *only* in that way; in particular, it cannot be, normally, comp-avowed as a consequence of inferences from outside the module;

(S-2)   each type predication is correlated with specific proximal stimul-ation conditions (and immediately antecedent states of that stimulus system);

(S-3)   the predications are typically parameterized in specific ways: e.g. visual predications apparently are marked for hue, lightness, saturation, and relative position in a 2-dimensional grid; pains for intensity and bodily location;

(S-4)   tokenings of each type of restricted predicate enter into further *characteristic processing* (for a predicate of type ϕ let $\ulcorner CP(\phi) \urcorner$ abbreviate: that such processing characteristic for ϕ actually occurs). This may involve other comp-avowals (e.g. "warm" vs. "cool" colors) and comp-preferences (e.g. to scratch in the case of an itch);

(S-5)   comp-avowed tokenings of these restricted predications provide *sufficient* but *not necessary* conditions for comp-avowed *unrestricted* observation predications (if available).

On this basis, we can now define what it is to have a sensory experience of a certain kind:

(S-DF) x has an F experience iff

$(\exists \phi)(S\text{-}Res(\ulcorner It(\phi)s \urcorner \ \& \ x \ comp\text{-}avows \ \ulcorner It(\phi)s \urcorner \ \& \ CP(\phi) \ \& \ \phi \ means \ [F])$

That is: a sensory experience of type F consists of the processing peculiar to an S-restricted predicate, ϕ, that means [F],[14] a processing that is accompanied by a comp-avowal of the form $\ulcorner It(\phi)s \urcorner$. Thus, for example, a red sensory experience would involve comp-avowing a restricted predication, "It(R)s," as a result of the stimulation of pre-dominantly "red" (or, more exactly, L-wave) sensitive cones,[15] a comp-avowal that, by (S-1) could normally occur only in that way. It is this latter correlation that makes it, by (S-2), a *red* experience, and, by (S-3), one involving the hue, lightness, saturation, and relative position that seems part of that expe-rience. By (S-4), this comp-avowal characteristically causes processing, CP("R"), involving further comp-avowal of "warm," and "advancing" predications. By (S-5), it also provides a sufficient condition for comp-avowing the mentalese translations of, for example, "That looks red," "That feels painful"; i.e. predications that, while they are close to the output of sensory modules, are not subject to these restrictions. However, someone could make these latter *non*-S-restricted comp-avowal without having made the corresponding S-restricted one, just as (to return to the analogy with FPRTs) I could avow that *GR* is bored without avowing that *I* am bored. Presumably this happens often with the color blind, who, on this account, are led to make unrestricted predications about the apparent color of things on other than the usual sensory basis, perhaps, for example, by an inference from a restricted predication that means [It(reflect to degree n)s]. Since hue and comparative reflectivity apparently vary directly in most human environments, such a difference can go unnoticed behaviorally in those environments.[16]

A point we noted in discussing anchored functionalisms early on (§7.2.1) bears emphasis here. Mental states divide into "occurrent" as opposed to merely "dispositional" states, a distinction that functionalist theories often don't bother to observe. Some of the implausibility of particularly functionalist theories of sensations has to do with conceiving them too dispositionally: a pain, after all, isn't merely a disposition to enter certain further states, since pains could persist even when, for some extraneous reason, the actual disposition to cause further mental states were to be interrupted.[17] However, as their assimilation to the "occurrent" processing state of comp-avowing should already make clear, a sensory state on the proposed view is fully activated. Per restriction (S-4), the state involves some "characteristic processing": indeed, it is perhaps best viewed not as a single *state*, but as a *process* involving interactions among a variety of cognitive states. A qualitative experience is presumably a process involving the comp-avowing of a certain restricted predicate, a comparison of it with certain memories, involving restricted and unrestricted predicates and other associations, certain effects upon the non-cognitive (e.g. hormonal) sub-systems, and the production in that and other ways of certain other restricted and unrestricted avowals. (And, of course, much of this processing is probably normally in parallel.) Thus, red *experiences* are thought to be warmer, more advancing, and lighter than green ones.[18]

A related question that is raised but need not be settled by this account is about the nature and extent of "unconscious sensation," as in purported cases of "hemianopia," or "blindsight" in Weiskrantz et al. (1974), and of hypnotic analgesia in Hilgard (1977). Subjects in these experiments seem to be having sensory experiences of which they are unaware. The above definition of "sensing" in (S-DF) requires that the agent (comp-)avow the restricted predication. There was no reason to burden the definition of sensing with a further claim that the predications were also comp-judged).[19] Moreover, for anything that's been said so far, the converse is also possible, that someone might only comp-*judge* a restricted predication without comp-avowing it; it is an advantage of the proposed account that it leaves these possibilities open.[20]

A particularly interesting advantage of a sentential approach to sensations is its capacity for dealing with the phenomena of "seeing as" that is characteristic of much such experience. An elegant example was provided by the physicist Ernest Mach (1914) who noted that an experience of a square can involve precisely the same objective stimuli as an experience of a diamond:

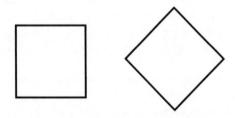

Figure 11.2   Mach's Square and Diamond (after Peacocke 1992:75).

but the experiences will still be different, depending upon how the subject "thinks" of it. I put "think" in scare-quotes, since it's not clear that it's any thing like what we call *thought* that is involved. As Peacocke (1992:75–7) stresses in discussing this example, someone (or perhaps an animal) could distinguish these two experiences without having the *concepts* [square] or [diamond]: they may not be able to reason about squares being equal sided and equal angled, and so might be regarded as lacking those concepts. Indeed, as Peacocke goes on to note:

> Intuitively, the difference between perceiving something as a square and perceiving it as a (regular) diamond is in part a difference in the way the symmetries are perceived. When something is perceived as a diamond, the perceived symmetry is about the bisection of its angles; when . . . as a square . . . about the bisection of its sides.   (1992:76)

But, as Peacocke again emphasizes, someone could have these different experiences without having the concept [symmetrical].

What the sentential approach permits us to do is to claim that a person might well represent, say, the property [square], but without having a representation that expresses the corresponding concept. The person may simply use a simple, restricted predicate, triggered by certain stimulus arrays, that might have the *content* [symmetry] – or [looks symmetrical], see below – but not an unrestricted one that expresses that *concept* and so allows her to *reason* about symmetry in the usual ways (hence the "if available" clause in (S-5)).[21]

11.4 Dealing with Some Standard Puzzles

Any such proposal about the nature of sensory experience is obliged to deal with some of the puzzling phenomena that we discussed in chapter 2. Sensory experiences seems to be peculiarly "private" to the subject of them, who enjoys a special "privileged access" to them, and a special epistemic state of "knowing what it's like" to be in them. I'll deal with each of these issues in turn.

11.4.1 Privacy

The special *privacy* of sensation (see §2.5.4 above) is a consequence of the same kind of restrictions that were placed on first-person reflexive terms. Just as a person can't judge that Sam is bored merely by comp-judging "I am bored," so a person can't avow that things look red to Sam by comp-avowing a restricted predication. According to (S-1) and (S-4), one person comp-avows a restricted predication only when a sensory module is excited in a specific way. At least normally, no other condition is sufficient. In particular, I can't comp-avow a restricted predication merely as a consequence of *your* sensory module being excited, nor can you do so as a consequence of mine, although each of us could comp-avow the corresponding *un*-restricted predications under those circumstances. Nor do either of our own comp-avowals give rise to the characteristic processing in the other. I can think "Things look red to you as they do to me," but not "It's R-ing to you as it does to me."[22] Of course, should two people become so computationally integrated that excitations from one of their modules causes entokenings in the other's central system, we should have some reason to think that they did in face have the "same sensation." But this is not a possibility that will even be clearly definable for most pairs of brains, any more than it is for arbitrary pairs of computers.[23]

11.4.2 Privileged access

The special privileges of knowing one's own state by and large fall out as features of a restricted predicate's characteristic processing. Insofar as they involve some further, usually second-order cognitive state, or disposition to acquire such a state, they are intimately tied to the sensational state itself: e.g. if x is in pain then x believes/knows of herself that she is in pain, and/or conversely. Any such state may simply be *included* in the characteristic processing of the restricted predicate associated with the state: the experience of pain may well include the avowal that one is (and perhaps the distinct preference that one no longer be).[24]

Indeed, what is perhaps the strongest argument for some kind of functionalist story is that it provides the right and even an illuminating account of the usual first-person privileges. Any non-functionalist account – i.e. any account that makes the connection between a sensory state and a thought that one has it, less tight, as in, for example, the biologistic and dualistic proposals – risks what seems to me intolerable first-person skepticism. If qualia are non-functionally defined objects, then their attachment to their role in my thought would seem to be *metaphysically accidental*. At any rate, it would seem metaphysically possible for me to *think* that I have one (of a certain kind) without it *being* one (of that kind); and for me to *have* one (of a certain kind) without *thinking* I do. For all I know now, what seems to me clearly a green experience is actually a red one, what seems to me a sharp pain is actually a tickle, what seems to me to be the sound of a Beethoven quartet is actually the smell of skunk. Indeed, *I might not have any qualia at all*! I might only *think* I do; but then how am I – or anyone – to know?

Worse, it would seem to be possible for there to be an *introspectively undetectable anaesthetic*: in principle, a surgeon could deprive you of the non-functional property, whatever it is, while leaving your functional cognitive system intact. *You* wouldn't be able to tell "from the inside": you would still avow that you're in, say, excruciating pain, but be assured by the surgeon that, having deprived you of the non-functional property, you were no long "really in pain." As Dennett (1978) writes about a similar case:

> It appears that [such a victim] will not know the difference, for after all, . . . he believes he in pain, he finds he is not immune to torture, he gladly takes aspirin and tells us, in one way or another, of the relief it produces. I would not want to take on the task of telling him how fortunate he was to be lacking the *je ne sais quoi* that constitutes real pain.   (1978:220).

While there seems to be some room for error in our qualitative thoughts, if such errors cannot be cashed out in terms of further comparisons and avowals I would make, it is utterly mysterious what I should be taken to be mistaken about.

11.4.3 *"What it's like"*

Lastly, there is the now well-worn problem of "knowing what it's like" (§2.6). As many writers have emphasized,[25] such "knowledge" may be more a matter of an *ability*: more a matter, for example, of *imagination* than of *cognition*. Comp-imagining, we surely have every reason to suppose, is a different relation from either comp-judging or comp-avowing: comp-judgments are the basis for action (the input to the decision system), and comp-avowings the basis for verbal expressions of belief, where mere comp-imaginings presumably are not. Roughly, to comp-imagine X-ing seems to involve being able to produce in certain addresses, protected from immediate consequences for action, many of the restricted predications that might result from actually X-ing. I can imagine what it's like to be on the coast at Big Sur, since I can comp-imagine many of the restricted predications that would be released by the sun, air, surf, and cliffs were I actually there. This is made particularly easy for me since I can remember (and so comp-remember many of the predications caused by) being there. But memory doesn't seem to be essential. Apparently, Stephen Crane in his novel, *The Red Badge of Courage*, provided what, according to veterans, were accurate depictions of what it was like to be in war, despite never having been in one; depictions that in turn seem to produce in readers similar comp-imaginings.

Thus, Nagel's and Jackson's problems of "Knowing what it's like to X" are the difficulties of being able to comp-imagine the restricted predications that are typically produced by X-ing. Insofar as we don't share such predications with bats, we can't know what it's like for them. The inability is not mysterious, but merely computational. Of course, the fact that we do not automatically enter such states as a result merely of learning an explanatory account of what goes on when one X-es is no argument against the truth or adequacy of that account. I don't need to have a heart attack in order to have a completely adequate account of heart attacks; nor do I have to be able to x (or be able to imagine, or "know what it's like" to X) in order to have a completely adequate theory of X-ing.

11.5 What is Represented in Sensation?[26]

CRTQ treats sensing as a species of propositional attitudes and/or the processing of them. As such, it is an attempt to vindicate another thesis associated with Brentano: that all *mental* phenomena are *intentional*, i.e. *representational* phenomena.[27] Besides its interest as a *possible* account of qualitative experience, one positive argument for this view as an *actual* account is that, by assimilating phenomenal experience to attitudes, we explain the essential *unity* of the mind, what it is that makes beliefs, desires, memories, hopes, fears, and sensations all states of *the same sort of entity*. We'll see that alternative views lack this unity.

Another interest of this approach is that it underwrites the independently plausible irreferentialist solution (§5.2.1–5.2.2) to the problem of phenomenal objects and properties that otherwise present peculiar metaphysical problems of spatiality (§2.5.3). Instead of treating phenomenal properties as some sort of real properties possessed by either queer things in some dualistic world or by physical things in some queer way, the suggestion is to treat them as simply a species of *intentional-objects and properties*. Instead of being special properties of the representation, they are simply properties of what the representation purports to represent. Our apparent descriptions of our experience are really merely *expressions* of it.

However, such treatment does require some account of just what the *intentional content* of an experience might be, as well as of why we don't ordinarily think of experience in this way. Shoemaker (1990) voices what many intuitively feel:

> [W]hat I like about [gustatory experiences of wine] is not that they have a certain intentional content, not that they are produced by certain sense organs (and are in that sense gustatory), and not a combination of these. What I like about them is what it is like to have them – and it is just saying the same thing in another way to say that what I like about them is their qualitative or phenomenal character, which must be distinguished from their intentional content. (1990:115)

Shoemaker is responding to the suggestion of Harman's (1990) that we cited in §5.2.2, which also advocates treating phenomenal properties as merely intentional. But it is important to notice the particular intentional content that Harman identifies with that of sensory experience:

> When you see a tree, you do not experience any features as intrinsic features of your experience. Look at a tree and try to turn your attention to intrinsic features of your visual experience. I predict you will find that the only features there to turn your attention to will be features of the presented tree, including relational features of the tree "from here." (1990:39)

The properties he selects are properties of *external* objects, "features of the presented tree" (cf. also Dretske 1995). He seems to assume that if philosophers think that experience doesn't involve reference to *external* properties, that they must have in mind "intrinsic" properties *of the representation* itself, and not properties of what gets represented. And it's certainly true that some philosophers (e.g. Jackson 1982, Nagel 1974/1991), take the properties of inner sensory experience to be the paradigms of non-physical, dualistic properties; and for others more materialistically inclined (e.g. Block 1978, Shoemaker 1981/1984, Loar 1996)[28] they are some neural or biological property of the realizer of a functional structure. After Dennett (1991), I shall call these latter philosophers (whether dualist or materialist) "qualiaphiles," invoking the word "qualia" as neutral between phenomenal objects or properties.

But Harman is presenting us with a wrong prediction and a false dichotomy. I think we can attend to "intrinsic" properties of our experience, but without indulging in qualiaphilia and regarding those properties as properties of the representation. "Intrinsic" properties themselves could be *intentional*-properties, i.e. properties specified in the *content* of the representation – and still not be properties actually instantiated anywhere, either in the world or in the mind.

Unfortunately, however, the issues here are much obscured by what seems to be a serious ambiguity in much of our vocabulary in describing experience. *Ordinarily we describe our experiences in the same terms with which we describe the external world.* For example, we might well describe both a tomato and an after-image as "red"; and in the above examples of squares and diamonds, it can seem natural to describe the experience using just those terms, "square" and "diamond." But a moment's thought (or, anyway, some of the problems we discussed in §2.5.3) shows we at least ought to be cautious here: whatever a "red after-image" might be, *it* isn't *colored* in the way tomatoes and barns are (it doesn't reflect light, it doesn't cause similar experiences in others, etc).[29] It is this ambiguity of sensation predicates that plagues discussions of the old question about whether a tree falling in an uninhabited forest does or doesn't make a sound.

In addition to being intuitively appealing, there are a number of reasons for insisting upon some sort of "internal" sense of introspective vocabulary. Firstly, if one adopted an *externalist* semantics for color words, so that "red" referred to whatever property *in the world* stood in the right causal relation to tokens of it (as in §9.2), there could be cases, analogous to "Twin-Earth" cases of "water" (§9.1.3), in which two molecular duplicates could use "red" to refer to different external properties.[30] Should we say that their *experiences* are different just because these external causes, and therefore the semantics of the words with which they describe them, are different? Perhaps. But one doesn't want to rush to this surprising conclusion simply because of this inner/outer ambiguity in our use of color words. Another possibility to be considered is that, while the use of "red" to refer to *outer* objects might well be tied to external causes, its use to describe one's inner experience is *not*: consequently, although these twins are describing *different external* properties in their different worlds, in their use of "red" to describe their *internal* experience, they are describing *the same* phenomenon. After all, many might claim: the character of one's inner experience depends (or "supervenes") only upon facts *inside* one's skin; not on facts *outside* of it. One doesn't *feel* differently *just because* one might have been transported to a different external environment in which, because of relations to different external phenomena, the semantics of one's words has changed.

Secondly, some kind of "inner" phenomenon seems apt for the intentional content of our restricted predicates. Consider again the Mach example of squares and diamonds. If "outer" square and diamond were what our experience was about, then it's a puzzle why both predicates aren't equally triggered by both stimuli – after all, both stimuli are both square and diamond shaped. Indeed, we can *think* that *both those* concepts apply to both shapes; but, despite that fact, both stimuli don't *look* equally square and diamond shaped; and it's the *look*, not the *thought*, that would seem to be the content of a visual experience. Moreover, in some cases, there would seem to be no *possible* property *of the world* we are representing, as in the case of many of Escher's prints and the impossible figures, for example, figure 3, discussed by Gregory (1970):[31]

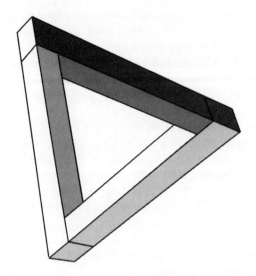

Figure 11.3   An Impossible Object (after Gregory 1966:227).

These considerations seem to me to undermine Harman's prediction about what we can attend to in our experience. They suggest that we should at least *allow* that phenomenal predicates, and thereby our introspected experience, *could* purport to refer to the property people take themselves to be experiencing when they are thinking about *themselves* in the above way, apart from their environment. "S" could purport to refer not to *square* but to *looking square*; "R" not to worldly redness, but to *looking red*, i.e. to the property a person ordinarily thinks she is experiencing as a causal consequence in our world (although not necessarily in all other worlds) of external redness. These "phenomenal" properties plausibly form the content of the restricted predicates whose activation constitutes our sensory experience.[32] It is when we attend to these contents that experience seems to consist in a veil of lively properties whose relation to the physical world seems so baffling.

Of course, as already emphasized, restricted predicates do not provide a conceptually rich way of expressing those properties (as others[33] have put a related point, they have "non-conceptual content"): although their *wide* content is the same as that of "property a person ordinarily thinks she is experiencing as a causal consequence in our world (although not necessarily in all other worlds) of external redness," their *narrow* content differs. This narrow content is provided merely by the restricted roles they play, much as the narrow content of "I" is provided by *its* role. And it's the narrow content of an experience that provides at least a crucial component of its intentional content.[34]

11.6   Are Qualia Real?

However, even if we can perfectly well attend to inner phenomenal properties, this doesn't for a moment entail that those properties are "intrinsic properties of the representation" of the sort that Harman rightly fears qualiaphiles take them to be. Indeed, the "intrinsic" properties of experience are intentional-properties, mere *constituents of the contents* of our experience, then they risk not being real (or, anyway, no more real than the property of being a winged horse, or a round square). But this does strike many people as outrageous. It seems as if it's one thing to deny the existence of phenomenal objects, quite another to deny the existence of *the very properties in which our experience seems to consist*. Knowledge of them can seem to be what distinguishes the color-sighted from the color-blind; they seem to enter into the well-confirmed laws relating perceived to actual stimulus amplitudes;[35] and for some, they can seem to be what makes life worth living at all. And one might think that they are precisely the sort of property that my sentential account invites as the referents of restricted predicates.

But such reference is an invitation that we saw in §5.1 it is possible to resist. Many predications might function in a language without there really being a property corresponding to the predicate.[36] One needs to ask whether the property postulated in addition to the predicate is required to do any explanatory work. I submit that in the present case the restricted predicates, their wide and narrow intentional content (the latter determined by the restrictions on their deployment), are all we need. After all, we still have the *states*: they are simply intentionally characterized. Intentionally characterized states could well be what distinguish the color-sight from the color-blind and enter into all manner of lawful relations with external stimuli. Psychophysical laws that relate "sensations" to external stimuli could be taken to relate not real to mysterious phenomenal properties, but simply *real* to mentally *represented* amplitudes, indeed, amplitudes as they are represented in the output of sensory modules, i.e. restricted sensory predications. And it's hard to see why life would be any more or less worth living depending on whether the representational state that is the object of one's sensory attitude really represents a quale or not. To think so would be a little like being an obsessive realist about paintings, insisting that a painting was beautiful only if *it actually did represent something real*. It's important to remember that, for anything that has been said so far, *intentionally characterized sensory states lacking real qualia may be every bit as intense, awful, or wonderful as any such states possessing them*! Indeed, one would be hard put introspectively to distinguish them – only your neurophysiologist (or expert epiphenomenalist) would know for sure. It may *seem* as though there is a rich panoply of phenomenal properties we are experiencing when we enjoy a day at the beach or a fine glass of wine – but that's *enough*: why insist that in addition to it seeming this way, that there actually *be* such a panoply?

An analogy that I think sheds light not only on qualia but on much of the debate between dualism and materialism is provided by the movies. Imagine that someone from a non-Western culture who has never seen or heard of movie theaters strolls inadvertently into one. She sits down and watches the proceedings (to avoid complications introduced by real actors, let us suppose it is a Mickey Mouse cartoon). She becomes interested in Mickey Mouse, so interested that, when he disappears from the screen, she attempts to pursue him.[37] Of course, her attempts would soon be frustrated by the presence of the screen: she would try to follow him out of it, only to notice that she can't possibly (as she might put it) "enter" it.

Imagine, now, the possible theories she might conceive: they are not unlike traditional theories of mind and body. She might first suppose that there is some mysterious space, like, but fundamentally different from physical space, in which such creatures as Mickey, Minnie, and their properties exist. This of course would certainly prove to be a limitation on physical theory: these creatures in this special space appear to interact with creatures in physical space – else how could she see them? And yet they seem to be inaccessible to those latter creatures in ways that physical theory can't explain. Finding that hypothesis too extravagant, she might try to be an identity theorist: but then she would notice that the identifications are very puzzling. There are Leibniz Law difficulties: does she really want to say that this set of dots on the screen loves that set? That the one set kissed the other set and then got slapped? And then there is the problem of multiple realizability: Mickey Mouse seems also to appear on canvas screens, wallpaper, tee-shirts, ... In the end the best thing for our stranger to do, of course, is to learn about the theory of projectors and the illusions they induce in us, special spaces and weird identifications be hanged: obviously when people talk about Mickey Mouse they are not meaning to refer to anything real. Of course, on that view, alas, Mickey Mouse simply doesn't exist. He only *appears* to, as a result of the interaction between the light, the screen, and the viewer (the viewer is put into a state a little like that of actually seeing a mouse . . .). Mickey Mouse and Minnie Mouse are not *real objects*; their kissing is not a real relation, nor are Mickey's happiness or embarrassment real properties in the world. They are simply part of the intentional content of the movie. Similarly, the apparent objects and properties of qualitative experience are simply part of the intentional content of the restricted predicates whose processing constitutes our experience.

Is this view *eliminativist* or *irreferentialist*? Well, it could be taken entirely irreferentially in the manner of §5.2.2: the claims we make about our experience, for example, that our after-images are green or our pains stabbing, could be taken to be merely expressive classifications of experiences according to their intentional content, much as one can classify cartoons in terms of being about Mickey Mouse and his embarrassed love for Minnie. Taken in this way, the claims are *true*. But if one took such claims to be *more* than classificatory, and to be purporting to refer to real things or properties – after-images, phenomenal colors – then the claims are false, and there is a point to being an eliminativist about them; just as there would be a point in telling the stranger to our movies that, no, there are no such mice, and there were no real episodes of embarrassed love between them. But the movies, no less our experiences, could be just as amusing, intense, or boring as if there were.

11.6.1   Reasons for CRTQ and denying qualia

In this denial of the reality of qualia, CRTQ can seem so counter-intuitive, it is worth summarizing some of the reasons that can be adduced for it:

(1)   while CRTQ may not exactly explain why experience has the particular qualities it has – CRTQ denies there are any qualities there to explain – it does go some way towards explaining why people *think* their experience has those qualities. Experience is presented with just such contents. It would certainly seem to make such thoughts unsurprising: they are just the thoughts one would expect any system that processed restricted predicates in the prescribed way would have. Of course, one thinks one is sensing a real internal red, just as one might think one is seeing a (peculiar sort of) mouse in watching a Mickey Mouse cartoon: that's precisely the content of those experiences! Moreover:

(2)   as we noted in discussing privileged access, the postulation of *further* phenomenal properties or qualia *distinct* from (and presumably the referents of) these intentional contents undermines the privileged access we ordinarily presume a person has to their qualitative states. Some people might in fact have the phenomenal properties attached to their states; others might only *think* they do. Who cares? Indeed, as we noted, the postulation of such further properties raises a possibility of first-person skepticism, but also the prospect of an introspectively undetectable anaesthetic.

(3)   we seem to have no non-tendentious evidence for their postulation: everything that can be explained by their postulation can be explained more clearly by the specific computational/representational states alone. Phenomenal objects and properties are no more needed to explain the (non-tendentiously described) workings of our mind than are angels needed to explain the motion of the planets. They are, to use a nice phrase Wittgenstein (1953) used precisely in this connection, "a wheel that can be turned though nothing else moves with it" (§271).[38]

(4)   the postulation of further phenomenal properties produces many of the problems – about spatiality, privacy – that we encountered in chapter 2 but which we observed above aren't problems for CRTQ: the sense of spatiality is produced by the specific contents of certain predications that encode "phenomenal" space; the "privacy" consists in the fact that this coded space is not one to which others – or even oneself, given its unreality – have any access. And sensory *states* are private just in the way that thoughts that essentially involve a predication subject to computational restrictions would inevitably be.

307

(5)   some phenomenal properties are *impossible*, for example, those represented in figure 11.3. One could, of course, postulate a world of properties that couldn't possibly be instantiated – *being a round square*, a *spherical cube, wise and not wise, even and odd* – but, for lack of any independent motivation for such postulations, this seems like property profligacy, gratuitous metaphysics;

(6)   lastly, to return to the "second Brentano thesis" with which I began this section, the sentential treatment of qualitative experience helps explain the essential *unity* of the mind: qualitative experience is just a particular species of propositional attitudes; and propositional attitudes are computational relations to representations in fairly integrated computational systems. Rival accounts lack this unity. For example, the biologistic or dualistic accounts that regard qualia either as biological or as entirely non-physical properties of a computationally organized brain have trouble explaining how a mind that thinks by computing manages to feel by being in some as yet unspecified relation to such further properties.

11.6.2*   Kripke's Cartesian argument answered

The denial of the reality of qualia also permits a surprisingly concessive, but still materialist response to Kripke's ingenious version of Descartes' argument against materialism that we discussed in §2.5.7. Kripke's argument, recall, proceeded as follows:

(K1)   The very thing that is pain P is necessarily painful, just as the very thing that is a stone is necessarily matter;

(K2)   The very thing that is brain state B is not necessarily painful, just as the very thing that is a stone is not necessarily a doorstop.

therefore

(K3)   The very thing that is pain P ≠ the very thing that is brain state B.

Now, I want to argue that the plausibility of (K1) turns entirely on precisely what one takes "pain" to be. If it is a phenomenal object, and being painful is a phenomenal property, then I am prepared to think that (K1) is true: *pains* in that sense *are* essentially painful, just as cats are necessarily cats: if something that was a cat ceased being a cat then, arguably, *it* would cease to exist. If it's a cat in this world, it's a cat in all possible worlds.[39] Or, anyway, a fairly clear contrast can be drawn between what might be called such "deep kind" terms (which Kripke would regard as "rigid designators," naming the *same thing* in all possible worlds) and "role" terms like, say, "president" ("non-rigid designators," which name *different things* in all possible worlds). Whereas it's hard to imagine (apart from fairy tales, where *anything* is possible) cats surviving their ceasing to be cats, presidents can quite easily cease being presidents – it happens all the time! For example, *that very thing*, Ronald Reagan, who was a president, continued to exist even after he ceased being the president. But could Tabby really survive failing to be cat? Only, it would seem, if she was never in fact a cat in the first place. Just so, says Kripke: "pain" is a "deep kind" word, and consequently a pain could not survive failing to be a pain:

> Thus [contingent identity theories] assert that a certain pain X might have existed yet not have been a pain. This seems to me self-evidently absurd. Imagine any pain: is it possible that *it itself* could have existed, yet not have been a pain? (1981:146 n. 1)

But, it would seem, a *particular brain-state* could survive failing to be a pain: some stimulation of c-fibers, or some 40 Hz oscillation could continue to occur, even though the organism is in fact quite dead.[40]

So (K1) is plausible on the assumption that pain is a phenomenal object. However, I claimed in the previous section that there is no reason to posit such objects; the *state* of *being in pain*, and in particular standing in the appropriate computational relations to a suitably restricted predication will suffice.[41] If "pain," taken loosely, can be taken to refer to such a *state*, then (K1) is by no means obviously true: why should we believe that this very state of being a pain is necessarily such a state, that *it* couldn't survive ceasing to be a pain? Kripke's insistence that "pain (state)" is a "deep kind" term, not a "role" term, simply denies what the functionalist is asserting. Functionalism just is the view that mental terms in general should be understood as *role* words, and we saw in chapters 5–7 that there was considerable reason to take such a proposal seriously. Indeed, it has been the burden of our discussion since chapter 8 that a specific functionalist hypothesis, CRTQ, offered the best framework for a mentalistic psychology that anyone has ever proposed. Kripke owes us an argument that (K1) really is true, when "pain" is taken in this broader way to refer to a functional state of being in pain.

Moreover, as with any mere insistence on linguistic intuitions, it's always open to the functionalist to give Kripke the word "pain." Suppose pain states were indeed necessarily pain states; so much the worse, one could say, for the concept [pain state]: it's as badly off as the concept of pain as a phenomenal object. What exist instead are "functional-pain states." They'll do all the explanatory work of "pain" states without the further modal commitments. If they will, then what reason does Kripke or anyone have to apply the old notion? Maybe, for all its appearance of enjoying certain certitudes, the notion is just as mistaken as other old notions about the mind, such as an immortal soul, or reason that transcends any physical constraints. To make this more than a verbal issue, Kripke needs to

309

show that the old notion has some important explanatory work to do. That, I submit, he cannot do.

11.7   Further Problems

Given all the above attractions of CRTQ, why do so many people (including myself) find it difficult to accept?[42] Well, it does seem frankly incredible, despite the above arguments, that merely the right program for manipulating representations could eventuate in the richness of our conscious experience. And there remain two problems that give voice to this intuition, pointing to a possible lack not only in CRTQ, but in most any functionalist account. The first is a version of the old chestnut about "reverse qualia"; the other, the problem of "absent qualia," occasioned by the possibility of arbitrary realizations of CRTQ that is both the pride and the despair of most any functionalist account.

11.7.1   Reverse qualia and other functional isomorphisms

"Couldn't one person see red where another person sees green?" This possibility occurs to many people spontaneously during childhood, and is supported by the following observation:

> color experience is a function of three basic features: hue, brightness, and saturation. Color quality space can be modeled then as a three dimensional solid; in fact, a cone. The vertical dimension represents brightness, the horizontal represents saturation, and the circular dimension represents hue. Given this model, there seems to be a mapping of points in the space onto their complements around an axis that bisects the cone through the middle. Reds would be mapped onto greens, blues onto yellows, etc. The resulting cone would be isomorphic to the original in the sense that all the distance/similarity relations among points would be maintained.   (Levine (forthcoming))

Now, suppose there existed a pair of glasses that produced this rotation in our experience, switching every color with its complement – red with green, yellow with blue. And now suppose these were implanted surreptitiously as contact lenses in an infant's eyes at birth. Wouldn't the infant grow up thinking and speaking like the rest of us, about roses being red and violets blue, but in fact be having, therefore, the complementary experiences?

Such "reverse spectrum" cases need to considered very gingerly. For starters, we need to distinguish such cases as they might arise as an objection against an analytic behaviorist (ABist), and as they might arise for a fully functionalist theory like CRTQ. Recall that ABism (§5.3) is motivated essentially by *epistemological* concerns, specifically a verificationism that in general ties the nature of a phenomenon to the evidence adducible for it (§5.4). Most forms of functionalism are *not* so motivated.[43] Their motivation is *metaphysical*: e.g. what sort of state could do the work that mental states are supposed to do, and how might they supervene on the physical world? Indeed, it is because it is a reasonable metaphysical conjecture that qualitative states supervene on the states of an agent's *brain* that we are entitled to take seriously the possibility of reverse qualia in the merely *behavioral* case of *external lenses* implanted from birth: we have reason to suppose that the subject's brain would be in a relevantly similar state to us when we wear the lenses, despite her otherwise speaking and behaving normally. However, when we imagine cases in which people are not only *behaviorally* indistinguishable, but have *functionally* indistinguishable brains, that presumption is no longer reasonable: if qualitative states supervene on the brain, then a change in its functional organization could *well* entail a change in them. It all depends upon *which* functional features are supposed to be relevant to *which* qualitative experiences. And who of us is able to say what those might be?

At any rate, the possibility of qualitative reversals for *functionally identical* creatures is not nearly as obvious as it can reasonably be claimed to be for merely *behaviorally* identical ones. The burden is on the skeptic about the functional analysis to produce a reason for supposing that this possibility is a real one. Until such a reason is provided, the postulation of the *metaphysical* possibility of CRTQ-transcendent qualia seems as gratuitous as the supposition of role-transcendent political properties, for example, that some senator "really is" a congressman, despite there being absolutely no difference in his political role (how he is elected, how he votes) from a normal senator.

However, as Ned Block has pointed out to me, although it may be difficult for the skeptic to mount a positive case, setting out in detail two functionally isomorphic brain states that could correspond to two different qualitative ones, there is still a problem for (most) any functionalist theory like CRTQ insofar as it can't *rule* such a possibility *out*. Functionalist theories, after all, purport to be strategies for the ultimate *analysis* of mental phenomena. If, according to CRTQ, qualitative states are specified entirely by computational roles, then the apparent, epistemic possibility of qualia reversals with respect to computational roles cannot be a genuine metaphysical possibility. But at this point how can we be in a position to establish such a claim? What, aside from philosophical prejudice, do we know about the mind that rules out the possibility of the computational role for one restricted predicate being perfectly isomorphic with that of another, their "characteristic processing," for example, displaying precisely the same *pattern* of causes and effects? Ramsify that pattern and you would come up with the same Ramsey sentence in both cases, just as it was once feared ramsifying positrons would yield the same Ramsey sentence as ramsifying electrons (§6.3.1). It would seem to be simply an accident, if it's true at all, that there aren't such states.

Color is not the only example philosophers have used for such functional isomorphs. As Bealer (1984) has ingeniously showed, many of the examples Quine (1960:chapter 2) marshaled as cases of indeterminate translation – say, "There's a rabbit" vs. "Rabbithood is again instantiated" (see §2.1 and §9.2.4) – could as well be raised in a functionalist one. Now, again, at this still early point in psychology, it's not as though we should take Bealer, much less Quine to have exhausted the possible differences in functional role that might be relevant to distinguishing the different contents.[44] But, again, the issue is not whether this or that example can be made to work, but *what reason is there to suppose at this point that no such case could ever be produced?*

We seem, then, to be left with still a trace of Levine's explanatory gap (§2.1): insofar as there could be functional isomorphs of different qualitative and intentional states, our functional descriptions of a system don't yet fully *necessitate* being in one specific qualitative or intentional state or the other. Perhaps it's some consolation to CRTQ that supplementing it with any other property doesn't seem to help. As Levine (1983) emphasizes, the same gap appears between *any* non-mental property – whether physical or functional – and the respective qualitative or intentional one.

Moreover, were we presented with such a case of isomorphism, it's not clear what we should do with it. As in the imagined case of electrons and positrons, we would have to *indexically* pick out one of the two properties that happen to be functional isomorphs: that is, we appeal in our definition to the one kind of element a functional definition cannot include, a demonstrative that points to the particular occupier of a role, and no longer to the property of being a particular role itself (§6.3.1). Functionalism about qualia would be an "anchored functionalism" (§7.2.1), anchored in some particular realization. But the victory of the qualiaphile here would seem pyrrhic: we have no reason to suppose that whether one had picked that property or its functional isomorph would make any difference whatsoever to our introspective lives, how things seem to us, the comparisons we make, what we love or loathe, relish or disdain.[45] For all these latter facts would presumably be capturable by functional/computational role. The further indexed property would seem to involve a distinction without a real difference, much as a positron world would be only technically different from the usual electron one. The temptation, of course, would be to suppose that one has some *special epistemic access* to them, that one is "directly acquainted" with them, in some fashion unmediated by fallible representations.[46] But, of course, the mere possibility of functional isomorphs establishes no such thing.

However, there is a worse problem, also pressed by Block.

11.7.2   *Arbitrary realizability and absent qualia*

In the above discussion, we considered the problem of reverse qualia as it arises among human beings. Within the anticipated circle of readers, it is pretty safe to assume that no serious questions arise about which of them are persons.[47] When we pass beyond humans, however, no such agreement can be presumed. But CRTQ could most surely have non-human realizations, at least some of which most readers[48] wouldn't count as persons, indeed, as having any consciousness or qualitative states at all. Perhaps the most famous example of such a realization is Block's (1980a) example of arranging the nation of China so that it realizes a person's functional architecture. For simplicity, let as assume (what is assumed by many functionalist neuropsychologists) that all of a person's psychology supervenes on the patterns of firing among the billion neurons of the brain. Essentially what Block imagines is arranging for the billion inhabitants of China to send radio signals to one another in precisely the same pattern, on precisely the same contingencies on which the billion neurons in the brain send electrical impulses to one another. There can be no doubt that this would be extremely difficult to coordinate, and we would have to supply each Chinese citizen with some efficient filing system for presenting the right response when provided with a particular input. The important point is that such a system seems in principle possible. But then the problem is: would the whole nation of China thereby become the realization of a conscious mind, passing through all the mental states of the person whose brain was in this way being emulated? Most people understandably balk at the suggestion. This is the "absent-qualia" problem: couldn't there be systems like this that realized the functional organization of a functionalist psychology like CRTQ, but lacked any qualitative (and maybe even any other) mental states?

There have been many attempts to reply to Block's example. Some have stressed the incredible complexity of bringing off the Chinese emulation; others point out that we might have the same intuitive response were we to think of the brain on exactly the same scale as China. Indeed, Leibniz noted (in an early expression of an explanatory gap):

> Supposing that there were a machine whose structure produced thought, sensation, and perception; we could conceive it as increased in size with the same proportions until one was able to enter into its interior as he would into a mill. Now, on going into it he would find only pieces working on one another, but never would he find anything to explain perception. (1714/1962:§17)

Despite this thought experiment, most of us are prepared to regard our brain as nevertheless providing at least the basis for a mental life; if for the brain, why not for the nation of China?[49]

Although I think there is much to be said for these replies, they seem to me to miss the point of Block's example, which is the suspicion that many of us have that, somehow, somewhere, there has to be some constraint on what will count as a realization of a mind; *but that it's extremely difficult to see what a principled basis for such a constraint might be.* As Block (1980a:§3) points out, theories in this domain run the conflicting risks of being either too "liberal," including too many realizations as minds, or too "chauvinistic," including too few. Again, we seem to need an "anchored" functionalism, but, so long as we include "ourselves" (whoever these may include), there seems no good reason to cast our anchor at any one point rather than another. One thing that doesn't seem likely is that anyone is going to produce a *scientific* reason: at least, it's extremely hard to think of any non-tendentious – non-question-begging – evidence that could be adduced to rule out some realizations and not others. (But see Lycan 1981.)

11.7.3   Behavioral chauvinism

In an interesting passage, Wittgenstein (1953) also addresses (a version of) this problem. But he seems to rely on something very nearly amounting to an uncritical species chauvinism:

> But a machine surely could not think! – Is that an empirical statement? No. We only say of a human being and what is like one that it thinks . . . only of a living human being and what resembles (behaves like) a living human being can one say: it sees; is blind; hears; is deaf; is conscious or unconscious.   (1953:§359–60; §281; §283)

Although these remarks have a force that ought not be lightly dismissed, they do seem indefensible on reflection. Surely we have every reason to suppose that a certain look and behavior is largely *accidental* to the possession of a conscious state: as many have remarked, there could be creatures with mental lives who don't look or act like humans (e.g. someone disfigured and paralyzed from an accident;[50] a creature from a remote, perhaps parallel biology), and there could be things that look and act like humans that turn out to be cleverly contrived fakes (marionettes controlled electronically from Mars). In any case, we need an *argument* to restrict mental concepts in this way.[51]

Despite these defects in Wittgenstein's remarks, I nevertheless think that there's an important truth in them, a truth which, although it may not *justify* our reactions to the "absent qualia" cases, at least may explain them. Unlike the question of which things are "solid," the question of which things have a genuinely conscious life, experiencing pain, joy, sorrow, love has considerable importance for us outside of scientific explanation. Minds matter in a way that mere matter doesn't. We aren't willing to be simply "good scientists" about the mind, and concede to computational psychologists that the appropriately arranged people of China could form a mind, in the way that we might indifferently concede to chemists that glass is a liquid. There are not only the *moral* issues of chauvinism (racism, sexism), but issues tied to deep facts about how, in a pretty fixed and fundamental way, we react and feel about only certain kinds of creatures, what we get attached to, what we care about, which, not surprisingly, is focused upon things that look and act like our conspecifics. These reactions are so stable and involuntary[52] that they cause us to project a property into them correlative to these reactions in ourselves – but not into things, like computers, windmills, or the nation of China, that do not induce that reaction. We may not really be able to give up these reactions, or even the projection of what we might call these "strong," computationally transcendent properties. They may be too deeply rooted as a part of our biological and social lives, and we may not be able to give them up any more than we seem to be able to give up our conception of a "strong" personal identity criticized by Parfit (1984), or the kind of free-will that Kant and others have tried so hopelessly to save. And so we don't give up expecting somehow to find some appropriate property of just the creatures that induce this reaction in us, despite the lack of any independent reason for supposing it exists, or really any idea of how this projection is to be seriously applied. Perhaps our moral conceptions of ourselves depend upon this projection. But it would seem that no genuinely explanatory claim does.[53]

Indeed, from an *explanatory* view, despite these latter problems, all that seems essential to the possession of a mind are specific computational processes defined over representations. That, at any rate, has been the main contention of this book.

Notes

1 One reason for distinguishing CRTQ from CRTT is to not burden CRTT or its proponents with these extensions, some of which even Fodor has regarded as carrying the Language of Thought too far (despite the bravado of the epigraph at his 1975:197).

2 And there are many available. For views not far from those defended here, see Lycan (1987) and Tye (1992); for contrastng views, see Hill (1991), Strawson (1994), Block (1995).

3 Still others, e.g. Peacocke (1992:chapter 6), might insist that the concept of belief is rooted in first person reflection. More on this shortly (§11.2.2).

4 In order to separate and not beg any questions, I will use this term in a way that does not entail consciousness itself. On this usage someone could be unconsciously self-conscious (i.e. unconsciously self-reflective), in a way that I'm prepared to believe most people regularly are.

5 The convention is Casteneda's (1966). See also Frege (1965) and Perry (1979) for discussion.

6 The actual history of the ideas is somewhat the reverse of their presentation here: "two factor theories" have as part of their inspiration Kaplan's (1979) pioneering work on indexicals of at least natural language, wherein he distinguishes the "character" from the "content" of an expression. The following suggestion about first-person reflexive thoughts is an obvious application of his suggestion about natural language to expressions in a language of thought.

7 I present these conditions as *sufficient*; I suspect that they are not entirely necessary. The echoes of Kant's "Transcendental Synthetic Unity of Apperception" (1781/ 1968:B131ff) are not coincidental.

8 Or consider Laing et al.'s (1966) hypothesis about the psychology of family dynamics:

> From the point of view of the subject, the starting point is often between the second and third level of perspective. Jill thinks that Jack thinks that she does not love him, that she neglects him, that she is destroying him, and so on, although she says that she does not think she is doing any of these things. . . . She may express fears lest he think that she thinks he is ungrateful to her for all she is doing, when she wants him to know that she does *not* think that he thinks that she thinks he thinks she does not do enough.   (pp. 30–1)

These sorts of deeply nested thoughts probably affect our behavior efficiently only so long as we are *not* struggling to make ourselves conscious of them. In any case, the authors also go on to cite examples of responses on Rorschach and intelligence tests in which, they argue, the responses were often affected by "reciprocal" perspectives of which the subjects were unaware (pp. 42–4).

Another problem with an HOT account like Rosenthal's is that it appears to entail the possibility of a peculiar anaesthetic: simply persuade yourself of eliminativism, *et voila*, you're unconscious! After all, if you really are convinced there are no thoughts, then *a fortiori*, you don't think *you* have any; and therefore do not have the second-order thoughts that are supposed to be constitutive of consciousness. (A similar problem plagues the accounts of Jaynes (1977) and Dennett (1991a). See Rey (1995b:270) for discussion.)

9 Note also that "Moore's paradox" – "p is true but I don't believe it" – is only a paradox if the assertion of p is sufficient for believing it. See Rosenthal (1991) for further discussion of this and other issues surrounding expressions vs. reports of attitudes.

10 Horgan and Woodward (1985) propose a related reply to Stich. Cf. also Bach's (1981) distinction between "thinking" and "believing."

11 I develop this distinction in some detail in Rey (1988b) as an independently motivated basis for an account of such phenomena as *akrasia* (or "weakness of will") and self-deception, which become various species of discrepancies between the two sorts of attitudes. Dennett (1969:118–19 and 1978a:chapter 11) comes close to the account I have in mind here when he distinguishes between the contents of addresses for speech and introspection, and contents of addresses that more generally determine a person's behavior. Alas, in Dennett (1991a:270 n. 2, 358 n. 16) he scorns such "boxological" proposals since "they tend to blind functionalists to alternative decompositions of functions." It's hard to see here, however, any principled objection. Indeed, in Rey (1995b) I argue that his own "multiple drafts" account of consciousness is nevertheless committed to such boxology.

12 It certainly would seem to be what Block (1995) means to capture by his "A(ccess)-consciousness," and it seems a better candidate than Rosenthal's HOT account (see above) in terms of thoughts about thoughts, since it allows at least for the *possibility* that such thoughts that are thought about might be entirely *un*conscious.

13 See Lycan (1990a) and Leeds (1993) for similar proposals.

14 The precise classification of experience as to kind – e.g. between *red* and *looks red* (or "phenomenal red"), and which of these properties a sensational predicate is supposed to represent – is a complicated issue that I postpone to §11.5.

15 This is widely known to be a gross over-simplification. A better candidate for the meaning of "Red" and of the corresponding restricted predicate might be the sufficient condition provided by Hardin (1988:76): "Given an object, an illumination configuration whereby a spot of light of a particular size and spectral content and intensity and duration falls on a given retinal area, a fully specified visual surround and an observer in a particular adaptive state, the result of the interaction is determinate by nature . . .". I hope these further complexities are not germane to the issues at hand.

16 This latter possibility does raise, however, the interesting question of the extent to which "top-down" processing can sometimes interfere with and seem to create sensory experiences that do not have their usual proximal causes; see Fodor (1983:76–7) for subtle discussion of this issue in the context of the postulation of "informationally encapsulated" perceptual modules.

17 The importance of this point emerged from conversations with Michael Antony – see Antony (1994). Maudlin (1989) raises a similar issue.

18 See Hardin (1988:129) for a discussion of these associations and some suggestive theories of their cause. Some of my remarks here are amplifications of his insistence (p. 138) that these associations are constitutive of the identity of particular kinds of experiences. Boden (1988:53) goes so far as to suggest that "voluntary movement also is necessary for 'visual' perception," citing experiments of Bach-y-Rita (1984) in which blind subjects "referred to objects located in the space in front of them" only when they controlled the movement of a tactile-transduced TV camera. An important empirical question that bears upon the philosophical worry about interpersonal commonalities of experience is the degree to which characteristic processing can be isolated from the rest of cognition. The more it is integrated with it, the less likely, of course, it is to be shared. Fodor's arguments for the modularity – the "information encapsulation" – of perception is promising in this regard.

19 Allowing thereby for a limited sort of "epiphenomenalism" of qualitative experience: the sensory experiences we report would lack many of the effects we suppose them to have. For purported neurophysiological evidence for something along these latter lines with regard to the phenomenology of choice, see Libet (1985).

20 And with them the possibility that concerns Block (1995) that "P(henomenal)-consciousness" could exist without "A(ccess)-consciousness."

21 For these reasons, Peacocke goes on to distinguish "protopropositions" from "propositions" in ways that I'm not sure are actually required, but in any case which we need not discuss here.

22 Of course I can indirectly indicate that you might be doing so by thinking a mental representation of an English sentence, such as "It's R-ing to you," which is meant to illustrate the limitation in question. The point here is that, strictly speaking, "R" in "It's R-ing to you" does not have the same role meaning of any mentalese restricted predication; rather "R" simply stands in place of such a predicate to illustrate the specific *form* of the mentalese predication.

23 The one actual sort of case in which this *might* be thought to arise is that of Gazzaniga et al.'s (1962) "split-brain patients." For discussion that could, with the present claims, lead to conclusions about "shared sensations" see Rey (1976), Nagel (1979), and Parfit (1984:§100). But note that the prospect of gaining any insight into another's mind by means of neural connection is about as likely as gaining an insight into one computer by plugging it into another.

24 The extent to which such further states are in fact implicated in CP(φ) is a question that does not need to be settled here. I only want to indicate the resources of the present theory to include them as need be.

25 See Levin (1986), Lewis (1988/1990), and Nemirow (1990), all usefully gathered together in Lycan (1990b:478–518).

26 The discussion of this section diverges in some details from the (different) accounts presented in my previous articles in Rey (1992, 1993a). Despite our continuing disagreements, I have benefitted greatly from discussions of the issue with Ned Block, Joe Levine, and Bill Lycan.

27 Treating sensations (or, anyway, "percepts") as a species of representation (or "concepts") was characteristic of many rationalist discussions, see, for example, Leibniz (1714/1962:§14). Needless to say, one might accept this rationalist thesis of Brentano's without accepting his (or other rationalist) theses about the irreducibility of the intentional, against which most of the discussion of the last four chapters has been directed.

28 And my own earlier (1980c) appeals to merely physiological states the analysis of emotions, which I now regard as mistaken.

29 In order to keep this discussion manageably clear, I will assume, contrary to quite reasonable claims of many (e.g. Hardin 1988), that tomatoes are indeed colored and that this is entirely a fact about the wave lengths they reflect. In the end, I'm inclined to think that actually *nothing* is colored – neither tomatoes, nor after-images – but there is no need to so burden the discussion at this point.

30 Making a similar point to the one I'm making here against Harman's (1990) treatment, Block (1990b) imagines an "inverted earth," where all objects are colored (i.e. reflect the radiation of) the complement of their colors on earth (e.g. blood is green and grass is red). In a slight variant of his case, imagine, however, that some strange, temporary condition in the atmosphere causes the light waves of objects to switch to their complements, so that for a while, on inverted earth, blood which is in fact green actually ordinarily looks red.

31 Peacocke (1992:73–4) notes this advantage of representational (for him, a "protopropositional") account of perception.

32 Tye (1995:chapter 4) advocates an intentional theory of sensation similar to that proposed here, except that he takes sensory experiences to consist in the processing of ("non-conceptual") representations of either distal properties (such as being red or square) or – in the case of pains – of "disturbances" in one's own body (p. 113). At least this latter does seem to come closer to capturing the "inner" phenomena that I think we are after, but it would still seem to be not sufficiently "internal": just as a difference in external environments could change *the content* of a distally oriented representation without changing the kind of sensory state it is, so could differences in the physical

318

bodies in which type identical brains reside change the content of a more proximally oriented one, but again without changing the kind of sensory experience *it* might be (imagine the same type of brain in a body arbitrarily different from our own, but which provides the same pattern of afferent signals). I think the only way to avoid this kind of objection is to require the sensory states to be categorized by contents involving genuinely phenomenal properties, not either bodily or distal ones.

33 See many of the articles in Crane (1992a), particularly Crane (1992b) and Tye (1992). See also Peacocke (1992:chapter 3) and Tye (1995).

34 In this way, the present proposal addresses the worry Shoemaker (1990) raises against the intentionalist strategy, regarding "what sort of 'sense' an experience . . . can have, if sense-individuated intentional properties are to the objects of our likes and dislikes that are directed at our experience" (p. 115). He rightly insists that an experience must represent *in a certain way*, but that "representing something 'in a certain way' had better not represent it by means of having a certain qualitative character." The present proposal is that the "certain way" is defined by the functional role of the restricted predicate. It's unclear to me whether, given how finely individuated this role might be, Shoemaker might find such a proposal inadequate (see his pp. 120–1 for his objection to a coarser sense-individuated view).

35 There are, for example, the Weber-Fechner and Stevens laws relating experienced to actual stimulus intensities, e.g. of sights and sounds. See Coren and Ward (1989) for discussion.

36 Or, alternatively, if one wanted to insist that there just had to be a property for *every* predicate: there needn't be a causally or explanatorily interesting property.

37 As Mia Farrow does the hero in "Purple Rose of Cairo," and Buster Keaton does in "Sherlock Jr.," two films well worth seeing for their philosophical conundra in this regard.

38 A particularly striking example of such an idle (if rather large) wheel is provided by Chalmers' (1996) dualism, which posits a non-physical consciousness that, by his own admission, is "explanatorily irrelevant" (p. 165). Of course, there might be various ways to protect the claim that such a wheel exists and is *causally* relevant (see his pp. 150–60). But its idleness consists in the fact that *there are no non-tendentiously described data* that require its postulation (cf. §1.3 and §3.1.1 above).

In Rey (1994b) I try to show how an impressive number of Wittgenstein's remarks with regard to sensations can be enlisted on behalf of what I call this "otiosity argument" against "private objects," an argument that can be divorced from his much less plausible "private language argument" and (broadly) behaviorist and contextualist claims he makes about mental ascription. Indeed, his remarks offer strikingly apt diagnoses of many of the philosophical worries about qualia although, I argue, *only* against the background of the kind of realistic, functionalist theory, such as CRTQ, that he would otherwise deplore.

39 Note this is *not* the logical truth, "Necessarily (x)(if x is a cat then x is a cat)," a so-called mere "de dicto necessity" (a necessity due to the way we describe things). Rather it is the more interesting claim: "(x)(if x is cat then necessarily x is a cat)," a so-called *de re* necessity (or necessity "of the thing itself"). This latter is not a logical truth, since there are false instances: for example, as discussed in the text, "(x)(if x is a president

then necessarily x is a president)." Just for the record, I should mention that I'm indulging in these fairly strong *de re* claims just for the sake of the argument; I'm not prepared to go to the wall for them.

40 Another possible reply to Kripke that I won't explore here is to identify pain with such a complete state of the whole of a body – including, for example, it's being fully alive and functioning – that it might seem plausible to suppose that being painful might be an essential property of *it*. The trouble here is that this would seem like identifying the president, implausibly, with the whole institution of the government.

41 Although I think CRTQ helps clarify some of what is going on, this (limited) eliminativist reply to Kripke doesn't require it. Any eliminativism or irreferentialism about (talk of) *pains* would suffice. Note that the point could be made by employing one-place predicates such as "x has a pain in his foot," rather than "x has y in z": there is no need to quantify over pains *per se* (cf. §1.1.1, §5.2).

42 Having defended versions of the view in a variety of forums for about fourteen years now, I have found only two people (*not* including myself) who don't seem to find the view troublesome, David Papineau and Bill Lycan, who both defend substantially less constrained versions of it.

43 The exceptions are folk functionalism (§7.1.1) and superficialism (§7.2.4).

44 Quine notoriously was working only within behaviorist constraints; Bealer considers only a few, very general mentalistic laws. See Evans (1975) and Fodor (1994:chapter 3) for some features of conceptual role that both Quine and Bealer ignore. Some of Bealer's cases involving different external causes of internal functional roles may also yield to an externalist semantics.

45 Of course, whichever one it *is* will have its effects: so it's not as though this renders the phenomenon unknowable (as Block 1980b rightly pointed in reply to Shoemaker 1975/1984). But it's the *difference* between the one and the isomorph that we could never experientially appreciate. I discuss this issue in greater detail in Rey (1992).

46 See Bealer's (1985) and Searle's (1987) appeals to introspection to settle the matter.

47 With the possible exception of Richard Rorty (1979:190) who, we noted in the introduction (§4), draws from his eliminativism the conclusion that it "is not irrational to deny civil rights to aboriginal tribes" (1979:190).

48 I'd like to say "no readers"; but there are those who at least claim to be prepared to be "pan-psychics"; e.g. Nagel (1979).

49 In order to try to make the intuitions a little sharper, I have argued in a somewhat different way (Rey 1983a, 1988a) that it would not be at all unfeasible to realize the essential features of CRTQ on existing computers, which most people would not seriously regard for a moment as thereby having any qualitative mental states (as Joe Levine put it to me in response, "no one would try to form a society for the prevention of cruelty to computers"). Demonstrating that feasibility in convincing detail requires, however, combining surprisingly diverse areas of research in artificial intelligence, psychology, and philosophy in a way that I suspect will not be practically possible for some years.

50 Of course, the phrase "resembles (behaves like)" in Wittgenstein could be construed sufficiently broadly to include even the paralyzed and disfigured. Presumably such people *would* be disposed to look and act properly were the paralysis or disfigurement

removed. But suppose these misfortunes were due to problems in brain processes controlling motor functions, so that even this disposition were lost.

51 I fear I don't find his talk of "meaning as use," and his hints at a "criteriological" account of the meanings of mental terms serve this purpose adequately.

52 Indeed, probably innate. There seems, for example, to be dedicated processing for human face recognition (Yin 1969), human bodily motion (Bernstein 1967), natural language (Lieberman et al. 1967), and emotional expression (Darwin 1872/1965, Ekman 1972) many of which appear to be part of our earliest endowment. Indeed, imitation of human facial expressions occurs in infants only twelve minutes old (Meltzoff and Moore 1983)!

53 I develop some of the suggestions of this last section in greater detail in Rey (1995d).

Glossary

a priori   knowable, because justifiable "independently of experience" in the way that, for example, the propositions of arithmetic (e.g. "$23 + 27 = 50$") seem to be; contrasted with "empirical" (q.v.), which is said of claims knowable only on the basis of experience (e.g. that rats have fur).

a priori functionalism   the view that the proper functionalist analyses of mental phenomena can be known *a priori*. See §7.1.2.

Abduction   the process by which one reasons from premises expressing certain data to the "best explanation" of them, which often involves phenomena not mentioned in the data. For example, Newton reasoned abductively from data about the motion of various bodies to the theory of universal gravitation. It is not deductive (q.v.), since the explanatory conclusion may be false, even if the data premises are true; and it is not purely inductive (q.v.), since the conclusion may involve phenomena (e.g. gravitational forces) not mentioned in the premises. See §8.3.

ABism/ist   Analytical Behaviorism/ist (q.v.).

Analytical Behaviorism   the view that mental phenomena (terms, concepts, properties, states) can be *defined* or *analyzed* in terms of stimuli and (dispositions to) responses alone. See radical and methodological behaviorism (q.v.). See §5.3.

Anchored Functionalism   the view that the proper analysis of mental phenomena will involve not only inputs, outputs, and (causal) relations among the states, as in I/O-Functionalism (q.v.), but also certain further phenomena, such as distal (worldly) input and output, or certain physical properties of the brain. See §7.2.1.

Causal Break   a break in the causal sequence of events, such that no prior individual events explain the latter ones. See §3.1.1.

322

ceteris paribus "others things being equal"; often prefaced to a law, to hedge it from counterexamples due to extraneous "interfering" factors. For example, Kepler's laws claiming the planets move in elliptical orbits is a *ceteris paribus* law since it abstracts from, for example, passing comets, and the mutual gravitational attraction exerted among the planets themselves, especially as they come into close proximity to one another. See §10.3.

COG the "toy" example of a computer program that, run on an actual computer, would, I argue, be adequate to realize the conditions of Modest Mentalism (q.v.). See §8.5.

Computational/Representational Theory of Thought the view, defended in this book, that (to a first approximation) propositional attitudes consist in an agent's bearing corresponding computational relations to sentences encoded in the brain.

Computational/Representational Theory of Thought and Qualitative States the view, set out in chapter 11 (especially §11.3), according to which not only thought, but qualitative states (q.v.) consist in an agent bearing specific computational relations to sentences encoded in her brain.

Connectionist Machine a computer whose output is determined by the varying excitation levels of interconnected nodes; thought by radical connectionists (q.v.) to provide an alternative to a "classical" machine that operates along the lines of CRTT (q.v.) (see Radical Connectionism q.v.), but by liberal connectionists (q.v.) to merely provide a novel implementation of a classical machine. See §8.8.

CRTQ the Computational/Representational Theory of Thought and Qualitative States (q.v.).

CRTT the Computational/Representational Theory of Thought (q.v.).

Deduction the process by which one reasons from premises to a conclusion, which *must* be true if the premises are; contrasted with induction (q.v.) and abduction (q.v.). For example, one can reason deductively from the premises "All rats are mammals" and "All mammals have fur" to the conclusion, "All rats have fur." See §8.2.

Dualism the view that mental phenomena, such as propositional attitudes or qualitative states, cannot be identified with (or even be regarded as composed of) any physical phenomenon. See §1.2.2, and chapter 2 (especially 2.5.7.1).

Eliminativism in general, "eliminativism" about some phenomenon x, is the view that x's don't exist; e.g. atheists are eliminativists about gods. It has come to be restricted to just the mental case: eliminativists about the mind deny any mental phenomena exist; eliminativists about qualia (q.v.), that qualia exist; see 1.2.3 and chapter 3; see also irreferentialism (q.v.).

Empirical (or *a posteriori*) depending for its justification upon the character of sensory experience; as distinct from *a priori*, which is said of claims that do not so depend; e.g. "Rats have fur" is empirical; "23 + 27 = 50" is thought by many to be *a priori* (q.v.).

Epistemological having to do with what people can know about the world, and so with issues of reasons, evidence, proof. See metaphysical (q.v.) and §5.4.

Explanatory Gap the gap in explanation between physical and mental phenomena, whereby the former do not "upwardly necessitate" the latter; to be distinguished from a "causal break" (q.v.). See §2.1.

Folk Functionalism the view that the proper analysis of mental phenomena is provided by a ramsification of the "commonplaces" popularly believed about the mind. See §7.1.1.

Functionalism an approach to the analysis of mental phenomena that looks to relations of mental phenomena both among themselves, and to inputs and outputs. The common ideas of the approach are set out in chapter 6, the many varieties of it, distinguished in chapter 7.

Holistic Functionalism the view that the proper analysis of mental phenomena is provided by a theory of the *whole* of an agent's psychology. See §7.2.2.

Homuncular Functionalism essentially "molecular functionalism" (q.v.) where the functional molecules (or sub-parts) are thought of as "little men" obeying various instructions.

Identity Theory the thesis that any mental phenomenon is identical to some or other physical phenomenon. For example, "a pain is a stimuli of c-fibers," "visual consciousness is identical to a 40 Hz oscillation in a certain area in the visual cortex." See §2.4–2.5.

Ideology (of a theory) the set of a theory's predicates; or the things that a theory can say about the world; e.g. the ideology of physics includes such predicates as "x is an electron," "the distance in meters between x and y = z," "x is greater than y." See §6.4.

Indexical any singular term (q.v.) type (q.v.) whose intuitive meaning permits different of its tokens to refer to different individual things, depending upon features of the context in which the token is used: e.g. "I," "here," "now"; as opposed to "red," "square," "the largest prime less than 12." See §11.2.1.

Induction the process by which one reasons from a sample of *observed* instances of a certain phenomenon to predictions and generalizations about *unobserved* instances of the same phenomenon. For example, one might reason from (what one reasonably took to be) a random sample of swans, all of which were white, to the conclusion that all swans are white. As this example shows, this reasoning process is not deductive (q.v.), since it's possible for the conclusion to be false (which in this case it is) even if the premises are true. Some writers regard it as a species of abduction (q.v.), one in which no new phenomena (e.g. genes, molecules) are introduced. See §8.3.

Input/Output Functionalism   the view that the proper functional analysis of mental phenomena can be provided in terms purely of inputs, outputs, and (causal) relations among the states. Contrasted with Anchored Functionalism (q.v.). See §7.2.1.

Instrumentalism   the view that the claims of an explanation should not be understood as literally true about the world, but only as an instrument for making predictions. Thus, someone might regard the geocentric claims of Ptolemaic astronomy as not literally true, but as a useful instrument for navigating at sea. The view can go hand in hand with an irreferentialism (q.v.) about *the terms* of some explanation. See §3.1.3, §10.3.4.

Intensional(ity) ("with an 's'," to be distinguished from "inten*t*ionality" q.v.)   the property of phenomena whereby they cannot be individuated merely by reference to the *objects* in the *actual* world. Meanings are commonly thought to be intensional, since two expressions e.g. "renate" and "cordate" could be true of precisely the same things in the world (all and only renates are cordates) but have different meanings: they would have the same *extension* but a different *intension*. Although many believe that all inten*t*ional phenomena are inten*s*ional, some believe there are inten*s*ional phenomena – e.g. properties, causal explanation – that are *not* inten*t*ional. See §1.1.3.

Intentional(ity) ("with a 't'," to be distinguished from "inten*s*ionality" q.v.)   in the philosophy of mind, this word is unfortunately used in two quite distinct senses: (i) the ordinary meaning, which is a near synonym of "deliberate" (as in "He intentionally pulled the trigger"), which is not a specific concern of this book, and (ii) the special philosophical meaning that *is* a central concern of this book, which has to do with "aboutness": a phenomenon is *intentional* (or exhibits *intentionality*) iff it is "about something": for example, someone's desire for apples is intentional, since it is about apples. See referential opacity (q.v.). See §1.1.3, §2.5.6, chapter 9.

I/O Functionalism   Input/Output Functionalism (q.v.).

Irreferentialism   in general, "irreferentialism" about some term is the view that it shouldn't be understood as *even purporting* (or functioning) to refer to anything; e.g. "The average American family" does not even purport to refer to any actual family. Many philosophers think that "pain" should be understood irreferentially, as not even purporting to refer to anything. The difference with "eliminativism" (q.v.) is that this view permits claims like "I have a pain in my foot" to be true, even if there do not exist such *things* as pains. See §5.2, §11.6.

Kripkenstein the name for the fictitious holder of the views expressed in Kripke's (1982) interpretation of Wittgenstein (1953). See §3.1.2 and §10.3.

LCON Liberal Connectionism (q.v.).

Liberal Connectionism the view that the brain is a connectionist machine (q.v.), on which, however, a classical CRTT (q.v.) account is implemented. Contrasted with RCON (q.v.). See §8.8.

Materialism originally, the view that all that exists is matter in motion; but it is often used more loosely as synonymous with "*physicalism*" (q.v.). In §6.4, I suggest restricting "materialism" to merely the thesis that the ontology for any true theory at all (or set of objects needed for the theory to be true) need only consist of whatever objects are needed for physics, where physicalism is a much stronger doctrine, that all the properties and truths about the world can be expressed in the terms of physics.

Mental this term is not defined here. Along the lines of §1.5.2, an adequate definition awaits an adequate empirical psychology (just as the definition of a chemical element would be provided by chemistry). A speculation explored in the latter chapters of this book (especially §11.6.1) is Brentano's claim that all mental phenomena are *intentional* (q.v.).

Metaphysical having to do with the way the world actually *is*, whether or not anyone knows, or has any good reasons for believing it is one way or another. See epistemological (q.v.) and §1.1.1, §5.4.

Methodological Behaviorism the view that the only *evidence* for any psychological or mental state is the evidence of overt responses to external stimuli. This entails neither analytical nor radical behaviorism (q.v.), but is closely related to "superficialism" (q.v.). See §7.2.4.

Modest Mentalism the sketch of the structure of a normal mind, set out at the end of chapter 7 (§7.3.2).

Molecular Functionalism the view that the proper analysis of mental phenomena is provided by a theory about various proper sub-portions of an agent's psychology. See §7.2.2.

Ontology (1) In general, issues surrounding what things (construed broadly) exist. Thus, the question whether properties like *being red* or *being square* exist as well as ordinary material objects is an ontological question. Ontological questions are a subset of *metaphysical* (q.v.) ones, which concern the broadest issues of what the world is like. (2) The "ontology of a theory" are the objects that the theory says exists (the "values of its variables"). Thus, the ontology of physics includes such things as electrons, protons, gravitational and electromagnetic fields; contrasted with its *ideology* (q.v.). See §6.4.

Physicalism   the view that all the truths, properties, and objects in the world are truths, properties, and objects that can be expressed or named by the terms of physics; see materialism (q.v.). See §1.2.1, §2.3, and §6.4.

Predicate   intuitively, a piece of language that is true of certain objects. Strictly: a predicate is formed by substituting in any indicative sentence a variable ("u," "v," "w," "x," "y," "z" with or without subscripts) for one or more occurrences of a singular term (q.v.). See §1.1.

Propositional Attitude (term)   any mental state that involves a relation to either a sentence or a proposition that expresses the meaning of a sentence. A propositional attitude term is a term that signifies such a relation, and that, as a verb, takes a sentence complement (e.g. a "that . . ." or "to . . ." clause) as its direct object. For example, "thinks that" and "wants to . . ." are propositional attitude terms (as in "John thinks that God exists," "Mary wants to buy peanuts") signifying corresponding propositional attitudes. See §1.1.2.

Psycho-functionalism   the view that the proper functional analysis of mental phenomena will emerge only from an adequate empirical psychology. See §7.1.3.

Qualia   the purported phenomena we are aware of when we are in a qualitative state, as distinct from the properties in the world that might correspond to that state: e.g. the look of red (as opposed to the actual color red), the way beer tastes (as opposed to the properties of beer itself). There is considerable controversy about whether qualia exist at all: see §2.6, §5.2.2, and §1.1.6.

Qualitative State   a state that has a certain feeling associated with it: there is "something it is like" to be in that state; for example, seeing red, tasting beer, being in pain. See §1.1.2.

Quantifier   in first order predicate logic, the expressions meaning "all" (the universal quantifier) or "some" (or "there exists at least one" – the existential quantifier). Quantifiers "bind" variables that they govern, or that are in their scope: thus, in "$\exists x(ex)$" – "There exists at least one x such that x is an even number" – the quantifier "(ex)" binds both the occurrences of "x." See §1.1.1.

Radical Behaviorism   the view, associated with the view of Watson and Skinner, that intelligent human and animal behavior can be explained in terms of the conditioning of responses to stimuli, especially via the Law of Effect. See §4.1.

Radical Connectionism   the view that mental phenomena can be understood *without* positing representations with causally efficacious constituent logical structure; the chief rival to CRTT (q.v.). Contrasted also with LCON (q.v.). See §8.8.

Ramsification   a logical technique for defining theoretical terms, developed by Frank Ramsey and David Lewis. See §6.3.

RBism   Radical Behaviorism (q.v.).

RCON   Radical Connectionism (q.v.).

Reductionism   broadly, the thesis that the phenomena of one domain can be explained entirely in terms of the phenomena of another domain (especially physics). See §1.2.1.

Referential Opacity   the phenomena whereby co-referential terms cannot in general be substituted into a sentence *salva veritate* (without changing the truth value of the sentence). The occurrence of "Mark Twain" in "Sue thinks Mark Twain is smart" is referentially opaque, since one can't substitute the co-referential "Sam Clemens" without risking change of truth value. See §1.1.3.

Singular Term   any expression in language that functions to refer to some unique individual thing: e.g. "Julius Caesar," "the largest prime less than 12," "the present king of France," "this," "now," "I." See §1.1.1.

Superficialism   the view that all the evidence for any even functionally defined state must be available in a person's ordinary behavior or introspections. The view is a cross between methodological behaviorism (q.v.) and folk functionalism (q.v.). See §7.2.4.

Teleo-functionalism   the view that the proper analysis of mental phenomena involves reference to the role of the phenomena in some selection process, especially natural selection. See §7.2.3.

Tokens   individual things that have a specific space/time location, as contrasted with *types* (q.v.) or classes of them, that do not. Originally, it was a way of distinguishing actual spatio-temporal linguistic items, like the word "the" that is written between "like" and "word" on the line above, from the type, or class of such items (there are many different tokens of the type word "the" on this page). But it has been extended to treatments especially of objects and events. See §2.4 and §6.4.

Transcendental Arguments   arguments that purport to demonstrate some conclusion without relying on any empirical evidence, particularly ones that show that some claim is necessary for the possibility of the truth of any claims at all. See §3.2.1.

Turing Machine   an abstract characterization of a particular method of computing a function. See §6.2.

Types   sets of tokens (q.v.).

References

Albritton, R. (1959/1968), "On Wittgenstein's Use of the Term 'Criterion'," in *Wittgenstein: the Philosophical Investigations*, Notre Dame: University of Notre Dame Press, pp. 231–50

Allen, F. (1994), "Unreasonable Facsimile," *Atlantic Monthly*, 274 (2):20–3

Alston, W. (1967), "Motives and Motivation," in P. Edwards, *The Encyclopedia of Philosophy*, New York: Macmillan, pp. 399–409

Anderson, J.A. and Mozer, M.C. (1981), "Categorization and Selective Neurons," in G.E. Hinton and J.A. Amderson (eds), *Parallel Models of Associative Memory*, Hillsdale, NJ: Erlbaum, pp. 213–36

Antony, L. (1987), "Attributions of Intentional Action," *Philosophical Studies*, 51:311–23

Antony, L. (1989), "Anomalous Monism and the Problem of Explanatory Force," *Philosophical Review*, XCVIII (2):153–87

Antony, L. and Levine, J. (1991), "The Nomic and the Robust," in Loewer and Rey (1991), pp. 1–16

Antony, M. (1994), "Against Functionalist Theories of Consciousness," *Mind and Language*, 9:105–23

Armstrong, D. (1968), *A Materialist Theory of the Mind*, London: Routledge and Kegan Paul

Attneave, F. (1960), "In Defense of Homunculi," in W. Rosenblith (ed.), *Sensory Communication*, Cambridge: MIT Press

Austin, J.L. (1956/1964), "A Plea for Excuses," in V.C. Chappell (ed.), *Ordinary Language*, Englewood Cliffs: Prentice Hall, pp. 41–63

Ayer, A.J. (1934/1952), *Language, Truth and Logic*, New York: Dover

Bach, K. (1981), "An Analysis of Self-deception," *Philosophy and Phenomenological Research*, 41:351–70

Bach-y-Rita, P. (1984), "The Relationship Between Motor Processes and Cognition in Tactile Visual Substitution," in W. Prinz and A. Sanders (eds), *Cognition and Motor Processes*, Berlin: Springer-Verlag, pp. 149–60

Baker, L. (1987), *Saving Belief: a Critique of Physicalism*, Princeton: Princeton University Press

Barwise, J. and Perry, J. (1983), *Situation Semantics*, Cambridge: MIT Press

Bealer, G. (1982), *Quality and Concept*, Oxford: Clarendon Press

Bealer, G. (1984), "Mind and Anti-Mind," in *Midwest Studies in Philosophy*, IX:283–328

Bealer, G. (1987), "The Philosophical Limits of Scientific Essentialism," in J. Tomberlin (ed.), *Philosophical Persepctives I, Metaphysics*, Atascadero: Ridgeview Press, pp. 289–365

Bechtel, W. and Abrahamson, A. (1991), *Connectionism and the Mind: an Introduction to Parallel Processing in Networks*, Oxford: Blackwell

Berlyne, D. (1950), "Novelty and Curiosity as Determinants of Exploratory Behavior," *British Journal of Psychology*, 41:68–80

Bernstein, N. (1967), *The Coordination and Regulation of Movement*, Oxford: Oxford University Press

Berwick, R. (1985), *The Acquisition of Syntactic Knowledge*, Cambridge: MIT Press

Bigelow, J. and Pargetter, R. (1987), "Functions," *Journal of Philosophy*, LXXXXIV (4):181–96

Bilgrami, A. (1992), *Belief and Meaning: the Unity and Locality of Mental Content*, Oxford: Blackwell

Bisiach, E. and Luzzatti, C. (1978), "Unilateral Neglect, Representational Schema and Consciousness," *Cortex*, 14:129–33

Block, N. (1978/1980), "Troubles with Functionalism," in Block (1980a), vol. I:268–306

Block, N. (ed.), (1980a), *Readings in the Philosophy of Psychology*, 2 vols., Cambridge: Harvard University Press

Block, N. (1980b), "Are Absent Qualia Impossible?", *The Philosophical Review*, 89:257–74

Block, N. (ed.), (1981a), *Imagery*, Cambridge: MIT Press/Bradford Books

Block, N. (1981b), "Psychologism and Behaviorism," *Philosophical Review*, LXXXX:5–43

Block, N. (1986), "Advertisement for a Semantics for Psychology," in P. French, T. Euhling and H. Wettstein (eds), *Studies in the Philosophy of Mind*, vol. 10 of *Midwest Studies in Philosophy*, pp. 615–78

Block, N. (1990a), "The Computer Model of the Mind," in D. Osherson and E. Smith (eds) *Thinking*, Cambridge: MIT Press

Block, N. (1990b), "Inverted Earth," in J. Tomberlin (ed.), *Philosophical Perspectives, vol. 4: Action Theory and Philosophy of Mind*, Atascadero: Ridgeview Press

Block, N. (1991), "What Narrow Content Is Not," in Loewer and Rey (1991a), pp. 33–64

Block, N. (1995), "On a Confusion about a Function of Consciousness," *Behavioral and Brain Sciences*, 18:227–87

Block, N. (forthcoming), "The Relativity of Kinds," in J. Tomberlin (ed.), *Philosophical Perspectives*, Oxford: Blackwell

Block, N. and Fodor, J.A. (1972), "What Psychological States are Not," *Philosophical Review*, 81:159–81

Blodgett, H. (1929), "The Effect of the Introduction of Reward Upon the Maze Performance of Rats," *University of California Publications in Psychology*, 48(8):113–34

Boden, M. (1988), *Computer Models of the Mind*, Cambridge: Cambridge University Press

Boghossian, P. (1990a), "The Status of Content," *Philosophical Review*, 99:157–84

Boghossian, P. (1990b), "The Status of Content Revisited," *Pacific Philosophical Quarterly*, 71 (1990):264–78

Brentano F. (1874/1973), *Psychology from an Empirical Standpoint*, trans. by A. Rancurello, D. Terrell, and L. McAlister, London: Routledge and Kegan Paul

Brown, D. (1995), "Pseudo Memories: the Standard of Science and the Standard of Care in Trauma Treatment," *American Journal of Clinical Hypnosis*, 37:1–24

Brown, R. and Hanlon, C. (1970), "Derivational Complexity and Order of Acquisition of Speech in Children," in J. Hayes (ed.), *Cognition and the Development of Language*, New York: Wiley, pp. 11–53

Burge, T. (1977), "Belief De Re," *Journal of Philosophy*, 74:338–62

Burge, T. (1978), "Belief and Synonymy," *Journal of Philosophy*, 75:119–38

Burge, T. (1979), "Individualism and the Mental," *Midwest Studies in Philosophy*, IV:73–121

Burge, T. (1986), "Individualism and Psychology," *Philosophical Review*, XCV (1):3–46

Buxton, C. (1940), "Latent Learning and the Goal Gradient Hypothesis," in *Contributions to Psychological Theory*, 2 (2):1–75

Caldwell, W. and Jones, H. (1954), "Some Positive Results on a Modified Tolman and Honzik Insight Maze," *Journal of Comparative Physiological Psychology*, 47 (5):416–18

Campbell, N. (1987), *Biology*, Menlo Park, CA: Benjamin/Cummings

Carey, S. (1985), *Conceptual Change in Childhood*, Cambridge: MIT Press

Carroll, L. (1895/1995), "What the Tortoise Said to Achilles," *Mind*, 4:278–80 (reprinted in *Mind*, 104:691–3

Cartwright, N. (1983), *How the Laws of Physics Lie*, Oxford: Clarendon Press

Cartwright, N. (1989), *Nature's Capacities and Their Measurement*, Oxford: Oxford University Press

Casteneda, H. (1966), "'He': A Study in the Logic of Self-Consciousness," *Ratio*, 8:130–57

Chalmers, D. (1996), *The Conscious Mind: in Search of a Fundamental Theory*, Oxford: Oxford University Press

Cherniak, C. (1986), *Minimal Rationality*, Cambridge: MIT Press/Bradford Books

Chihara, C. and Fodor, J.A. (1965), "Operationalism and Ordinary Language," in Fodor (1981), pp. 35–62

Chisholm, R. (1957), *Perceiving: a Philosophical Study*, Ithaca: Cornell University Press

Chomsky, N. (1957), *Syntactic Structures*, The Hague: Mouton

Chomsky, N. (1959/1964), "Review of Skinner's *Verbal Behavior*," in J. Fodor and J. Katz (eds), *The Structure of Language: Readings in the Philosophy of Language*, Englewood Cliffs: Prentice Hall, pp. 547–78

Chomsky, N. (1968), *Language and Mind*, New York: Harcourt, Brace and World

Chomsky, N. (1980), *Rules and Representations*, New York: Columbia University Press

Chomsky, N. (1988), *Language and Problems of Knowledge*, Cambridge: MIT Press

Chomsky, N. (1995a), "Language and Nature," *Mind*, 104 (413):1–62

Chomsky, N. (1995b), *The Minimalist Program*, Cambridge: MIT Press

Church, A. (1946), Review of Morton White's "A Note on the 'Paradox of Analysis'," Max Black's "The 'Paradox of Analysis' Again: A Reply," Morton White's "Analysis and Identity: a Rejoinder," and Max Black's "How Can Analysis Be Informative?," *Journal of Symbolic Logic*, 11:132–3

Churchland, Patricia (1986), *Neurophilosophy: Toward a Unified Science of the Mind-Brain*, Cambridge: MIT Press/Bradford Books

Churchland, Paul (1979), *Scientific Realism and the Plasticity of Mind*, Cambridge: Cambridge University Press

Churchland, Paul (1981), "Eliminative Materialism and Propositional Attitudes," in Lycan (1990b), pp. 206–23

References

Churchland, Paul (1984), *Matter and Consciousness*, Cambridge: MIT Press
Churchland, Paul (1995), *The Engine of Reason, the Seat of the Soul*, Cambridge: MIT Press
Clark, A. (1989), *Microcognition: Philosophy, Cognitive Science and Parallel Distributed Processing*, Cambridge: MIT Press
Clark, H. and Clark, E. (1977), *Psychology and Language*, New York: Harcourt Brace Jovanovich
Coffa, J. (1991), *The Semantic Tradition from Kant to Carnap: to the Vienna Station*, Cambridge: Cambridge University Press
Coren, S. and Ward, L. (1989), *Sensation and Perception*, 3rd edn, San Diego: Harcourt Brace Jovanovich
Crane, T. (1992a), *The Contents of Experience*, Cambridge: Cambridge University Press
Crane, T. (1992b), introduction to Crane (1992a)
Crick, F. (1994), *The Astonishing Hypothesis*, New York: Scribner's
Crick, F. and Koch, C. (1990), "Towards a Neurobiological Theory of Consciousness," *Seminars Neurose*, 2:263–75
Cummins, R. (1983), *The Nature of Psychological Explanation*, Cambridge: MIT Press
Cummins, R. (1986), "Inexplicit Information," in M. Brand and R. Harnish, *The Representation of Knowledge and Belief*, Tucson: University of Arizona Press
Cummins, R. (1989), *Meaning and Mental Representation*, Cambridge: MIT Press/Bradford Books
Cummins, R. and Schwarz, G. (1987), "Radical Connectionism," *Southern Journal of Philosophy*, XXVI (Supplement):43–61
Damasio, A. (1994), *Descartes' Error*, New York: Putnam
Danto, A. (1960), "On Consciousness in Machines," in S. Hook (ed.), *Dimensions of Mind*, New York: Free Press, pp. 180–7
Danto, A. (1963), "What We Can Do," *Journal of Philosophy*, 60:435–45
Darley, J. and Berschied, E. (1967), "Increased Liking as a Result of the Anticipation of Personal Contact," *Human Relations*, 20:29–40
Darwin, C. (1872/1965), *The Expression of Emotions in Man and Animals*, Chicago: University of Chicago Press
Dashiel, J.F. (1930), "Direction Orientation in Maze Running by the White Rat," *Comparative Psychology Monographs*, 7 (2):1–72
Davidson, D. (1963/1980), "Actions, Reasons and Causes," in Davidson (1980), pp. 3–20
Davidson, D. (1968/1984), "On Saying That," in Davidson (1984), pp. 93–108
Davidson, D. (1970/1980), "Mental Events," in Davidson (1980), pp. 207–28
Davidson, D. (1973/1980), "Freedom to Act," in Davidson (1980), pp. 64–81
Davidson, D. (1973/1984), "Radical Interpretation," in Davidson (1984), pp. 125–40
Davidson, D. (1974/1980), "Intending," in Davidson (1980), pp. 83–102
Davidson, D. (1974/1984), "Thought and Talk," in Davidson (1984), pp. 155–70
Davidson, D. (1980), *Essays on Actions and Events*, Oxford: Oxford University Press
Davidson, D. (1984), *Inquiries into Truth and Interpretion*, Oxford: Clarendon Press
Davidson, D. (1987), "Knowing One's Own Mind," *Proceedings and Addresses of American Philosophical Association*, 60:441–58
Davidson, D. and Hintikka, J. (1969), *Words and Objections*: Dordrecht: Reidel
Davies, M. (1991), "Concepts, Connectionism, and the Language of Thought," in W. Ramsey et al. (eds), *Philosophy and Connectionist Theory*, Hillsdale: Erlbaum, pp. 229–56

332

Davies, M. (1994), "The Mental Simulation Debate," in C. Peacocke (ed.), *Objectivity, Simulation, and the Unity of Consciousness*, Oxford: Oxford University Press

DeGroot, J. and Chusid, J. (1991), *Correlative Neuroanatomy*, East Norwalk: Appleton & Lange

Dennett, D. (1969), *Content and Consciousness*, London: Routledge & Kegan Paul

Dennett, D. (1971/1978), "Intentional Systems," in Dennett (1978a), pp. 3–22

Dennett, D. (1976/1978), "Conditions of Personhood," in Dennett (1978a), pp. 267–85

Dennett, D. (1978a), *Brainstorms*, Cambridge: MIT Press/Bradford Books

Dennett, D. (1978b), "Towards a Cognitive Theory of Consciousness," in Dennett (1978a), pp. 149–73

Dennett, D. (1978c), "Skinner Skinned," in Dennett (1978a), pp. 53–70

Dennett, D. (1978d), "Towards a Cognitive Theory of Consciousness," in Dennett (1978a), pp. 149–73

Dennett, D. (1978e), "Why the Law of Effect Won't Go Away," in Dennett (1978a), pp. 71–89

Dennett, D. (1978f), "Towards a Cognitive Theory of Consciousness," in Dennett (1978a), pp. 149–73

Dennett, D. (1981a), "A Cure for the Common Code," in Dennett (1978a), pp. 90–108

Dennett, D. (1981b), "True Believers: The Intentional Strategy and Why it Works," in A. Heath (ed.), *Scientific Explanation*, Oxford: Oxford University Press

Dennett, D. (1981c), "Three Kinds of Intentional Psychology," in R. Healy (ed.), *Reduction, Time and Reality*, Cambridge: Cambridge University Press

Dennett, D. (1986), "Julian Jaynes' Software Archeology," *Journal of Canadian Psychology*, XXVII (2):149–54

Dennett, D. (1987), *The Intentional Stance*, Cambridge: MIT Press/Bradford Books

Dennett, D. (1988a), "Quining Qualia," in A. Marcel and E. Bisiach (eds), *Consciousness in Contemporary Science*, New York: Oxford University Press

Dennett, D. (1988b), "Review of *Psychosemantics*," *Journal of Philosophy*, 85:384–9

Dennett, D. (1991a), *Consciousness Explained*, New York: Little Brown

Dennett, D. (1991b), "Real Patterns," *Journal of Philosophy*, 88 (1):27–51

Dennett, D. (1991c), "Lovely and Suspect Properties," in E. Villanueva (ed.), *Consciousness*, Atascadero: Ridgeview Press, pp. 37–44

Dennett, D. (1993), "The Message Is: There is no Medium," *Philosophy and Phenomenological Research*, 53:919–31

Dennett, D. (1995a), *Darwin's Dangerous Idea*, New York: Simon and Schuster

Dennett, D. (1995b), "Superficialism vs. Hysterical Realism," in *Philosophical Topic*, 22 (1–2):530–6

Dennett, D. and Kinsbourne, M. (1992), "Time and the Observer: the Where and When of Consciousness in the Brain," *Behavioral and Brain Sciences*, 15 (2):183–201

Descartes, R. (1637/1970), "Discourse on the Method," in *The Philosophical Works of Descartes*, vol. I, trans. by E.S. Haldane and G.R.T. Ross, Cambridge: Cambridge University Press, pp. 79–130

Descartes, R. (1641a/1970), "Meditations on First Philosophy," in *The Philosophical Works of Descartes*, vol. I, trans. by E.S. Haldane and G.R.T. Ross, Cambridge: Cambridge University Press, pp. 131–200

Descartes, R. (1641b/1970), "Replies to Objections," in *The Philosophical Works of Descartes*, vol. II, trans. by E.S. Haldane and G.R.T. Ross, Cambridge: Cambridge University Press, pp. 329–428

Descartes, R. (1649/1911), "The Passions of the Soul," in *The Philosophical Works of Descartes*, vol. I, trans. by E.S. Haldane and G.R.T. Ross, Cambridge: Cambridge University Press

DeSousa, R. (1971), "How to Give a Piece of Your Mind; or, a Logic of Belief and Assent," *Review of Metaphysics*, 25:52–79

Devitt, M. (1981), *Designation*, New York: Columbia University Press

Devitt, M. (1984), *Realism and Truth*, Oxford: Blackwell

Devitt, M. (1989), "A Narrow Representational Theory of the Mind," in S. Silvers (ed.), *Readings in the Philosophy of Mental Representation*, Dordrecht, Kluwer

Devitt, M. (1990), "Transcendentalism About Content," *Pacific Philosophical Quarterly*, 71:247–63

Devitt, M. (1991), "Why Fodor Can't Have It Both Ways," in Loewer and Rey (1991)

Devitt, M. and Rey, G. (1991), "Transcending Transcendentalism," *Pacific Philosophical Quarterly*, 64:354–61

Devitt, M. and Sterelny, K. (1987), *Language and Reality*, Cambridge: MIT Press/Bradford Books

Dinsmore, J. (1992), "Thunder in the Gap," in J. Dinsmore (ed.), *The Symbolic and Conncetionist Paradigms: Closing the Gap*, Hillsdale: Erlbaum, pp. 1–23

Dretske, F. (1981), *Knowledge and the Flow of Information*, Cambridge: MIT Press/Bradford Books

Dretske, F. (1988), *Explaining Behavior: Reasons in a World of Causes*, Cambridge: MIT Press/Bradford Books

Dretske, F. (1995), *Naturalizing the Mind*, Cambridge: MIT Press

Dreyfus, H. (1972/1979), *What Computers Can't Do*, New York: Harper and Row

Dreyfus, H. and Dreyfus, S. (1986), *Mind Over Machine*, New York: Free Press

Duhem, P. (1906/1964), *The Aim and Structure of Physical Theory*, New York: Atheneum

Dummett, M. (1975), "What Is a Theory of Meaning," in S. Guttenplan (ed.), *Mind and Language*, Oxford: Clarendon Press, pp. 97–138

Dummett, M. (1976), "What Is a Theory of Meaning (II)," in G. Evans and J. McDowell (eds), *Truth and Meaning: Essays in Semantics*, Oxford: Clarendon Press, pp. 67–137

Eccles, J. (1966), "Conscious Experience and Memory," in J. Eccles (ed.), *Brain and Conscious Experience*, Berlin: Springer-Verlag

Ekman, P. (1972), *Emotion in the Human Face*, New York: Pergamon Press

Elster, J. (1983), *Sour Grapes: Studies in the Subversion of Rationality*, Cambridge: Cambridge University Press

Elvee, R. (ed.), (1982), *Mind in Nature*, (Nobel Conference XVII), San Francisco: Harper and Row

Emlen, S. (1969), "The Development of Migratory Orientation in Young Indigo Buntings," *Living Bird*, 8:113–26

Ericsson, K. (1993), "Recall or Regeneration of Past Mental States: Toward an Account in Terms of Cognitive Processes," *Behavioral and Brain Sciences*, 16 (1):41–2

Ericsson, K. and Simon, H. (1984/1993), *Protocol Analysis: Verbal Reports as Data*, Cambridge: MIT Press/Bradford Books

Evans, G. (1975), "Identity and Predication," *Journal of Philosophy*, 72:343–63

Evans, G. (1977), "The Causal Theory of Names," in S.P. Schwartz (ed.), *Naming, Necessity, and Natural Kinds*, Ithaca: Cornell University Press

Festinger, L. (1957), *Cognitive Dissonance*, Standford: Stanford University Press

Feyerabend, P. (1963/1971), "Mental Events and the Brain," in Rosenthal (1971), pp. 172–3

Field, H. (1977), "Logic, Meaning, and Conceptual Role," *Journal of Philosophy*, LXXIV:379–408

Field, H. (1978a), "Mental Representation," in N. Block (ed.), *Readings in Philosophy of Psychology*, vol. II, Cambridge: Harvard University Press, pp. 78–114

Field, H. (1978b), *Science Without Numbers*, Princeton: Princeton University Press

Fodor, J.A. (1968), *Psychological Explanation*, New York: Random House

Fodor, J.A. (1975), *The Language of Thought*, New York: Crowell

Fodor, J.A. (1978/1981), "Propositional Attitudes," in Fodor (1981a), pp. 177–203

Fodor, J.A. (1980), "Methodological Solipcism as a Research Strategy in Cognitive Psychology," *Behavioral and Brain Sciences*

Fodor, J.A. (1980/1990), "Psychosemantics or Where Do Truth Conditions Come From?," in Lycan (1990b), pp. 312–38

Fodor, J.A. (1981a), *RePresentations*, Cambridge: MIT Press/Bradford Books

Fodor, J.A. (1981b), "Tom Swift and his Procedural Grandmother," in Fodor (1981a), pp. 204–24

Fodor, J.A. (1981c), "The Present Status of the Innateness Controversy," in Fodor, (1981a), pp. 257–316

Fodor, J.A. (1981d), "Three Cheers for Propositional Attitudes," in Fodor (1981a), pp. 100–23

Fodor, J.A. (1983), *The Modularity of Mind*, Cambridge: MIT Press/Bradford Books

Fodor, J.A. (1986), "Why paramecia don't have mental representations," *Midwest Studies In Philosophy*, X, pp. 3–24

Fodor, J.A. (1987), *Psychosemantics*, Cambridge: MIT Press/Bradford Books

Fodor, J.A. (1990), *A Theory of Content*, Cambridge: MIT Press

Fodor, J.A. (1991a), "Replies," in Loewer and Rey (1991), pp. 255–319

Fodor, J.A. (1991b), "A Modal Argument for Narrow Content," *Journal of Philosophy*, 88:5–26

Fodor, J.A. (1991c), "After Thoughts: Ying and Yang in the Chinese Room," in D. Rosenthal, *The Nature of Mind*, New York: Oxford University Press, pp. 424–5

Fodor, J.A. (1994), *The Elm and the Expert*, Cambridge: MIT Press

Fodor, J.A. and Bever, T. (1965), "The Psychological Reality of Linguistic Segments," *Journal of Verbal Learning and Verbal Behavior*, 4:414–20

Fodor, J.A., Garrett, M.F., Walker, E.C.T., and Parkes, C.H. (1980), "Against Definitions," *Cognition*, 8 (3): 265–367

Fodor, J.A. and LePore, E. (1992), *Holism: a Shopper's Guide*, Oxford: Blackwell Publishers

Fodor, J.A. and Mclaughlin, B. (1991), "Connectionism and the Problem of Systematicity: Why Smolensky's Solution Won't Work," *Cognition*, 35 (2):185–204

Fodor, J.A. and Pylyshyn, Z. (1981), "How Direct Is Visual Perception? Some Reflections on Gibson's 'Ecological Approach'," *Cognition*, 9:139–96

Fodor, J.A. and Pylyshyn, Z. (1988), "Connectionism and Cognitive Architecture: a Critical Analysis," in S. Pinker and J. Mehler (1988), pp. 3–72

Fodor, J.D., Fodor, J.A., and Garrett, M.F. (1975), "The Psychological Unreality of Semantic Representations," *Linguistic Inquiry*, 6:515–31

Frankfurt, H. (1971), "Freedom of the Will and the Concept of a Person," *Journal of Philosophy*, LXVIII:5–20

Frege, G. (1892/1952), "On Sense and Reference," in P. Geach and M. Black (eds), *Translations from the Work of Gottlob Frege*, Oxford: Blackwell, pp. 56–78

Frege, G. (1965), "The Thought: a Logical Inquiry," trans. by A.M. and Marcelle Quinton, *Mind*, 65:289–311

French, P., Uehling, T., and Wettstein, H. (1979), *Contemporary Perspectives in the Philosophy of Language*, Minneapolis: University of Minnesota Press

French, P., Uehling, T., and Wettstein, H. (1992), *Midwest Studies in Philosophy, XVII: The Wittgenstein Legacy*, Notre Dame: University of Notre Dame Press

Gallistel, C. (1990), *The Organization of Learning*, Cambridge: MIT Press

Gazzaniga, M., Bogen, J., and Sperry, R. (1962), "Some Functional Effects of Sectioning the Cerebral Commisures in Man," *Proceedings of National Academy of Sciences*, 48 (part 2):1,765

Gibson, J. (1979), *The Ecological Approach to Visual Perception*, Boston: Houghton Mifflin

Glanzer, M. (1958), "Curiosity, Exploratory Drive and Stimulus Satiation," *Psychological Bulletin*, 55 (5):302–15

Gleitman, H. (1963), "Place-learning," *Scientific American*, 209:116–22

Gleitman, H. (1986), *Psychology*, New York: Norton & Co., 2nd ed.

Globus, G. (1976), "Mind, Structure and Contradiction," in G. Globus, G. Maxwell, and I. Savodnik (eds), *Consciousness and the Brain*, New York: Plenum Press

Gödel, K. (1930), "Der Vollständigkeit der Axiom des logischen Funktionenkalküls," *Monatshefte für Mathematik und Physik*, 37:349–60

Gödel, K. (1931/1970), "On Formally Undecidable Propositions of *Principia Mathematica* and Related Systems I," in J. van Heijenoort (ed.), *Frege to Gödel: two Fundamental Texts in Mathematical Logic*, Cambridge: Harvard University Press

Godfrey-Smith, P. (1994), "A Continuum of Semantic Optimism," in S. Stich and T. Warfield (eds), *Mental Representation*, Oxford: Blackwell, pp. 259–77

Godfrey-Smith, P. (1996), *Complexity and the Function of Mind in Nature*, Cambridge: Cambridge University Press

Goldfarb, W. (1992), "Wittgenstein on Understanding," in P. French et al. (1992), pp. 109–22

Goldman, A. (1970), *A Theory of Human Action*, Englewood Cliffs: Prentice Hall

Goldman, A. (1986), *Epistemology and Cognition*, Cambridge: Harvard University Press

Goldman, A. (1993), "The Psychology of Folk Psychology," *Behavioral and Brain Sciences*, 16 (1):15–28

Goodman, N. (1951), *The Structure of Appearance*, Indianapolis: Bobbs-Merrill

Goodman, N. (1956), *Fact, Fiction, and Forecast*, Indianapolis: Bobbs-Merrill

Goodman, N. (1968), *Languages of Art*, Indianapolis: Bobbs-Merrill

Goodman, N. (1970), "Seven Strictures on Similarity," in L. Foster and J. Swanson (eds), *Experience and Theory*, Amherst: University of Massachusetts Press, pp. 19–30

Goodman, N. (1978), *Ways of Worldmaking*, Indianapolis: Hackett

Gopnik, A. (1994), "How We Know Our Own Minds: the Illusion of First-person Knowledge of Intentionality," *Behavioral and Brain Sciences*, 16 (1):1–14

Gordon, R. (1986), "Folk Psychology as Simulation," *Mind and Language*, 1:158–71

Gould, S. and Lewontin, R. (1979), "The Spandrels of San Marco and the Panglossian Paradigm: a Critique of the Adaptionist Paradigm," in *Proceedings of the Royal Society*, B205:581–98

Gregory, R. (1966), *Eye and Brain: the Psychology of Seeing*, New York: McGraw Hill

Grice, H.P. (1957), "Meaning," *Philosophical Review*, LXVI (3):377–88

Grice, H.P. (1965), "The Causal Theory of Perception," in R.J. Swartz (ed.), *Perceiving, Sensing and Knowing*, New York: Doubleday

Grice, H.P. and Strawson, P. (1956), "In Defense of a Dogma," *Philosophical Review*, 65:141–58

Haegeman, L. (1994), *Introduction to Government and Bonding Theory*, 2nd edn, Oxford: Blackwell

Hagueland, J. (1981), *Mind Design*, Cambridge: MIT Press/Bradford Books

Hagueland, J. (1985), *Artificial Intelligence: the Very Idea*, Cambridge: MIT Press

Hannan, B. (1993), "Don't Stop Believing: the Case Against Eliminative Materialism," *Mind and Language*, 8 (2):165–79

Hansel, C. (1980), *ESP and Parapsychology: a Critical Re-evaluation*, Buffalo: Prometheus Books

Hardin, C. (1988), *Color for Philosophers: Unweaving the Rainbow*, Indianapolis: Hackett

Harlow, H. (1950), "Learning and Satiation of Response in Intrinsically Motivated Complex Puzzle Performance in Monkeys," *Journal of Comparative and Physiological Psychology*, 43:289–94

Harlow, H.F. (1959), "Learning Set and Error Factor Theory," in S. Koch (ed.), *Psychology: a Study of Science*, vol. 2, New York: McGraw Hill, pp. 492–537

Harman, G. (1972), *Thought*, Princeton: Princeton University Press

Harman, G. (1982), "Conceptual Role Semantics," *Notre Dame Journal of Formal Logic*, 23:242–56

Harman, G. (1990), "The Intrinsic Quality of Experience," in J. Tomberlin, *Philosophical Perspectives 4: Action Theory and Philosophy of Mind*, Atascadero: Ridgeview Press

Harris, Z. (1951), *Methods in Structural Linguistics*, Chicago: University of Chicago Press

Harrison, B. (1973), *Form and Content*, Oxford: Oxford University Press

Hawking, S. (1980), *Is the End in Sight for Theoretical Physics?: An Inaugural Lecture*, New York: Cambridge University Press

Heidegger, M. (1924/1962), *Being and Time*, New York: Harper and Row

Hempel, C. (1965), *Aspects of Scientific Explanation*, New York: Free Press

Hess, R. (1975), "The Role of Pupil Size in Communication," *Scientific American*, 233 (5):110–18

Hilgard, E. (1977), *Divided Consciousness: Multiple Controls in Human Thought and Action*, New York: Wiley & Sons

Hill, C. (1991), *Sensations: a Defense of Type Materialism*, New York: Cambridge University Press

Hintikka, J. (1962), *Knowledge and Belief: an Introduction to the Logic of the Two Notions*, Ithaca: Cornell University Press.

Hobbes, Thomas (1651/1965), *Hobbes's Leviathan*, Oxford: Clarendon Press

Hodges, A. (1983), *Alan Turing: the Enigma*, New York: Simon and Schuster

Holzman, S. and Leich, C. (1981), *Wittgenstein: to Follow a Rule*, Oxford: Routledge & Kegan Paul

Hookway, C. (1984), *Minds, Machines and Evolution*, Cambridge: Cambridge University Press

Horgan, T. and Woodward, J. (1985), "Folk Psychology is Here to Stay," *Philosophical Review*, XCIV (2):197–225

Horwich, P. (1990), *Truth*, Oxford: Blackwell

Hull, C. (1943), *Principles of Behavior*, New York: Appleton-Century-Crofts

Hume, D. (1734/1978), *A Treatise of Human Nature*, L.A. Selby-Bigge (ed.), Oxford: Clarendon Press

Hursthouse, R. (1991), "Arational Action," *Journal of Philosophy*, LXXXVIII (2):57–68

Huxley, T. (1893), *Method and Results*, New York: Appleton-Century-Crofts

Jackendoff, R. (1987), *Consciousness and the Computational Mind*, Cambridge: MIT Press/ Bradford Books

Jackendoff, R. (1989), "What is a Concept that a Person May Grasp It?," *Mind and Language*, 4 (1&2):68–102

Jackson, F. (1982), "Epiphenomenal Qualia," *Philosophical Quarterly*, 32:127–32

Jackson, F. (1986/1992), "What Mary Didn't Know," in Lycan (1990), pp. 392–4

Jackson, F. and Pettit, P. (1993), "Folk Belief and Commonplace Belief," *Mind and Language*, 8:298–305

Jaynes, J. (1976), *The Origins of Consciousness in the Breakdown of the Bicameral Brain*, Boston: Houghton Mifflin

Jesperson, O. (1924), *The Philosophy of Grammar*, London: Allen and Unwin

Johnson, M. (1993), *Moral Imagination: Implications of Cognitive Science for Ethics*, Chicago: University of Chicago Press

Johnson-Laird, P. (1983), *Mental Models: Towards a Cogntive Theory of Language, Inference and Consciousness*, Cambridge: Cambridge University Press

Josephson, J. and Josephson, S. (eds), (1994), *Abductive Inference: Computation, Philosophy, Technology*, Cambridge: Cambridge University Press

Kahneman, D., Slovic, P., and Tversky, A. (1982), *Judgment Under Uncertainty: Heuristics and Biases*, Cambridge: Cambridge University Press

Kamil, A. (1978), "Systematic Foraging by a Nectar-Feeding Bird, the Amakihi *(Loxops virens)*," *Journal of Comparative and Physiological Psychology*, 92:388–96

Kant, I. (1781/1968), *Critique of Pure Reason*, trans. by N.K. Smith, New York: St. Martin's Press

Kaplan, D. (1969), "Quantifying In," in D. Davidson and J. Hintikka (1969), pp. 178–214

Kaplan, D. (1975), "How to Russell a Frege-Church," *Journal of Philosophy*, 72:716–29

Kaplan, D. (1979), "On the Logic of Demonstratives," in P. French et al. (1979), pp. 401–14

Katz, J. (1971), *The Underlying Reality of Language and Its Philosophical Import*, New York: Harper and Row

Keil, F. (1989), *Concepts, Kinds and Conceptual Development*, Cambridge: MIT Press

Kim, J. (1969), "Events and Their Descriptions: Some Considerations," in N. Rescher et al. (eds), *Essays in Honor of C.G. Hempel*, Dordrecht: Reidel, pp. 198–215

Kim J. (1976), "Events and Property Exemplifications," in M. Brand and D. Walton (eds), *Action Theory*, Dordrecht: Reidel, pp. 159–77

Kim, J. (1993), *Supervenience and Mind: Selected Philosophical Essays*, Cambridge: Cambridge University Press

Kluender, R. and Kutas, M. (1993), "Bridging the Gap: Evidence from ERPs on the Processing of Unbounded Dependencies," *Journal of Cognitive Neuroscience*, 5 (3):196–355

Köhler, W. (1926), *The Mentality of Apes*, New York: Harcourt, Brace and World

Kornblith, H. (1985), *Naturalising Epistemology*, Cambridge: MIT Press/Bradford Books

Kosslyn, S. (1980), *Image and Mind*, Cambridge: Harvard University Press

Kripke, S. (1972), "Naming and Necessity," in D. Davidson and G. Harman (1972), *Semantics of Natural Language*, Dordrecht: Reidel, pp. 253–355

Kripke, S. (1979), "A Puzzle About Belief," in A. Margalif (ed.), *Meaning and Use*, Dordrecht: Reidel, pp. 239–83

Kripke, S. (1981), "Identity and Necessity," in N. Block (ed.), *Readings in the Philosophy of Psychology*, vol. 1, Cambridge: Harvard University Press, pp. 144–68

Kripke, S. (1982), *Wittgenstein on Rules and Private Language*, Cambridge: Harvard University Press

Kuhn, T. (1962), *The Structure of Scientific Revolutions*, Chicago: University of Chicago Press

Lachter, J. and Bever, T. (1988), "The Relation Between Linguistic Structure and Associative Theories of Language Learning – A Constructive Critique of Some Connectionist Learning Models," in S. Pinker and J. Mehler (1988), pp. 195–247

Lackner, J.R. and Garrett, M. (1972), "Resolving Ambiguity: Effects of Biasing Context in the Unattended Ear," *Cognition*, I:359–72

Laing, R., Phillipson, H., and Lee, A. (1966), *Interpersonal Perception: a Theory and Method of Research*, London: Tavistock

Landau, B. and Gleitman, L. (1985), *Language and Experience: Evidence from the Blind Child*, Cambridge: Harvard University Press

Lasnik, H. (1989), *Essays on Anaphora*, Boston: Kluwer Academic Publishers

Latané, B. and Darley, J.M. (1970), *The Unresponsive Bystander: Why Doesn't He Help?*, New York: Appleton-Century-Crofts

Leeds, S. (1993), "Qualia, Awareness and Sellars," *Nous*, XXVII (3):303–29

Leibniz, G. (1714/1962), "Monadology," in *Basic Writings*, trans. by G. Montgomery, LaSalle: Open Court, pp. 251–72

LePore, E. and Loewer, B. (1987), "Dual Aspect Semantics," in E. LePore (ed.), *New Directions in Semantics*, Amsterdam: Kluwer Academic Press, pp. 83–112

Lettvin, J., Maturana, H., McCulloch, W., and Pitts, W. (1951), "What the Frog's Eye Tells the Frog's Brain," *Proceedings of the IRE*, 47 (11):1940–59

Levin, J. (1986), "Could Love Be Like a Heatwave? Physicalism and the Subjective Character of Experience," *Philosophical Studies*, 49 (2):245–61

Levine, J. (1983), "Materialism and Qualia: the Explanatory Gap," *Pacific Philosophical Quarterly*, 64:354–61

Levine, J. (1991), "Cool Red," *Philosophical Psychology*, 4:27–40

Levine, J. (1993), "On Leaving Out What It's Like," in M. Davies and G. Humphreys (eds), *Consciousness*, Oxford: Blackwell, pp. 121–36

Levine, Joseph (forthcoming), "Color," entry in *Encyclopaedia of Philosophy*, Oxford: Routledge

Lewis, D. (1969), "Lucas Against Mechanism," *Philosophy*, 44:231–3

Lewis, D. (1970), "How to Define Theoretical Terms," *Journal of Philosophy*, 67:427–44

Lewis, D. (1972/1980), "Psychophysical and Theoretical Identifications," *Australasian Journal of Philosophy*, 50 (3):249–58; also in N. Block (1980a), pp. 207–15

Lewis, D. (1979a), "Attitudes *de dicto* and *de se*," *Philosophical Review*, LXXXVIII:513–43

Lewis, D. (1979b), "Lucas Against Mechanism II," *Canadian Journal of Philosophy*, IX (3):373–5

Lewis, D. (1994), "David Lewis: Reduction of Mind," in S. Guttenplan (ed.), *A Companion to the Philosophy of Mind*, Oxford: Blackwell

Liberman, A., Cooper, F., Shankweiler, D., and Studdert-Kennedy, M. (1967), "The Perception of the Speech Code," *Psychological Review*, 74:431–61

Libet, B. (1985), "Unconscious Cerebral Initiative and the Role of Conscious Will in Voluntary Action," *Behavioral and Brain Sciences*, 8:529–66

Lightfoot, D. (1982), *The Language Lottery: Toward a Biology of Grammars*, Cambridge: MIT Press

Loar, B. (1981), *Mind and Meaning*, New York: Cambridge University Press

Loar, B. (1987a), "Subjective Intentionality," *Philosophical Topics*, Spring, 15 (1):89–124

Loar, B. (1987b), "Social Content and Psychological Content," in R. Grimm and D. Merrill (eds), *Contents of Thought: Proceedings of the 1985 Oberlin Colloquium in Philosophy*, Tucson: University of Arizona Press, pp. 39–139

Loar, B. (1996), "Phenomenal States," in Block et al., *The Nature of Consciousness*, Cambridge: MIT Press

Locke, John (1690/1977), *Locke on Human Understanding: Selected Essays*, I. C. Tipton (ed.), New York: Oxford University Press

Lockwood, M. (1989), *Mind, Brain and the Quantum: the Compound "I"*, Oxford: Blackwell

Loewer, B. (1987), "From Information to Intentionality," *Synthèse*, 70:287–317

Loewer, B. and Rey, G. (ed.), (1991a), *Meaning in Mind: Fodor and his Critics*, Oxford: Blackwell

Loewer, B. and Rey, G. (1991b), introduction to Loewer and Rey (1992), pp. xi–xxxvii

Loftus, E., Polonsky S., and Fullilove, M.T. (1994), "Memories of Childhood Sexual Abuse: Remembering and Repressing," *Psychology of Women Quarterly*, 18:67–84

Lorenz, K. (1981), *The Foundations of Ethology*, trans. by K.Z. Lorenz and R.W. Kickert, New York: Springer-Verlag

Lucas, J. (1961), "Minds, Machines and Gödel," *Philosophy*, 36:112–27

Ludwig, J. (1978), *Philosophy and Parapsychology*, Buffalo: Prometheus Books

Lycan, W. (1981), "Form, Function, and Feel," *Journal of Philosophy*, 78:24–50

Lycan, W. (1987), *Consciousness*, Cambridge: MIT Press

Lycan, W. (1988), *Judgment and Justification*, Cambridge: Cambridge University Press

Lycan, W. (1990a), "What is the 'Subjectivity of the Mental'?," in J. Tomberlin (ed.), *Philosophical Perspectives*, 4: *Action Theory and the Philosophy of Mind*, Atascadero: Ridgeview, pp. 109–30

Lycan, W. (ed.), (1990b), *Mind and Cognition*, Oxford: Blackwell

Lycan, W. (1993), "A Deductive Argument for the Language of Thought," *Mind and Language*, 8 (3):404–22

Lycan, W. (forthcoming), *Consciousness and Experience*, Cambridge: MIT Press/Bradford Books

Mach, E. (1914), *The Analysis of Sensations*, Chicago: Open Court

Maier, N. (1931), "Reasoning in Humans: II. The Solution of a Problem and its Appearance in Consciousness," *Journal of Comparative Psychology*, 12:181–94

Malcolm, N. (1968), "The Conceivability of Mechanism," *Philosophical Review*, 77:45–72

Malcolm, N. (1972), "Thoughtless Brutes," in *Proceedings and Addresses of the American Philosophical Association*, pp. 5–20

Malcolm, N. (1977), *Thought and Knowledge*, Ithaca: Cornell University Press

Maloney, J. (1989), *The Mundane Matter of the Mental Language*, Cambridge: Cambridge University Press

Marcus, Mitchell (1980), *A Theory of Syntactic Recognition for Natural Language*, Cambridge: MIT Press

Marler, P. (1970), "A Comparative Approach to Vocal Learning: Song Development in White-Crowned Sparrows," *Journal of Comparative and Physiological Psychology Monographs*, 71 (2):1–25

Marr, D. (1982), *Vision*, San Francisco: Freeman & Co.

Mates, B. (1951), "Synonymity," *University of California Publications in Philosophy*, 25:201–26, reprinted in *Semantics and the Philosophy of Language*, ed. by L. Linsky, Chicago: University of Chicago Press, 1952

Maudlin, T. (1989), "Computation and Consciousness," *Journal of Philosophy*, 86:407–32

McGinn, C. (1991), *The Problem of Consciousness*, Oxford: Blackwell

McNamara, H.J., Long, J.B., and Wike, F.L. (1956), "Learning without Response Under Two Conditions of External Cues," *Journal of Comparative Physiological Psychology*, 49 (5):477–80

Mehler, J. and Dupoux, E. (1994), *What Infants Know*, Oxford: Blackwell

Meltzoff, A.N. and Borton, R.W. (1979), "Intermodal Matching by Neonates," *Nature*, 264:746–8

Meltzoff, A. and Moore, M. (1983), "New Born Infants Imitate Adult Facial Gestures," *Child Development*, 54:702–9

Millikan, R. (1984), *Language, Thought, and Other Biological Categories*, Cambridge: MIT Press/Bradford Books

Millikan, R. (1991), "Speaking Up for Darwin," in Loewer and Rey (1991a), pp. 151–64

Minsky, M. (1967), *Computation: Finite and Infinite Machines*, Englewood Cliffs: Prentice-Hall

Monk, R. (1990), *Ludwig Wittgenstein: The Duty of Genius*, New York: Free Press

Morris, C. (1946/1955), *Signs, Language, and Behavior*, New York: G. Braziller

Munn, N. (1950), *Handbook of Psychological Research on the Rat*, Boston: Houghton Mifflin

Nagel, E. and Newman, J. (1958), *Gödel's Proof*, New York: New York University Press

Nagel, T. (1965/1971), "Physicalism," in Rosenthal (1971), pp. 96–110

Nagel, T. (1974/1991), "What Is It Like To Be A Bat?" in Rosenthal (1991a), pp. 422–8

Nagel, T. (1979), "Pan-Psychism," in *Mortal Questions*, Cambridge: Cambridge University Press, pp. 181–95

Nagel, T. (1986), *The View from Nowhere*, Oxford: Oxford University Press

Nagel, T. (1994a), "Freud's Permanent Revolution," *New York Review of Books*, May 12, 1994, pp. 34–8

Nagel, T. (1994b), "Reply," *New York Review of Books*, August 11, 1994, pp. 55–6

Neander, K. (1991), "Functions as Selected Effects," *Philosophy of Science*, 58:168–84

Neander, K. (1995), "Misrepresenting and Malfunctioning," *Philosophical Studies*, 79:109–41

Nemirow, L. (1990), "Physicalism and the Cognitive Role of Acquiantance," in Lycan (1990b), pp. 490–9

Neville, H., Nicol, J.L., Barss, A., Forster, K.I., and Garrett, M.F. (1991), "Syntactically Based Sentence Processing Classes: Evidence from Event-Related Brain Potentials," *Journal of Cognitive Neuroscience*, 3:151–65

Newall, A. and Simon, H. (1981), "Computer Science as an Empirical Inquiry," in J. Haguealand (ed.), *Mind Design*, Cambridge: MIT Press/Bradford Books

Nisbett, R. and Wilson, T. (1977), "On Telling More Than We Can Know," *Psychological Review*, 84 (3):231–59

Nissen, P. (1954), "The Nature of Drive as Innate Determinant of Behavioral Organization," *Nebraska Symposium on Motivation*, Lincoln: University of Nebraska Press, pp. 281–321

Olton, D. and Samuelson, R. (1976), "Remembrance of Places Past: Spatial Memory in Rats," *Journal of Experimental Psychology: Animal Behavior Processes*, 2:97–116

Osherson, D. and Smith, E. (1981), "On the Adequacy of Prototype Theory as a Theory of Concepts," *Cognition*, 9:35–58

Papineau, D. (1987), *Reality and Representation*, Oxford: Blackwell

Parfit, D. (1984), *Reasons and Persons*, Oxford: Oxford University Press

Passmore, J. (1965), *Priestley's Writings on Philosophy of Science and Politics*, New York: Collier-Macmillan

Peacocke, C. (1986), "Explanation in Computational Psychology: Language, Perception and Level 1.5," *Mind and Language*, 1:101–23

Peacocke, C. (1992), *A Study of Concepts*, Cambridge: MIT Press

Peirce, C. (1897–1906/1966), *Collected Papers*, C. Hartshorne and P. Weiss (eds), Cambridge: Belknap Press of Harvard University Press

Penrose, R. (1989), *The Emperor's New Mind: Concerning Computers, Minds, and the Laws of Physics*, New York: Oxford University Press

Penrose, R. (1994), *Shadows of the Mind: a Search for the Missing Science of Consciousness*, New York: Oxford University Press

Perry, J. (1979), "The Problem of the Essential Indexical," *Nous*, 13:3–21

Pietroski, P. (1992), "Intentionality and Teleological Error," *Pacific Philosophical Quarterly*, 73:367–82

Pietroski, P. and Rey, G. (1995), "When Other Things Aren't Equal: Saving Ceteris Paribus Laws from Vacuity," *British Journal for the Philosophy of Science*, 46:81–110

Pinker, S. (1994), *The Language Instinct: How the Mind Creates Language*, New York: Harper and Row

Pinker, S. and Mehler, J. (1988), *Connections and Symbols*, Cambridge: MIT Press

Pinker, S. and Prince, A. (1988), "On Language and Connectionism: Analysis of a Parallel Distributed Processing Model of Language Acquisition," in S. Pinker and H. Mehler, *Connections and Symbols*, Cambridge: MIT Press, pp. 73–194

Place, U. (1956/1991), "Is Consciousness a Brain Process?," in Lycan (1990b), pp. 29–36

Putnam, H. (1960/1975), "Minds and Machines," in Putnam (1975a), pp. 362–85

Putnam, H. (1962a), "It Ain't Necessarily So," *Journal of Philosophy*, 59 (22):658–71

Putnam, H. (1962b), "Dreaming and 'Depth Grammar'," in Putnam (1975a), pp. 304–24

Putnam, H. (1962/1975), "The Analytic and the Synthetic," in Putnam (1975a), pp. 33–69

Putnam, H. (1963/1975), "Brains and Behavior," in Putnam (1975a), pp. 325–41

Putnam, H. (1969/1975), "Logical Positivism and the Philosophy of Mind," in Putnam (1975a), pp. 441–51

Putnam, H. (1975a), *Mind, Language and Reality* (Philosophical Papers, vol. II), Cambridge: Cambridge University Press

Putnam, H. (1975b), "The Meaning of 'Meaning'," in Putnam (1975a), pp. 215–71

Putnam, H. (1978), *Meaning and the Moral Sciences*, London: Routledge & Kegan Paul

Putnam, H. (1983), "Computational Psychology and Interpretation Theory," in *Realism and Reason*, vol. 3, Cambridge: Cambridge University Press, pp. 134–54

Putnam, H. (1988), *Representation and Reality*, Cambridge: MIT Press

Putnam, H. (1990), *Realism with a Human Face*, with an introduction by J. Conant (ed.); Cambridge: Harvard University Press

Pylyshyn, Z. (1981), "The Imagery Debate: Analog Media vs. Tacit Knowledge," in Block (1981a)

Pylyshyn, Z. (1984), *Computation and Cognition*, Cambridge: MIT Press/Bradford Books

Quine, W. (1936/1976), "Truth by Convention," in Quine (1976), pp. 77–106

Quine, W. (1953a), *From a Logical Point of View and Other Essays*, New York: Harper & Row

Quine, W. (1953b), "Notes on the Theory of Reference," in Quine (1953a), pp. 130–8

Quine, W. (1953c), "Two Dogmas of Empiricism," in Quine (1953a), pp. 20–46

Quine, W. (1953d), "On What There Is," in Quine (1953a), pp. 1–9

Quine, W. (1955/1976), "Posits and Reality," in Quine (1976), pp. 246–54

Quine, W. (1956a/1976), "Quantifiers and Propositional Attitudes," in Quine (1976), pp. 185–96

Quine, W. (1956b/1976), "Carnap and Logical Truth," in Quine (1976), pp. 107–32

Quine, W. (1960), *Word & Object*, Cambridge: MIT Press

Quine, W. (1968), "Replies," *Synthèse*, 19 (1):264–322

Quine, W. (1969a), *Ontological Relativity and Other Essays*, New York: Columbia University Press

Quine, W. (1969b), "Natural Kinds," in Quine (1969a), pp. 114–38

Quine, W. (1969c), "Epistemology Naturalized," in Quine (1969a), pp. 69–90

Quine, W. (1970), *Philosophy of Logic*, Englewood Cliffs: Prentice Hall

Quine, W. (1972), *Methods of Logic*, 3rd edn, New York: Holt, Reinhart and Winston

Quine, W. (1973), *The Roots of Reference*, LaSalle: Open Court

Quine, W. (1976), *Ways of Paradox and other Essays*, 2nd edn, Cambridge: Harvard University Press

Quine, W. (1987), "Indeterminacy of Translation Again," *Journal of Philosophy*, LXXXIV (1):5–10

Quine, W. and Ullian, J. (1970/78), *The Web of Belief*, New York: Random House

Radford, A. (1988), *Transformational Syntax: a First Course*, 2nd edn, New York: Cambridge University Press

Ramsey, W., Stich, S., and Garon, S. (1990), "Connectionism, Eliminativism, and the Future of Folk Psychology," in C. Macdonald (ed.), *Connectionism: Debates on Psychological Explanation*, Cambridge: Blackwell

Rawls, J. (1971), *A Theory of Justice*, Cambridge: Harvard University Press

343

Rey, G. (1976), "Survival," in A. Rorty (ed.), *The Identities of Persons*, Berkeley: University of California Press, pp. 41–66

Rey, G. (1980a), "What Are Mental Images?" in N. Block (ed.) (1981), *Readings in the Philosophy of Psychology*, vol. II, Cambridge: Harvard University Press, pp. 117–27

Rey, G. (1980b), "Penetrating the Impenetrable," commentary on Pylyshyn, Z., "Computation and Cognition: Issues in the Foundation of Cognitive Science," *Behavioral and Brain Sciences*, 3 (1980):149–50

Rey, G. (1980c), "Functionalism and the Emotions," in A. Rorty (ed.), *Explaining Emotions*, Berkeley: University of California Press, pp. 163–95

Rey, G. (1980d), "The Formal and the Opaque," *Behavioral and Brain Sciences*, 3 (1980):290–2

Rey, G. (1983a), "A Reason for Doubting the Existence of Consciousness," in R. Davidson, G. Schwartz, and D. Shapiro (eds), *Consciousness and Self-Regulation*, vol. III, New York: Plenum, pp. 1–39

Rey, G. (1983b), "Concepts and Stereotypes," *Cognition*, 15:237–62

Rey, G. (1985), "Concepts and Conceptions," *Cognition*, 19:297–303

Rey, G. (1986), "What's Really Going On In Searle's 'Chinese Room'," *Philosophical Studies* 50:169–85

Rey, G. (1988a), "A Question About Consciousness," in H. Otto and J. Tuedio, *Perspectives on Mind*, Dordrecht: Reidel, pp. 5–24

Rey, G. (1988b), "Towards a Computational Theory of Akrasia and Self-Deception," in B. MacLaughlin and A. Rorty, *Essays in Self-Deception*, Berkeley: University of California Press, pp. 264–96

Rey, G. (1990), "Constitutive Causation and The Reality of Mind," commentary on John Searle, "Consciousness, Explanatory Inversion, and Cognitive Science," *Behavioral and Brain Sciences*, Jan. 1991

Rey, G. (1991b), "An Explanatory Budget for Connectionism and Eliminativism," in T. Horgan and J. Tienson (eds), *Connectionism and the Philosophy of Mind*, Dordrecht: Kluwer Academic Publishers, pp. 219–40

Rey, G. (1992), "Sensational Sentences Switched," *Philosophical Studies*, 67:73–103

Rey, G. (1993a), "Sensational Sentences," in M. Davies and G. Humphyries, *Consciousness*, Oxford: Blackwell, pp. 240–57

Rey, G. (1993b), Review of Colin McGinn, *The Problem of Consciousness*, *Philosophical Review*, 102 (2):274–8

Rey, G. (1993c), "Why Think Analyses Are On-Line?" commentary on Goldman, A., "The Psychology of Folk Psychology," *Behavioral and Brain Sciences*, 16 (1):74–5

Rey, G. (1993d), "The Unavailability of What We Mean I: A Reply to Quine, Fodor and LePore," in J. Fodor and E. LePore (eds), *Holism: a Consumer Update. Grazer Philosophica Studien*, 46:61–101

Rey, G. (1994), "Wittgenstein, Computationalism and Qualia," in R. Casati and G. White (eds), *Philosophy and the Cognitive Sciences*, Vienna: Hölder-Pichler-Tempsky, pp. 61–74

Rey, G. (1995a), "A Not 'Merely Empirical' Argument for the Language of Thought," *Philosophical Perspectives*, vol. 9, ed. by J. Tomberlin, pp. 201–22

Rey, G. (1995b), "Dennett's Unrealistic Psychology," in *Philosophical Topics* ("The Philosophy of Daniel Dennett"), 22 (1–2):259–90

Rey, G. (1995c), Review of Ray Jackendoff, *Consciousness and the Computational Mind*, in *Minds and Machines*, 3:444–8

Rey, G. (1995d), "Towards a Projectivist Account of Conscious Experience," in T. Metzinger (ed.), *Conscious Experience*, Paderborn: Ferdinand-Schöningh-Verlag

Rey, G. (1996), "Resisting Primitive Compulsions," *Philosophy and Phenomenological Research*, LVI(2), June

Richard, M. (1990), *Propositional Attitudes*, Cambridge: Cambridge University Press

Rorty, R. (1965), "Mind-Body Identity, Physicalism, and Categories," *Review of Metaphysics* XIX (1):24–54

Rorty, R. (1979), *Philosophy and the Mirror of Nature*, Princeton: Princeton University Press

Rosch, E. (1973), "On the Internal Structure of Perceptual and Semantic Categories," in T.E. Moore (ed.) *Cognitive Development and Acquisition of Language*, New York: Academic Press, pp. 111–44

Rosenthal, D. (ed.) (1971), *Materialism and the Mind-Body Problem*, Englewood Cliffs: Prentice Hall

Rosenthal, D. (ed.) (1991a), *The Nature of Mind*, Oxford: Oxford University Press

Rosenthal, D. (1991b), "Two Concepts of Consciousness," in D. Rosenthal (ed.), (1991a), pp. 462–77

Russell, B. (1904/1938), *Principles of Mathematics*, New York: Norton

Russell, B. (1912a), *The Problems of Philosophy*, Oxford: Oxford University

Russell, B. and Whitehead, A. (1912b/1960), *Principia Mathematica*, 2nd edn, Cambridge: Cambridge University Press

Ryle, G. (1949), *The Concept of Mind*, London: Hutcheson

Salmon, N. (1986), *Frege's Puzzle*, Cambridge: MIT Press/Bradford Books

Sartre, J. (1973), *Existentialism and Humanism*, trans. by P. Mairet, London: Eyre Methuen

Schank, R. (1984), *The Cognitive Computer*, Menlo Park: Addison-Wesley

Scheffler, I. (1963), *Anatomy of Inquiry*, Indianapolis: Bobbs-Merrill

Schiffer, S. (1981), "Truth and the Theory of Content," in H. Parret and J. Bouvaresse (eds), *Meaning and Understanding*, Berlin: Walter de Gruyter

Schiffer, S. (1987), *Remnants of Meaning*, Cambridge: MIT Press

Schwartz, G. and Shapiro, D. (eds), (1976), *Consciousness and Self-Regulation*, vol. 1, New York: Plenum Press

Searle, J. (1980a), "Minds, Brains, and Programs," *Behavioral and Brain Sciences*, 3:417–24

Searle, J. (1980b), "Author's Response," *Behavioral and Brain Sciences*, 3:450–7

Searle, J. (1984), *Minds, Brains, and Science*, Cambridge: Harvard University Press

Searle, J. (1987), "Indeterminacy, Empiricism, and the First-Person," *Journal of Philosophy*, 84:123–46

Searle, J. (1990a), "Consciousness, Explanatory Inversion, and Cognitive Science," *Behavioral and Brain Sciences*, 13 (4):585–642

Searle, J. (1990b), "Author's Response," *Behavioral and Brain Sciences*, 13 (4):610–42

Searle, J. (1992), *The Rediscovery of the Mind*, Cambridge: MIT Press

Sellars, W. (1956), "Empiricism and the Philosophy of Mind," in M. Scriven, P. Feyerabend, and G. Maxwell (eds), *Minnesota Studies in the Philosophy of Science*, vol. I, Minneapolis: University of Minnesota Press, pp. 253–329

Shaffer, J. (1963/1991), "Mental Events and the Brain," in Rosenthal (1991a), pp. 177–80

Shepard, J. (1933), "Higher Processes in the Behavior of Rats," *Proceedings of National Academy of Science*, 19, pp. 149–52

Shepard, R. (1982), *Mental Images and their Transformations*, Cambridge: MIT Press

Sherrington, C. (1906/1947), *The Integrative Action of the Nervous System*, 2nd edn, New Haven: Yale University Press

Shoemaker, S. (1969/1984), "Time Without Change," in Shoemaker (1984), pp. 49–66

Shoemaker, S. (1975/1984), "Functionalism and Qualia," in Shoemaker (1984), pp. 184–205

Shoemaker, S. (1977/1984), "Immortality and Dualism," in Shoemaker (1984), pp. 139–58

Shoemaker, S. (1981/1984), "The Inverted Spectrum," in Shoemaker (1984), pp. 327–57

Shoemaker, S. (1984), *Identity, Cause, and Mind*, Cambridge: Cambridge University Press

Shoemaker, S. (1990), "Qualities and Qualia: What's in the Mind?," *Philosophy and Phenomenological Research*, L:109–31

Singer, P. (1979), *Practical Ethics*, New York: Cambridge University Press

Skinner, B. (1938), *The Behavior of Organisms*, New York: Appleton-Century-Crofts

Skinner, B. (1950), "Are Theories of Learning Necessary?," *Psychological Review*, 57:193–216

Skinner, B. (1953), *Science and Human Behavior*, New York: Macmillan

Skinner, B. (1957), *Verbal Behavior*, New York: Appleton-Century-Crofts

Skinner, B. (1963/1984), "Behaviorism at Fifty," *Behavioral and Brain Sciences*, 7 (4):615–21

Skinner, B. (1981), "Selection by Consequences," *Science*, 213:501–4

Slote, M. (1975), "Inapplicable Concepts," *Philosophical Studies*, 28:265–71

Slote, M. (1989), *Beyond Optimizing: a Study of Rational Choice*, Cambridge: Harvard University Press

Smart, J. (1962/1991), "Sensations and Brain Processes," *Philosophical Review*, LXVIII:141–56

Smith, D. (1986), "The Structure of (Self-)Consciousness," in *Topoi* 5/2

Smith, E. and Medin, D. (1981), *Categories and Concepts*, Cambridge: Harvard University Press

Smith, E., Medin, D., and Rips, L. (1984), "A Psychological Approach to Concepts: Comments on Rey's 'Concepts and Stereotypes'," *Cognition*, 17:265–74

Smolensky, P. (1988a), "On the Proper Treatment of Connectionism," *Behavioral and Brain Sciences*, 11:1–23

Smolensky, P. (1988b), "Putting Together Connectionism – Again," *Behavioral and Brain Sciences*, 11:59–74

Sober, E. (1985), *The Nature of Selection*, Cambridge: MIT Press

Sowa, J. (1984), *Conceptual Structures: Information Processing in Mind and Machine*, Menlo Park: Addison-Wesley

Spelke, E. (1991), "Physical Knowledge in Infancy: Reflections on Piaget's Theory," in S. Carey and R. Gelman (eds), *The Epigenesis of Mind*, Hillsdale: Erlbaum Associates, pp. 133–70

Stabler, Edward (1983), "How are Grammars Represented?," *Behavioral and Brain Sciences*, 6:391–421

Stalnaker, R. (1984), *Inquiry*, Cambridge: MIT Press/Bradford Books

Stampe, D. (1977), "Towards a Causal Theory of Linguistic Representation," *Midwest*

Studies in Philosophy, Minneapolis: University of Minnesota Press, pp. 42–63

Sterelny, K. (1990), *The Representational Theory of Mind: an Introduction*, Oxford: Blackwell

Stich, S. (1983), *From Folk Psychology to Cognitive Science*, Cambridge: MIT Press

Stich, S. (1984), "Relativism, Rationality and the Limits of Intentional Description," *Pacific Philosophical Quarterly*, 65:211–35

Strawson, G. (1987), *Freedom and Belief*, Oxford: Oxford University Press

Strawson, G. (1994), *Mental Reality*, Cambridge: MIT Press

Stromswold, K. (1990), "Learnability and the Acquisition of Auxiliaries," Doctoral Dissertation, Department of Brain and Cognitive Sciences, MIT

Tarski, A. (1956), "The Concept of Truth in Formalized Languages," in *Logic, Semantics, Metamathematics*, trans. by J. Woodger. Oxford: Oxford University Press

Taylor, C. (1964), *The Explanation of Behavior*, London: Routledge & Kegan Paul

Taylor, C. (1967), "Mind-Body Identity, a Side Issue?," *Philosophical Review*, LXXVI:201–13

Teller, P. (1984), "A Poor Man's Guide to Supervenience and Determination," *Southern Journal of Philosophy*, 22:137–67

Thagard, P. (1988), *Computational Philosophy of Science*, Cambridge: MIT Press

Thomson, J. (1964), "Private Language," *American Philosophical Quarterly*, I (1):20–31

Thomson, J. (1977), *Acts and Other Events*, Ithaca: Cornell University Press

Thorndike, E. (1911), *Animal Intelligence: Experimental Studies*, New York: Macmillan

Thorpe, W. (1950), "A Note on Detour Experiments with *Ammophila pubescens Curt*," *Behavior*, 2:257–63

Tienson, J. (1987), "Introduction to Connectionism," *Southern Journal of Philosophy*, XXVI (supplement):1–16

Tolman, E. (1948), "Cognitive Maps in Rats and Men," *Psychological Review*, 55:189–208

Tolman, E. and Gleitman, H. (1949), "Studies in Spatial Learning: VII. Place and Response Learning Under Different Degrees of Motivation," *Journal of Experimental Psychology*, 39:653–9

Tolman, E. and Honzik, C. (1930), "Introduction and Removal of Reward, and Maze Performance in Rats," *University of California Publications in Psychology*, 4:257–75

Tooley, M. (1983), *Abortion and Infanticide*, Oxford: Oxford University Press

Touretsky, D.S. & Hinton, G.E. (1985), "Symbols Among the Neurons: Details of a Connectionist Inference Architecture," *Proceedings of the International Joint Conference on Artificial Intelligence*, pp. 238–43

Tversky, A. (1977), "Features of Similarity," *Psychological Review*, 84 (4):327–52

Tye, M. (1984), "The Adverbial Approach to Visual Experience," *Philosophical Review*, 93:195–225

Tye, M. (1989), *The Metaphysics of Mind*, Cambridge: Cambridge University Press

Tye, M. (1991), *The Imagery Debate*, Cambridge: MIT Press

Tye, M. (1992), "Visual Qualia and Visual Content," in Crane (1992a), pp. 158–76

Tye, M. (1995), *Ten Problems of Consciousness*, Cambridge: MIT Press

Ullman, Shimon (1979), *The Interpretation of Visual Motion*, Cambridge: MIT Press

van Gelder, T. and Niklasson, L. (1994), "Classicism and Cognitive Architecture," *Proceedings of the Sixteenth Annual Conference of the Cognitive Science Society*, Hillsdale: Erlbaum, pp. 905–9

van Gulick, Robert (1989), "Metaphysical Arguments for Individualism, and Why They

Don't Work," in S. Silvers (ed.), *Re-Representations, Philosophical Studies*; Kluwer Academic Publishers, pp. 151–60

Velmans, M. (1991), "Is Human Information Processing Conscious?," *Behavioral and Brain Sciences*, 14:4

von St. Paul, U. (1982), "Do Geese Use Path Integration for Walking Home?," in F. Papi and H.G. Wallraff (eds), *Avian Navigation*, New York: Springer, pp. 298–307

Vuillemin, J. (1986), "On Quine's and Duhem's Theses," in L. Hahn and P. Schilpp, *The Philosophy of W.V. Quine*, LaSalle: Open Court, pp. 595–618

Wason, P. and Evans, J. (1975), "Dual Processes in Reasoning," *Cognition*, 3 (2):141–54

Wason, P. and Johnson-Laird (1972), *Psychology of Reasoning: Structure and Content*, London: Batsford

Watson, G. (1977), "Skepticism About Weakness of Will," *Philosophical Review*, 86:316–39

Weber, M. (1922/1978), "The Nature of Social Action," in W. Runciman (ed.), *Weber: Selections in Translation*, Cambridge: Cambridge University Press

Weinberg, Steven (1992), *Dreams of a Final Theory*, New York: Pantheon

Weiskrantz, L. (1986), *Blindsight: a Case Study and Implications*, Oxford: Oxford University Press

Weiskrantz, L., Warrington, E.K., and Saunders, M.D. (1974), "Visual Capacity in the Hemianopic Field Following a Restricted Occipital Ablation," *Brain*, 97:709–28

Weizenbaum, J. (1976), *Computer Power and Human Reason*, San Francisco: Freeman

Wheeler, J. (1982), "Bohr, Einstein, and the Strange Lesson of the Quantum," in R. Elvee (1982), pp. 1–30

White, S. (1982), "Partial Character and the Language of Thought," *Pacific Philosophical Quarterly* 63:347–65

Whiten, A. (1991), *Natural Theories of Mind*, Oxford: Blackwell

Whyte, L. (1967), "Unconscious," in *Encyclopedia of Philosophy*, New York: Macmillan, pp. 185–8

Wiggins, D. (1971), *Identity and Spatio-Temporal Continuity*, Oxford: Blackwell

Wigner, E. (1982), "The Limitation of the Validity of Present Day Physics," in R. Elvee (1982), pp. 118–33

Wilks, Y. (1984), "Machines and Consciousness," in Hookway (1984), pp. 105–28

Wilson, M. (1978), "Cartesian Dualism," in M. Hooker, *Descartes: Critical and Interpretive Essays*, Baltimore: Johns Hopkins University Press, pp. 197–211

Wimmer, H. and Hartl, M. (1991), "The Cartesian View and the Theory View of the Mind: Developmental Evidence from Understanding False Belief in Self and Other," *British Journal of Developmental Psychology*, 9:125–8

Wittgenstein, L. (1914–16/1979), *Notebooks 1914–16*, 2nd edn, G. Wright and G. Anscombe (eds), trans. by G. Anscombe, Chicago: University of Chicago Press

Wittgenstein, L. (1920/1961), *Tractatus Logico-Philosophicus*, trans. by D. Pears and B. McGuinness, Oxford: Routledge & Kegan Paul

Wittgenstein, L. (1929/1968), "A Lecture on Ethics," *Philosophical Review* LXXIV (1):4–14

Wittgenstein, L. (1937/1983), *Remarks on the Foundations of Mathematics*, G.H. von Wright, R. Rhees, and G.E.M. Anscombe (eds), Cambridge: MIT Press

Wittgenstein, L. (1953), *Philosophical Investigations*, trans. by G.E.M. Anscombe, New York: Macmillan

Wittgenstein, L. (1958), *Blue and Brown Books*, New York: Harper and Row

Wittgenstein, L. (1966), *Lectures and Conversations on Aesthetics, Psychology, and Religious Belief*, C. Barrett (ed.) from notes by Y. Smythies, R. Rhees, and J. Taylor, Berkeley: University of California Press

Wittgenstein, L. (1967) *Zettel*, G.E.M. Anscombe and G.H. von Wright (eds), Oxford: Blackwell

Wittgenstein, L. (1978), *Remarks on Color*, Berkeley: University of California Press

Wittgenstein, L. (1980-I), *Remarks on the Philosophy of Psychology, I*, G.E.M. Anscombe and G.H. von Wright (eds), Oxford: Blackwell

Wittgenstein, L. (1980-II), *Remarks on the Philosophy of Psychology, II*, G.E.M. Anscombe and G.H. von Wright (eds), Oxford: Blackwell

Wright, L. (1973), "Functions," *Philosophical Review*, 82:139–68

Wynn, K. (1992a), "Addition and Subtraction by Human Infants," *Nature*, 358:749–50

Wynn, K. (1992b), "Evidence Against Empiricist Accounts of the Origins of Mathematical Knowledge," *Mind and Language*, 7 (4):315–32

Yablo, S. (1987), "Identity, Essence, Indiscernability," *Journal of Philosophy*, 84:293–314

Yin, R. (1969), "Looking at Upside-Down Faces," *Journal of Experimental Psychology*, 81:141–5

Yin, R. (1970), "Face Recognition by Brain-Injured Patients: a Dissociable Ability?," *Neuropsychologia*, 8:395–402

Young, A. (1994), "Covert Recognition," in M. Farah & G. Ratcliff (eds), *The Neuropsychology of Higher Vision: Collected Tutorial Essays*, Hillsdale: Erlbaum

Zajonc, R. (1968), "The Attitudinal Effects of Mere Exposure," *Journal of Personality and Social Psychology*, 8:1–27

Ziff, P. (1967/1971), "On H.P. Grice's Account of Meaning," *Analysis*, XXVIII (1):1–8

Index

359